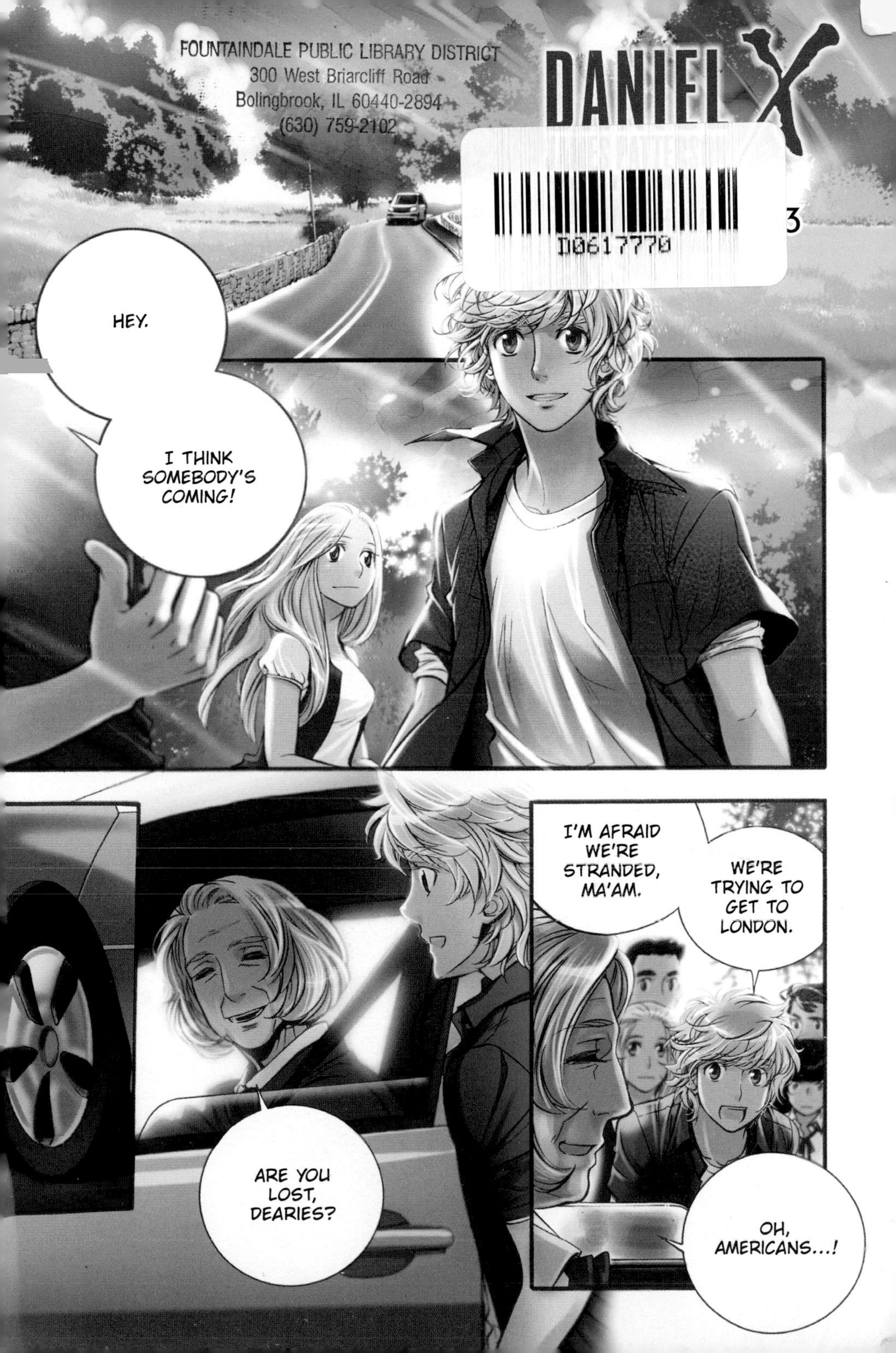
DANIEL X
HEY.
I THINK SOMEBODY'S COMING!
ARE YOU LOST, DEARIES?
I'M AFRAID WE'RE STRANDED, MA'AM.
WE'RE TRYING TO GET TO LONDON.
OH, AMERICANS...!

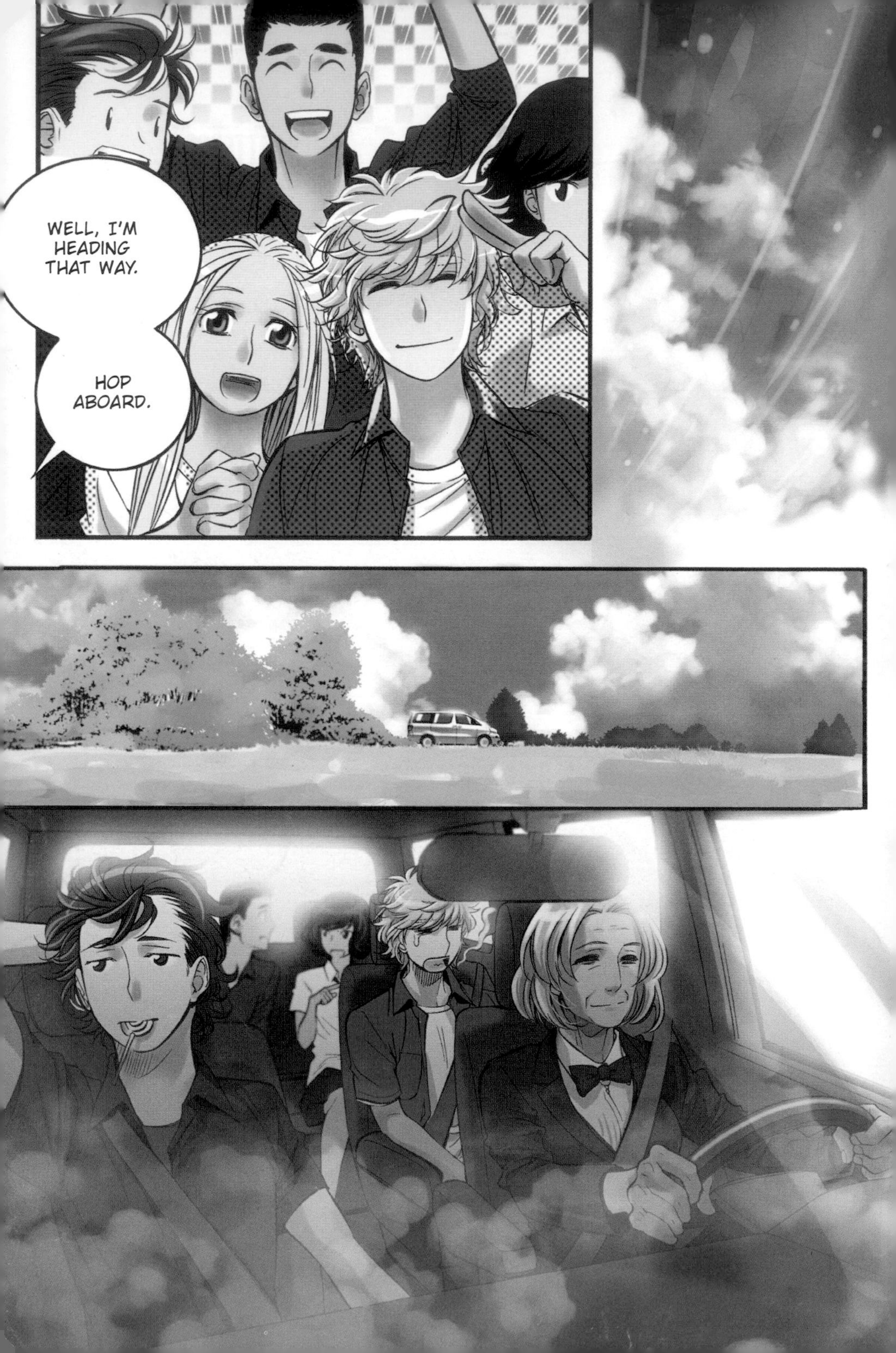
WELL, I'M HEADING THAT WAY.
HOP ABOARD.

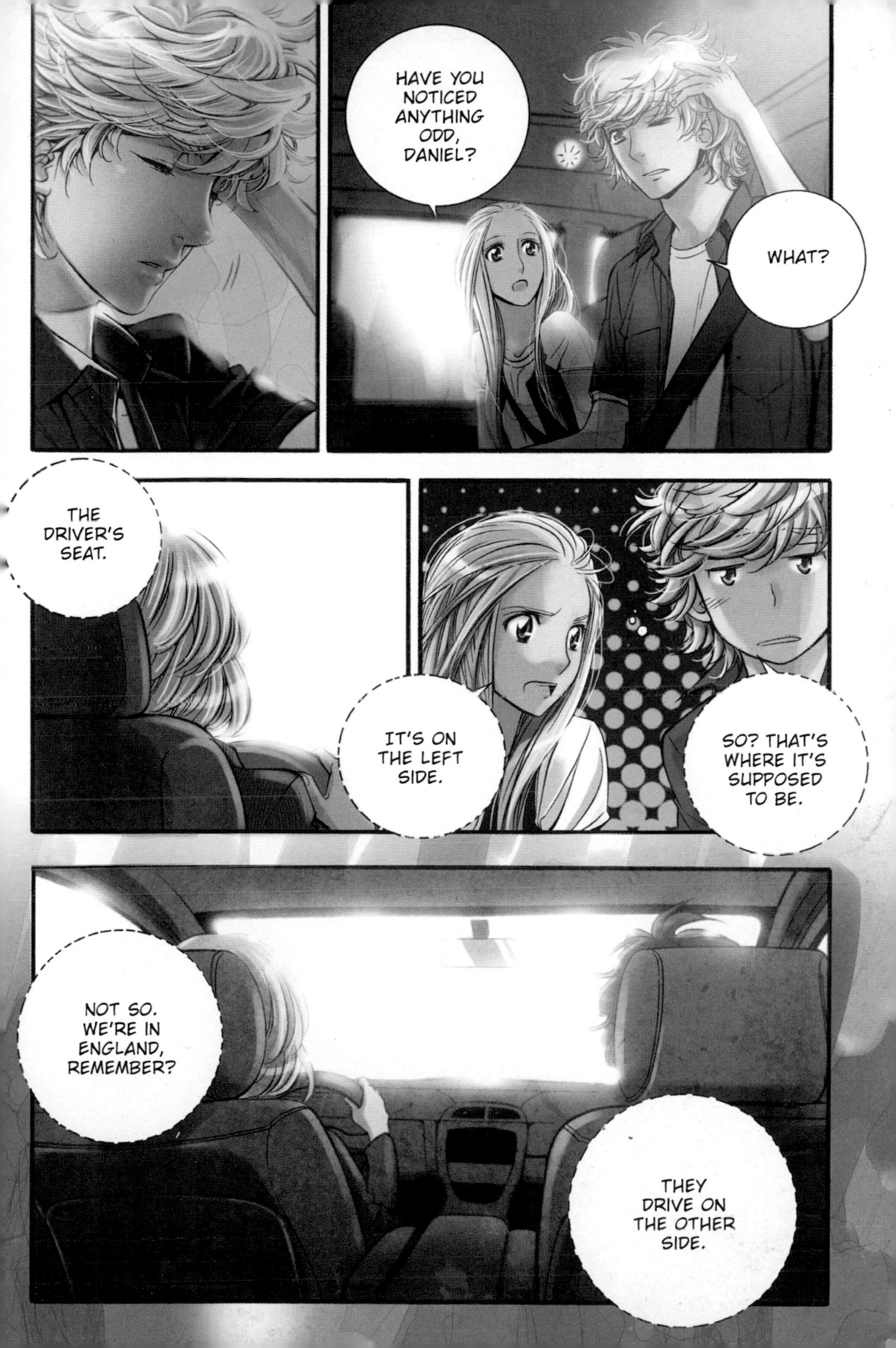
HAVE YOU NOTICED ANYTHING ODD, DANIEL?
WHAT?
THE DRIVER'S SEAT.
IT'S ON THE LEFT SIDE.
SO? THAT'S WHERE IT'S SUPPOSED TO BE.
NOT SO. WE'RE IN ENGLAND, REMEMBER?
THEY DRIVE ON THE OTHER SIDE.

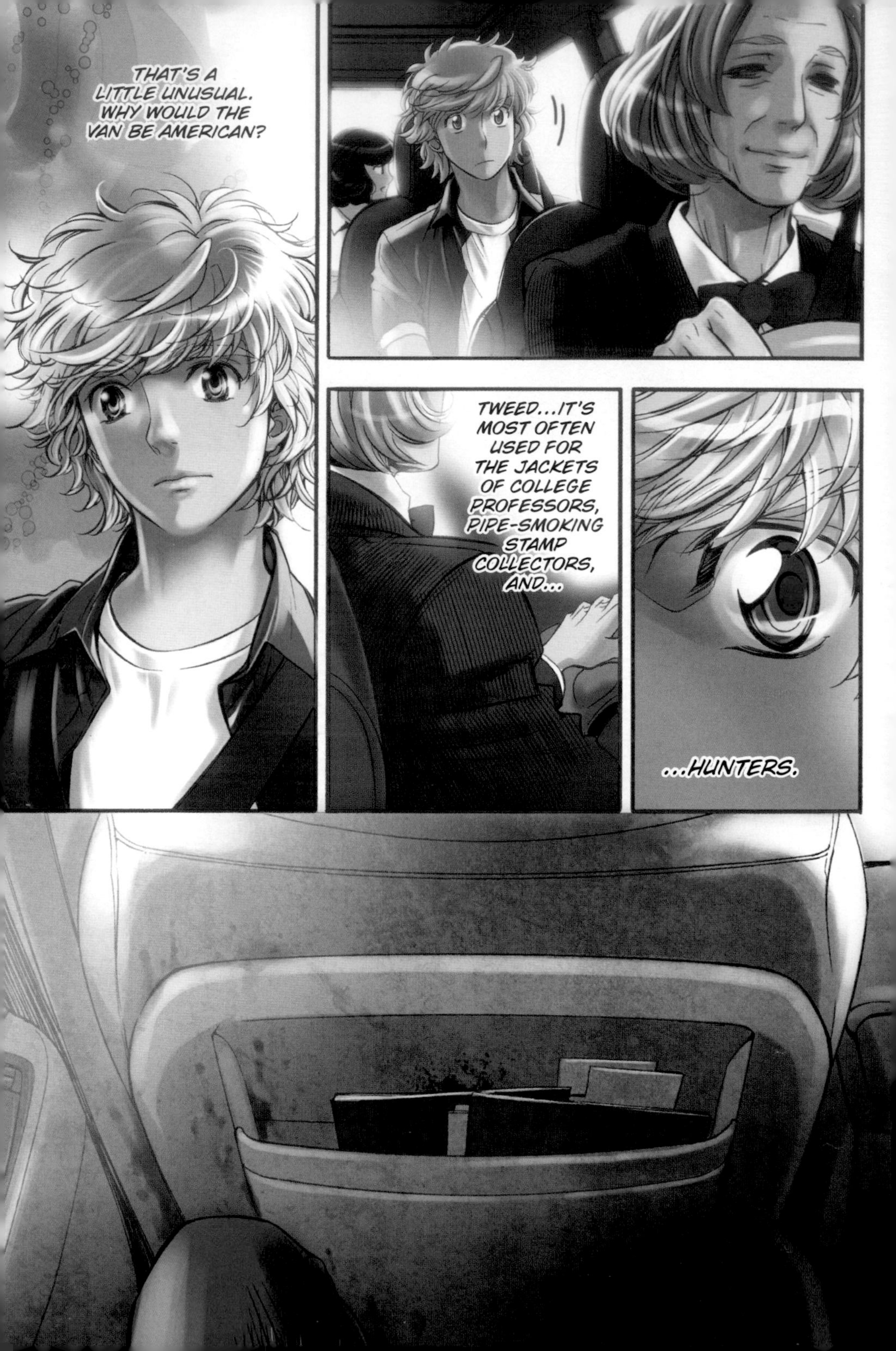
THAT'S A LITTLE UNUSUAL. WHY WOULD THE VAN BE AMERICAN?
TWEED...IT'S MOST OFTEN USED FOR THE JACKETS OF COLLEGE PROFESSORS, PIPE-SMOKING STAMP COLLECTORS, AND...
...HUNTERS.

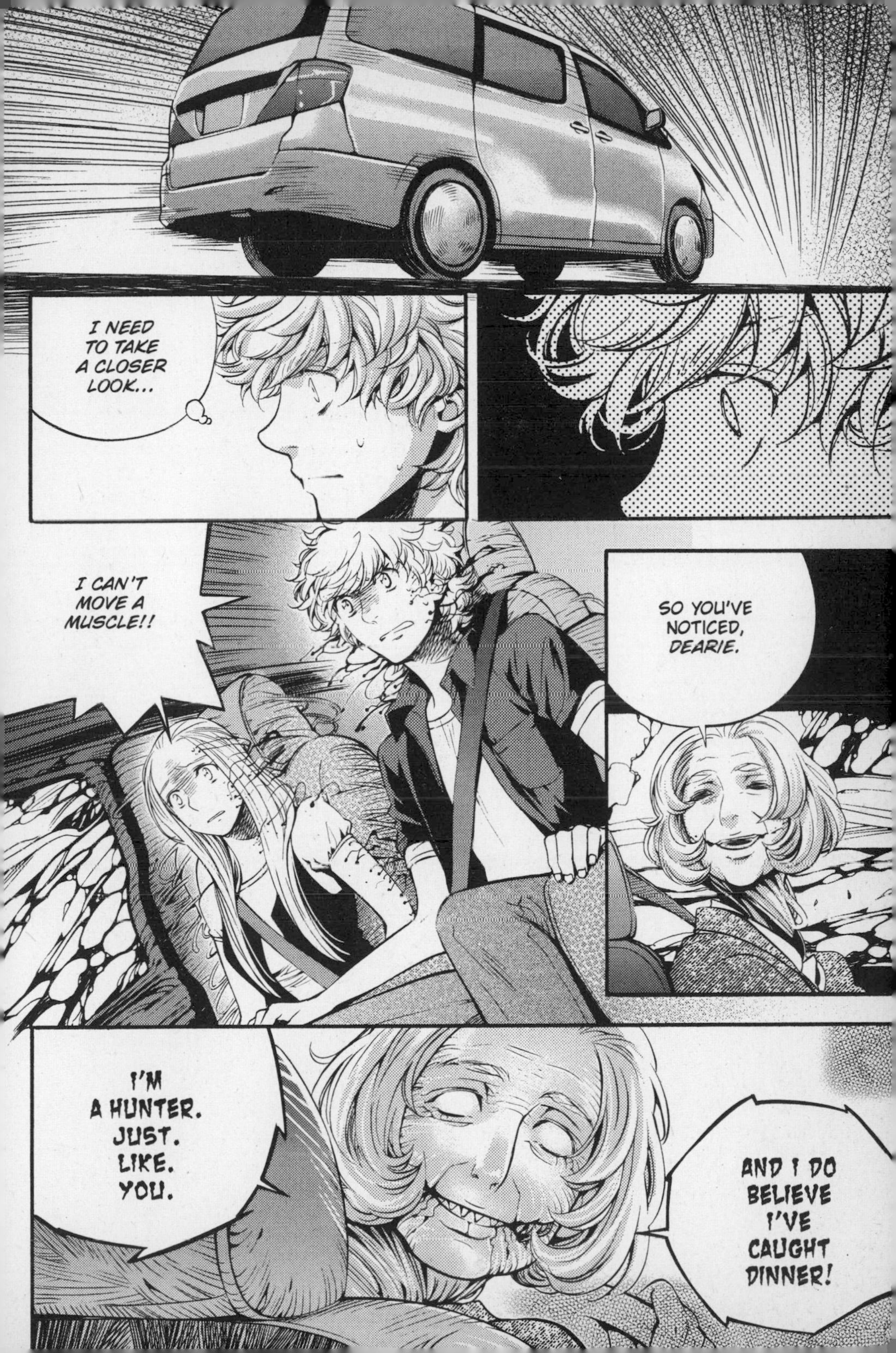
I NEED TO TAKE A CLOSER LOOK...
I CAN'T MOVE A MUSCLE!!
SO YOU'VE NOTICED, DEARIE.
I'M A HUNTER. JUST. LIKE. YOU.
AND I DO BELIEVE I'VE CAUGHT DINNER!

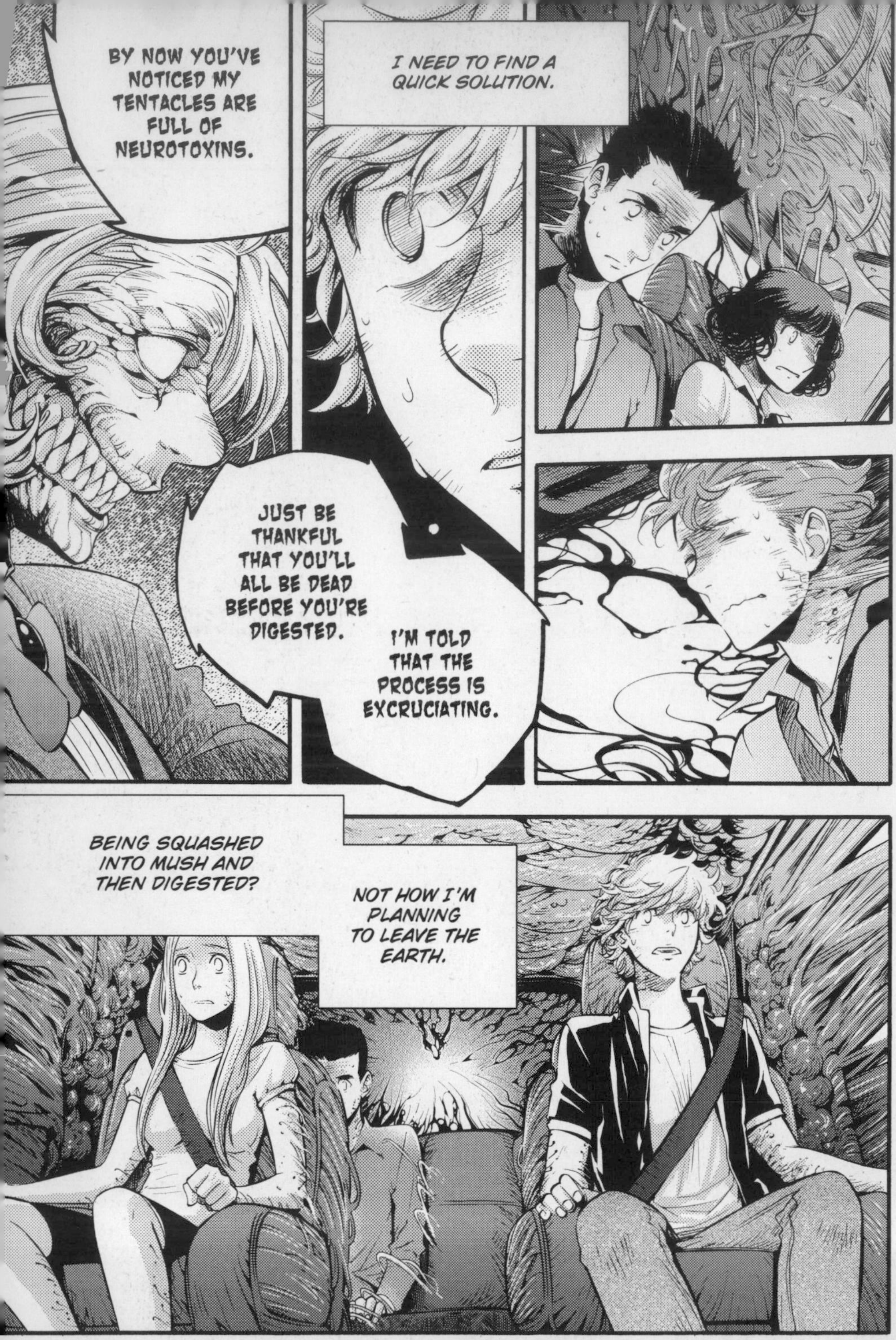
BY NOW YOU'VE NOTICED MY TENTACLES ARE FULL OF NEUROTOXINS.
I NEED TO FIND A QUICK SOLUTION.
JUST BE THANKFUL THAT YOU'LL ALL BE DEAD BEFORE YOU'RE DIGESTED.
I'M TOLD THAT THE PROCESS IS EXCRUCIATING.
BEING SQUASHED INTO MUSH AND THEN DIGESTED?
NOT HOW I'M PLANNING TO LEAVE THE EARTH.

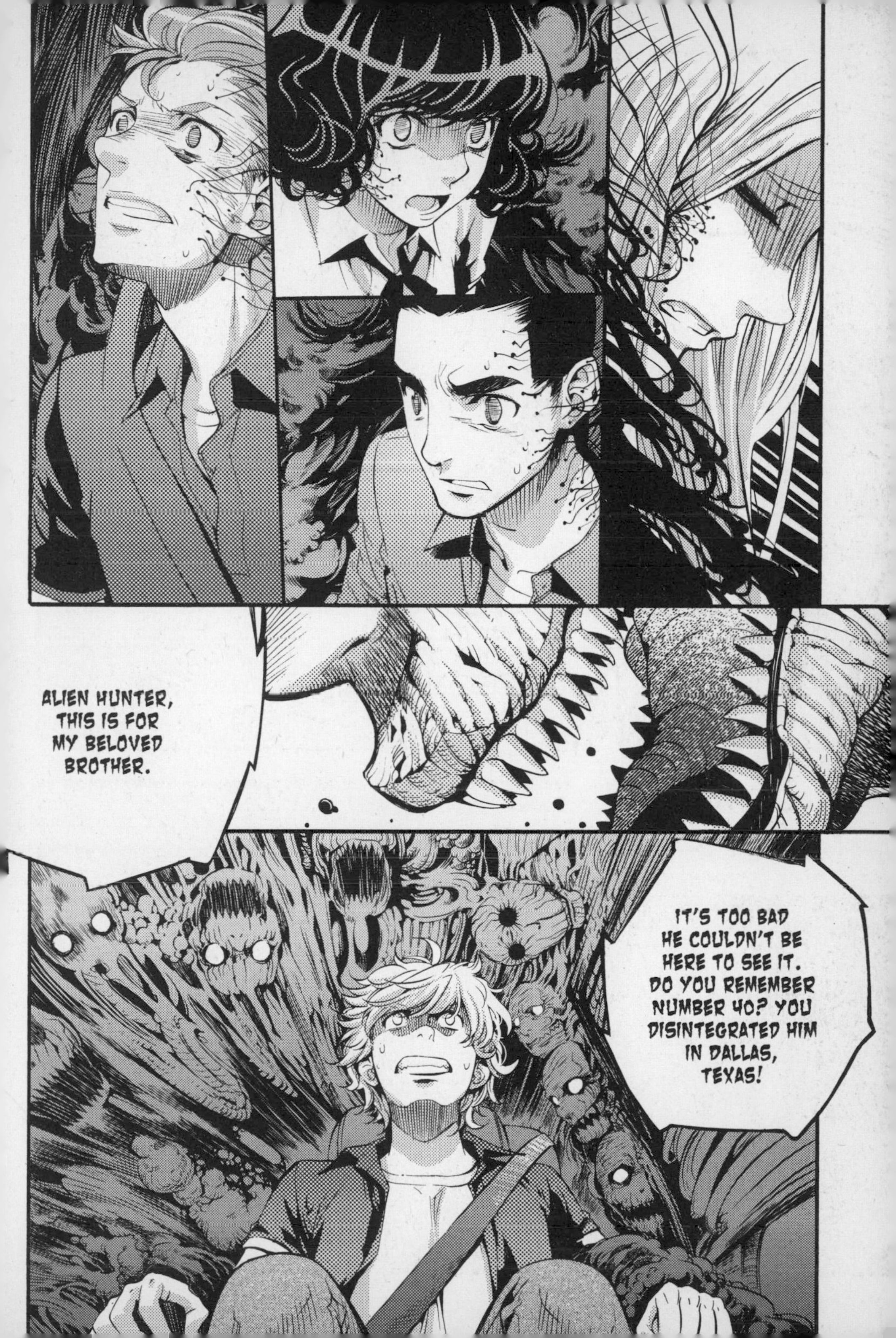
ALIEN HUNTER, THIS IS FOR MY BELOVED BROTHER.
IT'S TOO BAD HE COULDN'T BE HERE TO SEE IT. DO YOU REMEMBER NUMBER 40? YOU DISINTEGRATED HIM IN DALLAS, TEXAS!

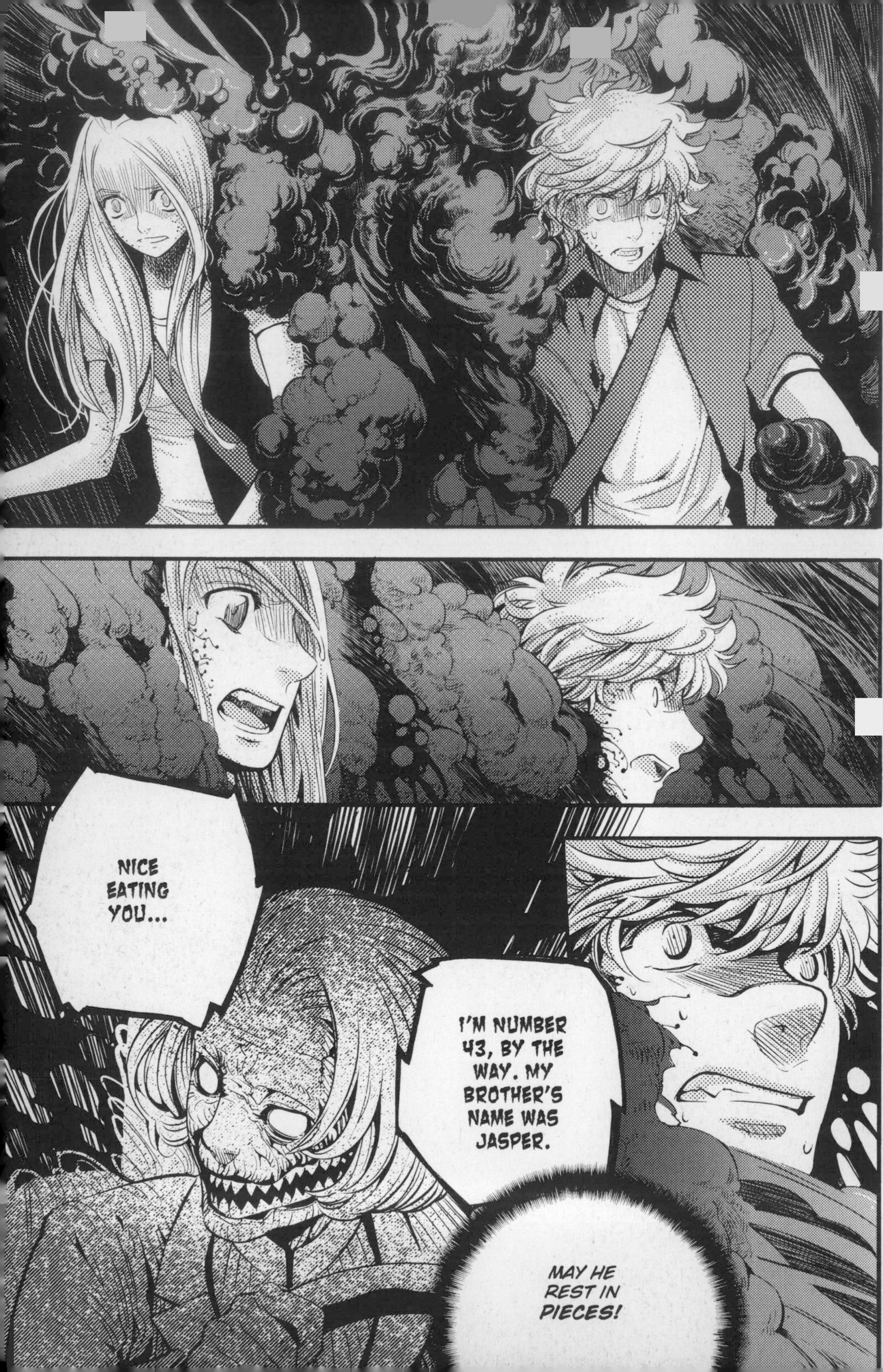
NICE EATING YOU...
I'M NUMBER 43, BY THE WAY. MY BROTHER'S NAME WAS JASPER.
MAY HE REST IN PIECES!

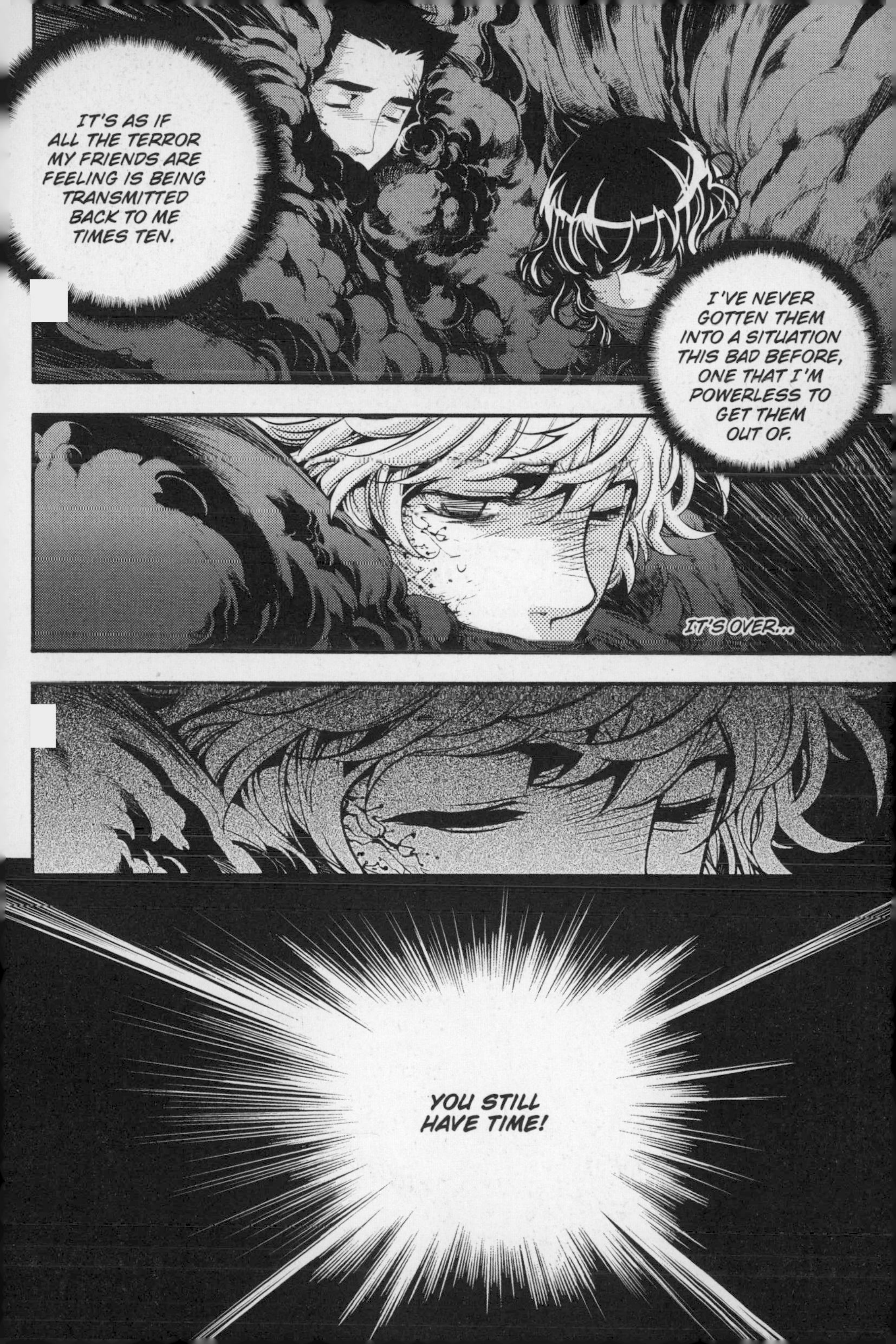
IT'S AS IF ALL THE TERROR MY FRIENDS ARE FEELING IS BEING TRANSMITTED BACK TO ME TIMES TEN.
I'VE NEVER GOTTEN THEM INTO A SITUATION THIS BAD BEFORE, ONE THAT I'M POWERLESS TO GET THEM OUT OF.
IT'S OVER...
YOU STILL HAVE TIME!

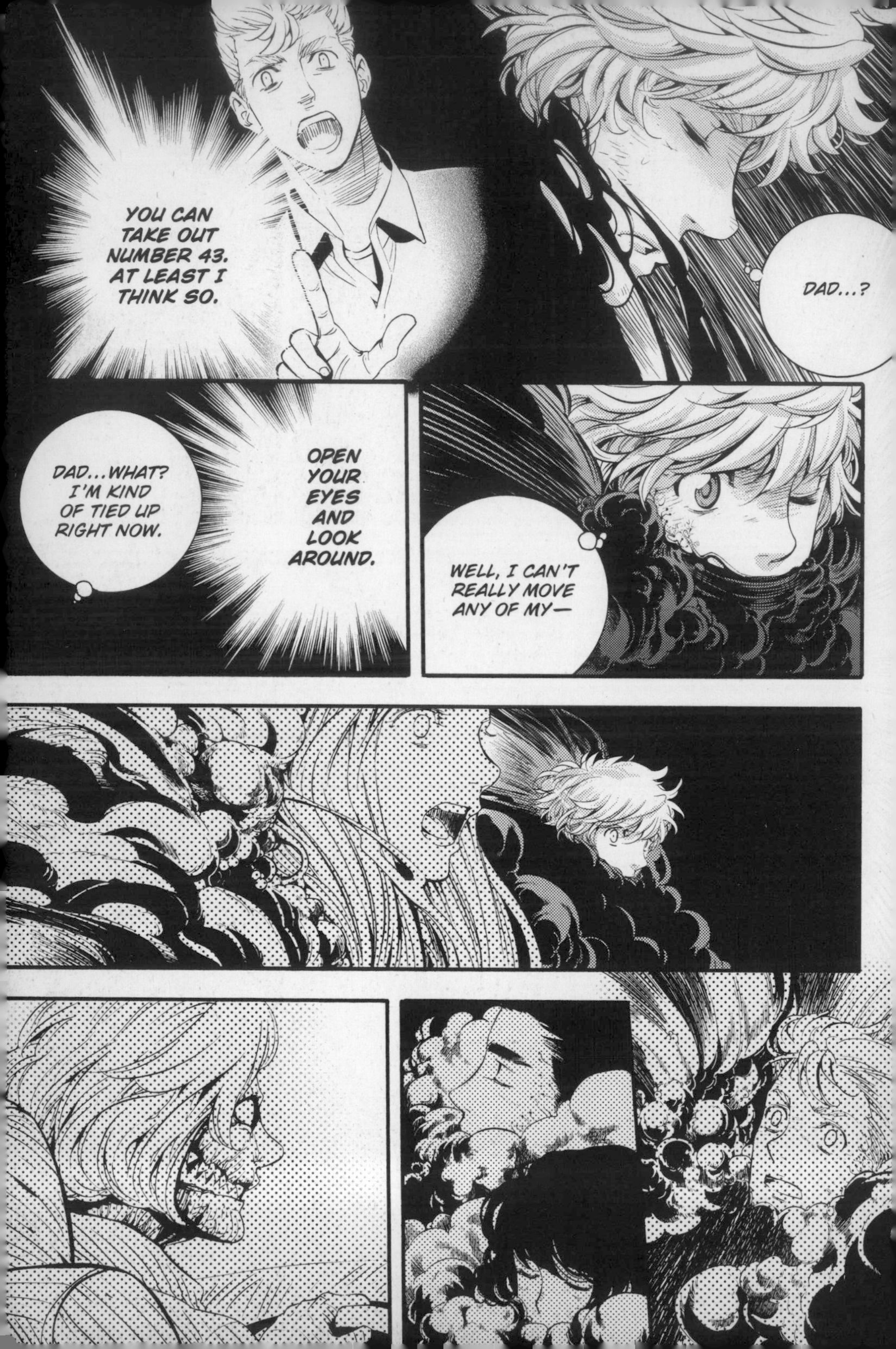
YOU CAN TAKE OUT NUMBER 43. AT LEAST I THINK SO.
DAD...?
DAD...WHAT? I'M KIND OF TIED UP RIGHT NOW.
OPEN YOUR EYES AND LOOK AROUND.
WELL, I CAN'T REALLY MOVE ANY OF MY—

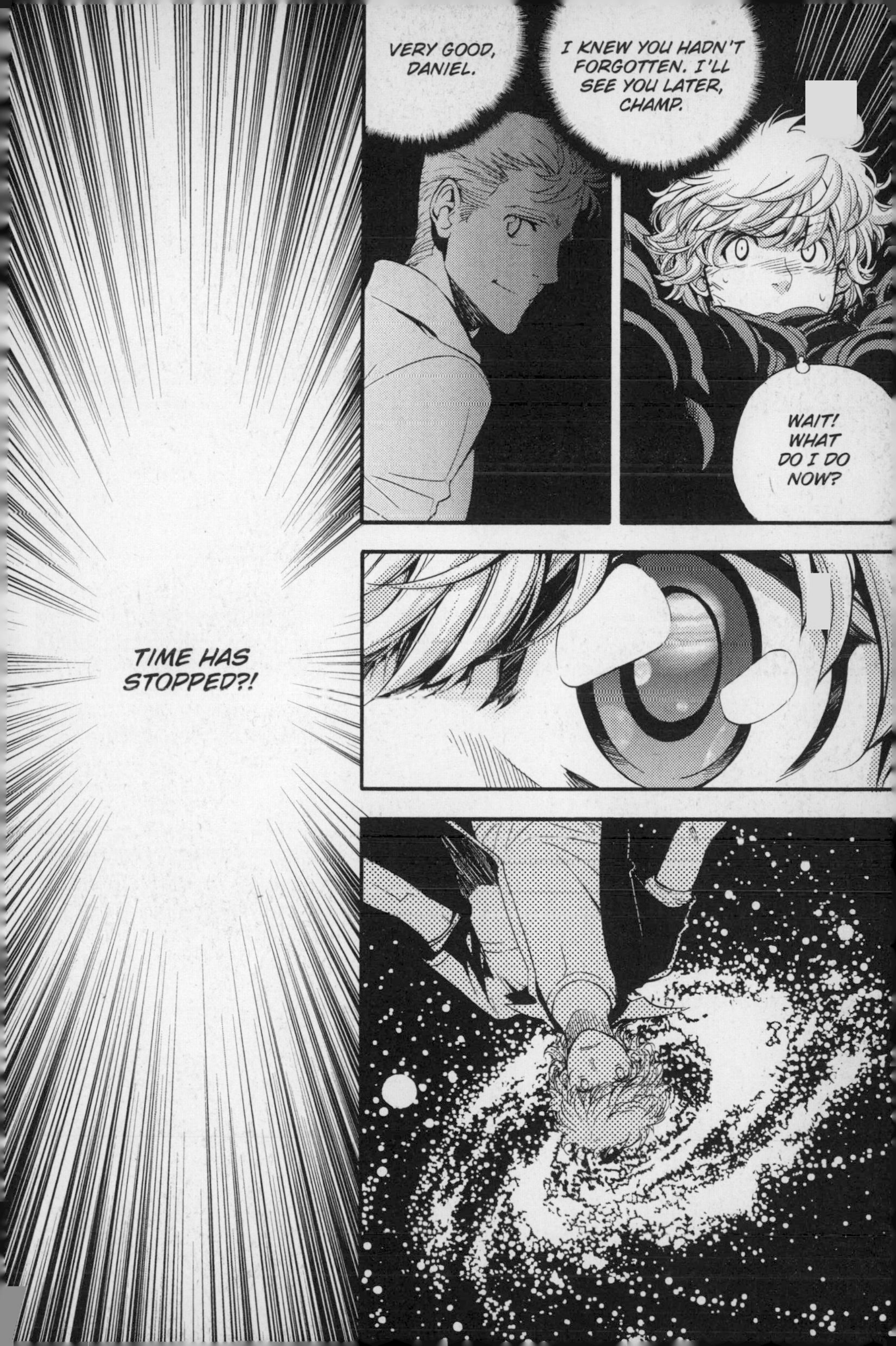
TIME HAS STOPPED?!
VERY GOOD, DANIEL.
I KNEW YOU HADN'T FORGOTTEN. I'LL SEE YOU LATER, CHAMP.
WAIT! WHAT DO I DO NOW?

USUALLY WHEN I USE MY POWERS, I HAVE TO CONCENTRATE...
...BUT THIS TIME IT'S JUST THE OPPOSITE.
FIRST I RELAX, LET MY MIND GO LIMP...

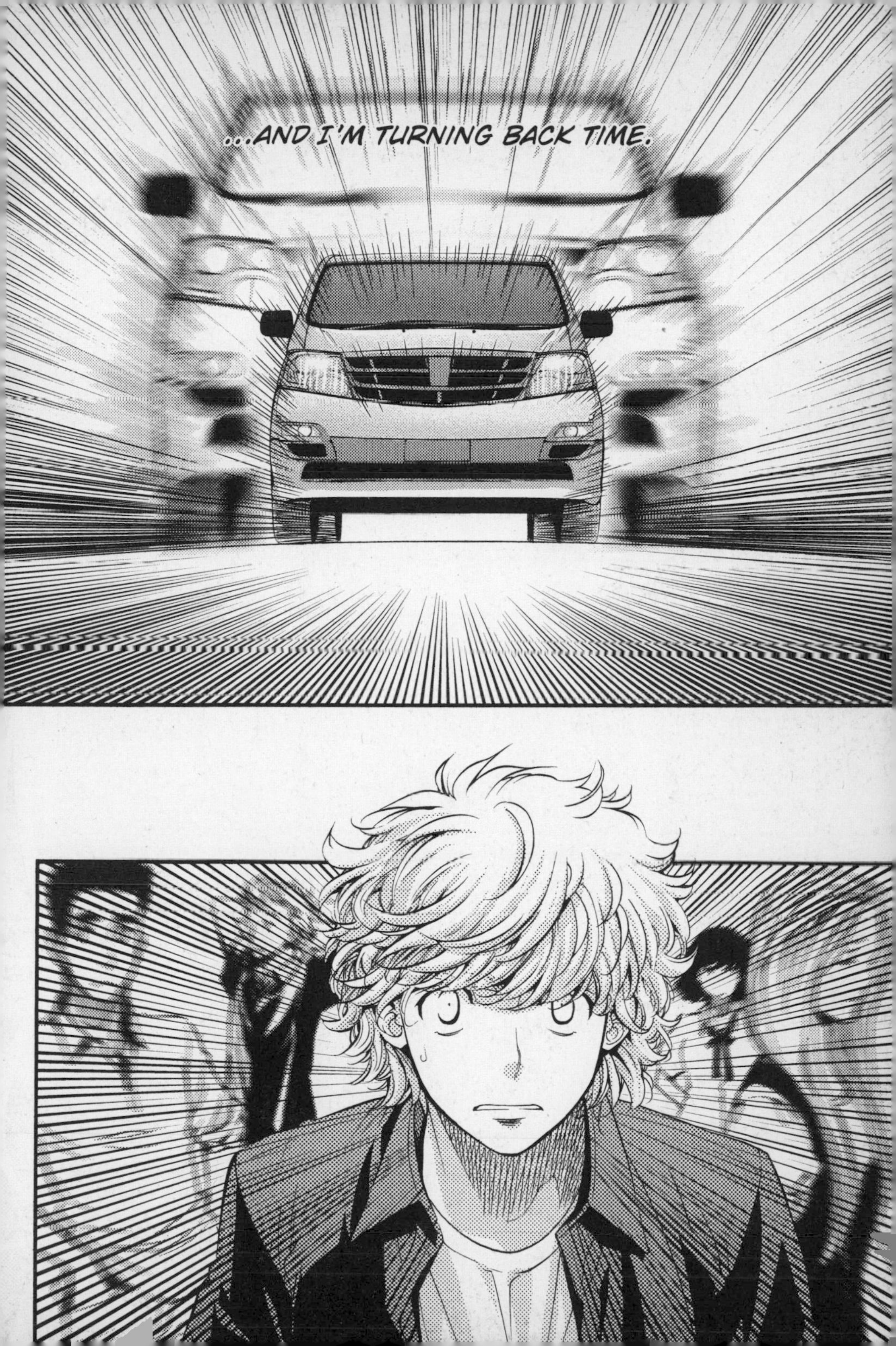
...AND I'M TURNING BACK TIME.

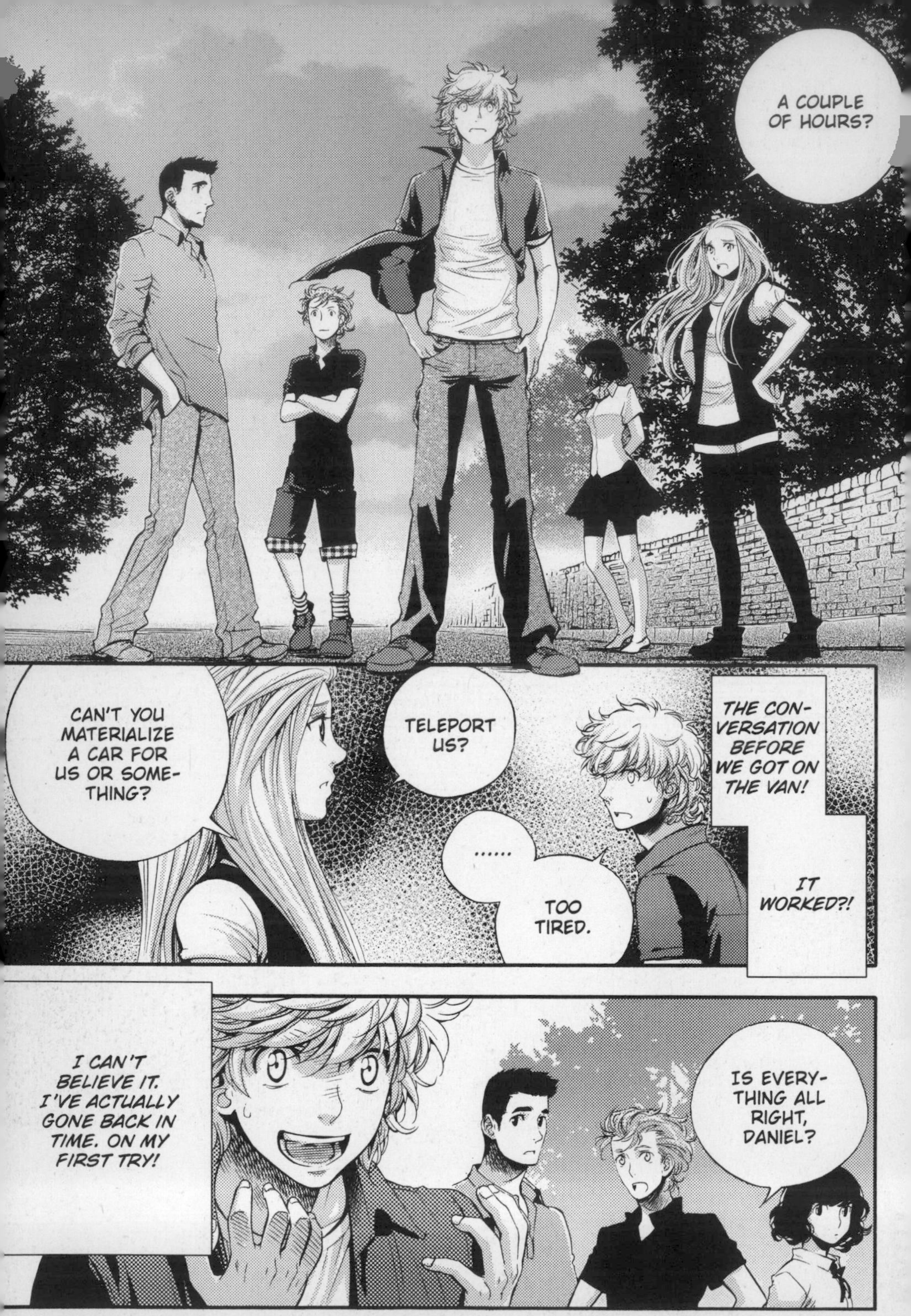
A COUPLE OF HOURS?
CAN'T YOU MATERIALIZE A CAR FOR US OR SOMETHING?
TELEPORT US?
......
TOO TIRED.
THE CONVERSATION BEFORE WE GOT ON THE VAN!
IT WORKED?!
I CAN'T BELIEVE IT. I'VE ACTUALLY GONE BACK IN TIME. ON MY FIRST TRY!
IS EVERYTHING ALL RIGHT, DANIEL?

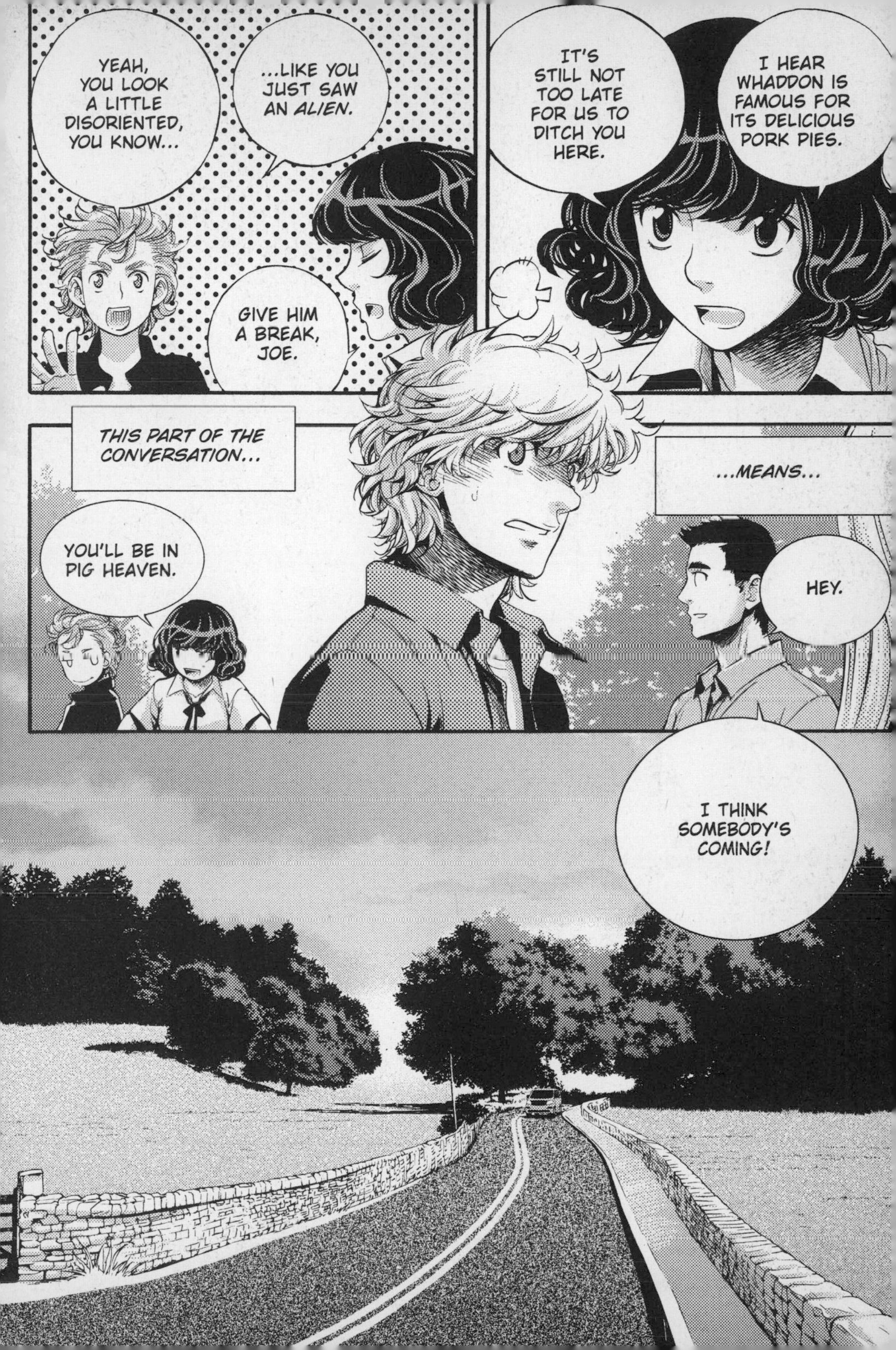
YEAH, YOU LOOK A LITTLE DISORIENTED, YOU KNOW...
...LIKE YOU JUST SAW AN *ALIEN*.
GIVE HIM A BREAK, JOE.
IT'S STILL NOT TOO LATE FOR US TO DITCH YOU HERE.
I HEAR WHADDON IS FAMOUS FOR ITS DELICIOUS PORK PIES.
THIS PART OF THE CONVERSATION...
YOU'LL BE IN PIG HEAVEN.
...MEANS...
HEY.
I THINK SOMEBODY'S COMING!

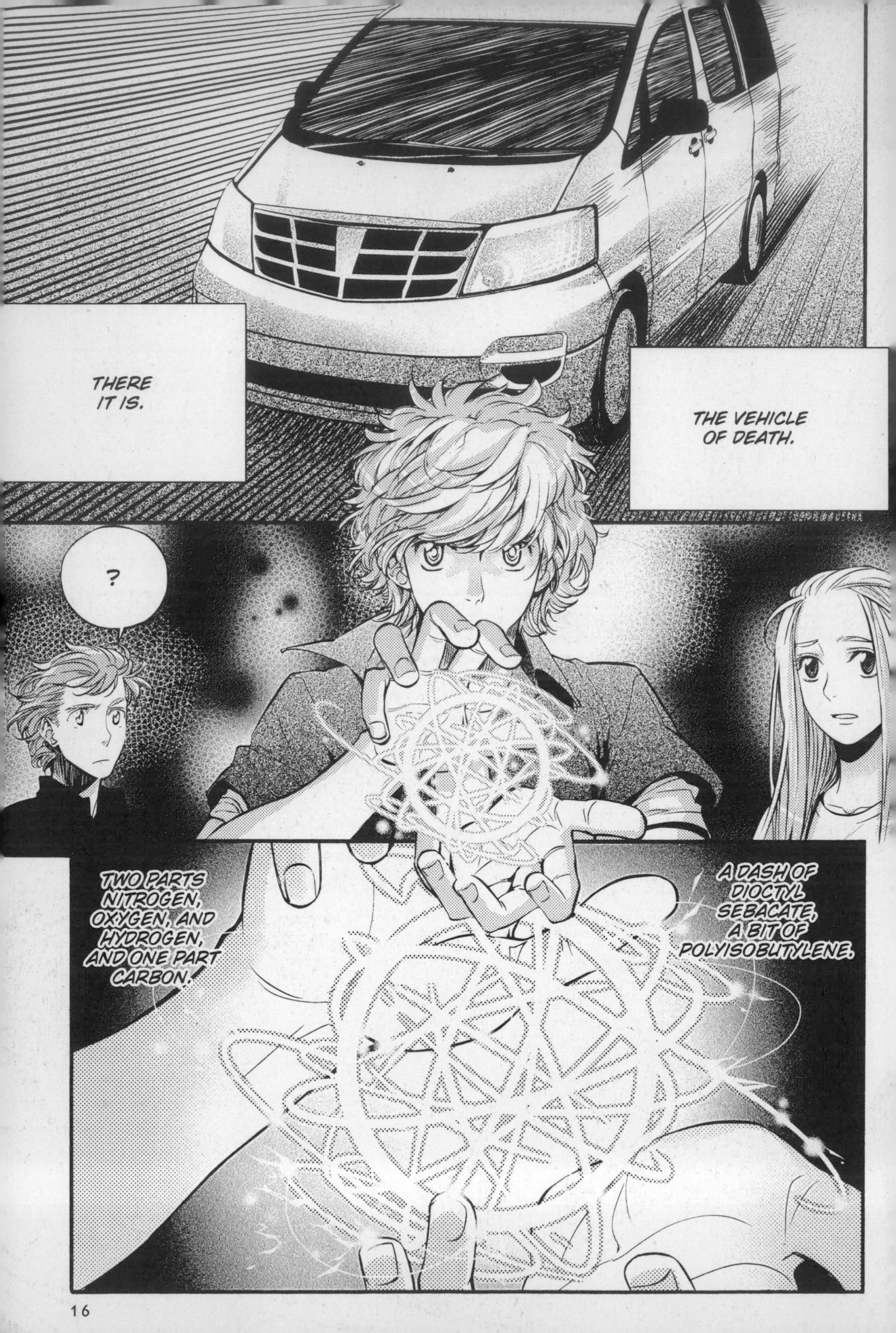
THERE IT IS.
THE VEHICLE OF DEATH.
?
TWO PARTS NITROGEN, OXYGEN, AND HYDROGEN, AND ONE PART CARBON.
A DASH OF DIOCTYL SEBACATE, A BIT OF POLYISOBUTYLENE.

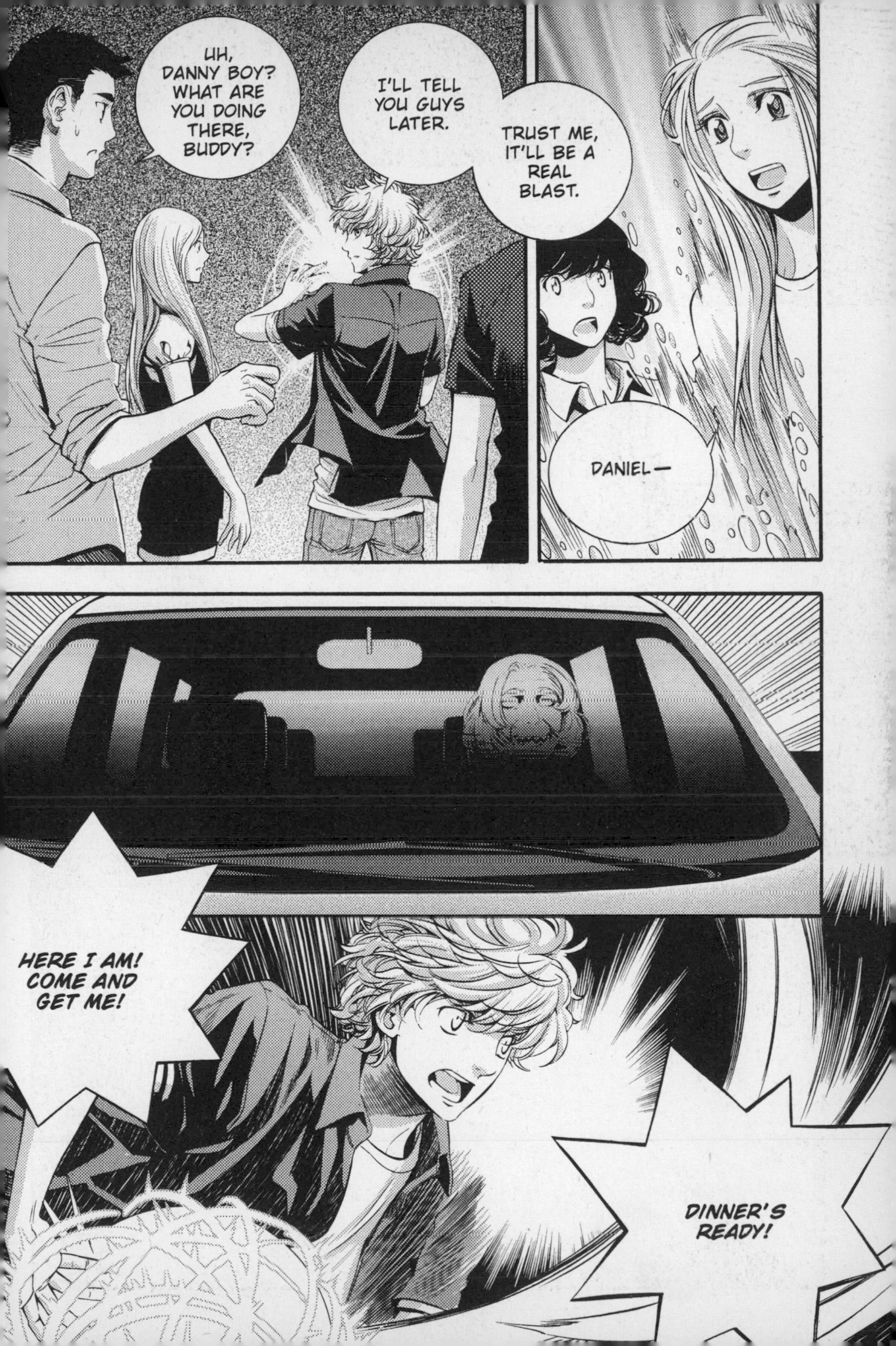
UH, DANNY BOY? WHAT ARE YOU DOING THERE, BUDDY?
I'LL TELL YOU GUYS LATER.
TRUST ME, IT'LL BE A REAL BLAST.
DANIEL—
HERE I AM! COME AND GET ME!
DINNER'S READY!

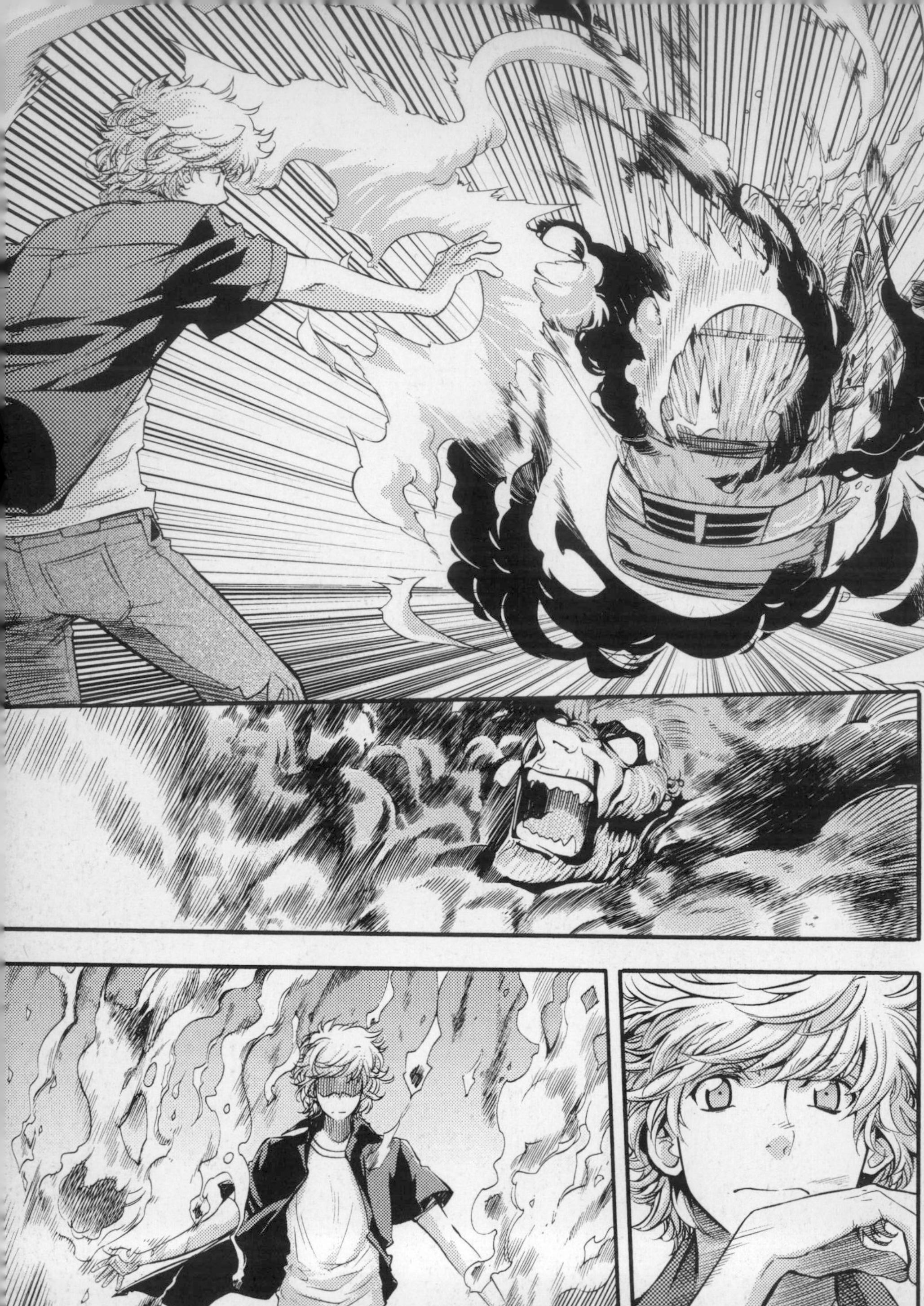

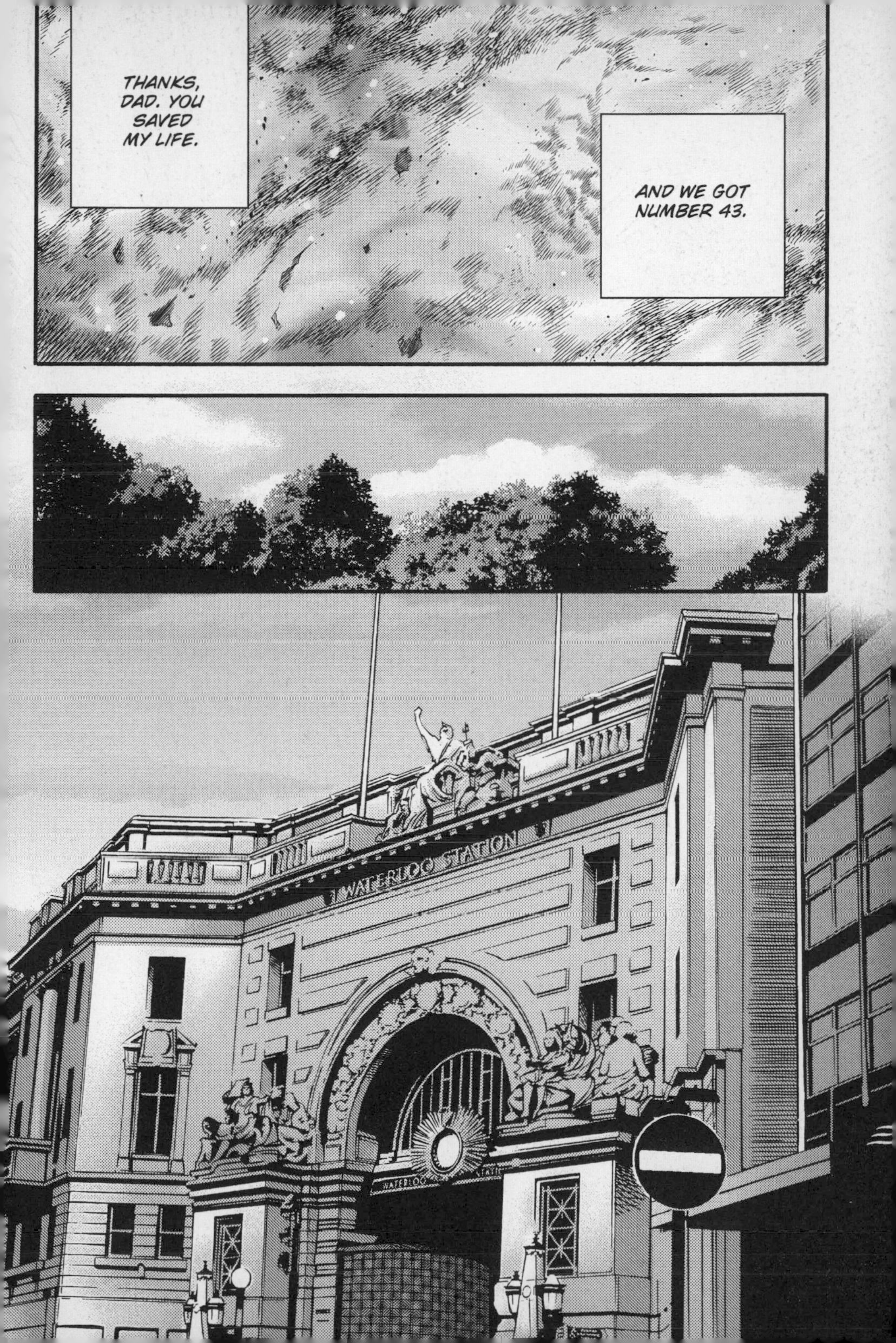
THANKS, DAD. YOU SAVED MY LIFE.
AND WE GOT NUMBER 43.
WATERLOO STATION

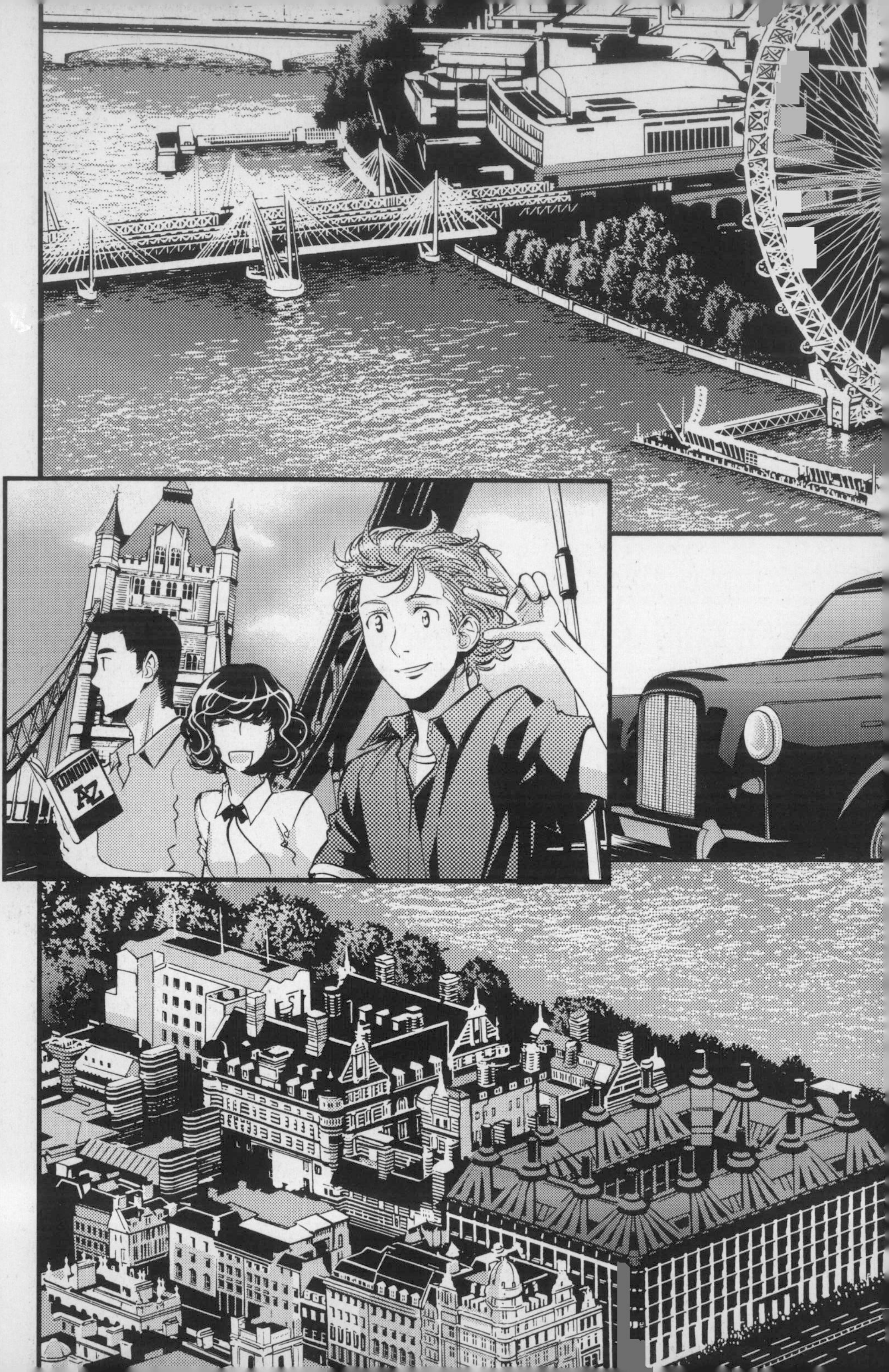
AZ

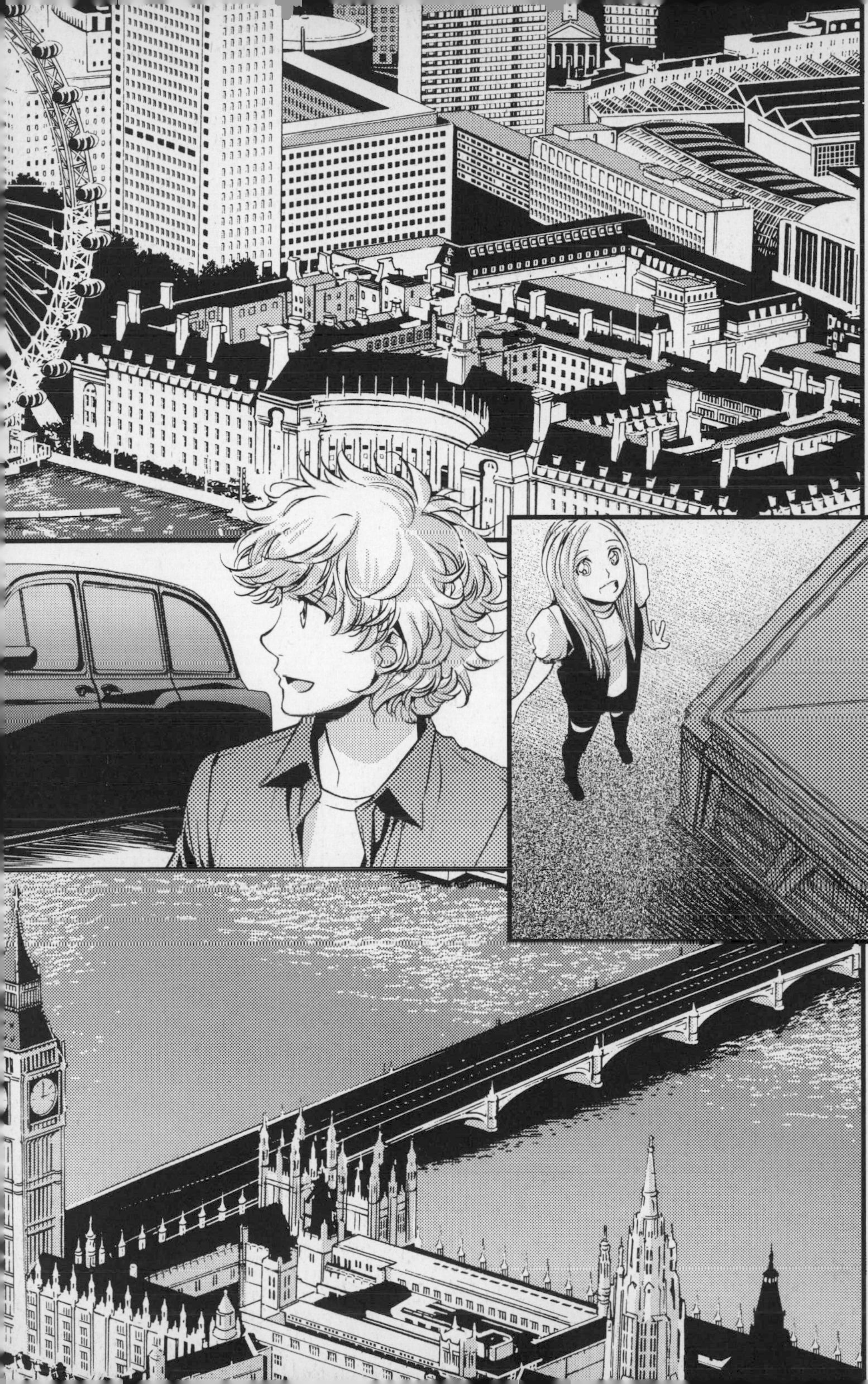

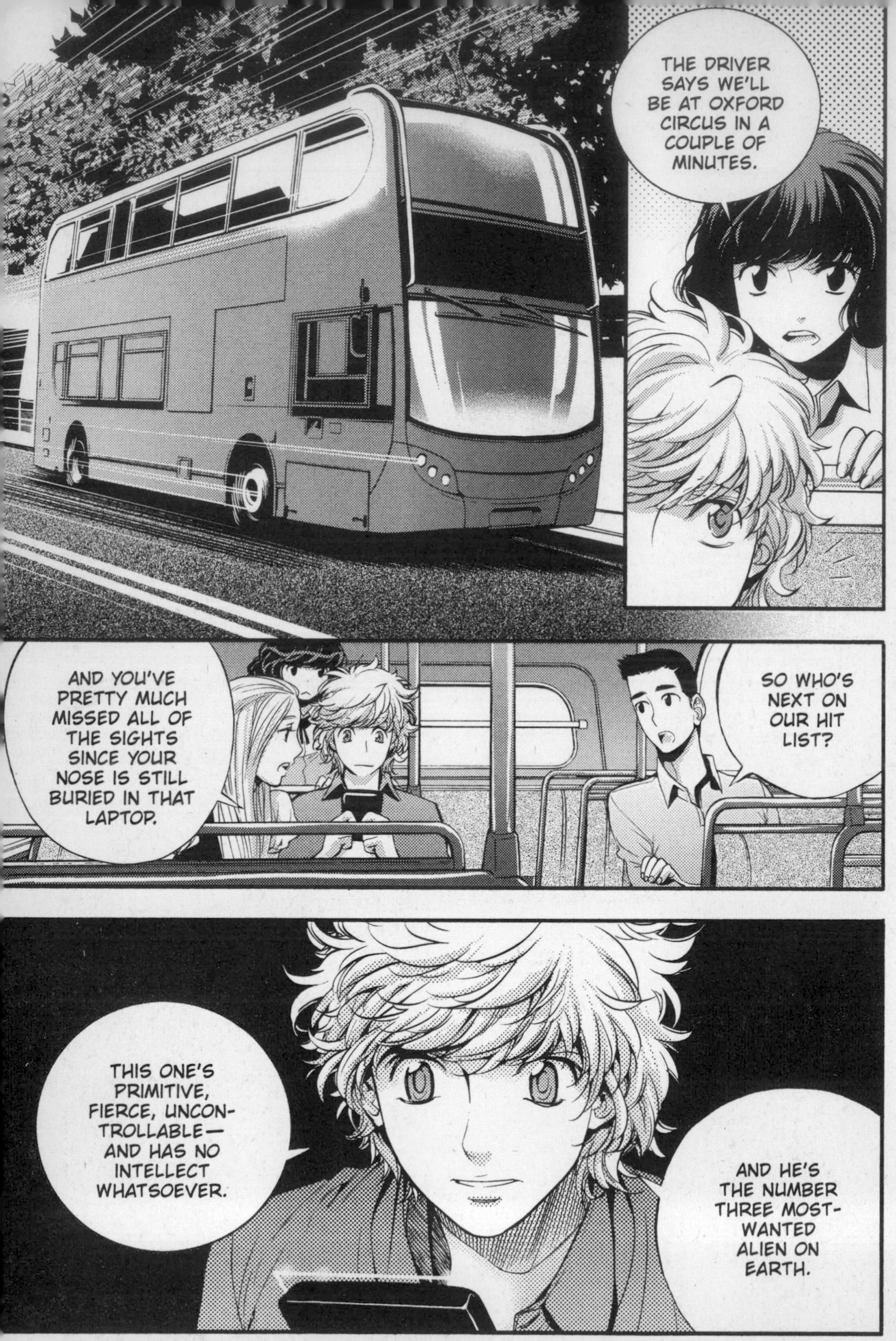
THE DRIVER SAYS WE'LL BE AT OXFORD CIRCUS IN A COUPLE OF MINUTES.
AND YOU'VE PRETTY MUCH MISSED ALL OF THE SIGHTS SINCE YOUR NOSE IS STILL BURIED IN THAT LAPTOP.
SO WHO'S NEXT ON OUR HIT LIST?
THIS ONE'S PRIMITIVE, FIERCE, UNCON-TROLLABLE— AND HAS NO INTELLECT WHATSOEVER.
AND HE'S THE NUMBER THREE MOST-WANTED ALIEN ON EARTH.

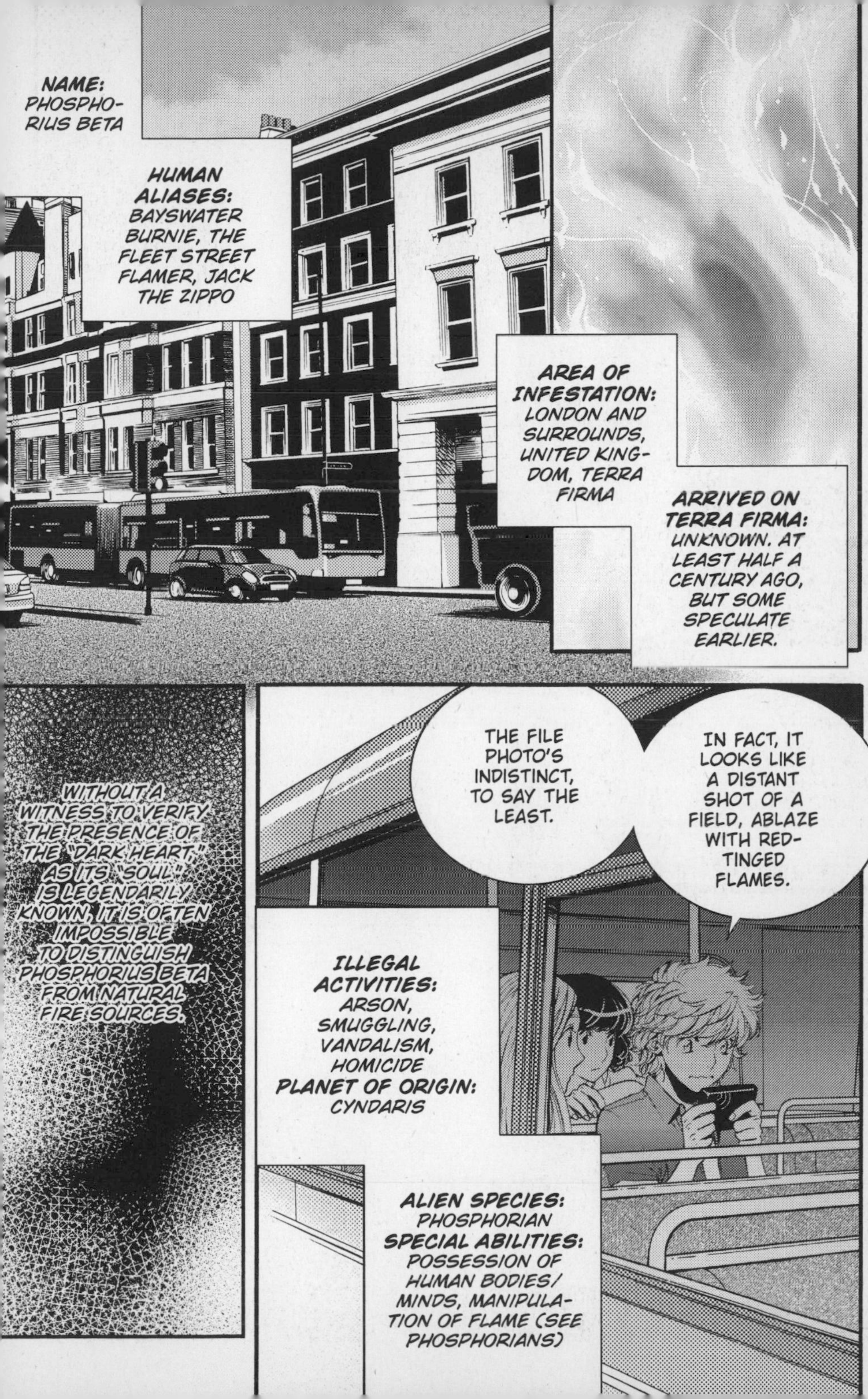
NAME: PHOSPHO-RIUS BETA
HUMAN ALIASES: BAYSWATER BURNIE, THE FLEET STREET FLAMER, JACK THE ZIPPO
AREA OF INFESTATION: LONDON AND SURROUNDS, UNITED KING-DOM, TERRA FIRMA
ARRIVED ON TERRA FIRMA: UNKNOWN. AT LEAST HALF A CENTURY AGO, BUT SOME SPECULATE EARLIER.
WITHOUT A WITNESS TO VERIFY THE PRESENCE OF THE "DARK HEART," AS ITS "SOUL" IS LEGENDARILY KNOWN, IT IS OFTEN IMPOSSIBLE TO DISTINGUISH PHOSPHORIUS BETA FROM NATURAL FIRE SOURCES.
THE FILE PHOTO'S INDISTINCT, TO SAY THE LEAST.
IN FACT, IT LOOKS LIKE A DISTANT SHOT OF A FIELD, ABLAZE WITH RED-TINGED FLAMES.
ILLEGAL ACTIVITIES: ARSON, SMUGGLING, VANDALISM, HOMICIDE
PLANET OF ORIGIN: CYNDARIS
ALIEN SPECIES: PHOSPHORIAN
SPECIAL ABILITIES: POSSESSION OF HUMAN BODIES/ MINDS, MANIPULA-TION OF FLAME (SEE PHOSPHORIANS)

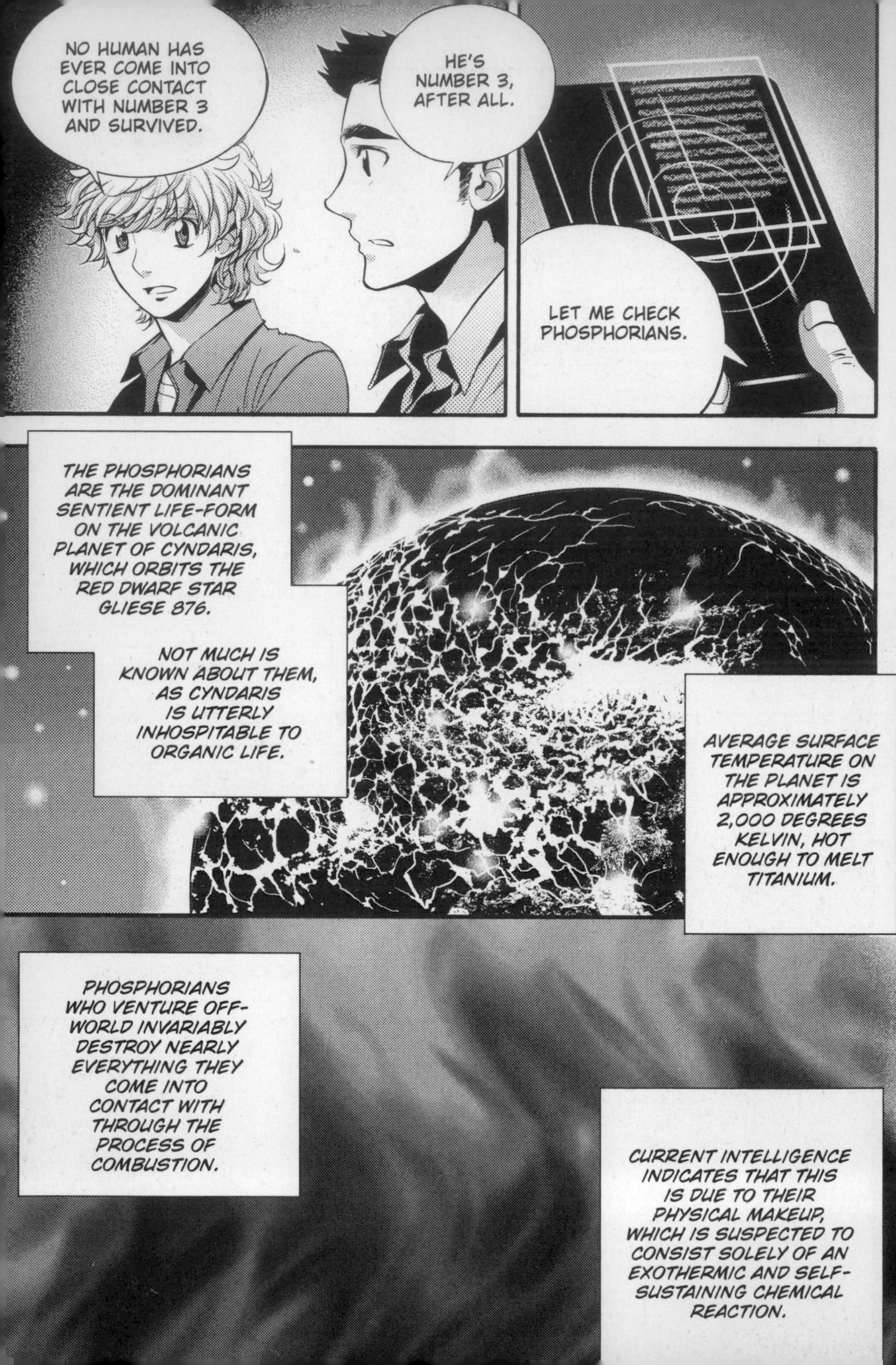
NO HUMAN HAS EVER COME INTO CLOSE CONTACT WITH NUMBER 3 AND SURVIVED.
HE'S NUMBER 3, AFTER ALL.
LET ME CHECK PHOSPHORIANS.
THE PHOSPHORIANS ARE THE DOMINANT SENTIENT LIFE-FORM ON THE VOLCANIC PLANET OF CYNDARIS, WHICH ORBITS THE RED DWARF STAR GLIESE 876.
NOT MUCH IS KNOWN ABOUT THEM, AS CYNDARIS IS UTTERLY INHOSPITABLE TO ORGANIC LIFE.
AVERAGE SURFACE TEMPERATURE ON THE PLANET IS APPROXIMATELY 2,000 DEGREES KELVIN, HOT ENOUGH TO MELT TITANIUM.
PHOSPHORIANS WHO VENTURE OFF-WORLD INVARIABLY DESTROY NEARLY EVERYTHING THEY COME INTO CONTACT WITH THROUGH THE PROCESS OF COMBUSTION.
CURRENT INTELLIGENCE INDICATES THAT THIS IS DUE TO THEIR PHYSICAL MAKEUP, WHICH IS SUSPECTED TO CONSIST SOLELY OF AN EXOTHERMIC AND SELF-SUSTAINING CHEMICAL REACTION.

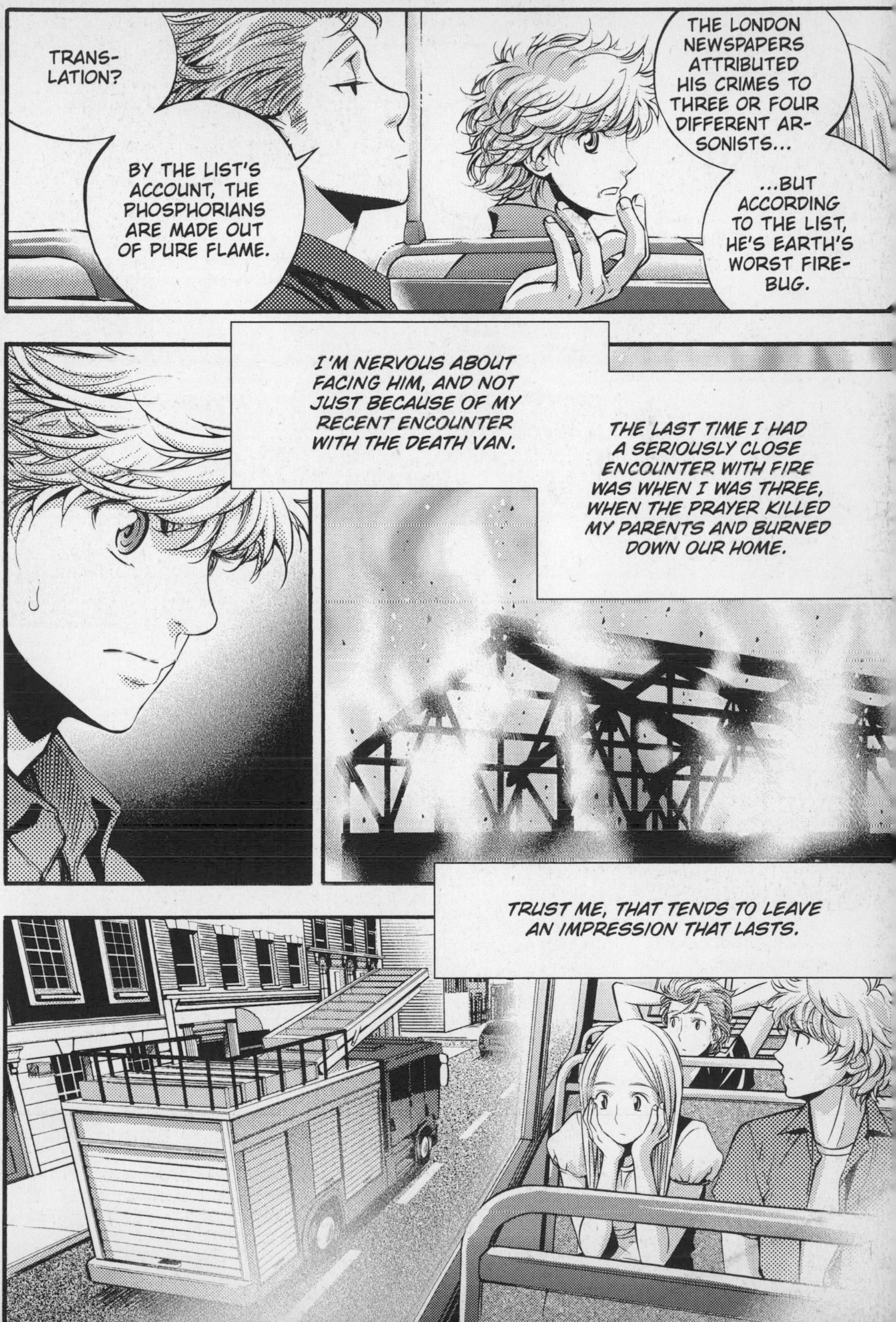
TRANS-LATION?
BY THE LIST'S ACCOUNT, THE PHOSPHORIANS ARE MADE OUT OF PURE FLAME.
THE LONDON NEWSPAPERS ATTRIBUTED HIS CRIMES TO THREE OR FOUR DIFFERENT AR-SONISTS...
...BUT ACCORDING TO THE LIST, HE'S EARTH'S WORST FIRE-BUG.
I'M NERVOUS ABOUT FACING HIM, AND NOT JUST BECAUSE OF MY RECENT ENCOUNTER WITH THE DEATH VAN.
THE LAST TIME I HAD A SERIOUSLY CLOSE ENCOUNTER WITH FIRE WAS WHEN I WAS THREE, WHEN THE PRAYER KILLED MY PARENTS AND BURNED DOWN OUR HOME.
TRUST ME, THAT TENDS TO LEAVE AN IMPRESSION THAT LASTS.

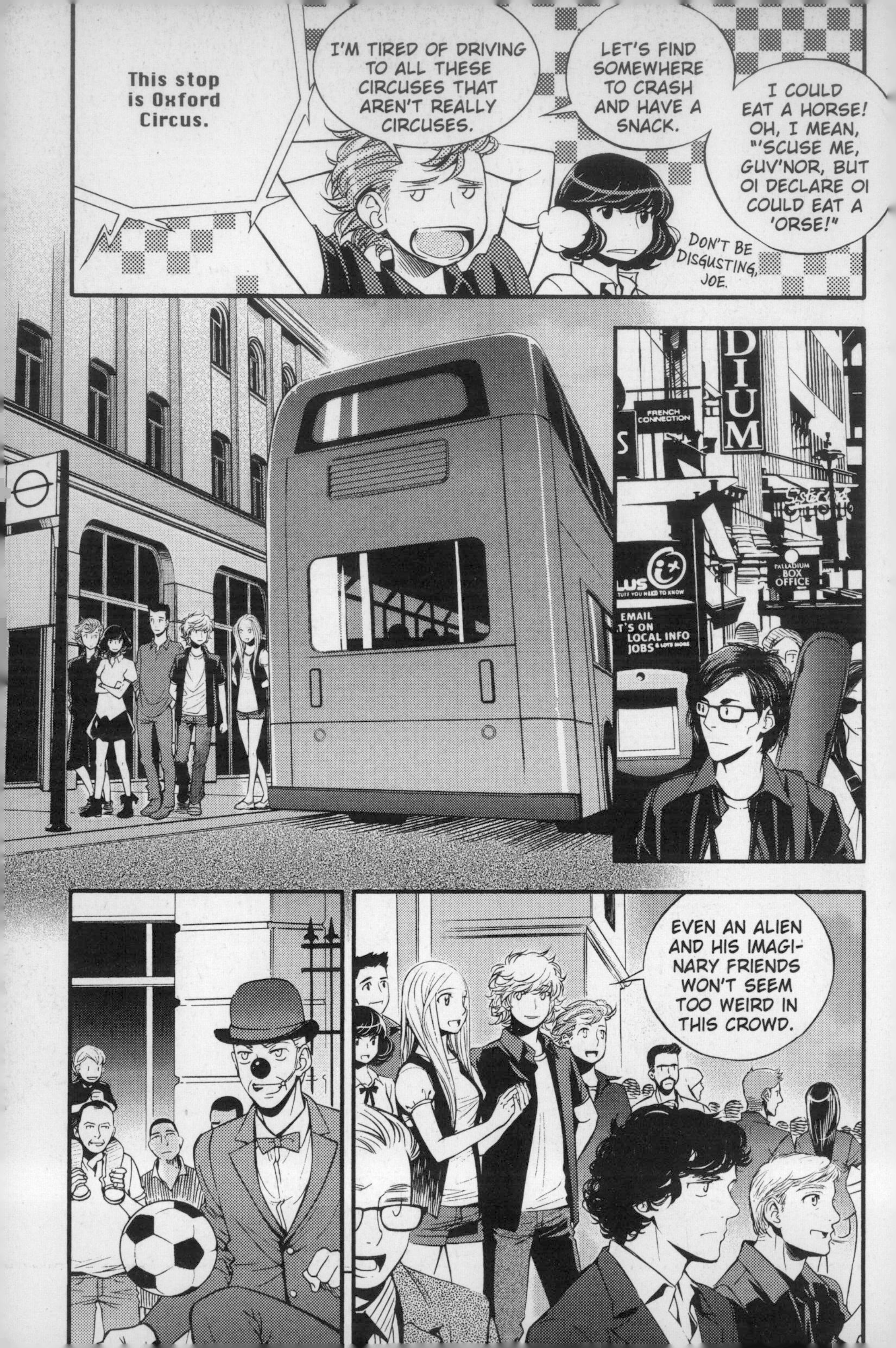
This stop is Oxford Circus.
I'M TIRED OF DRIVING TO ALL THESE CIRCUSES THAT AREN'T REALLY CIRCUSES.
LET'S FIND SOMEWHERE TO CRASH AND HAVE A SNACK.
I COULD EAT A HORSE! OH, I MEAN, "'SCUSE ME, GUV'NOR, BUT OI DECLARE OI COULD EAT A 'ORSE!"
DON'T BE DISGUSTING, JOE.
DIUM
FRENCH CONNECTION
PALLADIUM BOX OFFICE
EMAIL
LOCAL INFO
JOBS
EVEN AN ALIEN AND HIS IMAGINARY FRIENDS WON'T SEEM TOO WEIRD IN THIS CROWD.

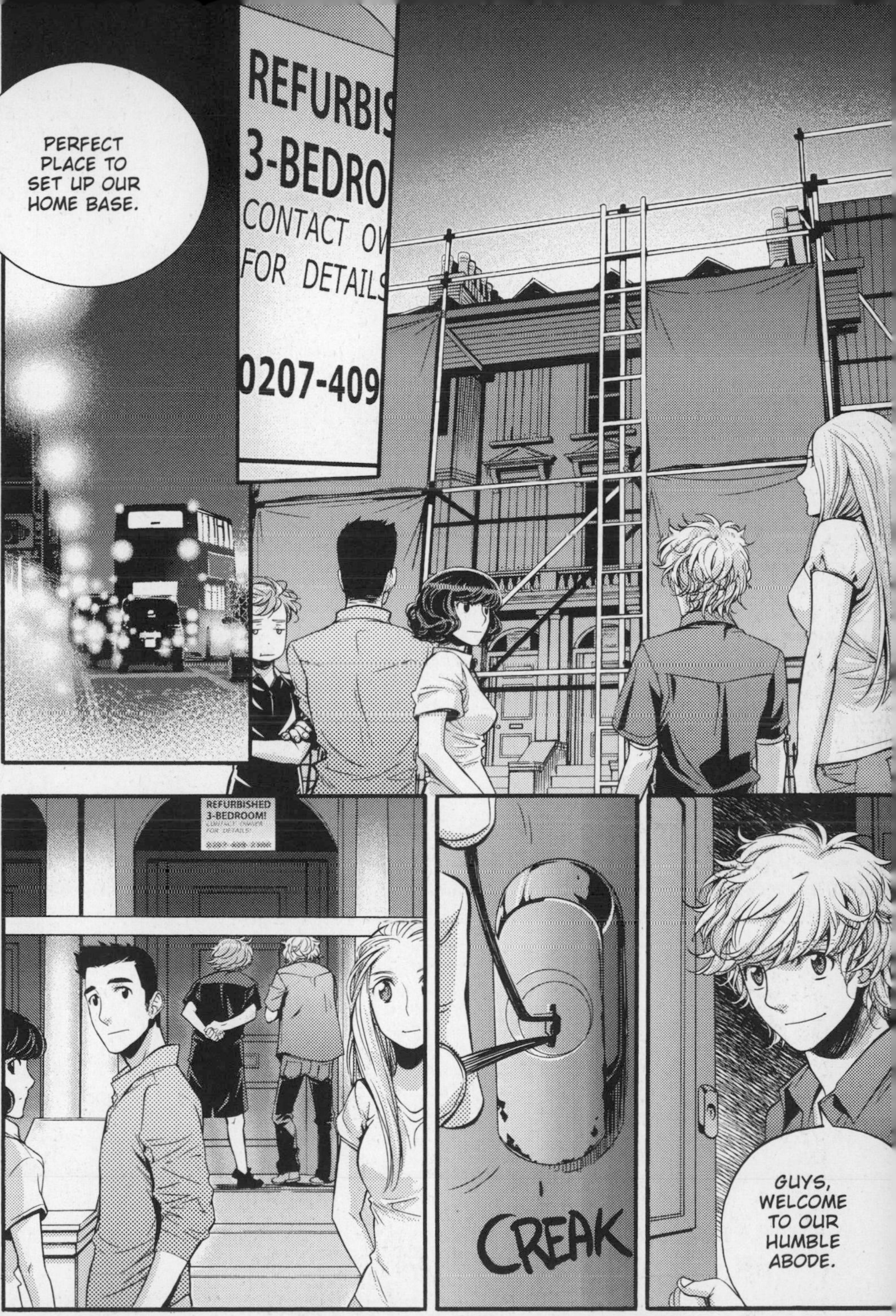
PERFECT PLACE TO SET UP OUR HOME BASE.
REFURBIS
3-BEDRO
CONTACT OV
FOR DETAILS
0207-409
REFURBISHED 3-BEDROOM!
CONTACT OWNER FOR DETAILS!
CREAK
GUYS, WELCOME TO OUR HUMBLE ABODE.

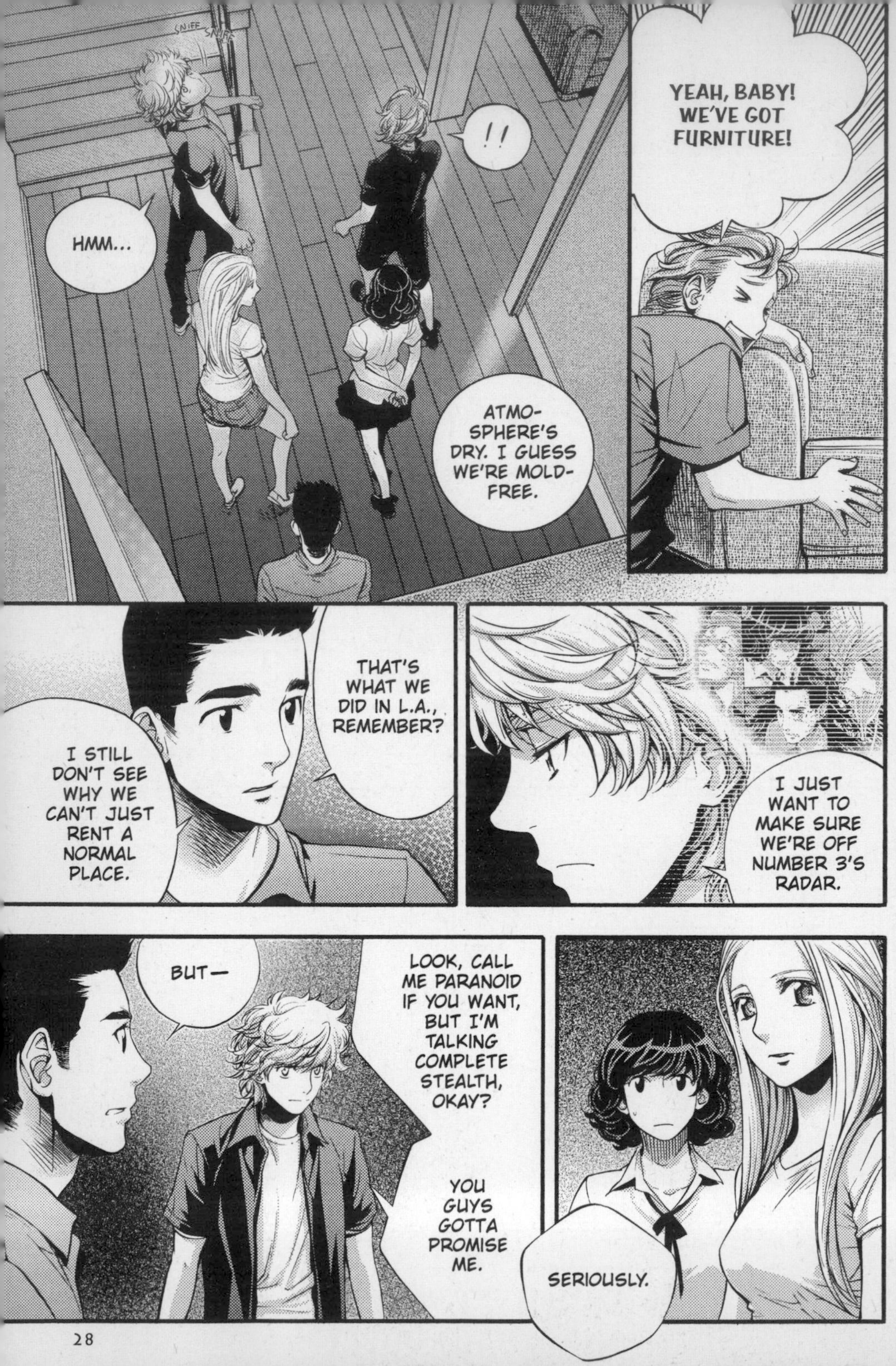
SNIFF SNIFF
!!
HMM...
ATMOSPHERE'S DRY. I GUESS WE'RE MOLD-FREE.
YEAH, BABY! WE'VE GOT FURNITURE!
I STILL DON'T SEE WHY WE CAN'T JUST RENT A NORMAL PLACE.
THAT'S WHAT WE DID IN L.A., REMEMBER?
I JUST WANT TO MAKE SURE WE'RE OFF NUMBER 3'S RADAR.
BUT—
LOOK, CALL ME PARANOID IF YOU WANT, BUT I'M TALKING COMPLETE STEALTH, OKAY?
YOU GUYS GOTTA PROMISE ME.
SERIOUSLY.

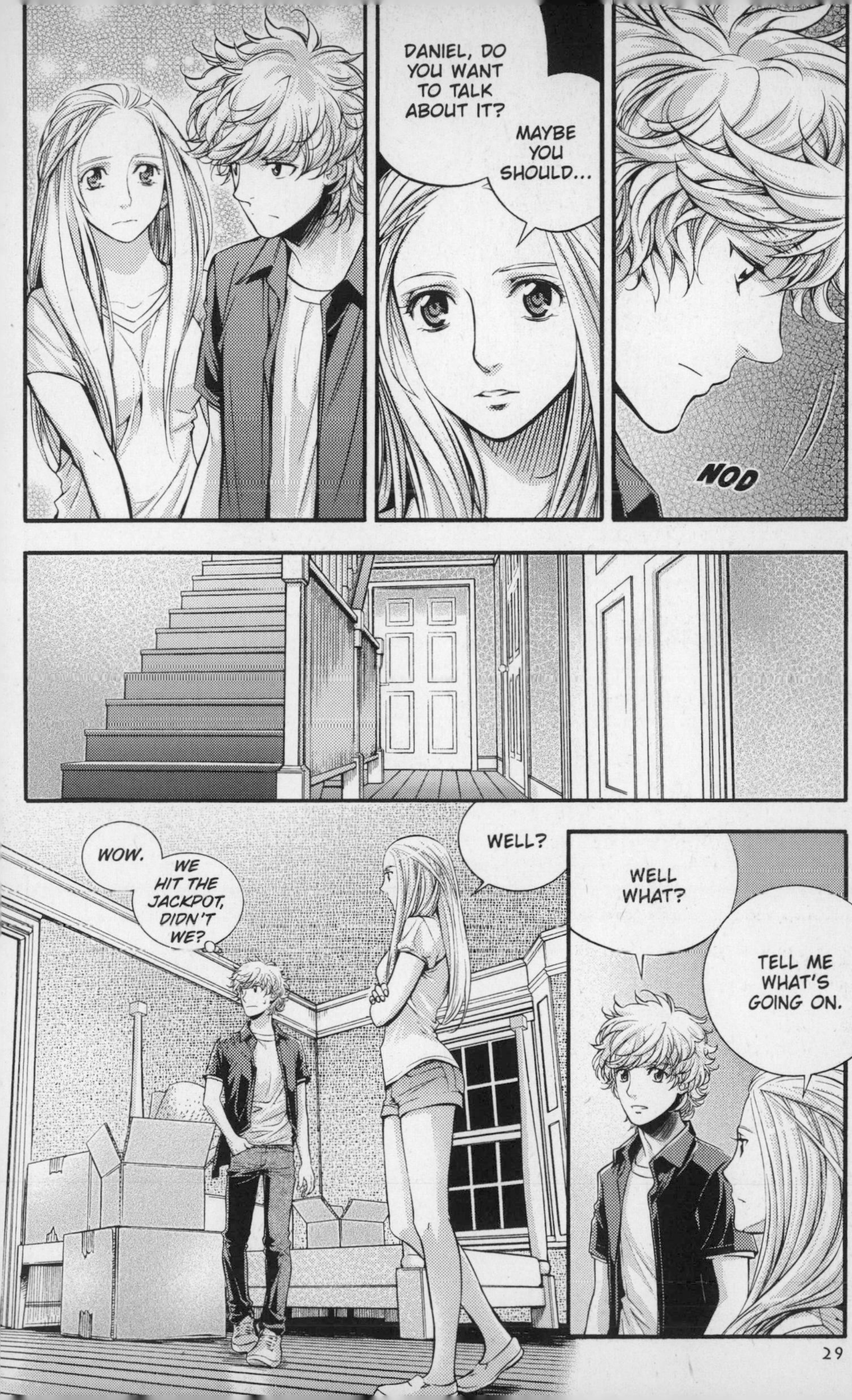
DANIEL, DO YOU WANT TO TALK ABOUT IT?
MAYBE YOU SHOULD...
NOD
WOW.
WE HIT THE JACKPOT, DIDN'T WE?
WELL?
WELL WHAT?
TELL ME WHAT'S GOING ON.

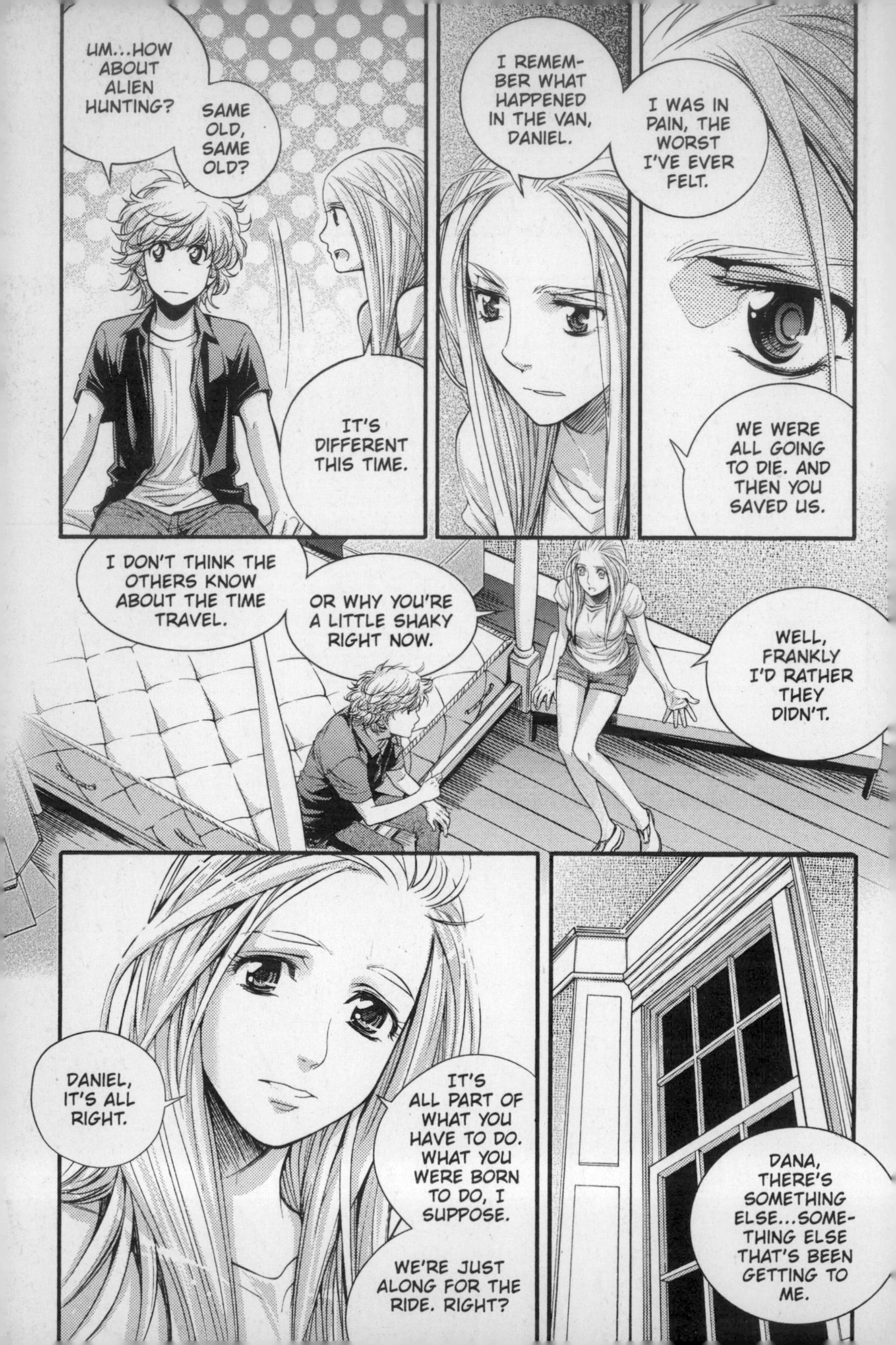

UM...HOW ABOUT ALIEN HUNTING?
SAME OLD, SAME OLD?
IT'S DIFFERENT THIS TIME.
I REMEMBER WHAT HAPPENED IN THE VAN, DANIEL.
I WAS IN PAIN, THE WORST I'VE EVER FELT.
WE WERE ALL GOING TO DIE. AND THEN YOU SAVED US.
I DON'T THINK THE OTHERS KNOW ABOUT THE TIME TRAVEL.
OR WHY YOU'RE A LITTLE SHAKY RIGHT NOW.
WELL, FRANKLY I'D RATHER THEY DIDN'T.
DANIEL, IT'S ALL RIGHT.
IT'S ALL PART OF WHAT YOU HAVE TO DO. WHAT YOU WERE BORN TO DO, I SUPPOSE.
WE'RE JUST ALONG FOR THE RIDE. RIGHT?
DANA, THERE'S SOMETHING ELSE...SOMETHING ELSE THAT'S BEEN GETTING TO ME.

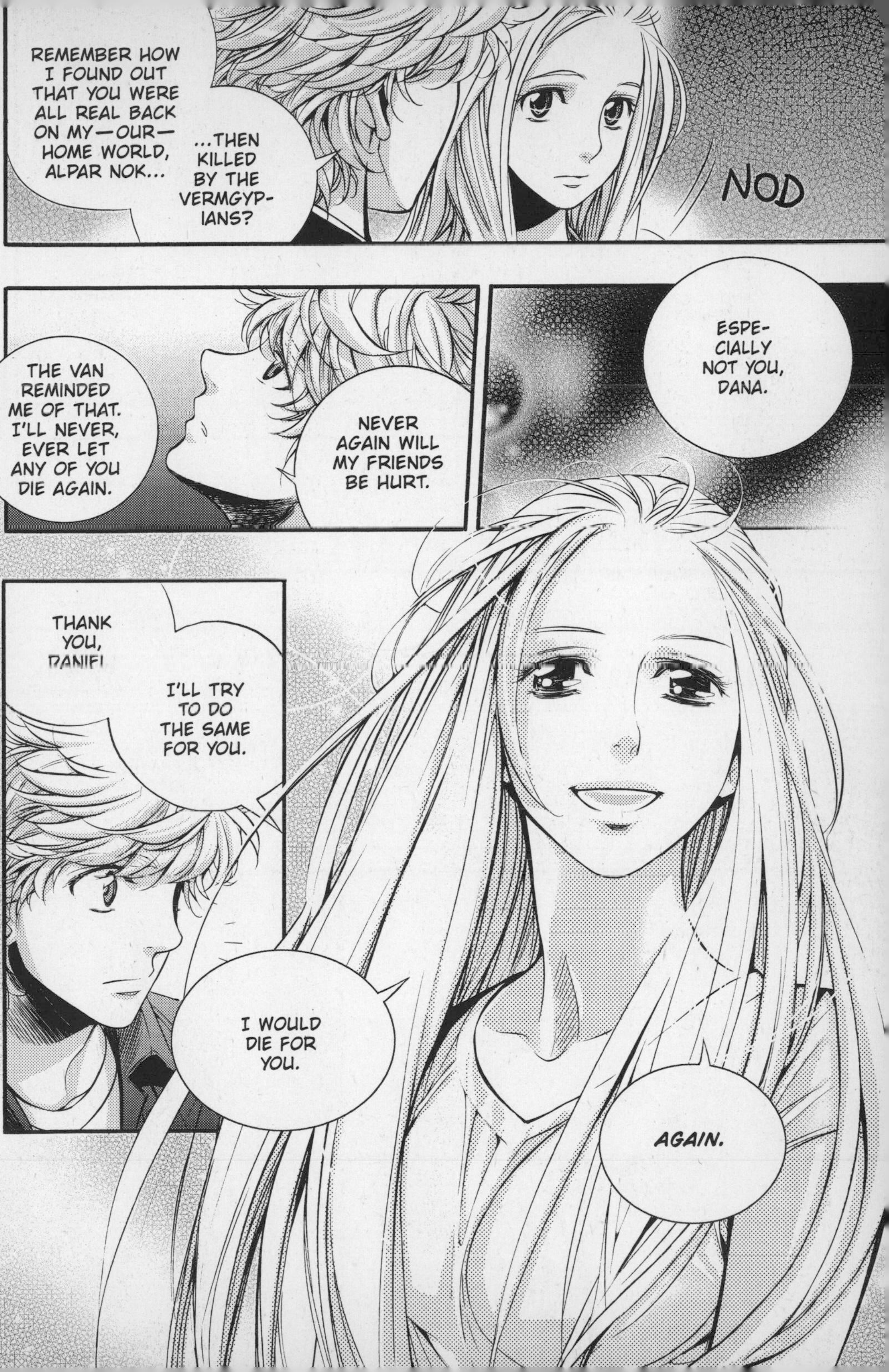
REMEMBER HOW I FOUND OUT THAT YOU WERE ALL REAL BACK ON MY—OUR—HOME WORLD, ALPAR NOK...
...THEN KILLED BY THE VERMGYP-IANS?
NOD
THE VAN REMINDED ME OF THAT. I'LL NEVER, EVER LET ANY OF YOU DIE AGAIN.
NEVER AGAIN WILL MY FRIENDS BE HURT.
ESPE-CIALLY NOT YOU, DANA.
THANK YOU, DANIEL.
I'LL TRY TO DO THE SAME FOR YOU.
I WOULD DIE FOR YOU.
AGAIN.

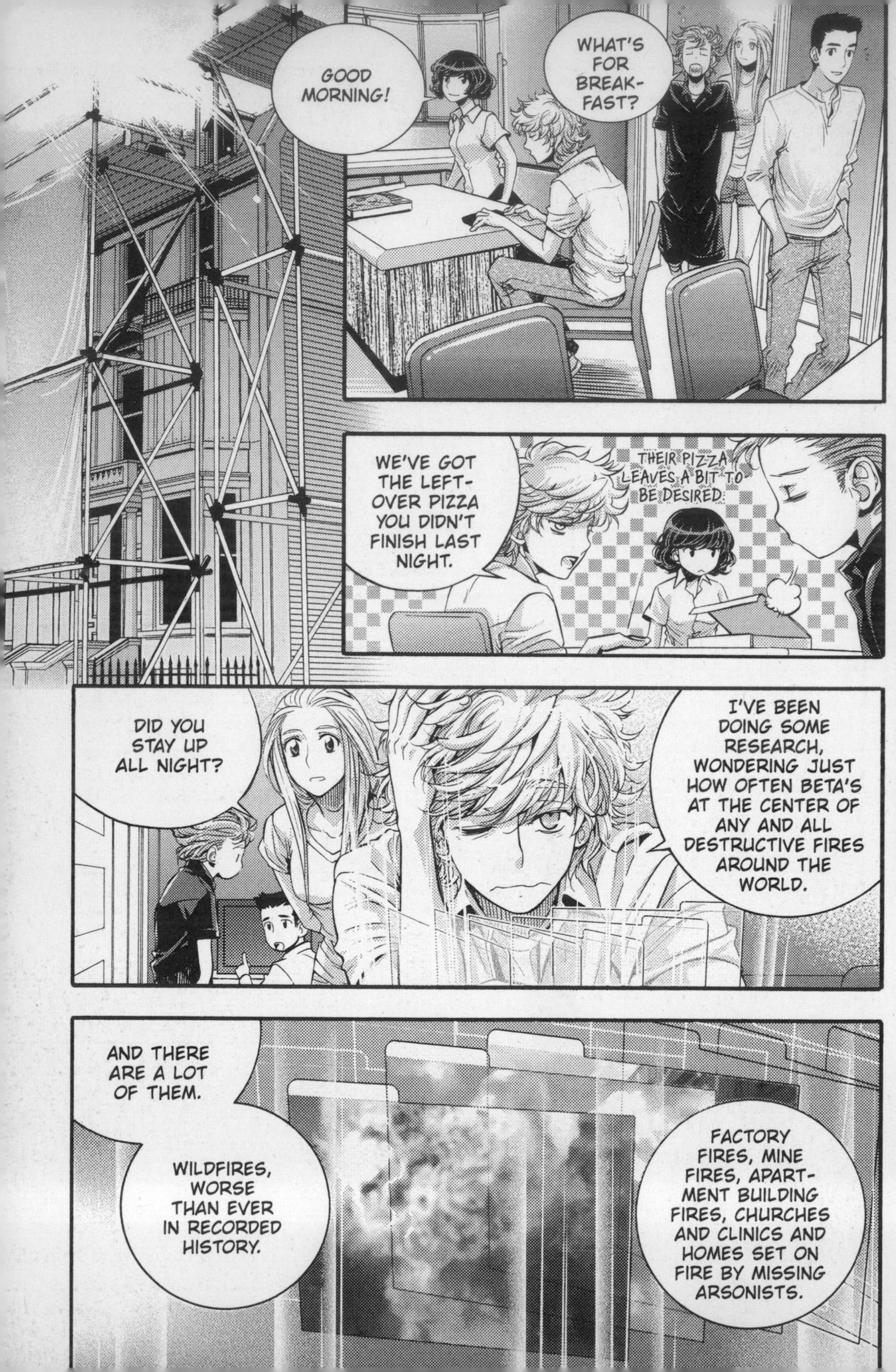
GOOD MORNING!
WHAT'S FOR BREAK-FAST?
WE'VE GOT THE LEFT-OVER PIZZA YOU DIDN'T FINISH LAST NIGHT.
THEIR PIZZA LEAVES A BIT TO BE DESIRED
DID YOU STAY UP ALL NIGHT?
I'VE BEEN DOING SOME RESEARCH, WONDERING JUST HOW OFTEN BETA'S AT THE CENTER OF ANY AND ALL DESTRUCTIVE FIRES AROUND THE WORLD.
AND THERE ARE A LOT OF THEM.
WILDFIRES, WORSE THAN EVER IN RECORDED HISTORY.
FACTORY FIRES, MINE FIRES, APARTMENT BUILDING FIRES, CHURCHES AND CLINICS AND HOMES SET ON FIRE BY MISSING ARSONISTS.

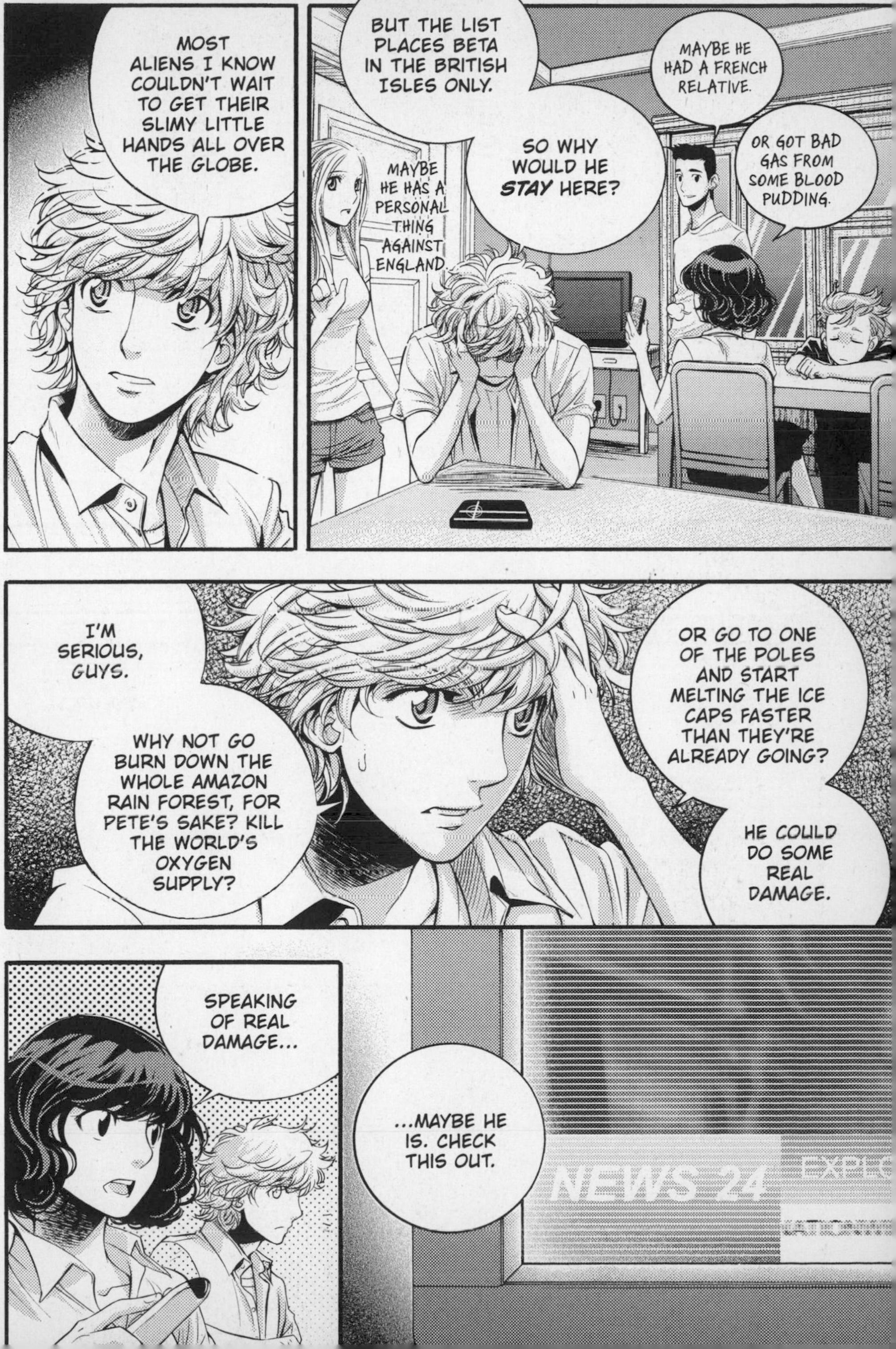
MOST ALIENS I KNOW COULDN'T WAIT TO GET THEIR SLIMY LITTLE HANDS ALL OVER THE GLOBE.
BUT THE LIST PLACES BETA IN THE BRITISH ISLES ONLY.
SO WHY WOULD HE *STAY* HERE?
MAYBE HE HAS A PERSONAL THING AGAINST ENGLAND.
MAYBE HE HAD A FRENCH RELATIVE.
OR GOT BAD GAS FROM SOME BLOOD PUDDING.
I'M SERIOUS, GUYS.
WHY NOT GO BURN DOWN THE WHOLE AMAZON RAIN FOREST, FOR PETE'S SAKE? KILL THE WORLD'S OXYGEN SUPPLY?
OR GO TO ONE OF THE POLES AND START MELTING THE ICE CAPS FASTER THAN THEY'RE ALREADY GOING?
HE COULD DO SOME REAL DAMAGE.
SPEAKING OF REAL DAMAGE...
...MAYBE HE IS. CHECK THIS OUT.
NEWS 24

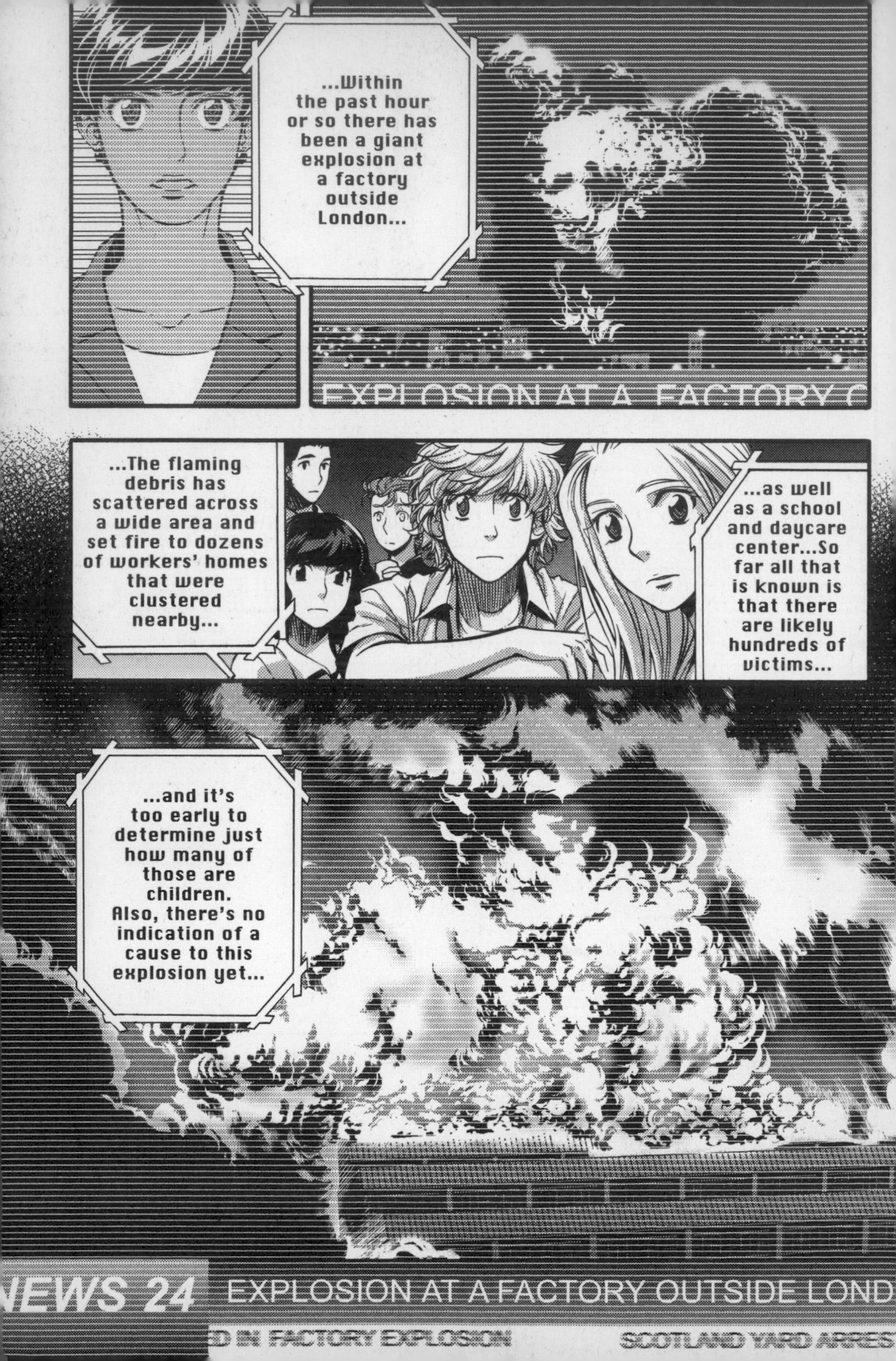
...Within the past hour or so there has been a giant explosion at a factory outside London...
EXPLOSION AT A FACTORY
...The flaming debris has scattered across a wide area and set fire to dozens of workers' homes that were clustered nearby...
...as well as a school and daycare center...So far all that is known is that there are likely hundreds of victims...
...and it's too early to determine just how many of those are children. Also, there's no indication of a cause to this explosion yet...
NEWS 24
EXPLOSION AT A FACTORY OUTSIDE LOND
D IN FACTORY EXPLOSION
SCOTLAND YARD ARRES

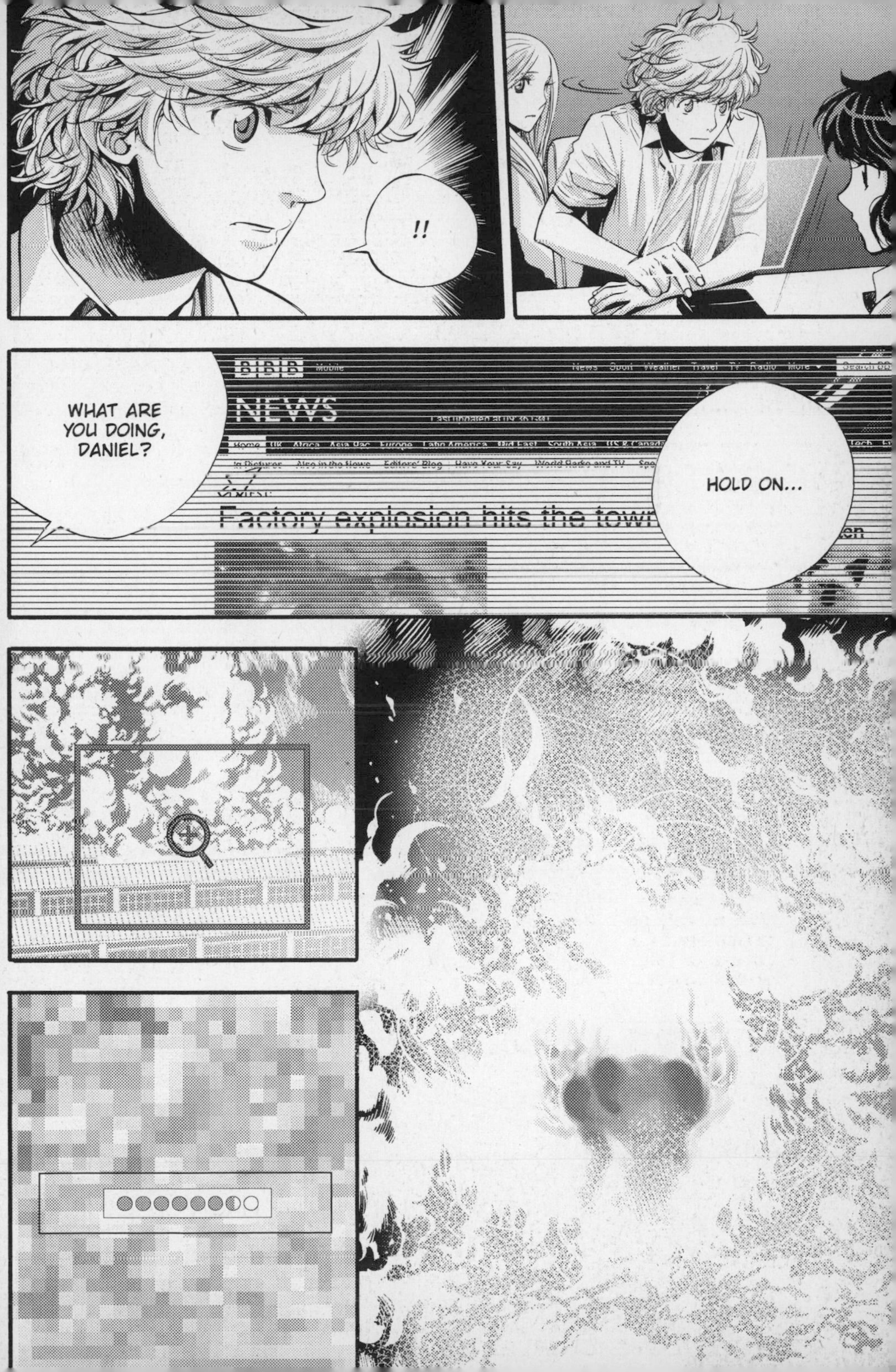
!!
WHAT ARE YOU DOING, DANIEL?
BBB Mobile
News Sport Weather Travel TV Radio More
NEWS
Factory explosion hits the towr
HOLD ON...

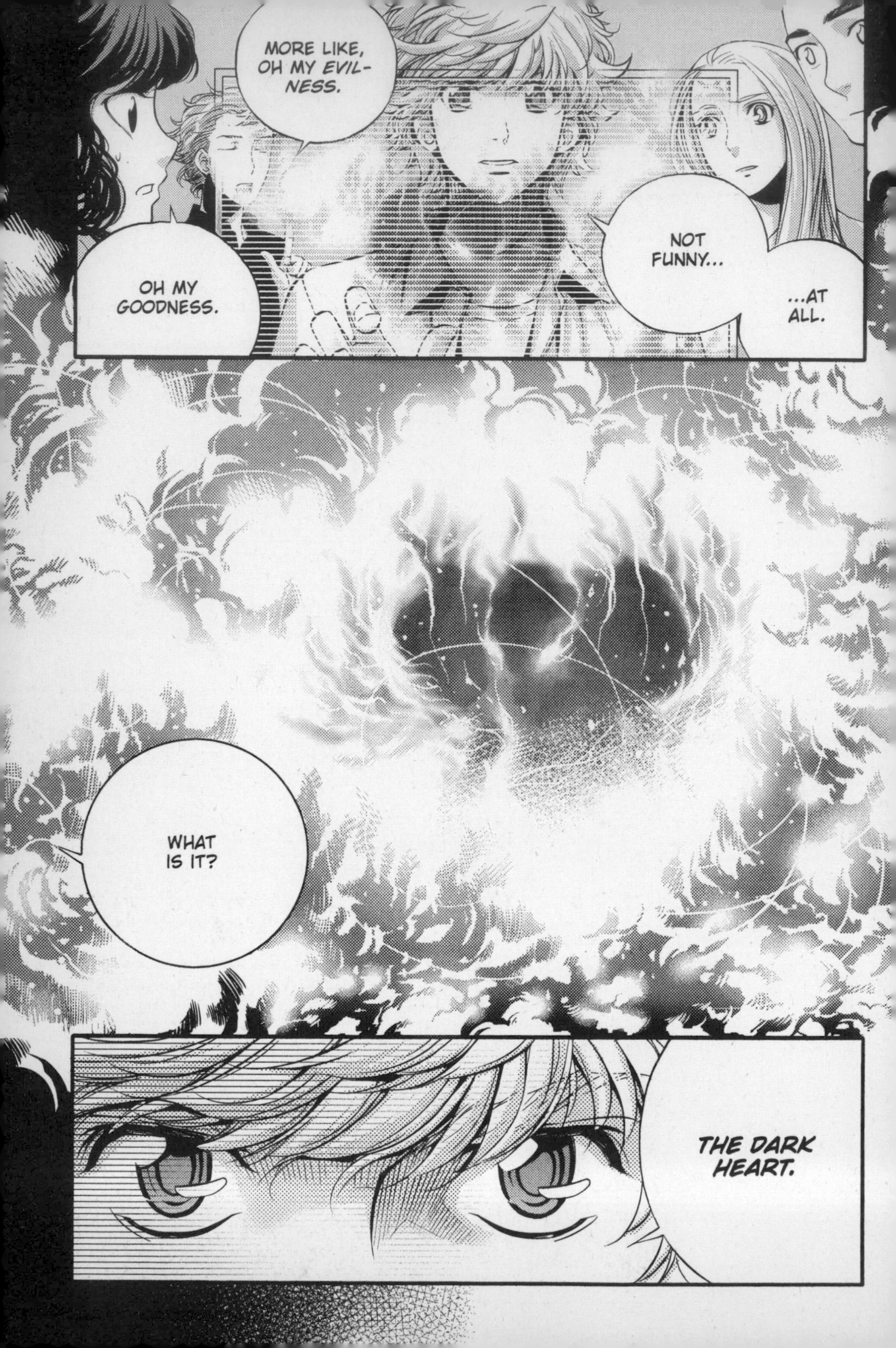
OH MY GOODNESS.
MORE LIKE, OH MY EVIL-NESS.
NOT FUNNY...
...AT ALL.
WHAT IS IT?
THE DARK HEART.

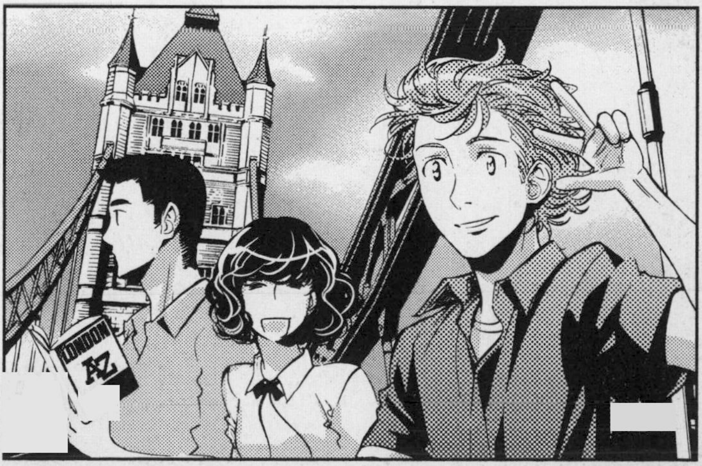
LONDON
AZ

DANIEL X

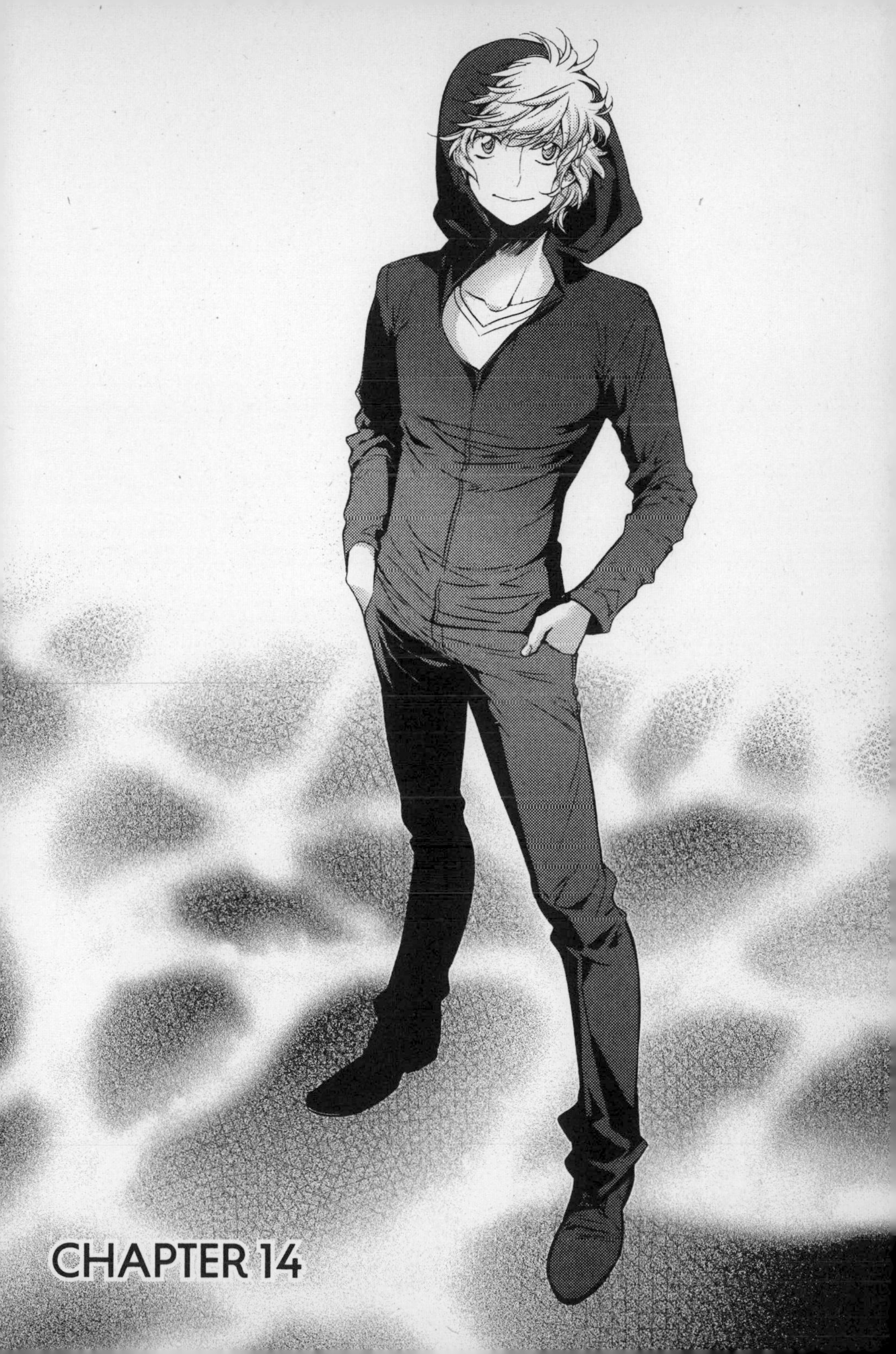
CHAPTER 14

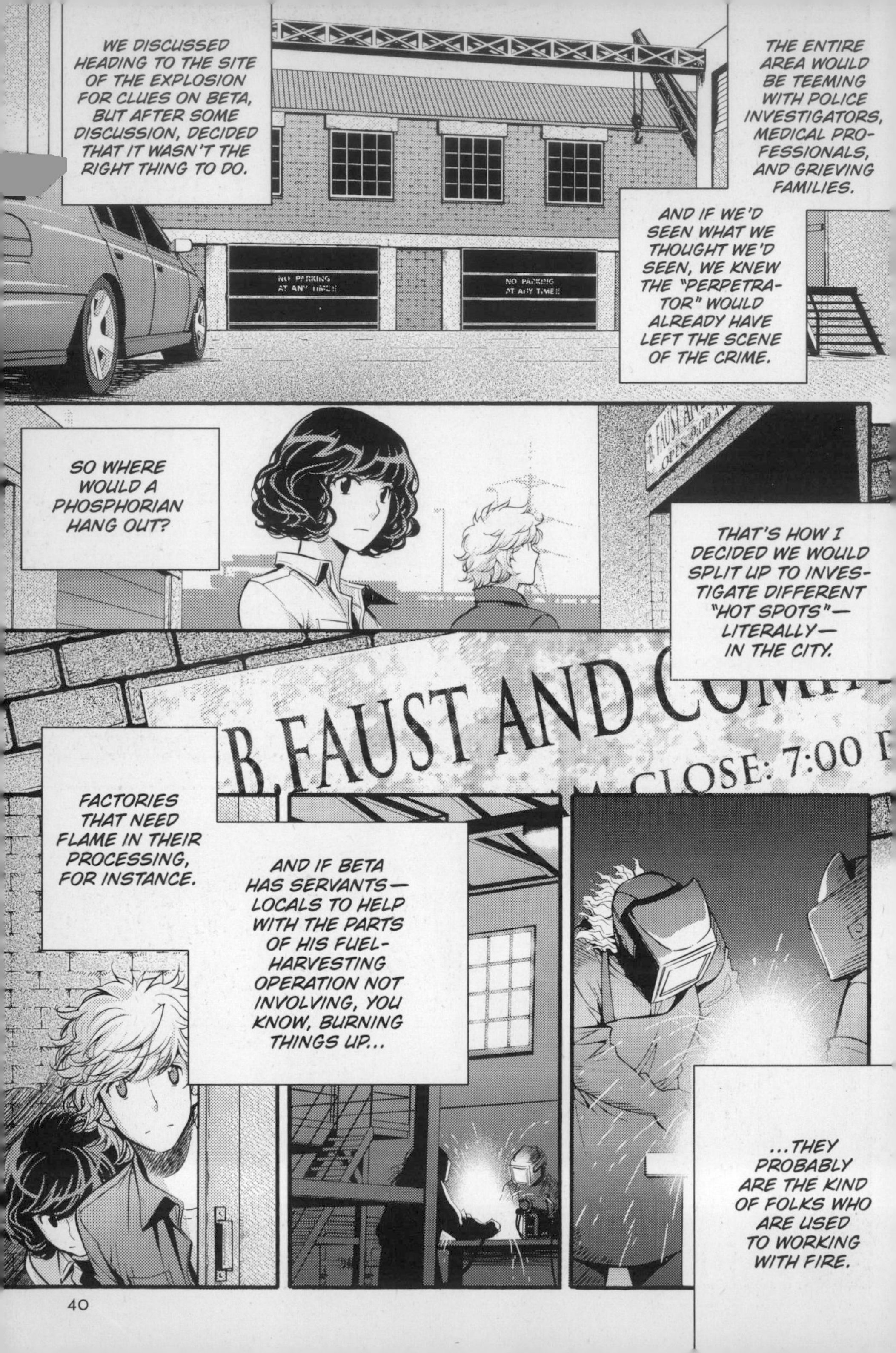
WE DISCUSSED HEADING TO THE SITE OF THE EXPLOSION FOR CLUES ON BETA, BUT AFTER SOME DISCUSSION, DECIDED THAT IT WASN'T THE RIGHT THING TO DO.
NO PARKING AT ANY TIME!!
NO PARKING AT ANY TIME!!
THE ENTIRE AREA WOULD BE TEEMING WITH POLICE INVESTIGATORS, MEDICAL PROFESSIONALS, AND GRIEVING FAMILIES.
AND IF WE'D SEEN WHAT WE THOUGHT WE'D SEEN, WE KNEW THE "PERPETRATOR" WOULD ALREADY HAVE LEFT THE SCENE OF THE CRIME.
SO WHERE WOULD A PHOSPHORIAN HANG OUT?
THAT'S HOW I DECIDED WE WOULD SPLIT UP TO INVESTIGATE DIFFERENT "HOT SPOTS"—LITERALLY—IN THE CITY.
B. FAUST AND COM
CLOSE: 7:00
FACTORIES THAT NEED FLAME IN THEIR PROCESSING, FOR INSTANCE.
AND IF BETA HAS SERVANTS—LOCALS TO HELP WITH THE PARTS OF HIS FUEL-HARVESTING OPERATION NOT INVOLVING, YOU KNOW, BURNING THINGS UP...
...THEY PROBABLY ARE THE KIND OF FOLKS WHO ARE USED TO WORKING WITH FIRE.

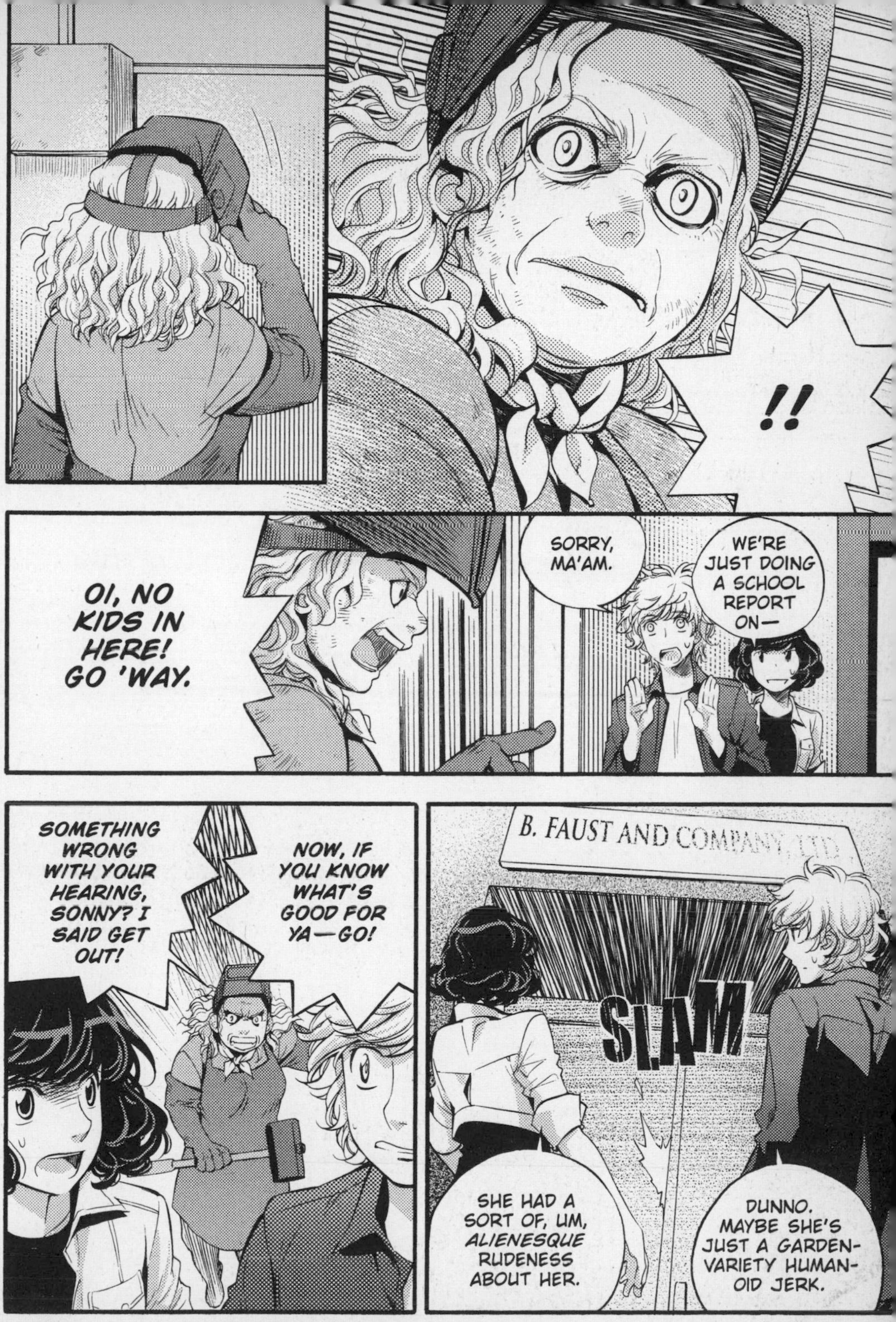
!!
OI, NO KIDS IN HERE! GO 'WAY.
SORRY, MA'AM.
WE'RE JUST DOING A SCHOOL REPORT ON—
SOMETHING WRONG WITH YOUR HEARING, SONNY? I SAID GET OUT!
NOW, IF YOU KNOW WHAT'S GOOD FOR YA—GO!
B. FAUST AND COMPANY, LTD
SLAM
SHE HAD A SORT OF, UM, *ALIENESQUE* RUDENESS ABOUT HER.
DUNNO. MAYBE SHE'S JUST A GARDEN-VARIETY HUMAN-OID JERK.

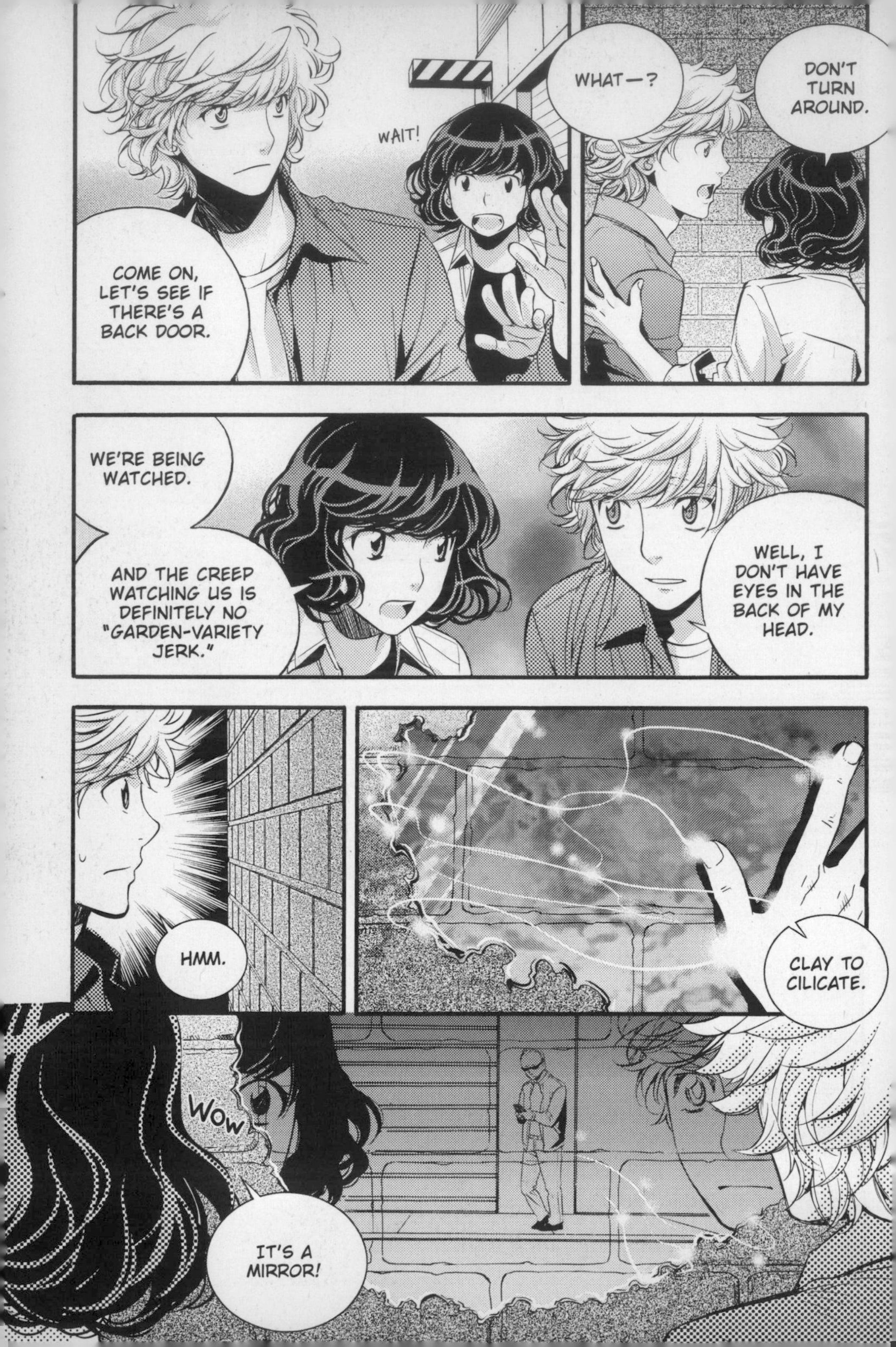
WAIT!
COME ON, LET'S SEE IF THERE'S A BACK DOOR.
WHAT—?
DON'T TURN AROUND.
WE'RE BEING WATCHED.
AND THE CREEP WATCHING US IS DEFINITELY NO "GARDEN-VARIETY JERK."
WELL, I DON'T HAVE EYES IN THE BACK OF MY HEAD.
HMM.
CLAY TO CILICATE.
WOW
IT'S A MIRROR!

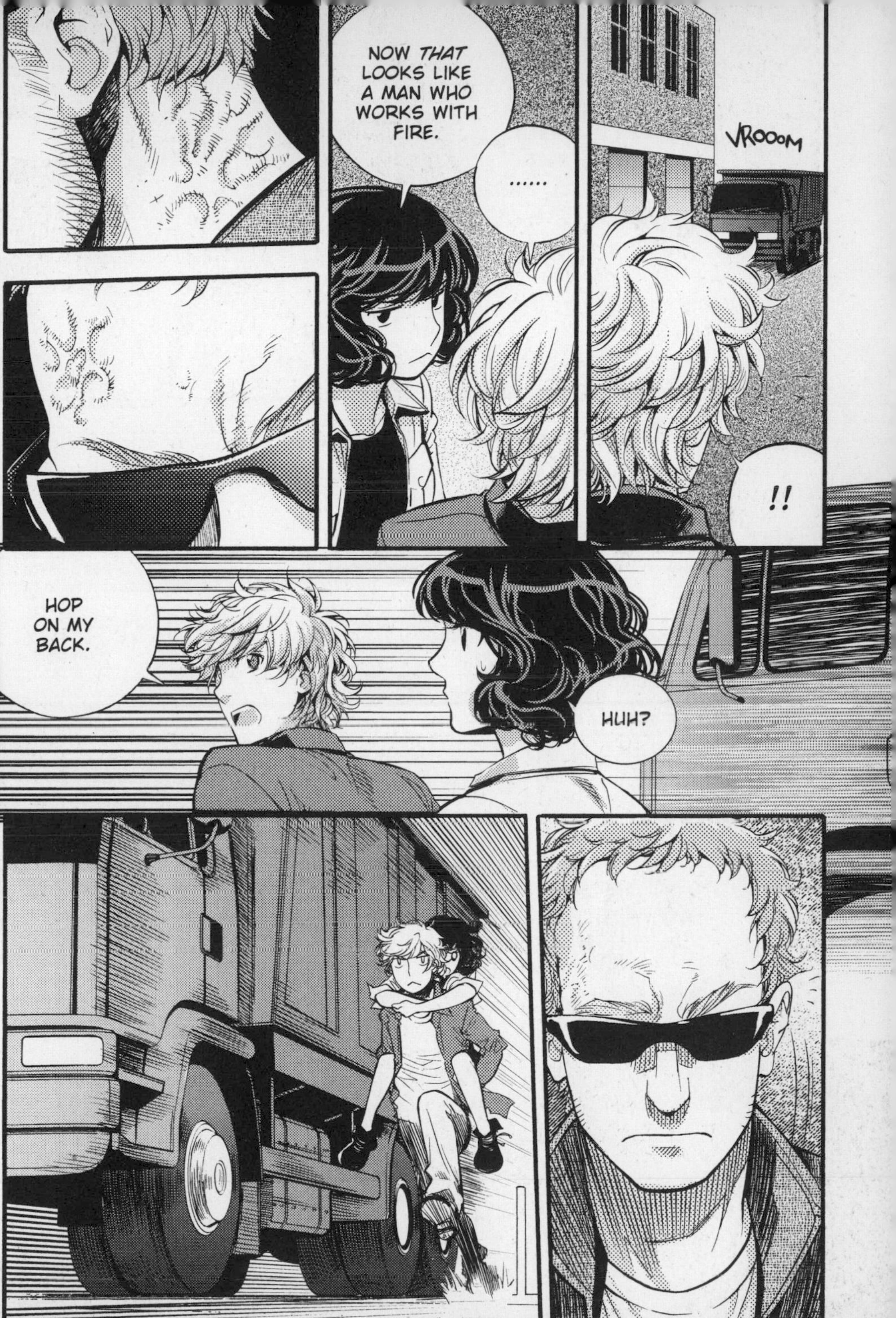
NOW *THAT* LOOKS LIKE A MAN WHO WORKS WITH FIRE.
......
VROOOM
!!
HOP ON MY BACK.
HUH?

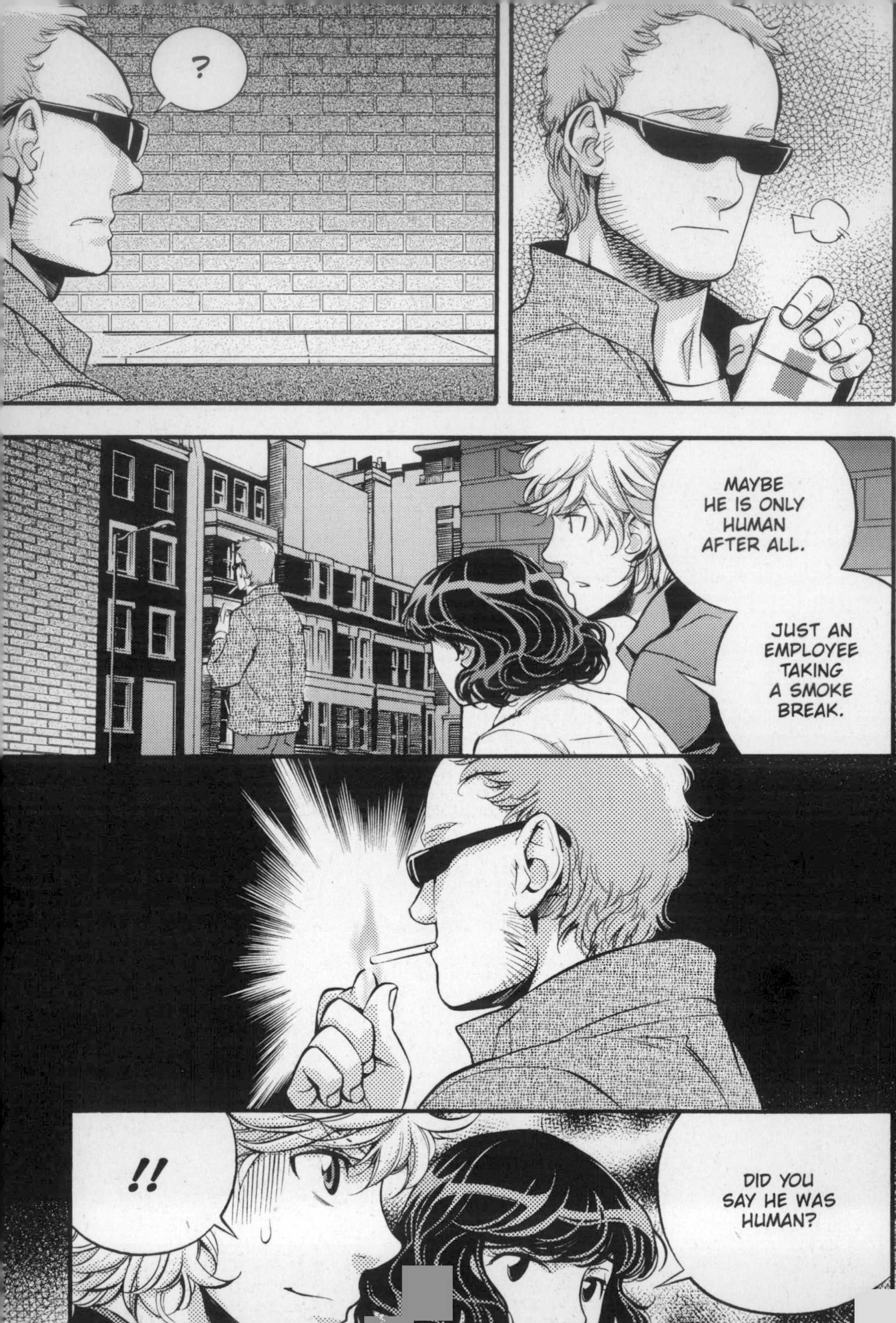
?
MAYBE HE IS ONLY HUMAN AFTER ALL.
JUST AN EMPLOYEE TAKING A SMOKE BREAK.
!!
DID YOU SAY HE WAS HUMAN?

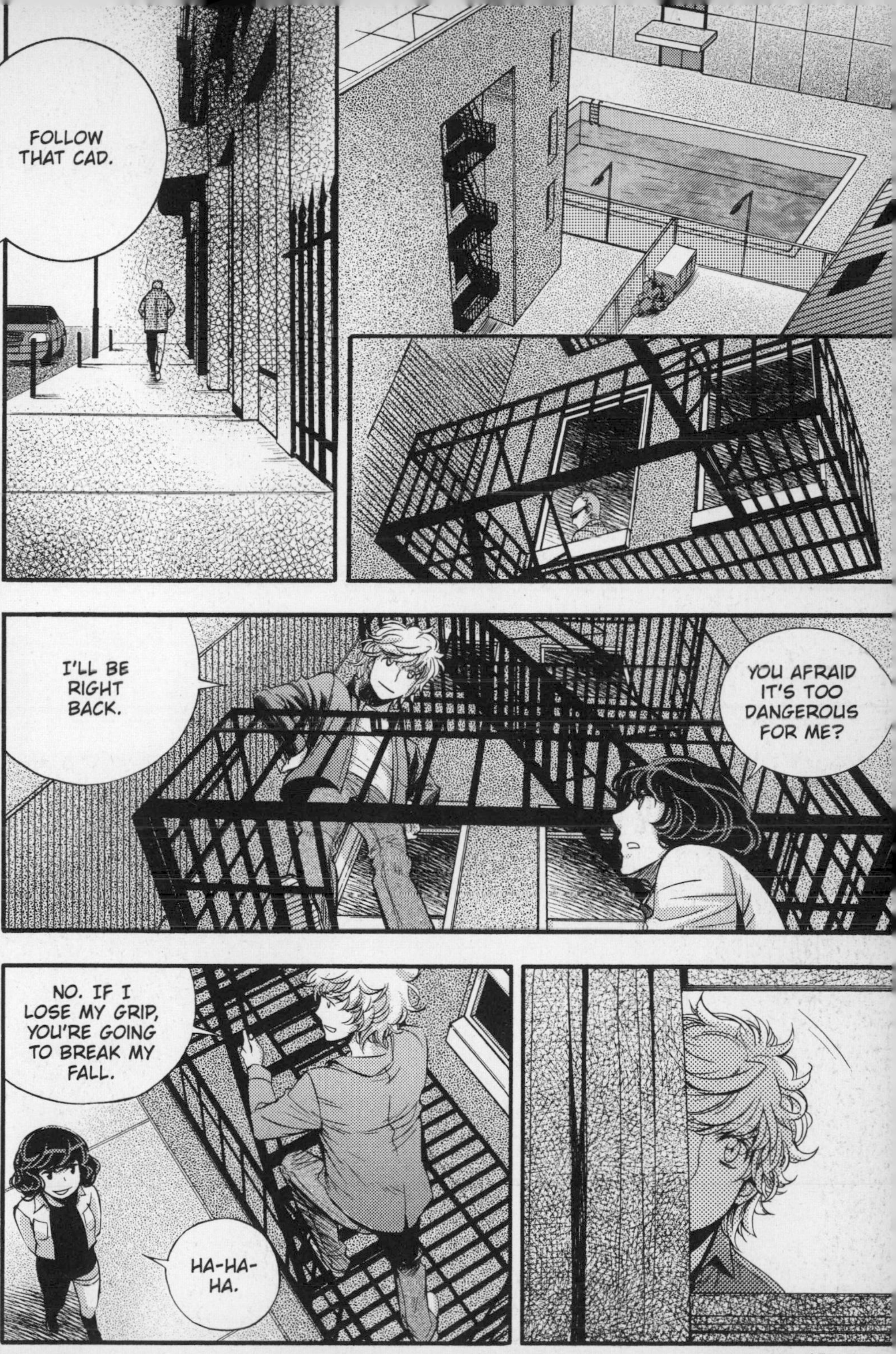
FOLLOW THAT CAD.
I'LL BE RIGHT BACK.
YOU AFRAID IT'S TOO DANGEROUS FOR ME?
NO. IF I LOSE MY GRIP, YOU'RE GOING TO BREAK MY FALL.
HA-HA-HA.

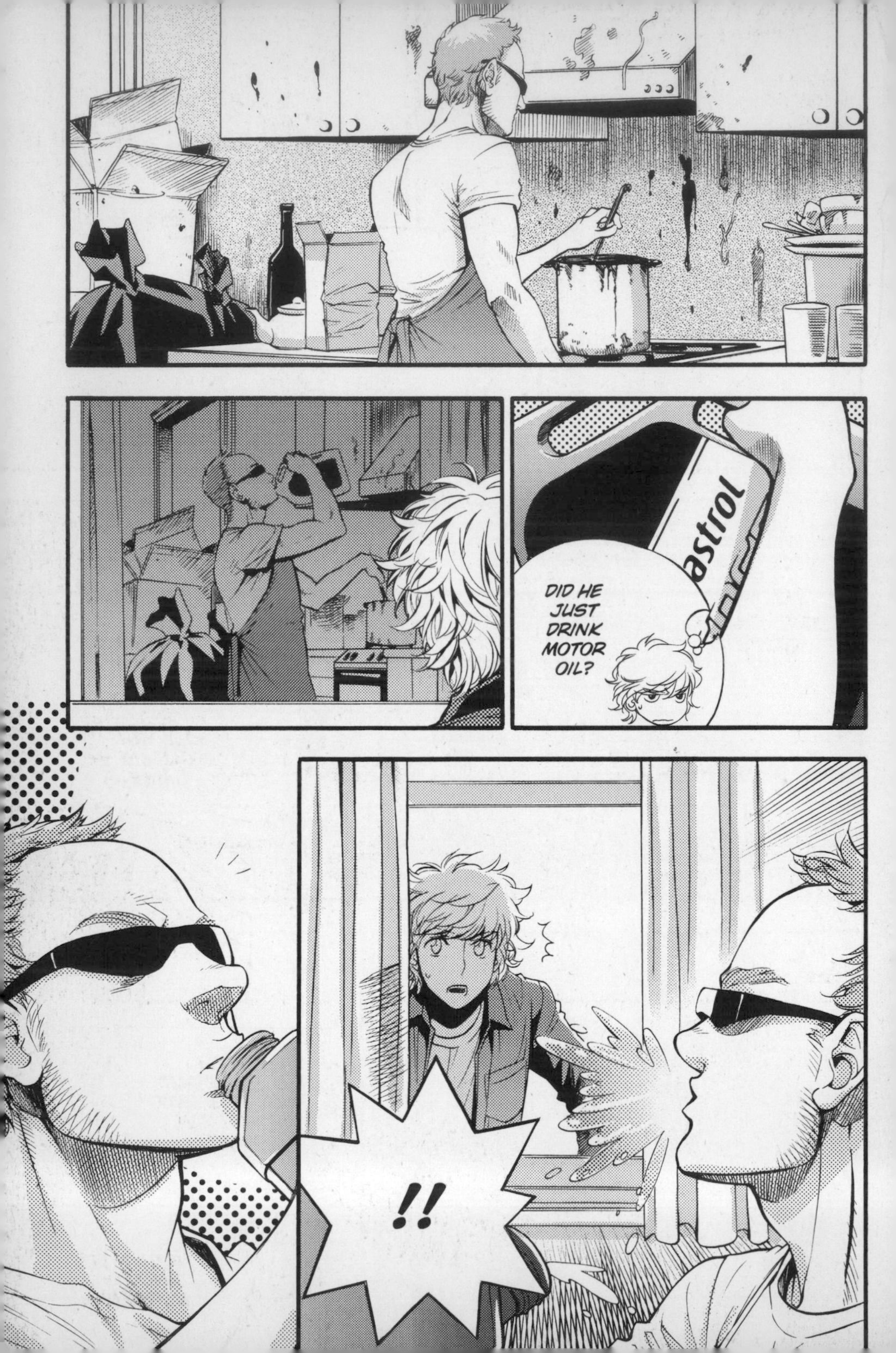

astrol
DID HE JUST DRINK MOTOR OIL?
!!

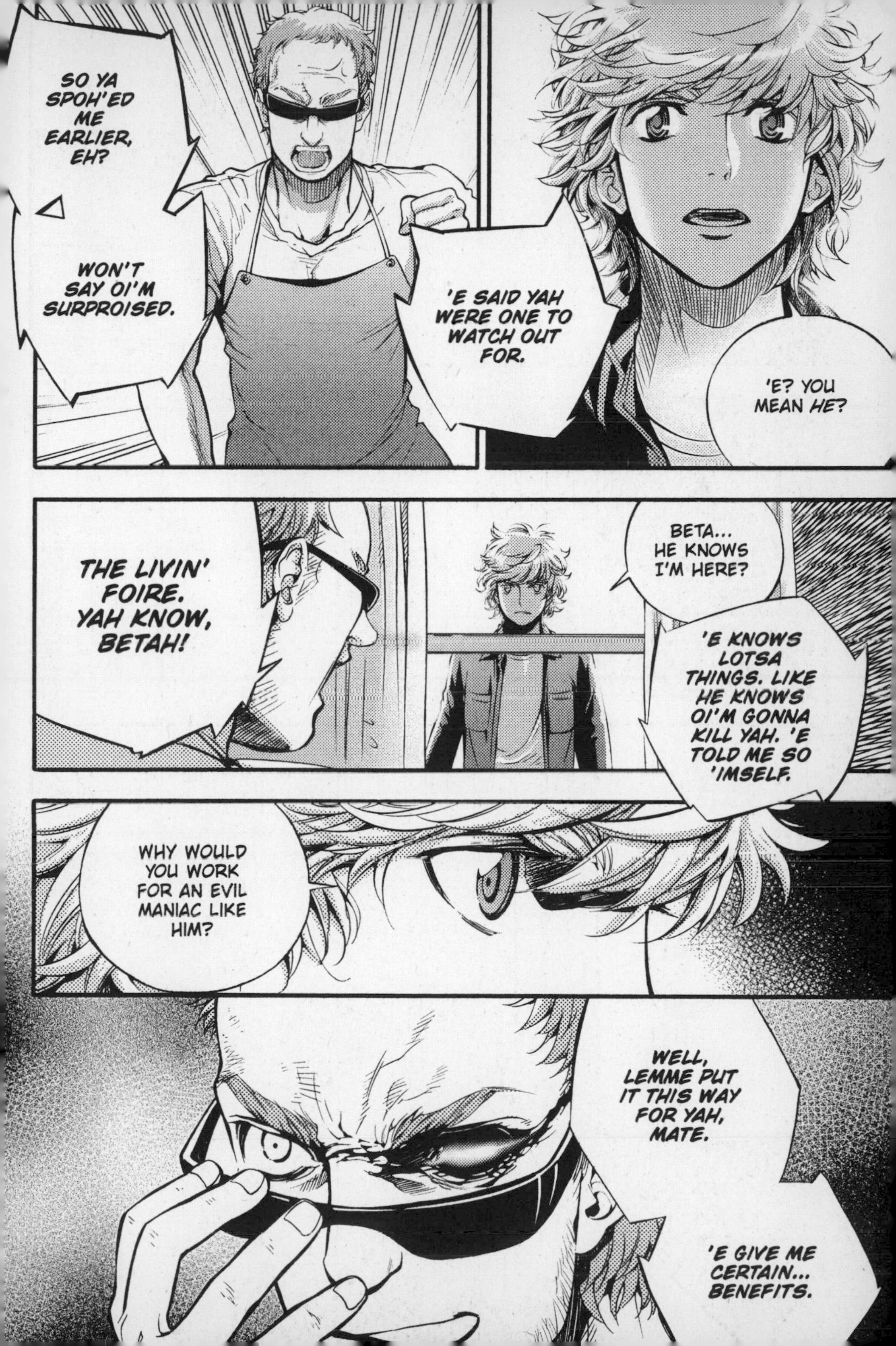
SO YA SPOH'ED ME EARLIER, EH?
WON'T SAY OI'M SURPROISED.
'E SAID YAH WERE ONE TO WATCH OUT FOR.
'E? YOU MEAN HE?
THE LIVIN' FOIRE. YAH KNOW, BETAH!
BETA... HE KNOWS I'M HERE?
'E KNOWS LOTSA THINGS. LIKE HE KNOWS OI'M GONNA KILL YAH. 'E TOLD ME SO 'IMSELF.
WHY WOULD YOU WORK FOR AN EVIL MANIAC LIKE HIM?
WELL, LEMME PUT IT THIS WAY FOR YAH, MATE.
'E GIVE ME CERTAIN... BENEFITS.

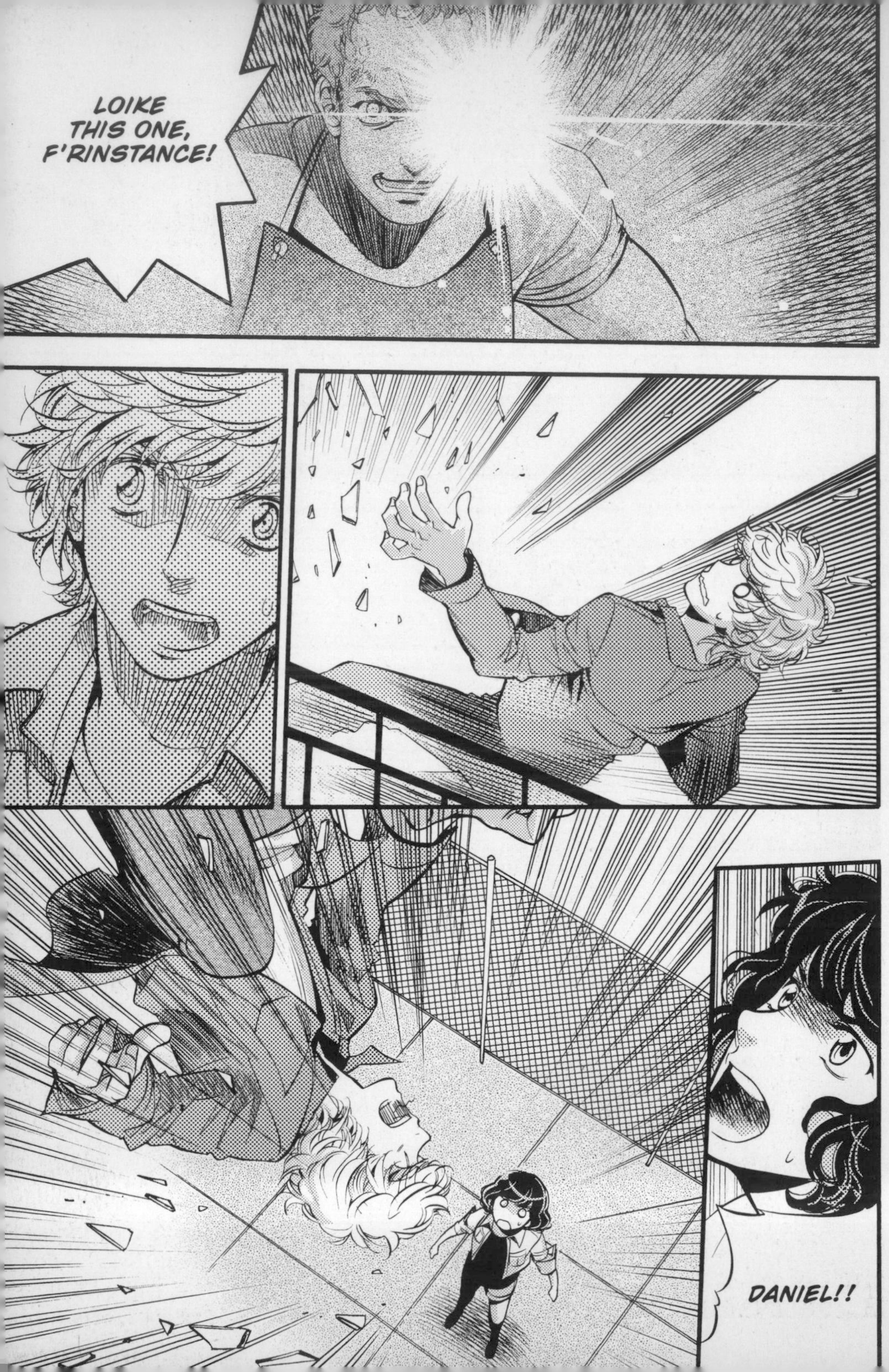
LOIKE THIS ONE, F'RINSTANCE!
DANIEL!!

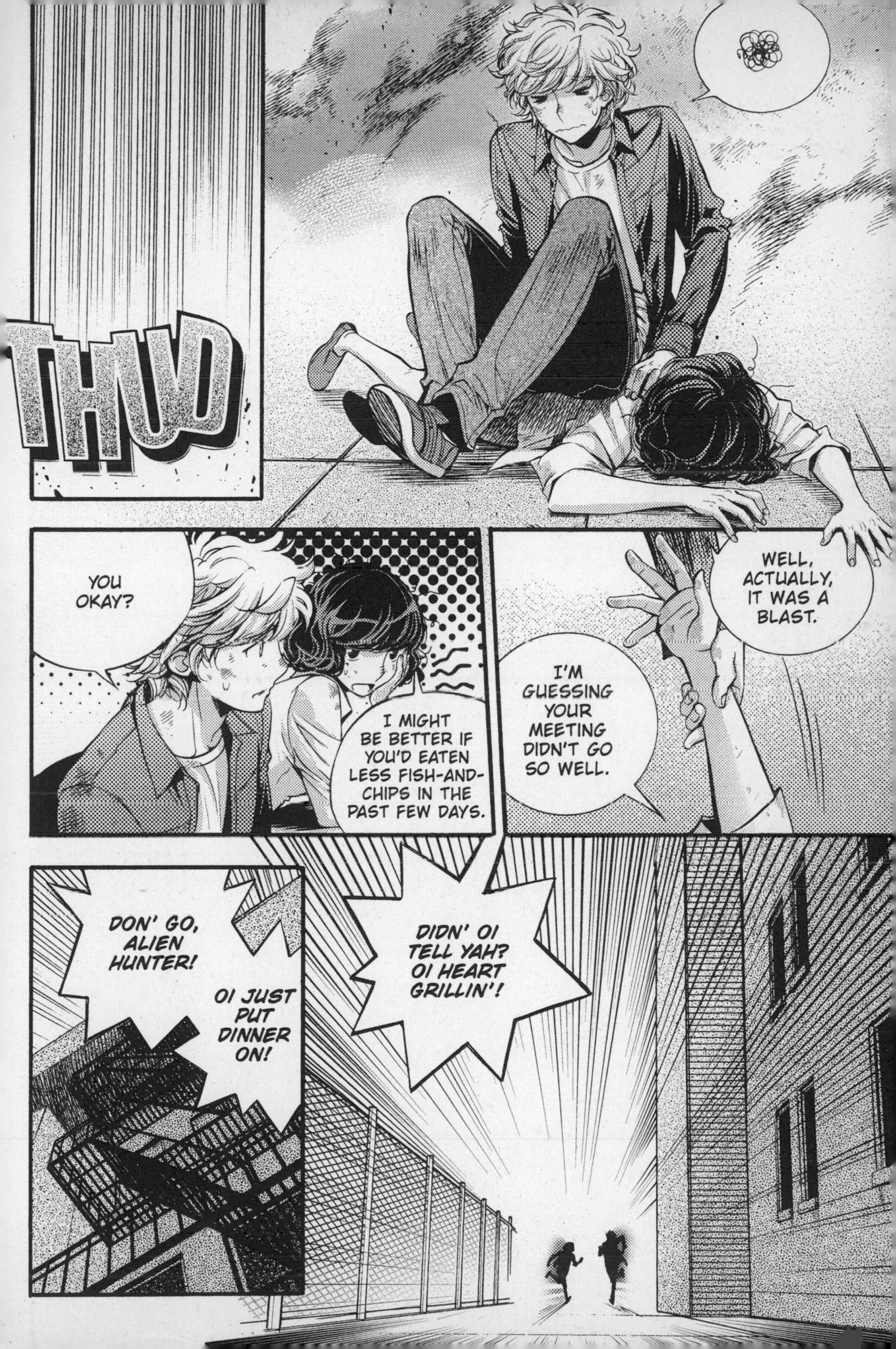
THUD
YOU OKAY?
I MIGHT BE BETTER IF YOU'D EATEN LESS FISH-AND-CHIPS IN THE PAST FEW DAYS.
I'M GUESSING YOUR MEETING DIDN'T GO SO WELL.
WELL, ACTUALLY, IT WAS A BLAST.
DON' GO, ALIEN HUNTER!
OI JUST PUT DINNER ON!
DIDN' OI TELL YAH? OI HEART GRILLIN'!

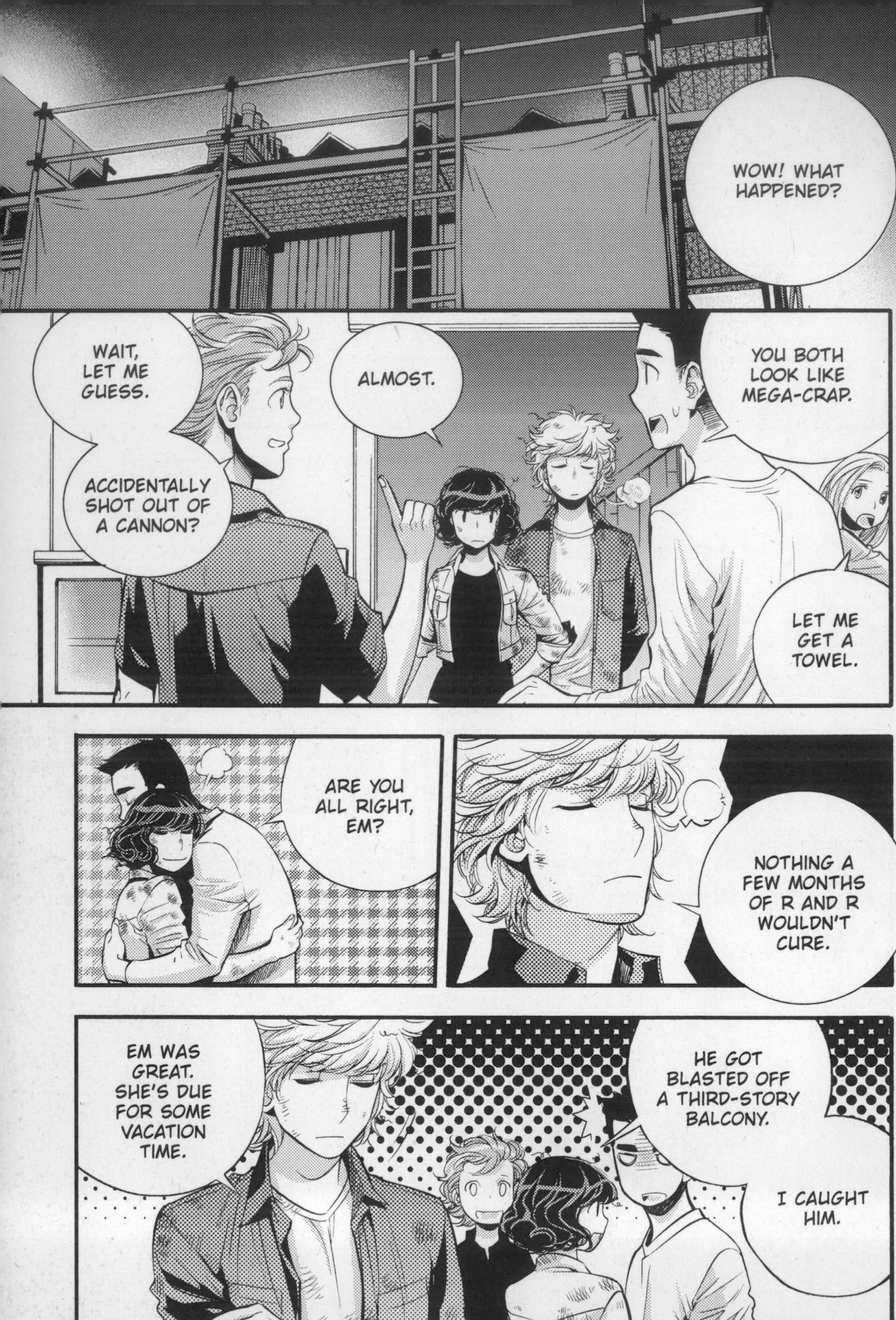
WOW! WHAT HAPPENED?
WAIT, LET ME GUESS.
ACCIDENTALLY SHOT OUT OF A CANNON?
ALMOST.
YOU BOTH LOOK LIKE MEGA-CRAP.
LET ME GET A TOWEL.
ARE YOU ALL RIGHT, EM?
NOTHING A FEW MONTHS OF R AND R WOULDN'T CURE.
EM WAS GREAT. SHE'S DUE FOR SOME VACATION TIME.
HE GOT BLASTED OFF A THIRD-STORY BALCONY.
I CAUGHT HIM.

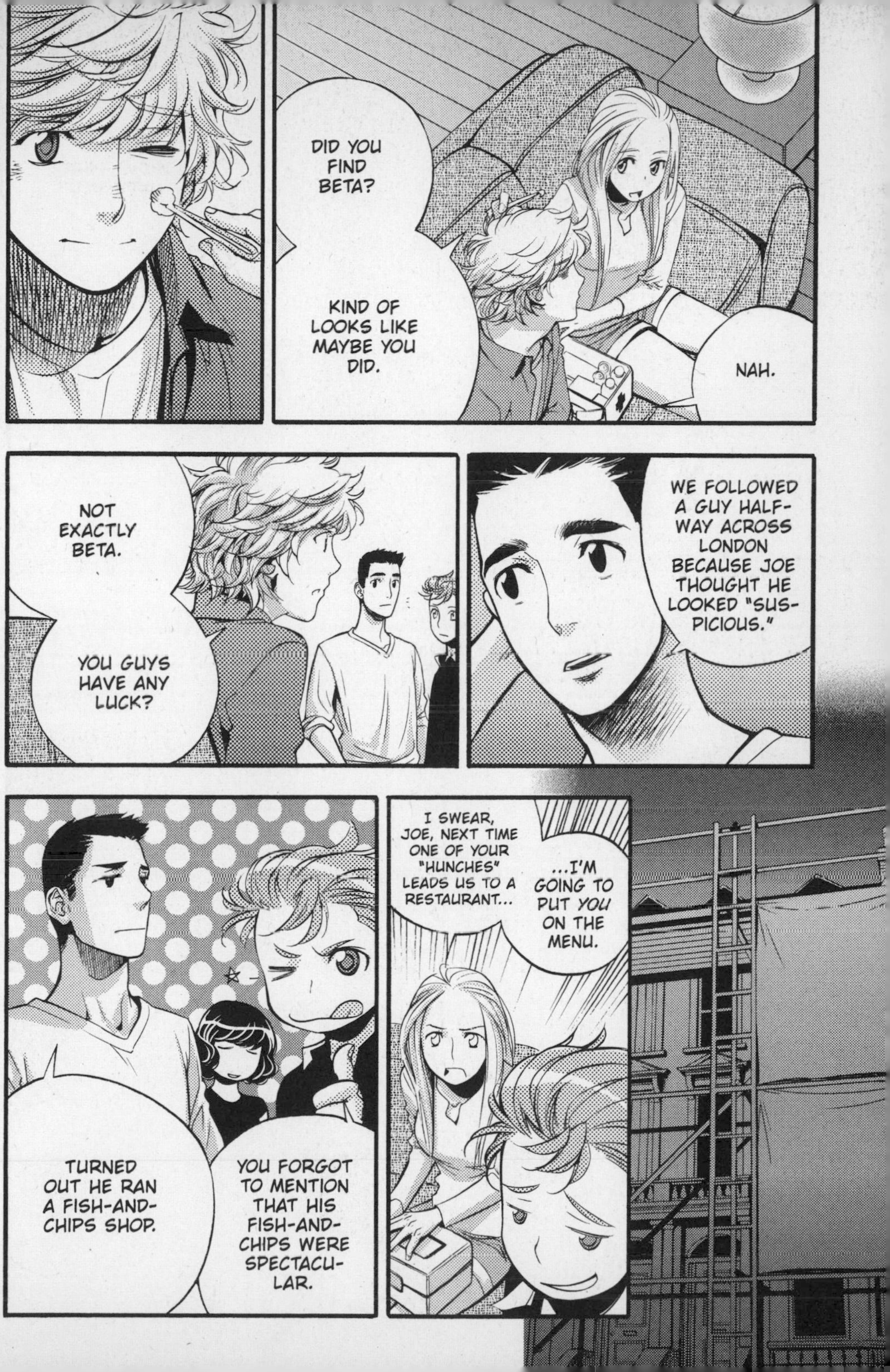
DID YOU FIND BETA?
KIND OF LOOKS LIKE MAYBE YOU DID.
NAH.
NOT EXACTLY BETA.
YOU GUYS HAVE ANY LUCK?
WE FOLLOWED A GUY HALF-WAY ACROSS LONDON BECAUSE JOE THOUGHT HE LOOKED "SUS-PICIOUS."
TURNED OUT HE RAN A FISH-AND-CHIPS SHOP.
YOU FORGOT TO MENTION THAT HIS FISH-AND-CHIPS WERE SPECTACU-LAR.
I SWEAR, JOE, NEXT TIME ONE OF YOUR "HUNCHES" LEADS US TO A RESTAURANT...
...I'M GOING TO PUT *YOU* ON THE MENU.

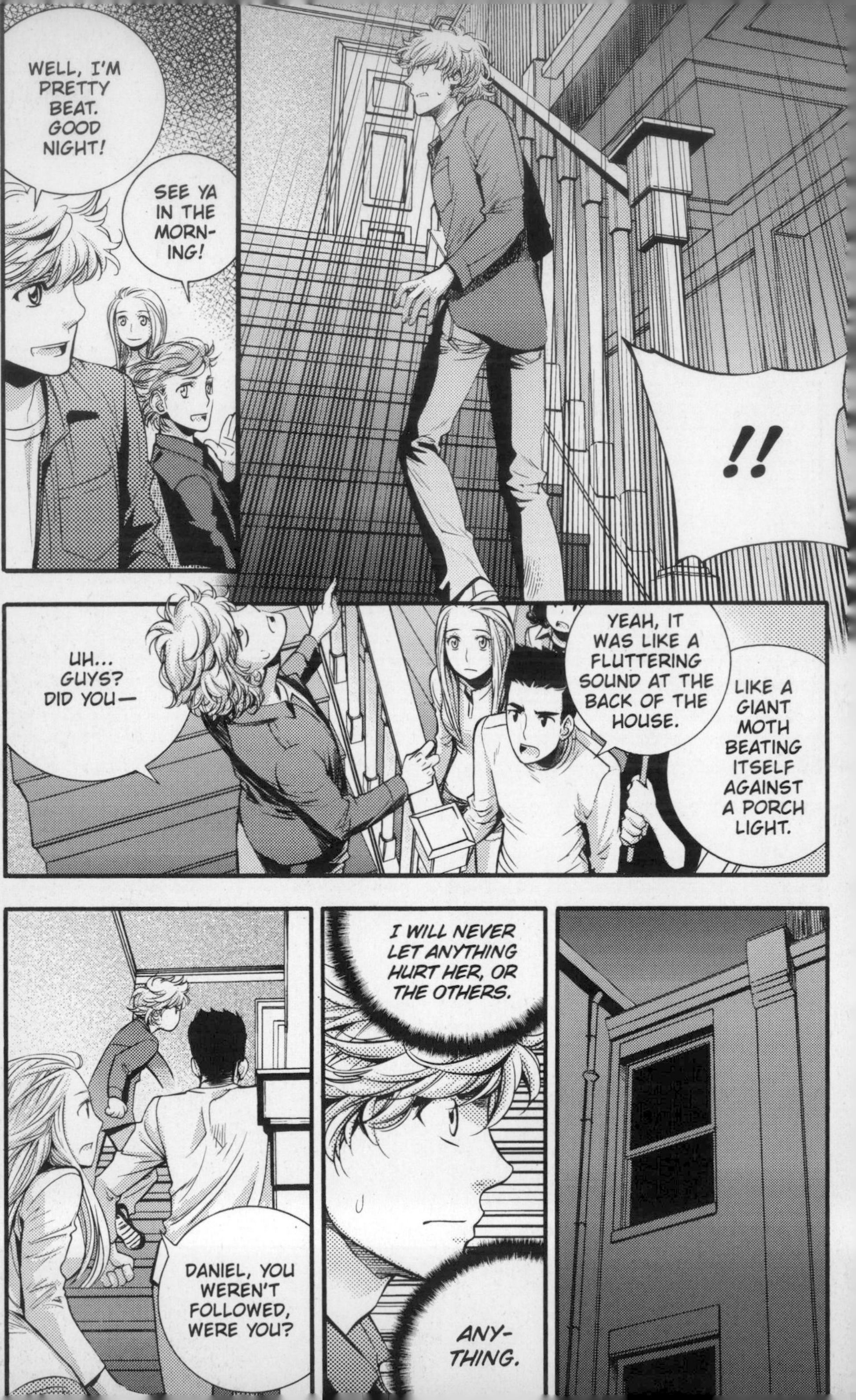
WELL, I'M PRETTY BEAT. GOOD NIGHT!
SEE YA IN THE MORN-ING!
!!
UH... GUYS? DID YOU—
YEAH, IT WAS LIKE A FLUTTERING SOUND AT THE BACK OF THE HOUSE.
LIKE A GIANT MOTH BEATING ITSELF AGAINST A PORCH LIGHT.
DANIEL, YOU WEREN'T FOLLOWED, WERE YOU?
I WILL NEVER LET ANYTHING HURT HER, OR THE OTHERS.
ANY-THING.

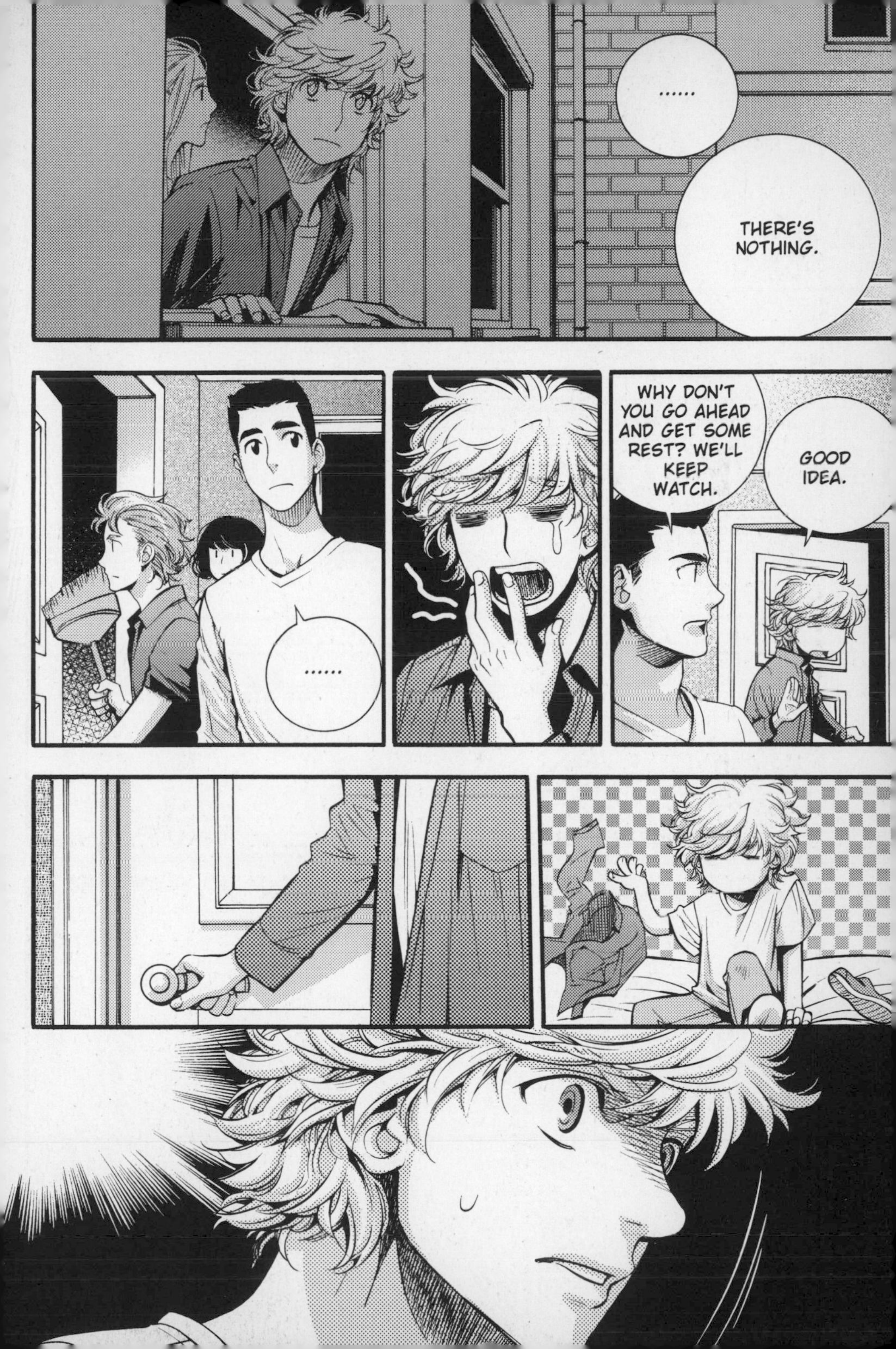
……
THERE'S NOTHING.
……
WHY DON'T YOU GO AHEAD AND GET SOME REST? WE'LL KEEP WATCH.
GOOD IDEA.

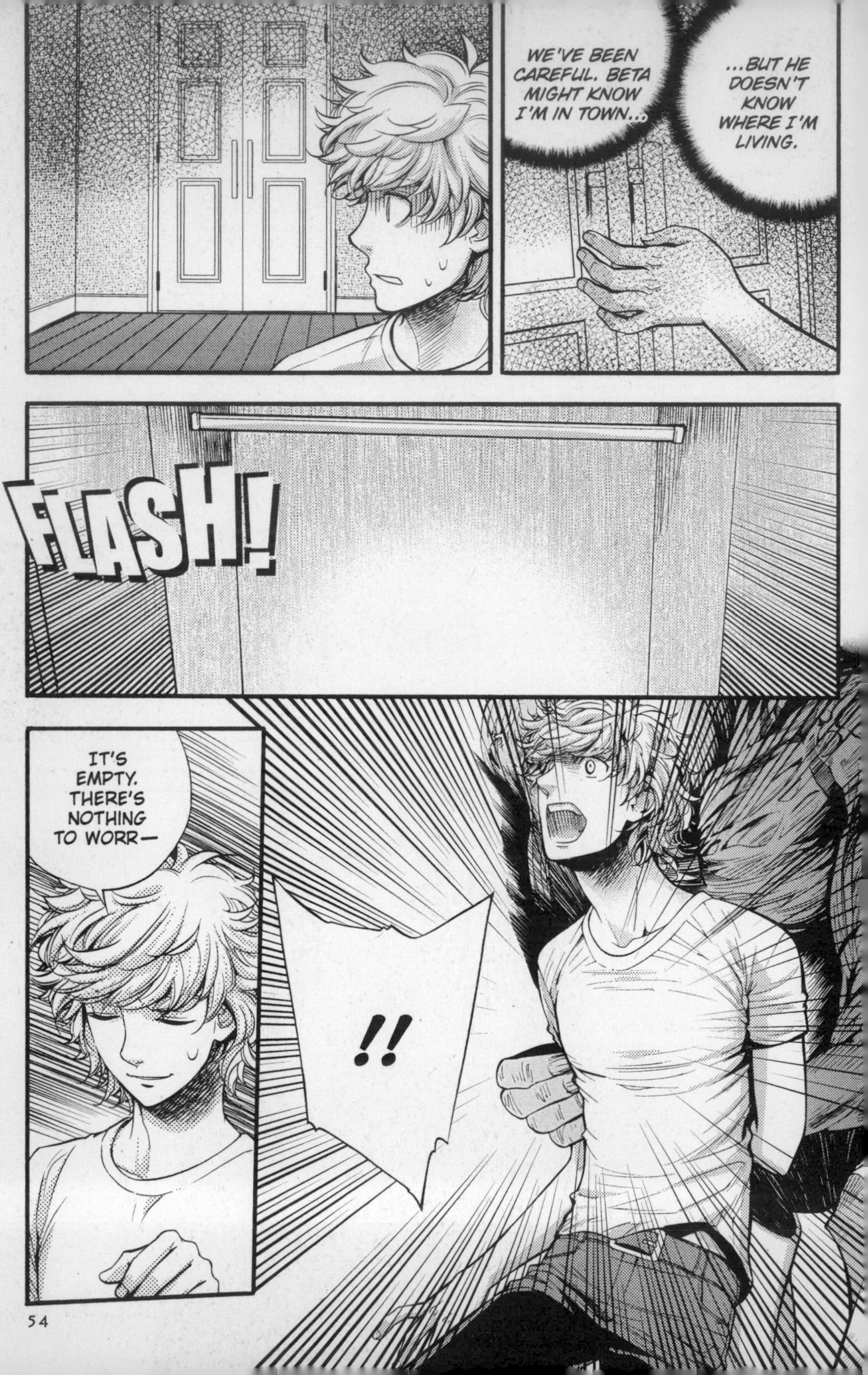

WE'VE BEEN CAREFUL. BETA MIGHT KNOW I'M IN TOWN...
...BUT HE DOESN'T KNOW WHERE I'M LIVING.
FLASH!
IT'S EMPTY. THERE'S NOTHING TO WORR—
!!

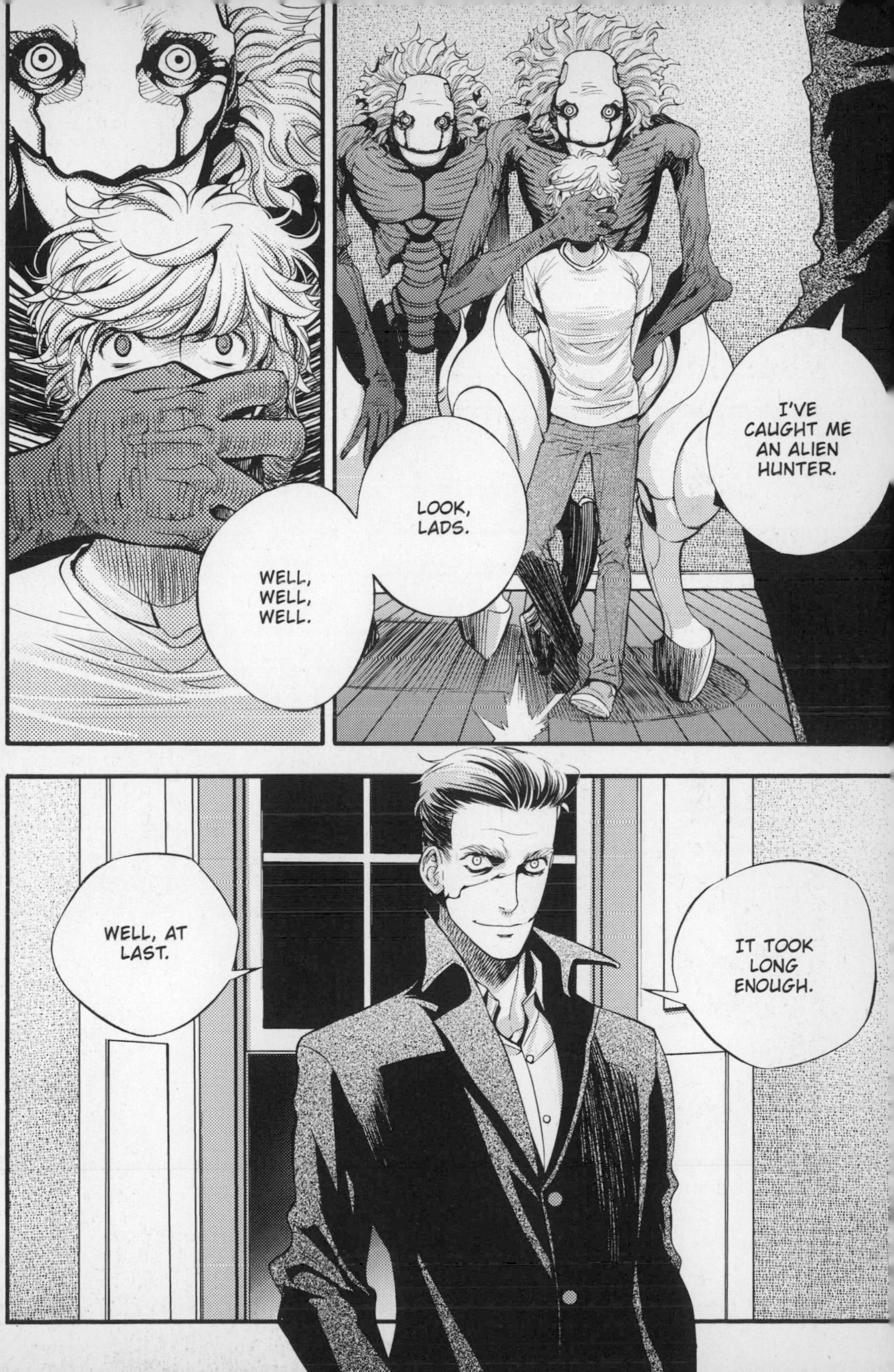
WELL, WELL, WELL.
LOOK, LADS.
I'VE CAUGHT ME AN ALIEN HUNTER.
WELL, AT LAST.
IT TOOK LONG ENOUGH.

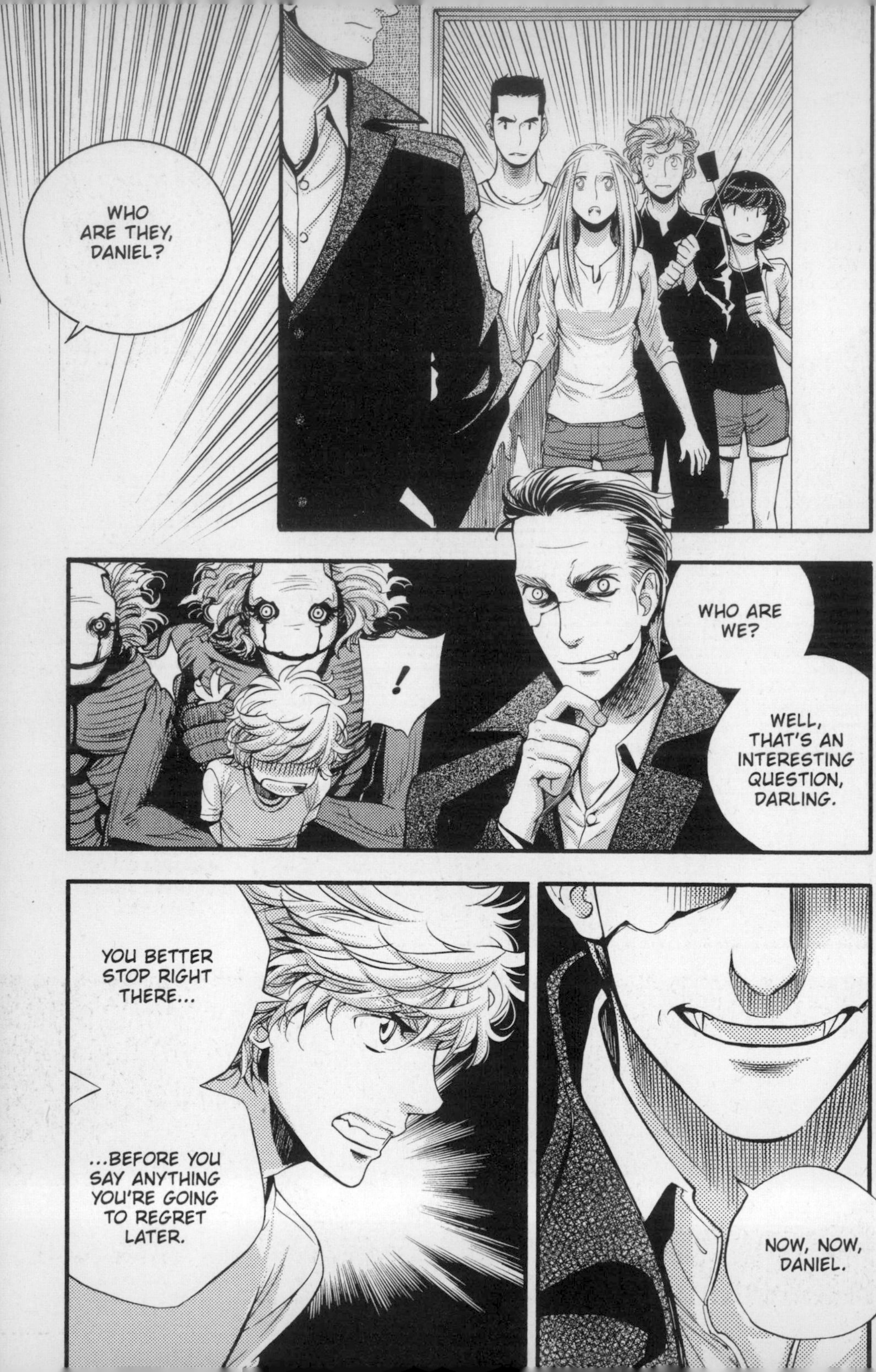
WHO ARE THEY, DANIEL?
WHO ARE WE?
WELL, THAT'S AN INTERESTING QUESTION, DARLING.
!
YOU BETTER STOP RIGHT THERE...
...BEFORE YOU SAY ANYTHING YOU'RE GOING TO REGRET LATER.
NOW, NOW, DANIEL.

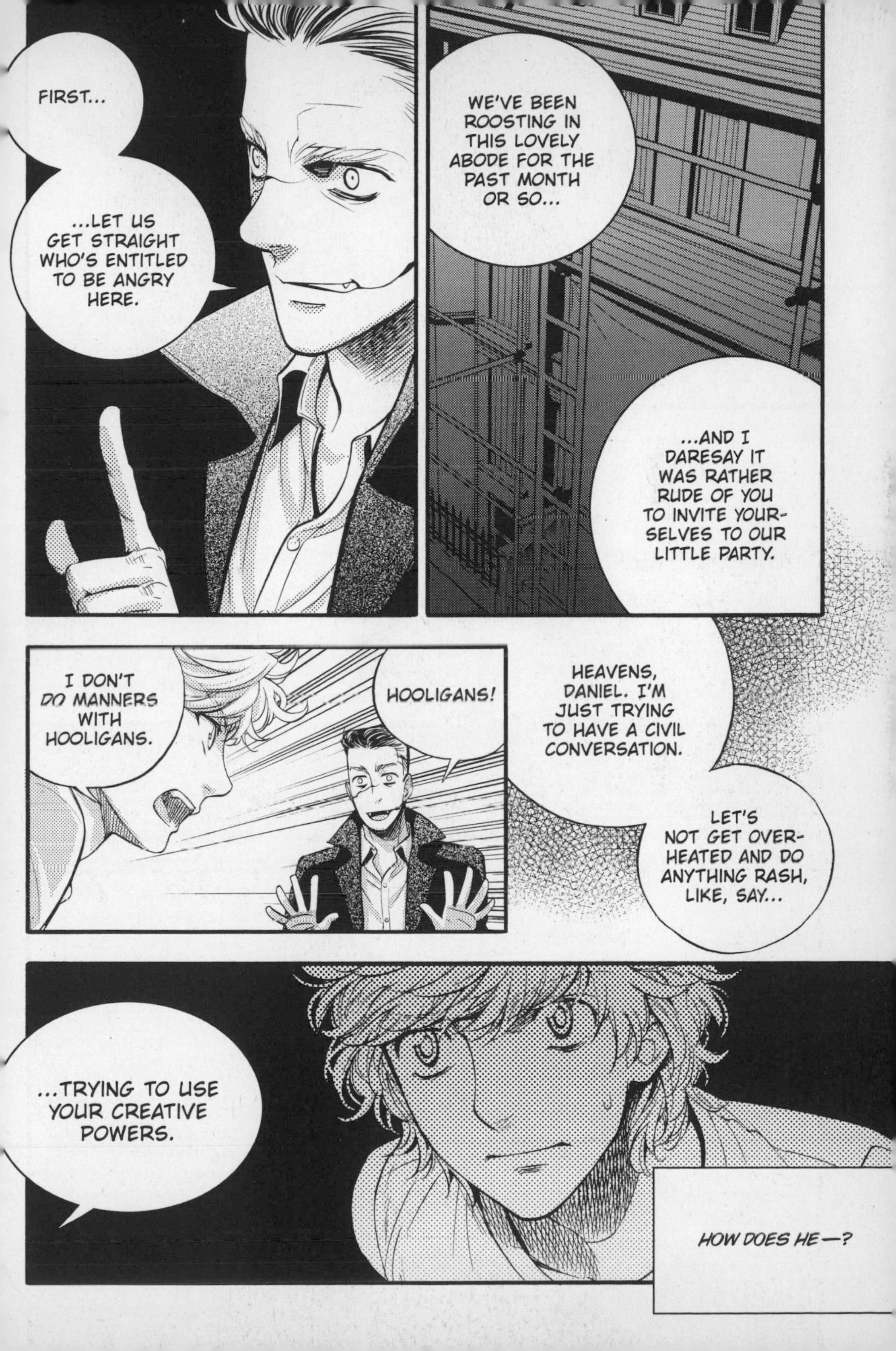
FIRST...
...LET US GET STRAIGHT WHO'S ENTITLED TO BE ANGRY HERE.
WE'VE BEEN ROOSTING IN THIS LOVELY ABODE FOR THE PAST MONTH OR SO...
...AND I DARESAY IT WAS RATHER RUDE OF YOU TO INVITE YOURSELVES TO OUR LITTLE PARTY.
I DON'T *DO* MANNERS WITH HOOLIGANS.
HOOLIGANS!
HEAVENS, DANIEL. I'M JUST TRYING TO HAVE A CIVIL CONVERSATION.
LET'S NOT GET OVERHEATED AND DO ANYTHING RASH, LIKE, SAY...
...TRYING TO USE YOUR CREATIVE POWERS.
HOW DOES HE—?

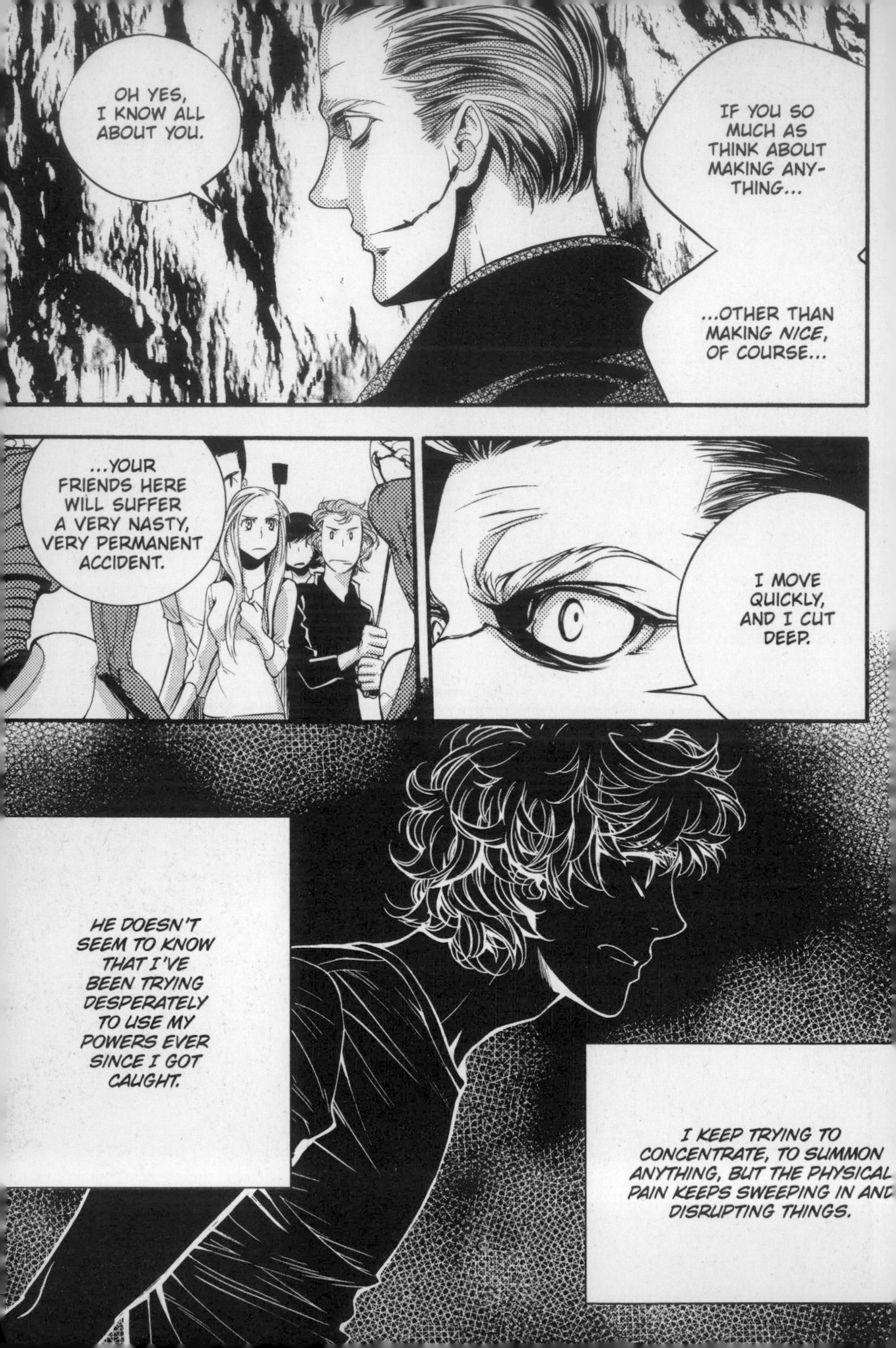
OH YES, I KNOW ALL ABOUT YOU.
IF YOU SO MUCH AS THINK ABOUT MAKING ANY-THING...
...OTHER THAN MAKING *NICE*, OF COURSE...
...YOUR FRIENDS HERE WILL SUFFER A VERY NASTY, VERY PERMANENT ACCIDENT.
I MOVE QUICKLY, AND I CUT DEEP.
HE DOESN'T SEEM TO KNOW THAT I'VE BEEN TRYING DESPERATELY TO USE MY POWERS EVER SINCE I GOT CAUGHT.
I KEEP TRYING TO CONCENTRATE, TO SUMMON ANYTHING, BUT THE PHYSICAL PAIN KEEPS SWEEPING IN AND DISRUPTING THINGS.

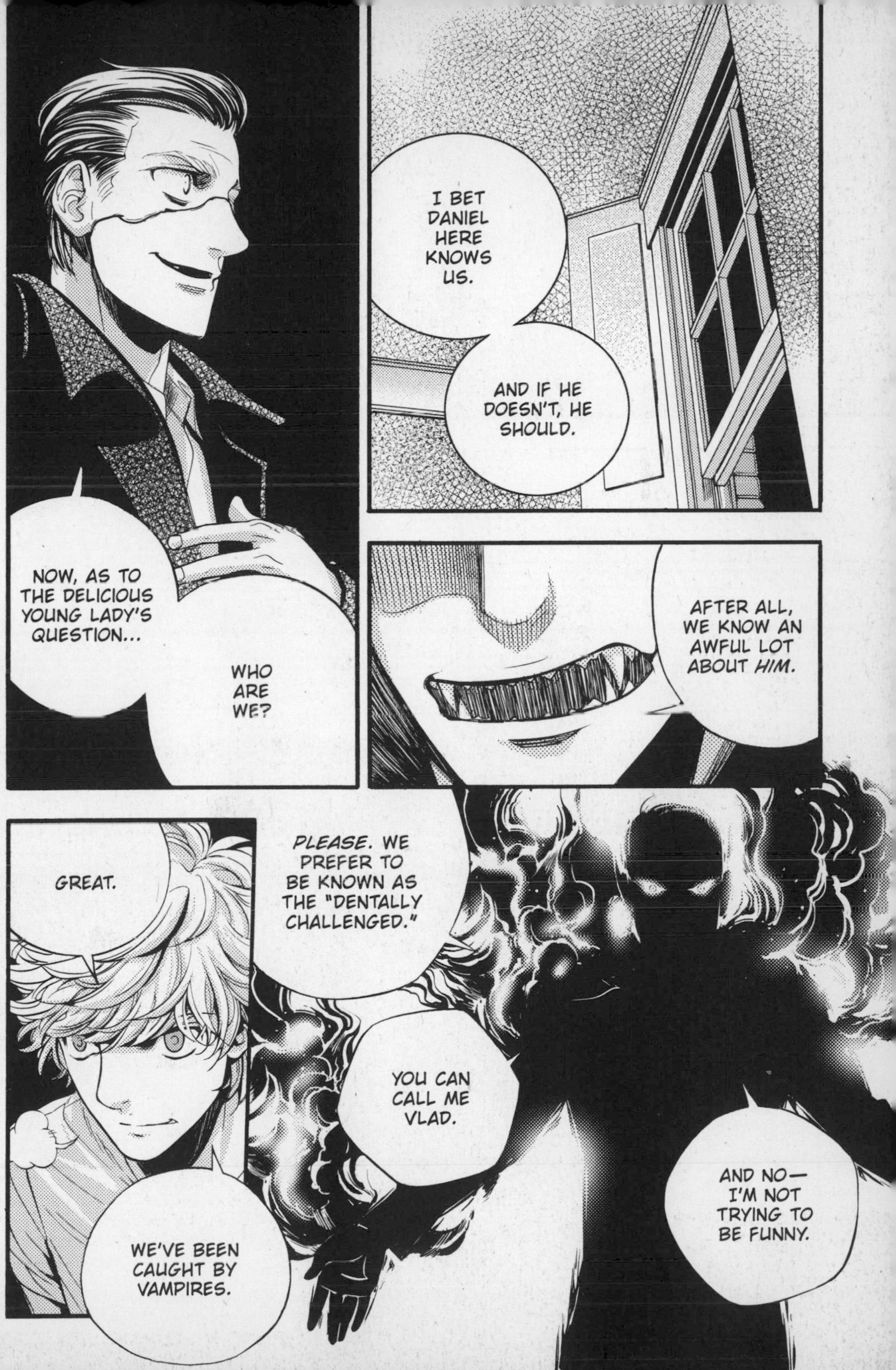
I BET DANIEL HERE KNOWS US.
AND IF HE DOESN'T, HE SHOULD.
NOW, AS TO THE DELICIOUS YOUNG LADY'S QUESTION...
WHO ARE WE?
AFTER ALL, WE KNOW AN AWFUL LOT ABOUT *HIM*.
GREAT.
PLEASE. WE PREFER TO BE KNOWN AS THE "DENTALLY CHALLENGED."
WE'VE BEEN CAUGHT BY VAMPIRES.
YOU CAN CALL ME VLAD.
AND NO— I'M NOT TRYING TO BE FUNNY.

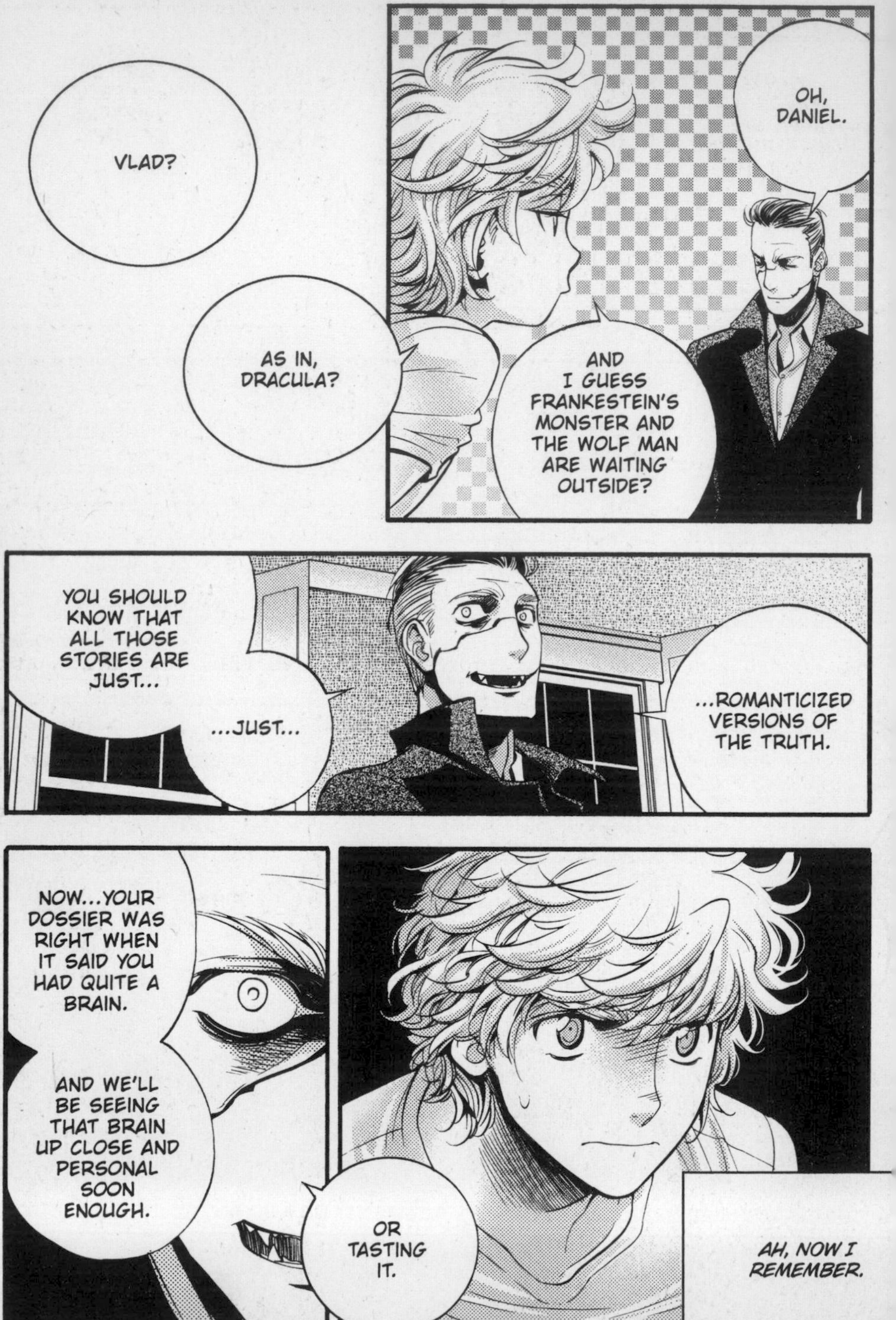
VLAD?
OH, DANIEL.
AS IN, DRACULA?
AND I GUESS FRANKESTEIN'S MONSTER AND THE WOLF MAN ARE WAITING OUTSIDE?
YOU SHOULD KNOW THAT ALL THOSE STORIES ARE JUST...
...JUST...
...ROMANTICIZED VERSIONS OF THE TRUTH.
NOW...YOUR DOSSIER WAS RIGHT WHEN IT SAID YOU HAD QUITE A BRAIN.
AND WE'LL BE SEEING THAT BRAIN UP CLOSE AND PERSONAL SOON ENOUGH.
OR TASTING IT.
AH, NOW I REMEMBER.

THIS IS SOMETHING I HAVE SEEN MENTIONED IN THE LIST.

YOU'RE PART OF THE SPECIES *VAMPIRUS SAPIENS.*

AND AS I RECALL, IT'S NOT BLOOD YOU'RE AFTER.

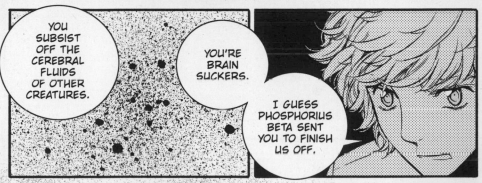

YOU SUBSIST OFF THE CEREBRAL FLUIDS OF OTHER CREATURES.

YOU'RE BRAIN SUCKERS.

I GUESS PHOSPHORIUS BETA SENT YOU TO FINISH US OFF.

BETA?

THAT NUTTER?

NEVER!

I SHOULD THINK HE SENT *YOU* HERE TO FINISH *ME* OFF.

AFTER ALL, WE GO BACK CENTURIES, MR. BETA AND I...

!!

61

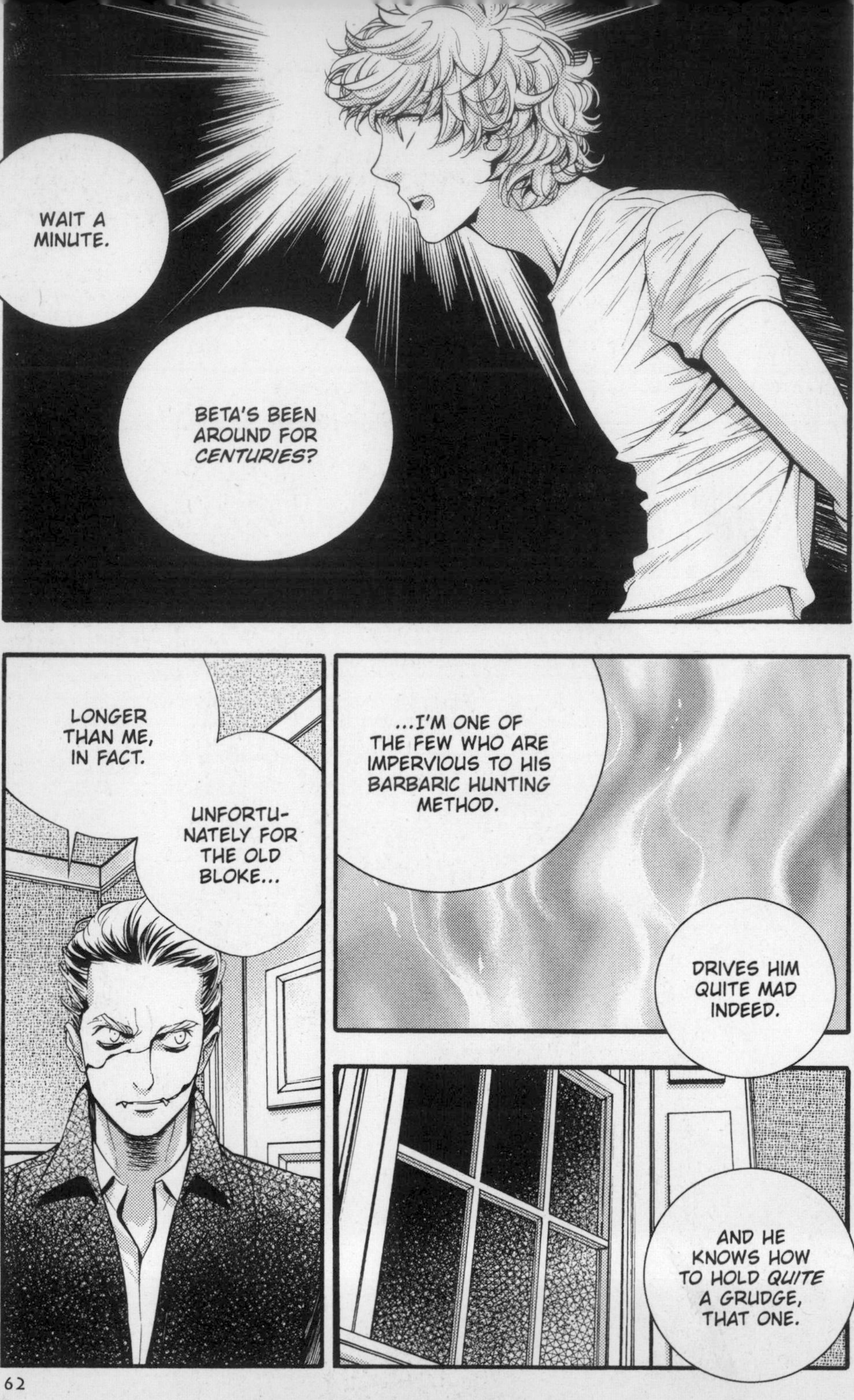
WAIT A MINUTE.
BETA'S BEEN AROUND FOR *CENTURIES?*
LONGER THAN ME, IN FACT.
UNFORTU-NATELY FOR THE OLD BLOKE...
...I'M ONE OF THE FEW WHO ARE IMPERVIOUS TO HIS BARBARIC HUNTING METHOD.
DRIVES HIM QUITE MAD INDEED.
AND HE KNOWS HOW TO HOLD *QUITE* A GRUDGE, THAT ONE.

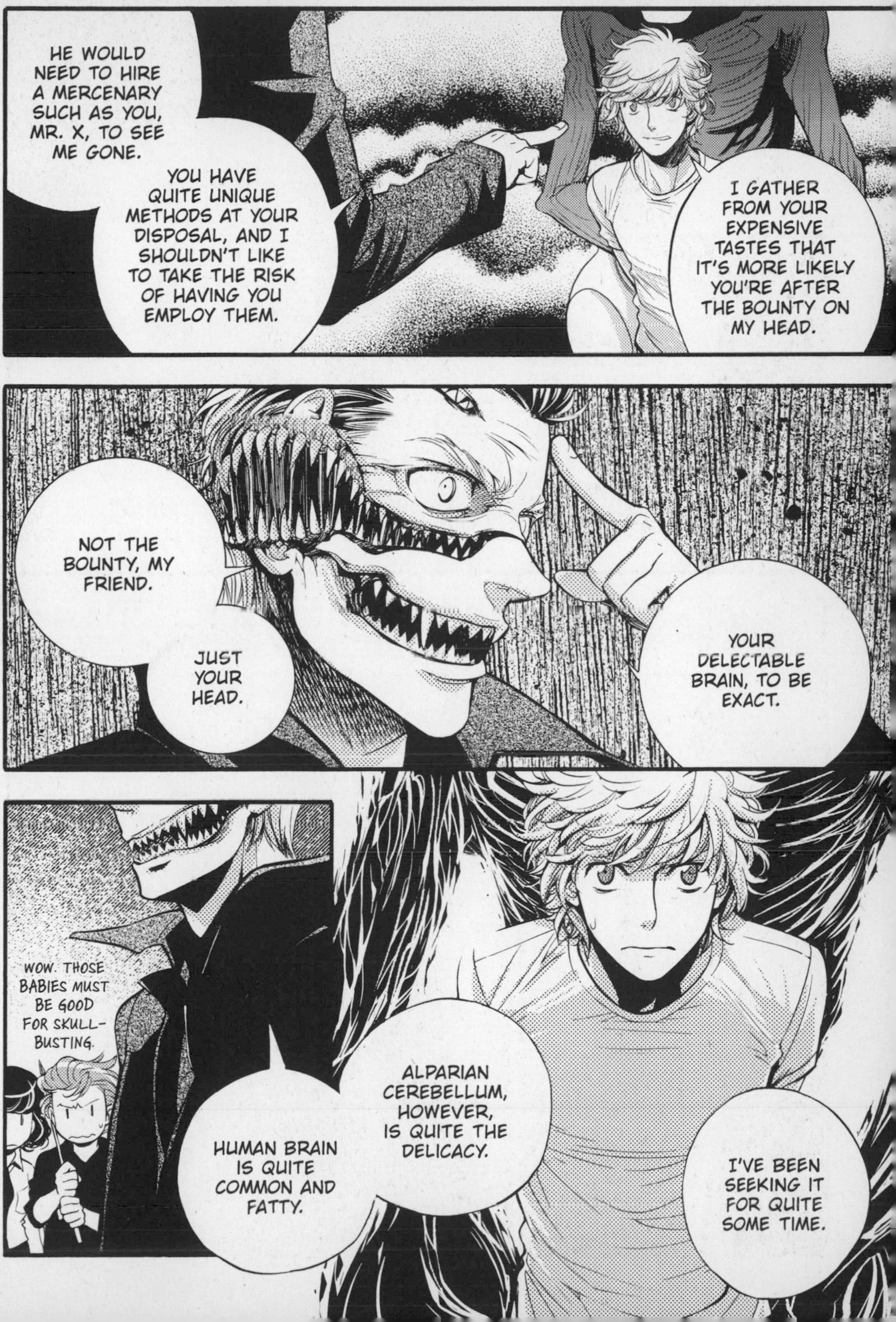
HE WOULD NEED TO HIRE A MERCENARY SUCH AS YOU, MR. X, TO SEE ME GONE.
YOU HAVE QUITE UNIQUE METHODS AT YOUR DISPOSAL, AND I SHOULDN'T LIKE TO TAKE THE RISK OF HAVING YOU EMPLOY THEM.
I GATHER FROM YOUR EXPENSIVE TASTES THAT IT'S MORE LIKELY YOU'RE AFTER THE BOUNTY ON MY HEAD.
NOT THE BOUNTY, MY FRIEND.
JUST YOUR HEAD.
YOUR DELECTABLE BRAIN, TO BE EXACT.
WOW. THOSE BABIES MUST BE GOOD FOR SKULL-BUSTING.
HUMAN BRAIN IS QUITE COMMON AND FATTY.
ALPARIAN CEREBELLUM, HOWEVER, IS QUITE THE DELICACY.
I'VE BEEN SEEKING IT FOR QUITE SOME TIME.

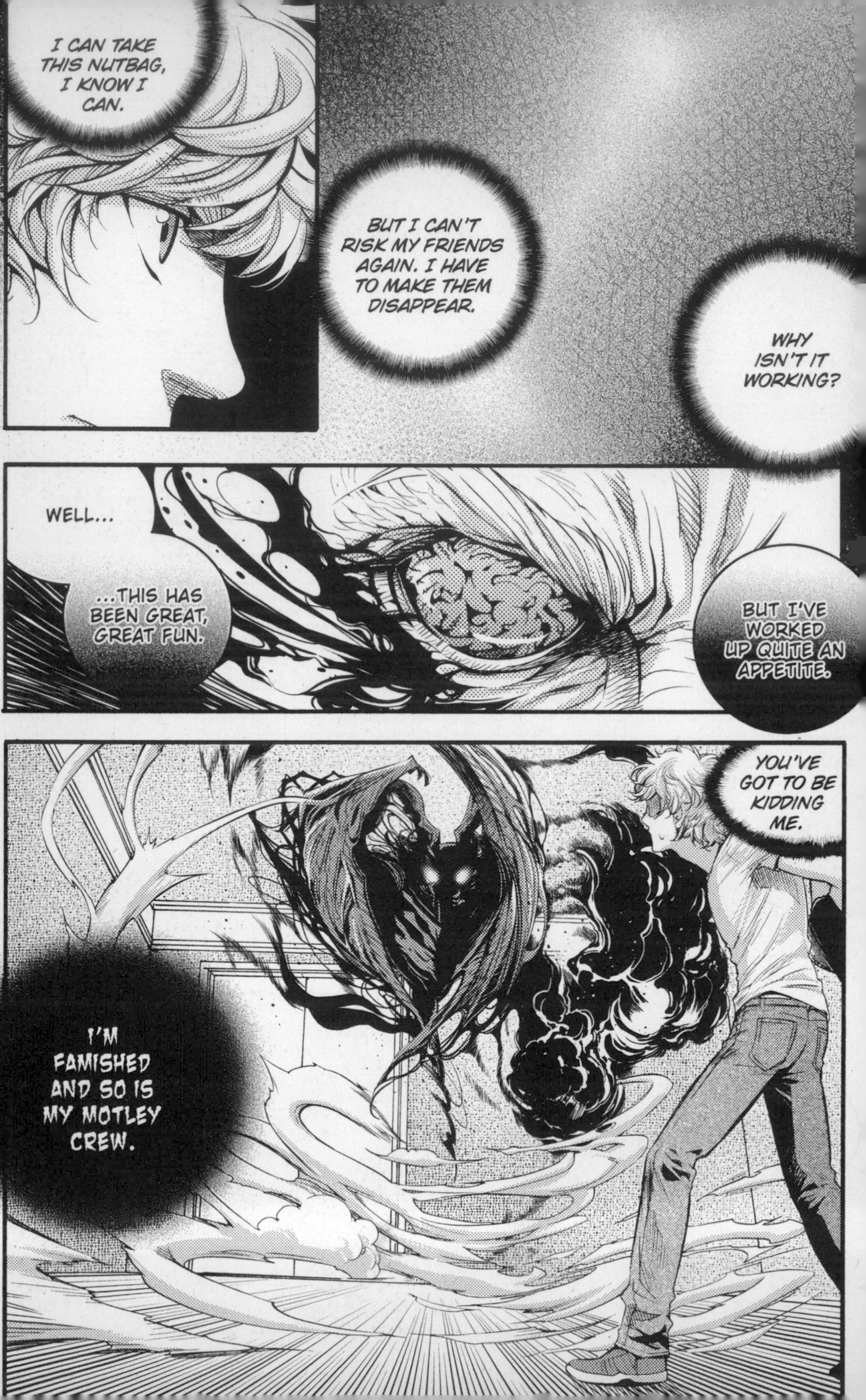
I CAN TAKE THIS NUTBAG, I KNOW I CAN.
BUT I CAN'T RISK MY FRIENDS AGAIN. I HAVE TO MAKE THEM DISAPPEAR.
WHY ISN'T IT WORKING?
WELL...
...THIS HAS BEEN GREAT, GREAT FUN.
BUT I'VE WORKED UP QUITE AN APPETITE.
YOU'VE GOT TO BE KIDDING ME.
I'M FAMISHED AND SO IS MY MOTLEY CREW.

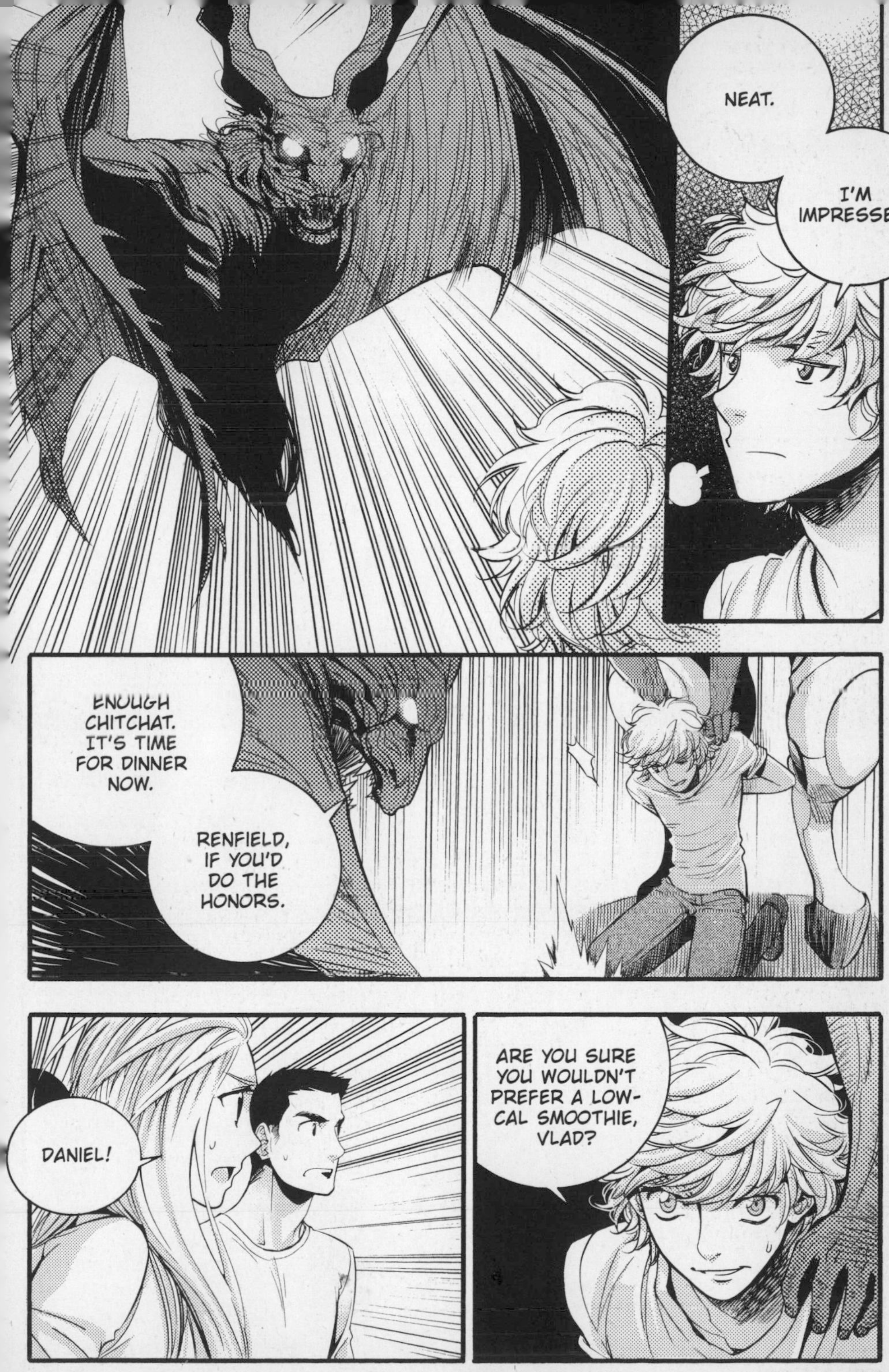
NEAT.
I'M IMPRESSED.
ENOUGH CHITCHAT. IT'S TIME FOR DINNER NOW.
RENFIELD, IF YOU'D DO THE HONORS.
DANIEL!
ARE YOU SURE YOU WOULDN'T PREFER A LOW-CAL SMOOTHIE, VLAD?

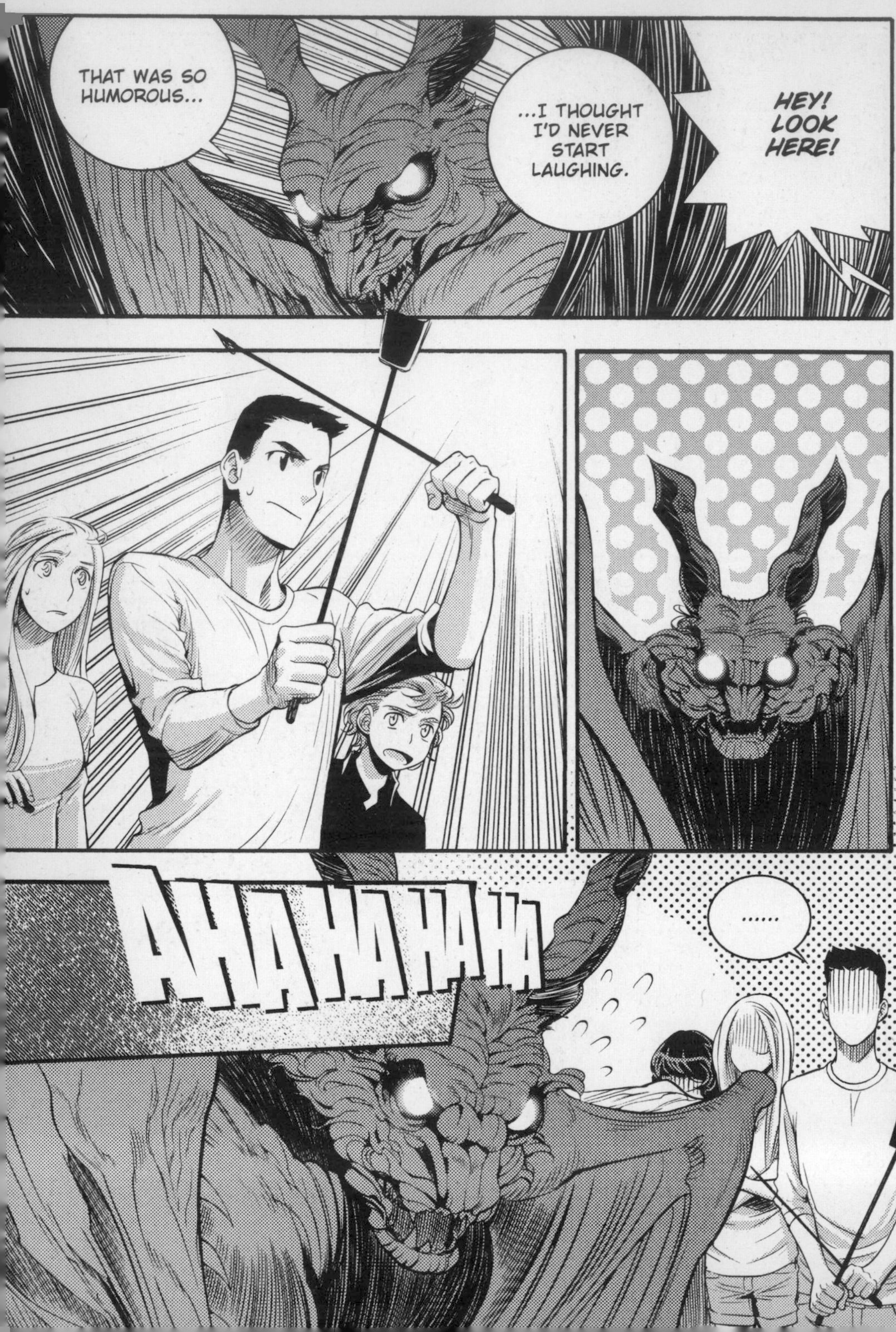
THAT WAS SO HUMOROUS...
...I THOUGHT I'D NEVER START LAUGHING.
HEY! LOOK HERE!
AHAHAHAHAHA
......

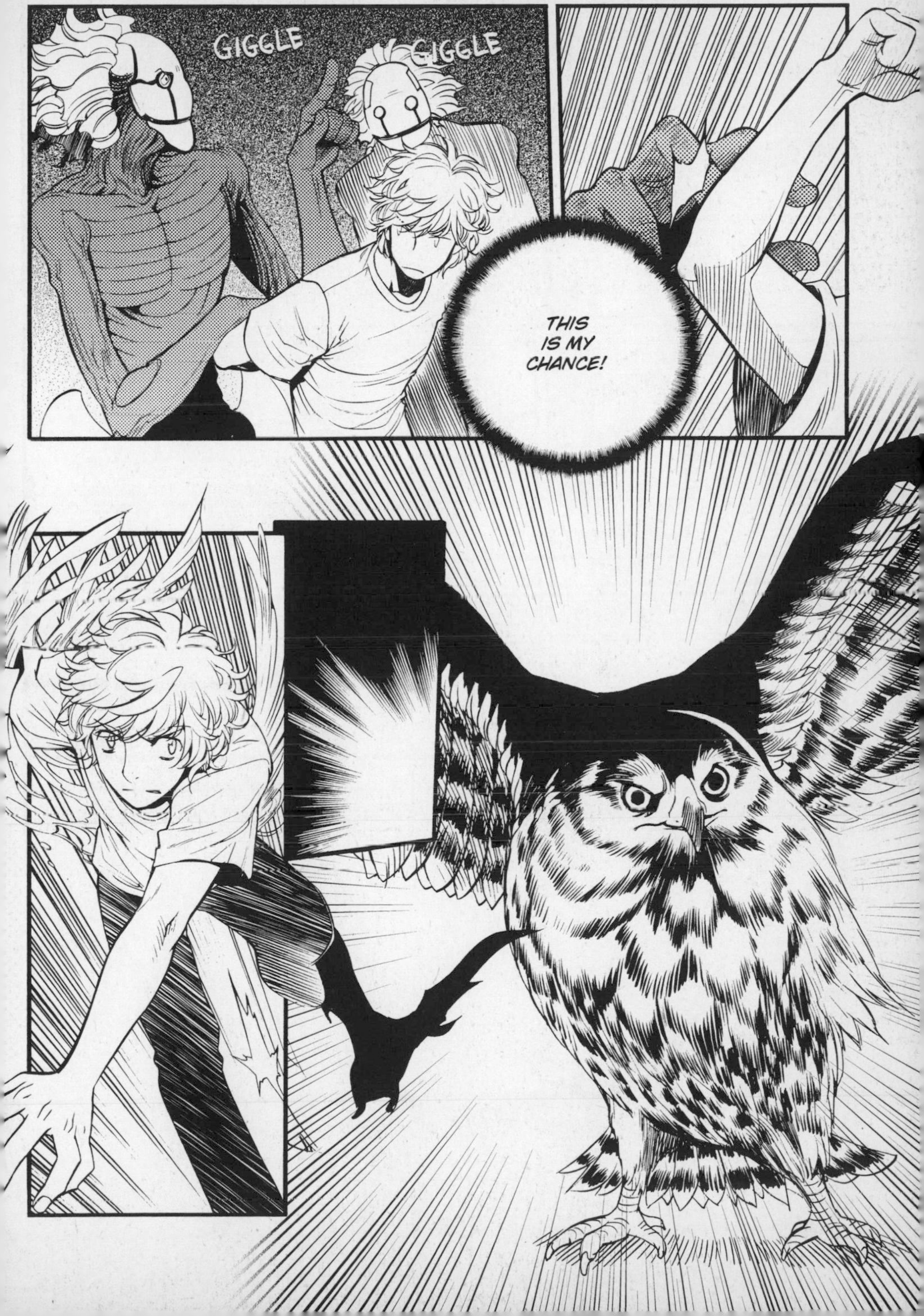
GIGGLE
GIGGLE
THIS IS MY CHANCE!

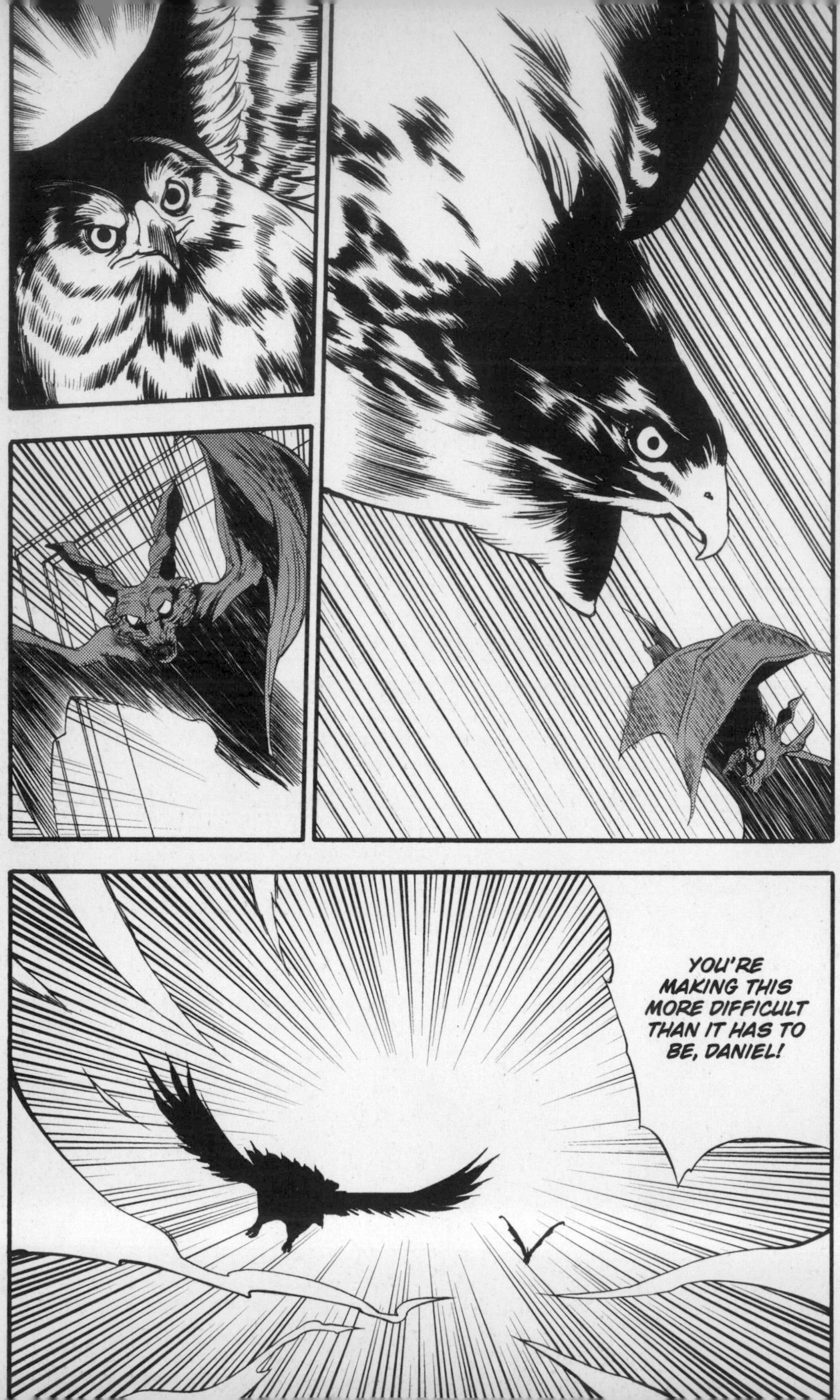
YOU'RE MAKING THIS MORE DIFFICULT THAN IT HAS TO BE, DANIEL!

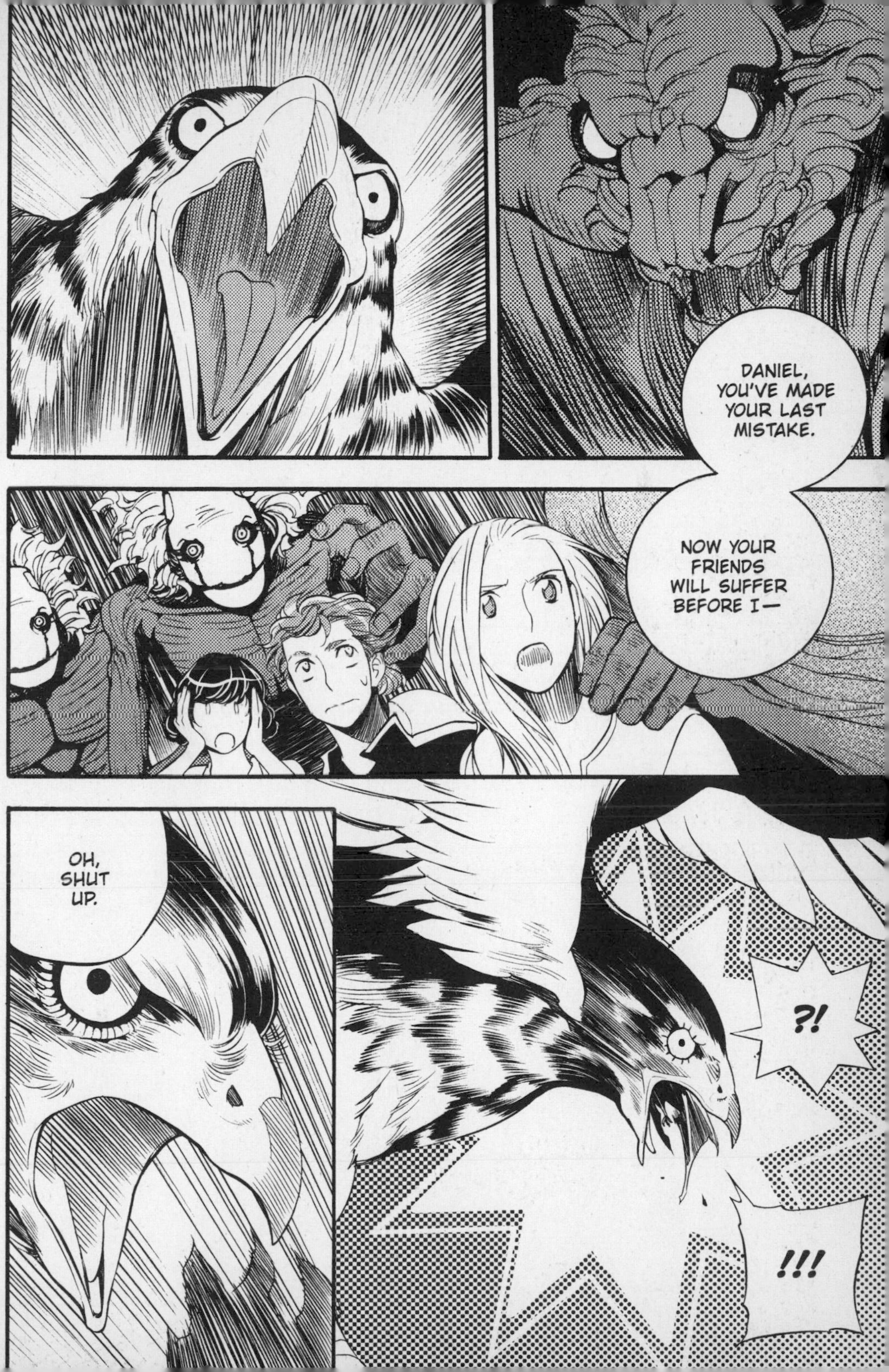
DANIEL, YOU'VE MADE YOUR LAST MISTAKE.
NOW YOUR FRIENDS WILL SUFFER BEFORE I—
OH, SHUT UP.
?!
!!!

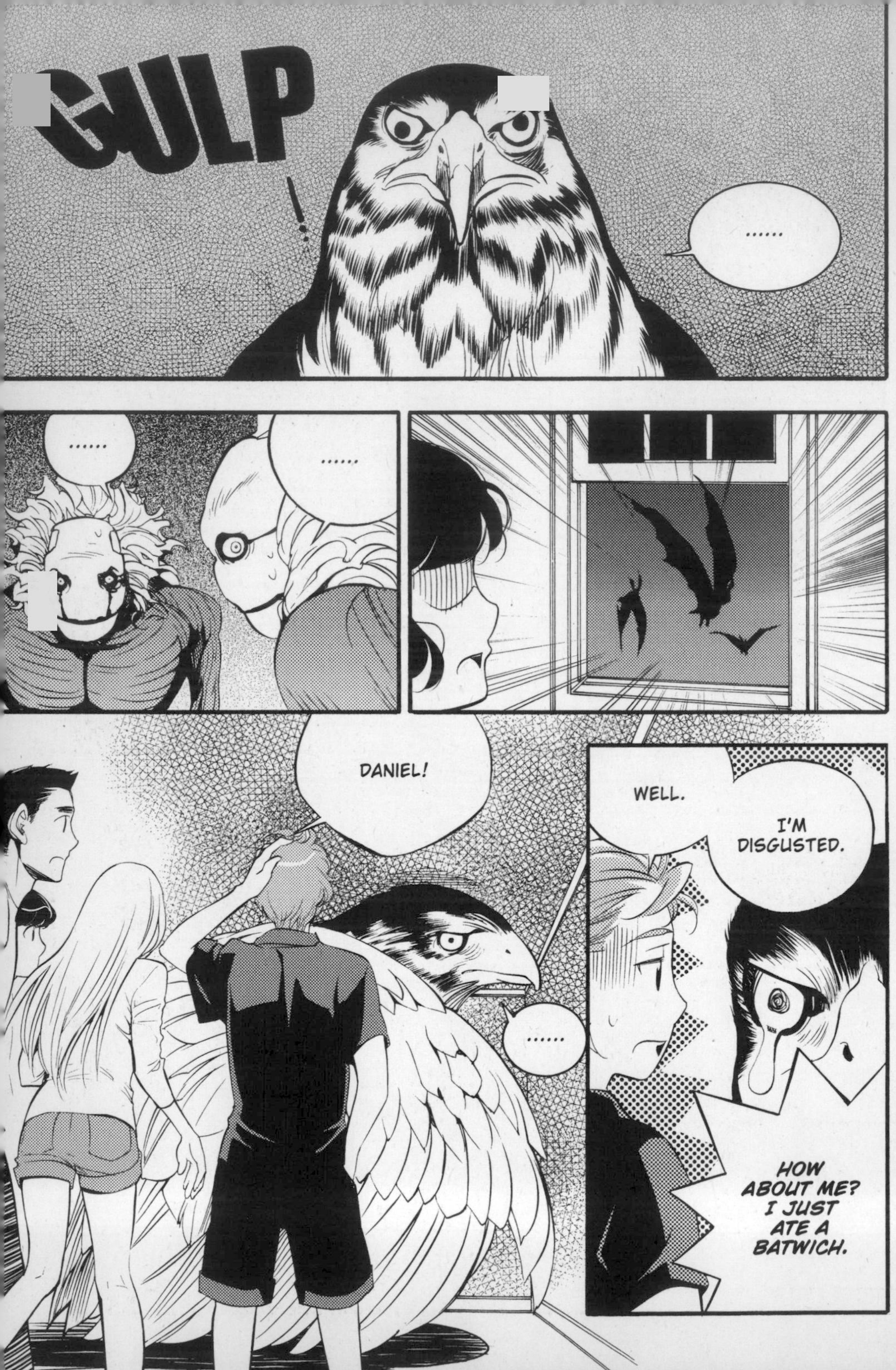
GULP
......
......
......
DANIEL!
......
WELL.
I'M DISGUSTED.
HOW ABOUT ME? I JUST ATE A BATWICH.

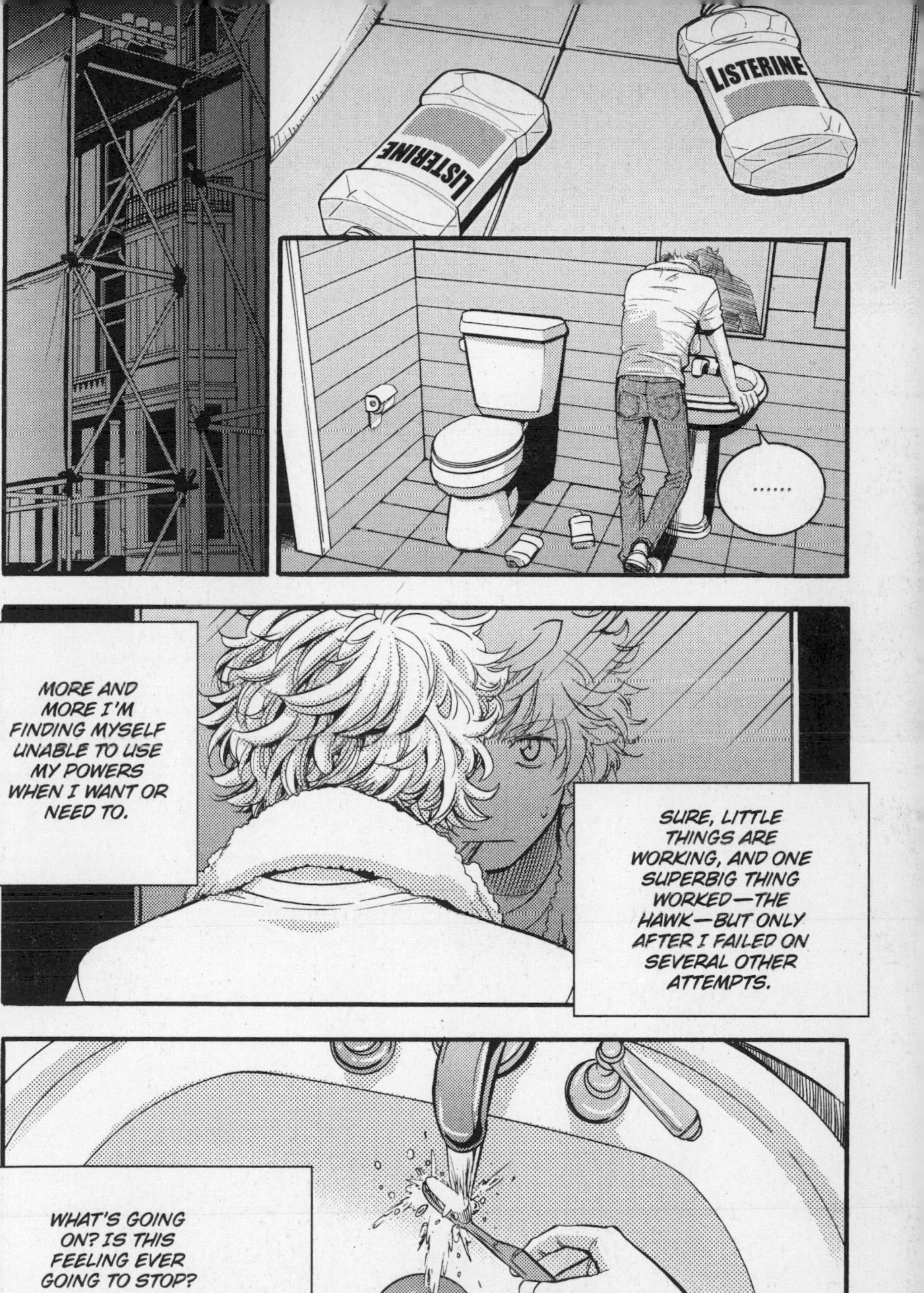
LISTERINE
LISTERINE
......
MORE AND MORE I'M FINDING MYSELF UNABLE TO USE MY POWERS WHEN I WANT OR NEED TO.
SURE, LITTLE THINGS ARE WORKING, AND ONE SUPERBIG THING WORKED—THE HAWK—BUT ONLY AFTER I FAILED ON SEVERAL OTHER ATTEMPTS.
WHAT'S GOING ON? IS THIS FEELING EVER GOING TO STOP?

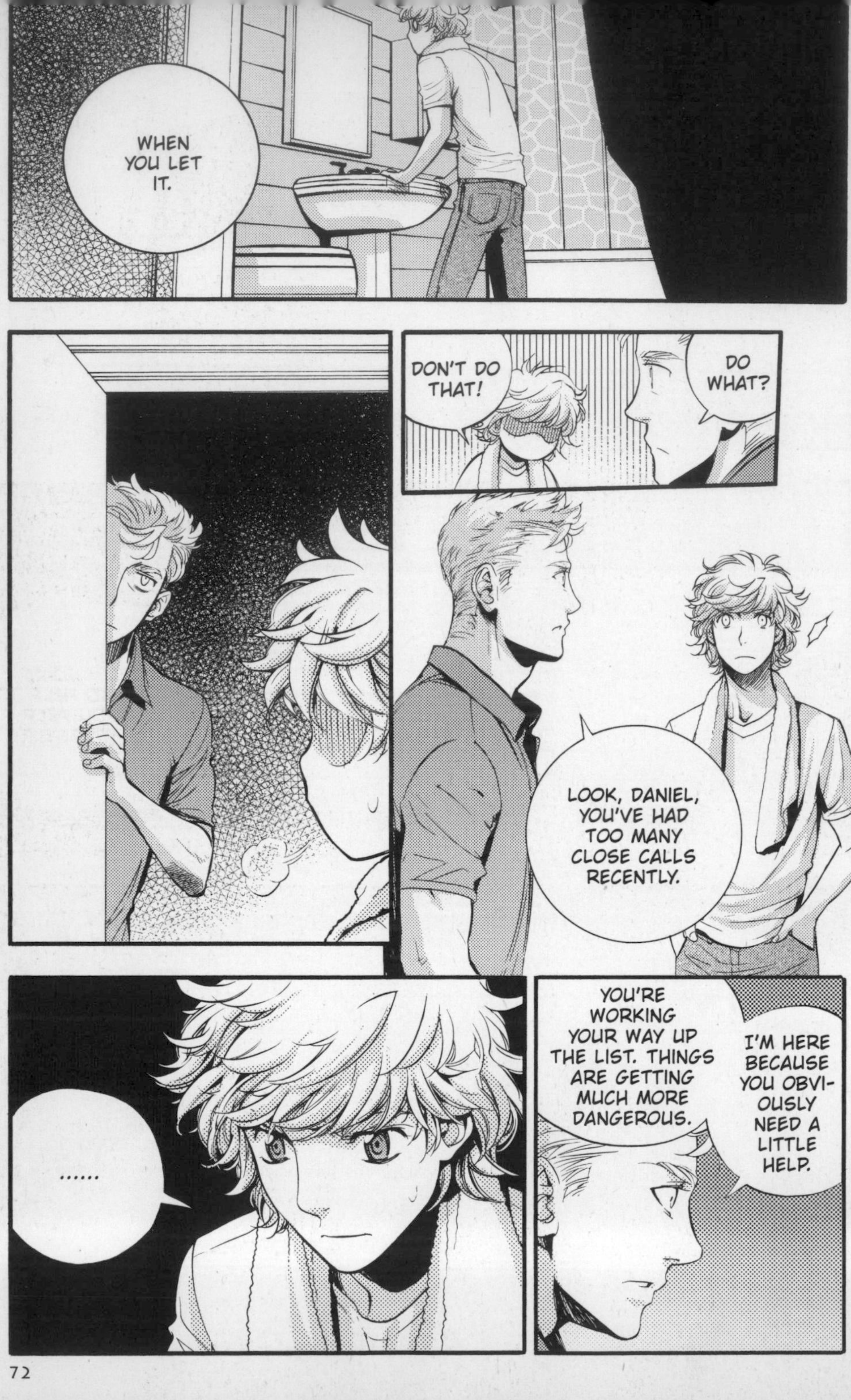
WHEN YOU LET IT.
DON'T DO THAT!
DO WHAT?
LOOK, DANIEL, YOU'VE HAD TOO MANY CLOSE CALLS RECENTLY.
......
YOU'RE WORKING YOUR WAY UP THE LIST. THINGS ARE GETTING MUCH MORE DANGEROUS.
I'M HERE BECAUSE YOU OBVI-OUSLY NEED A LITTLE HELP.

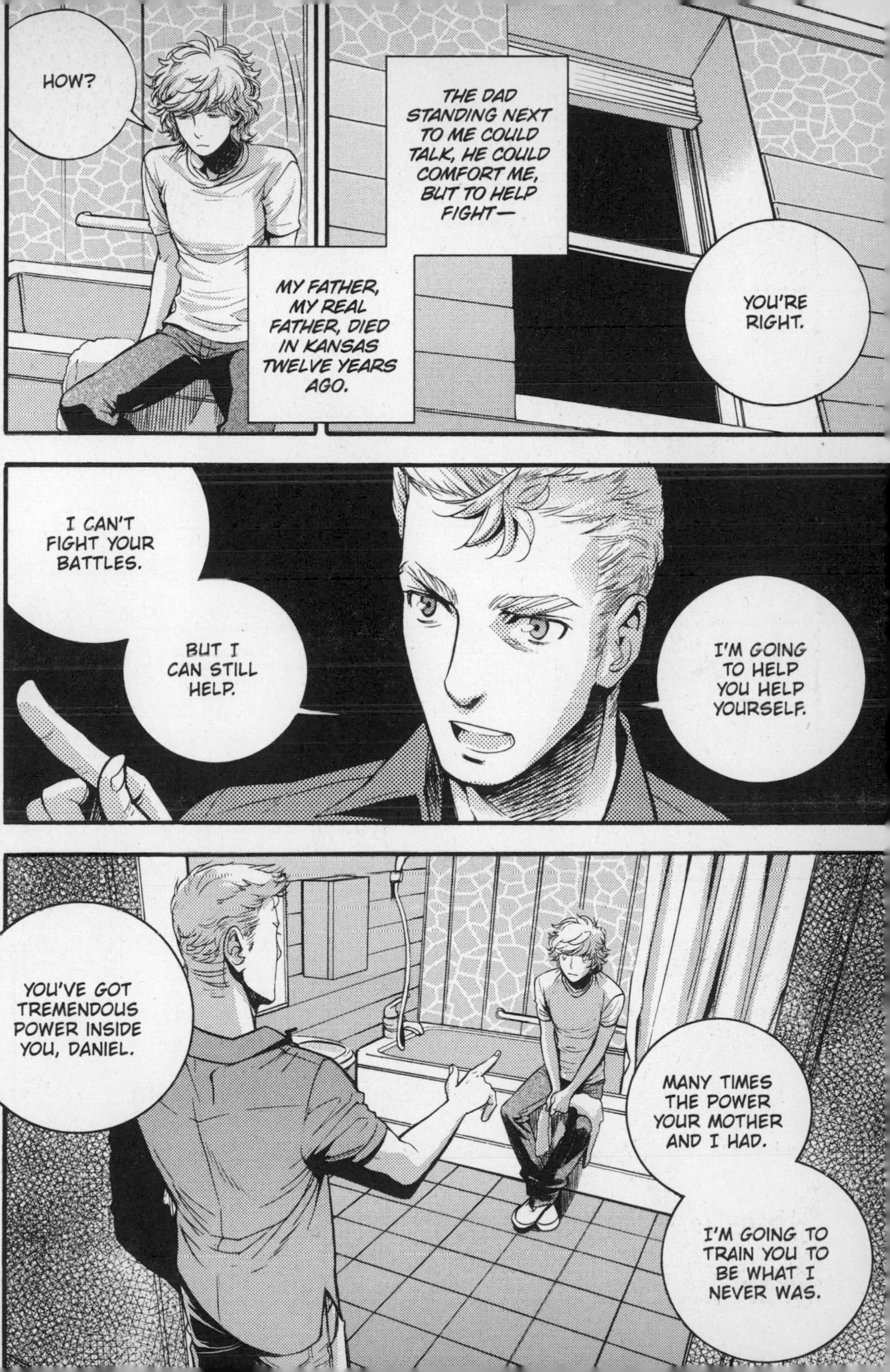
HOW?
THE DAD STANDING NEXT TO ME COULD TALK, HE COULD COMFORT ME, BUT TO HELP FIGHT—
MY FATHER, MY REAL FATHER, DIED IN KANSAS TWELVE YEARS AGO.
YOU'RE RIGHT.
I CAN'T FIGHT YOUR BATTLES.
BUT I CAN STILL HELP.
I'M GOING TO HELP YOU HELP YOURSELF.
YOU'VE GOT TREMENDOUS POWER INSIDE YOU, DANIEL.
MANY TIMES THE POWER YOUR MOTHER AND I HAD.
I'M GOING TO TRAIN YOU TO BE WHAT I NEVER WAS.

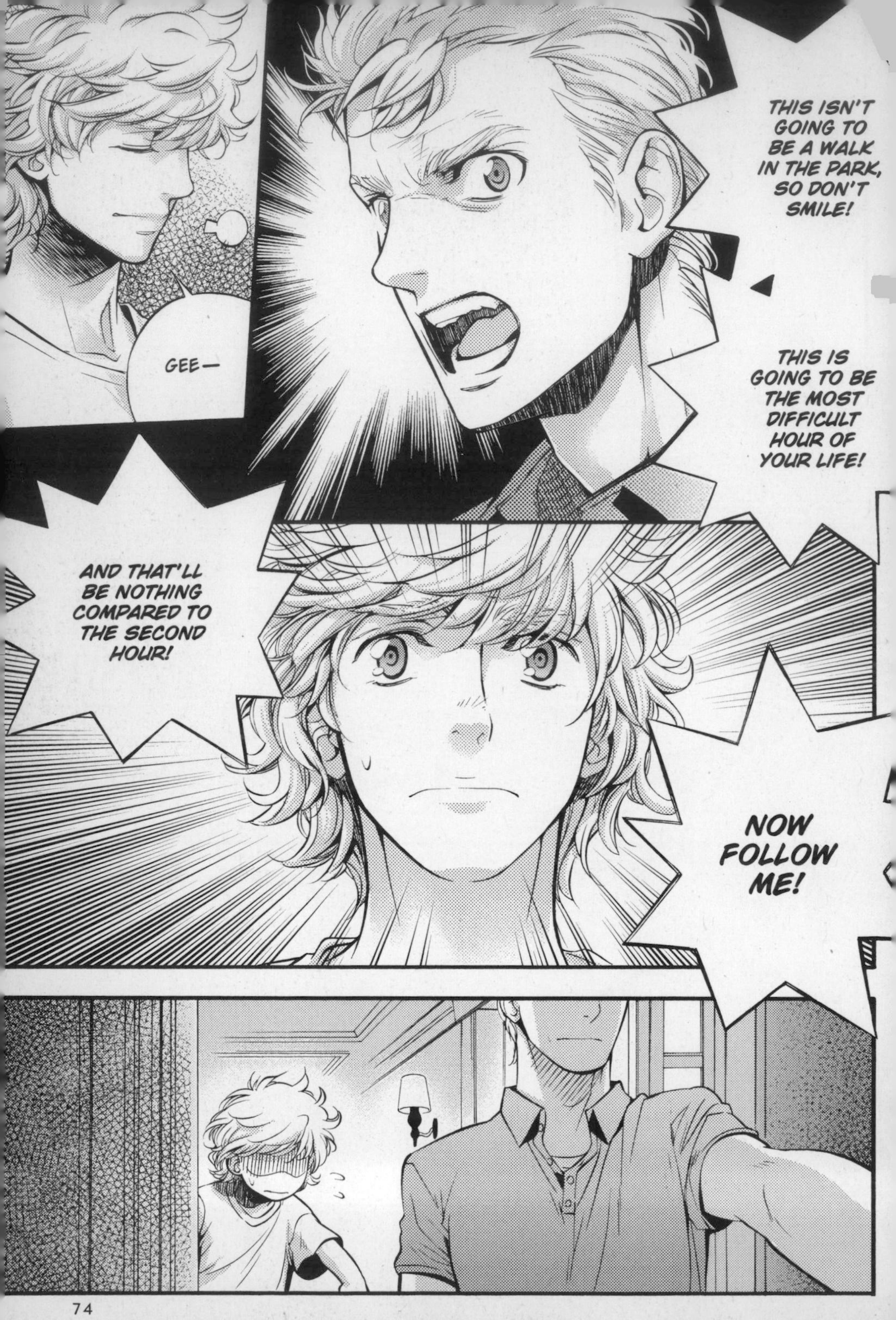
GEE—
THIS ISN'T GOING TO BE A WALK IN THE PARK, SO DON'T SMILE!
THIS IS GOING TO BE THE MOST DIFFICULT HOUR OF YOUR LIFE!
AND THAT'LL BE NOTHING COMPARED TO THE SECOND HOUR!
NOW FOLLOW ME!

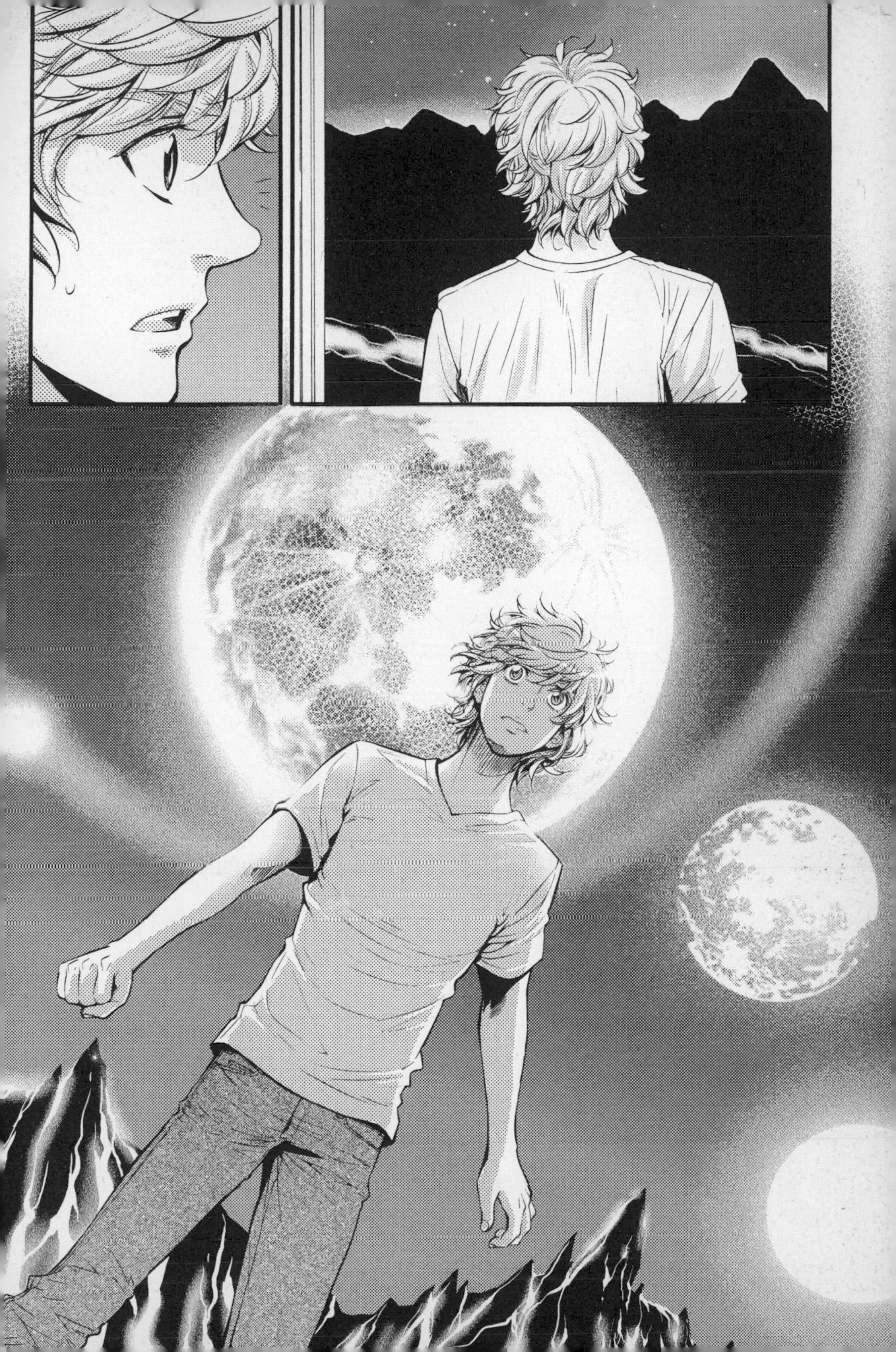

DANIEL X

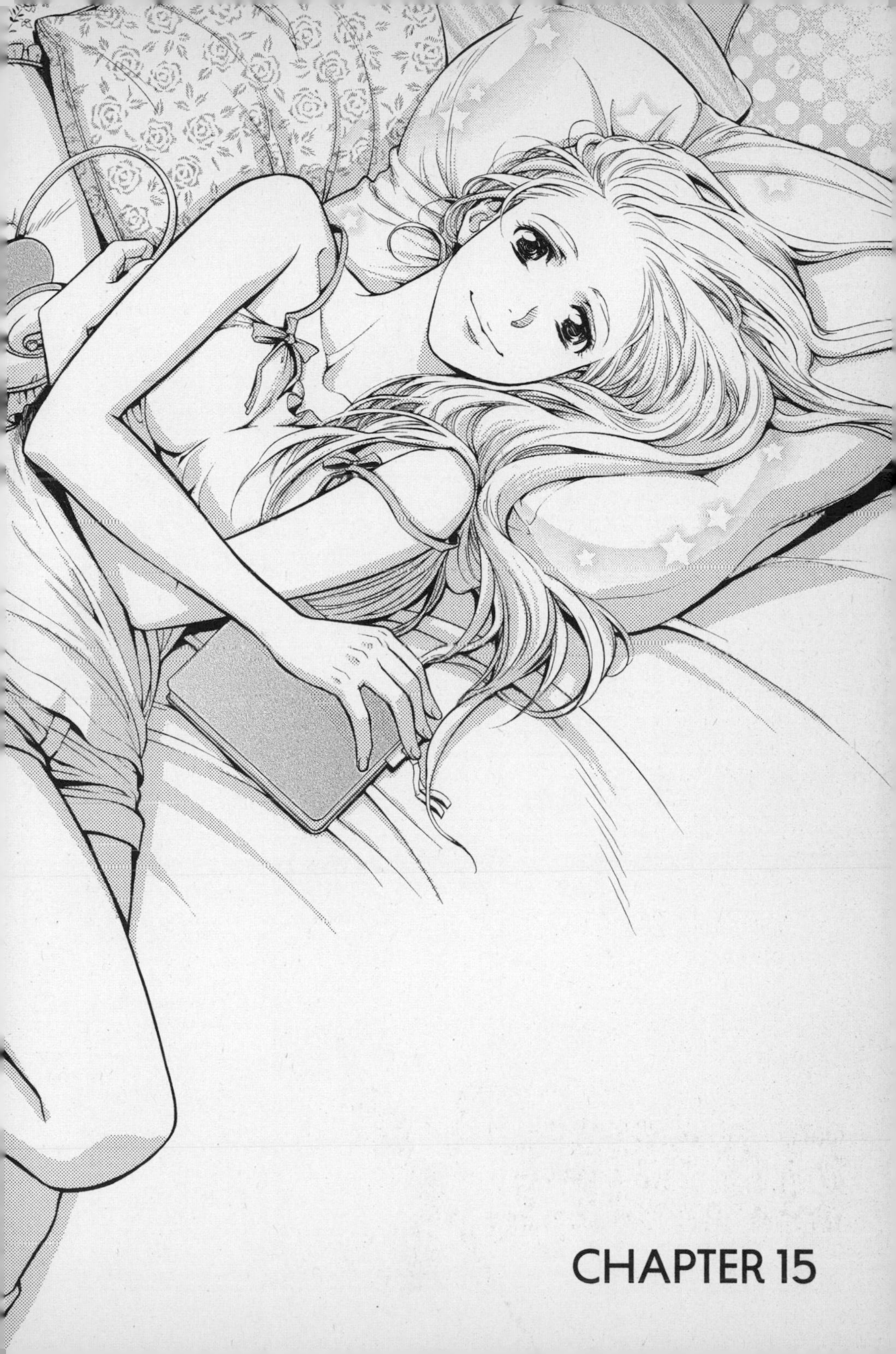

CHAPTER 15

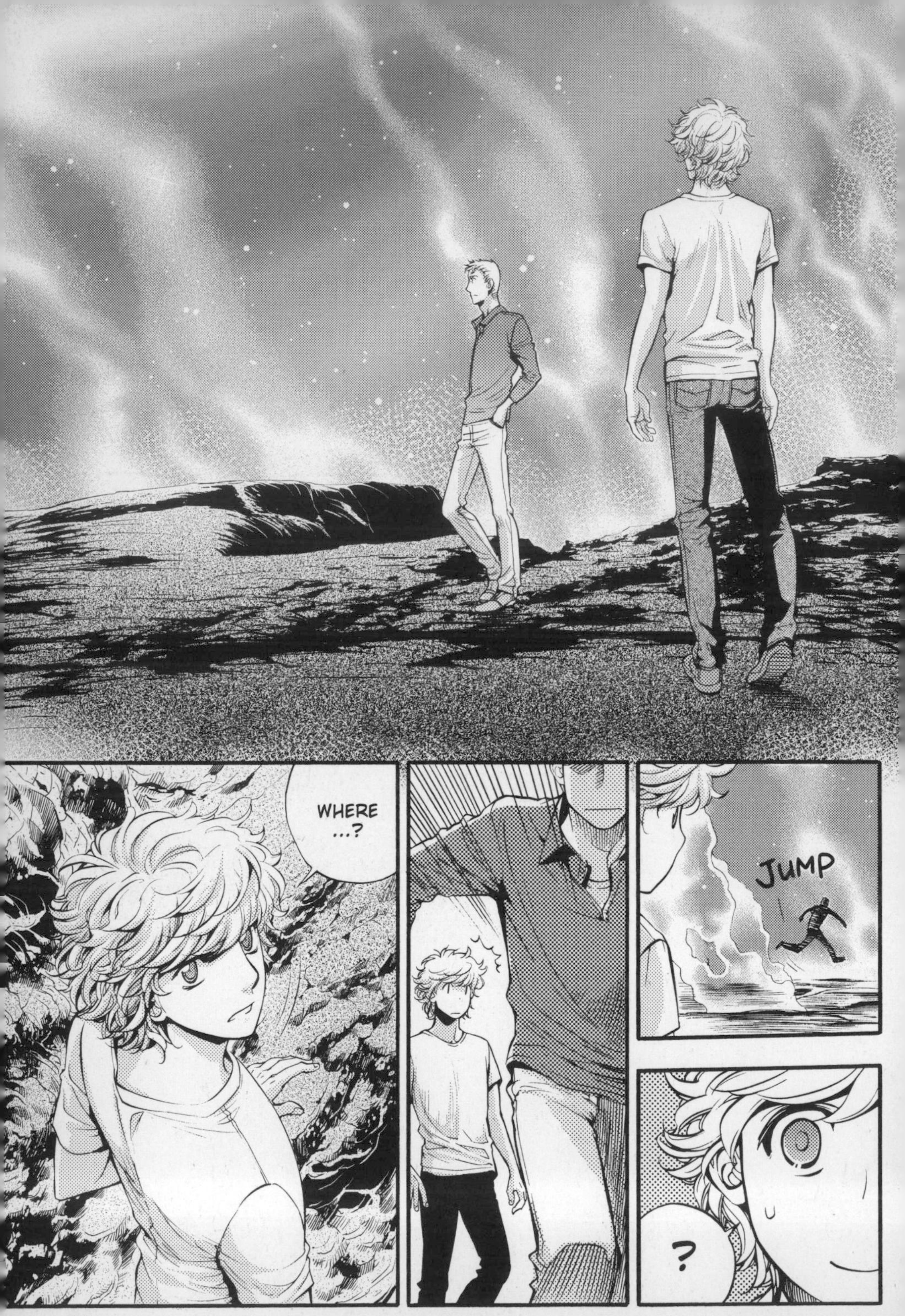
WHERE ...?
JUMP
?

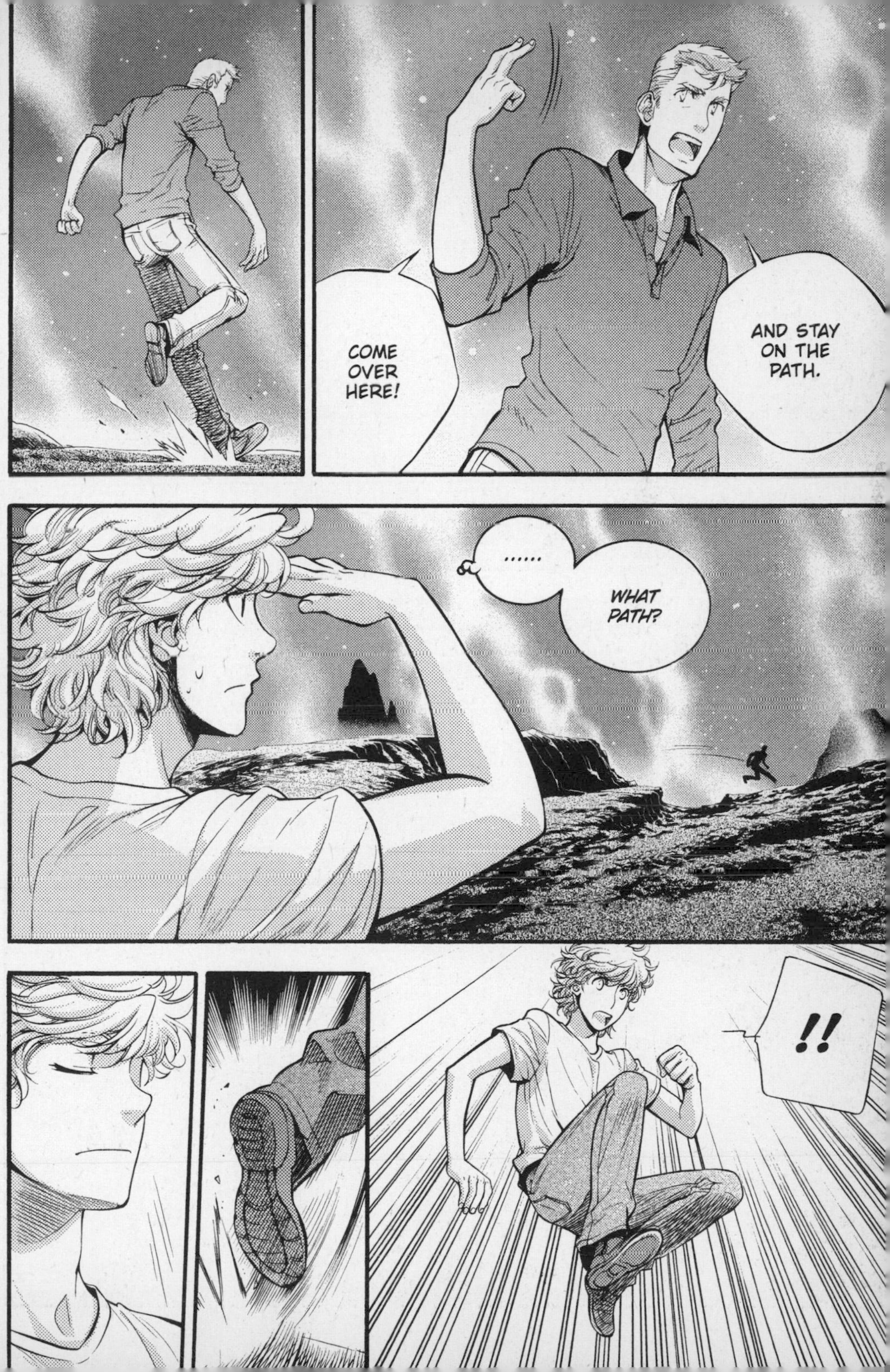
COME OVER HERE!
AND STAY ON THE PATH.
......
WHAT PATH?
!!

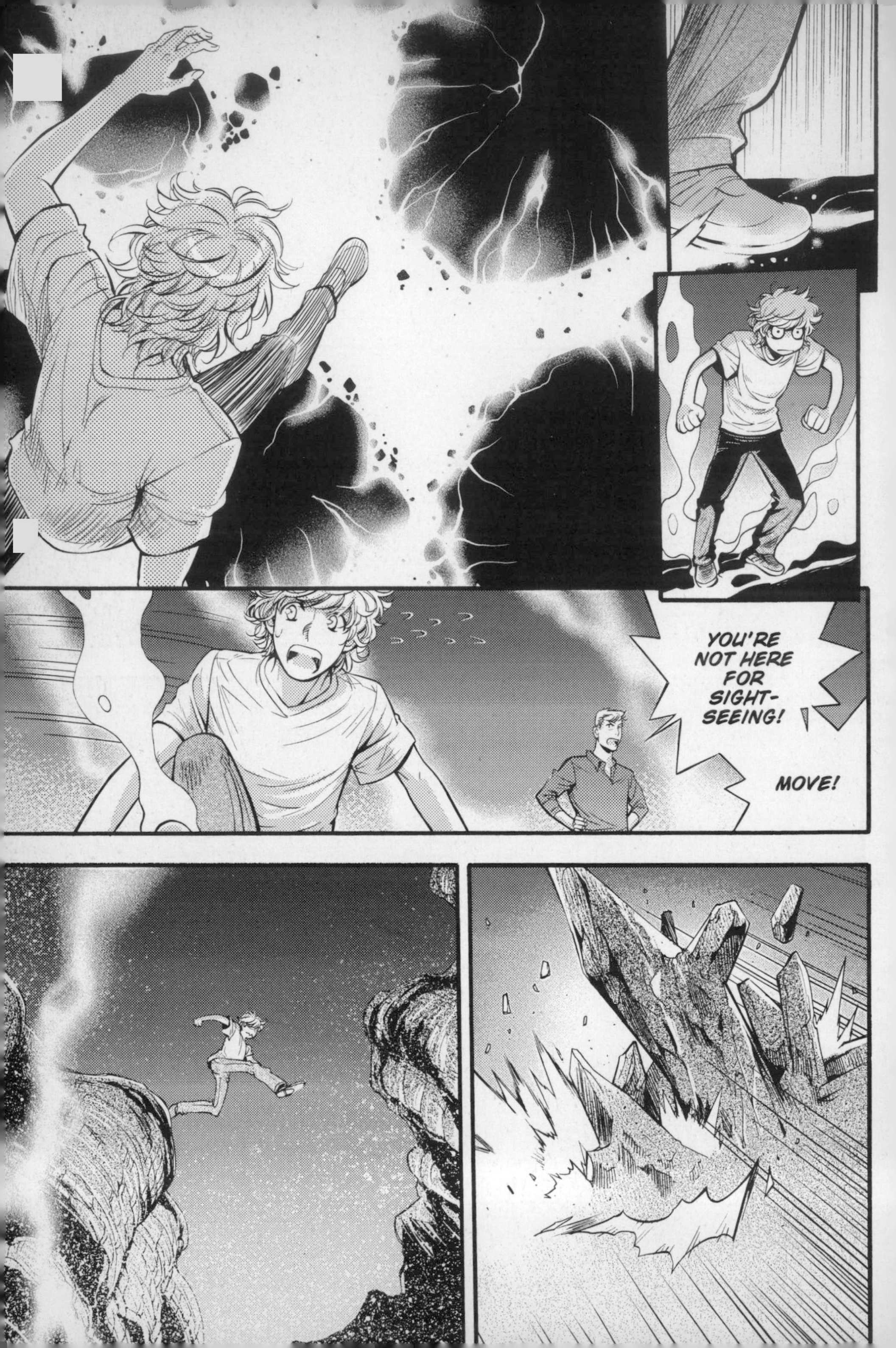
YOU'RE NOT HERE FOR SIGHT-SEEING!
MOVE!

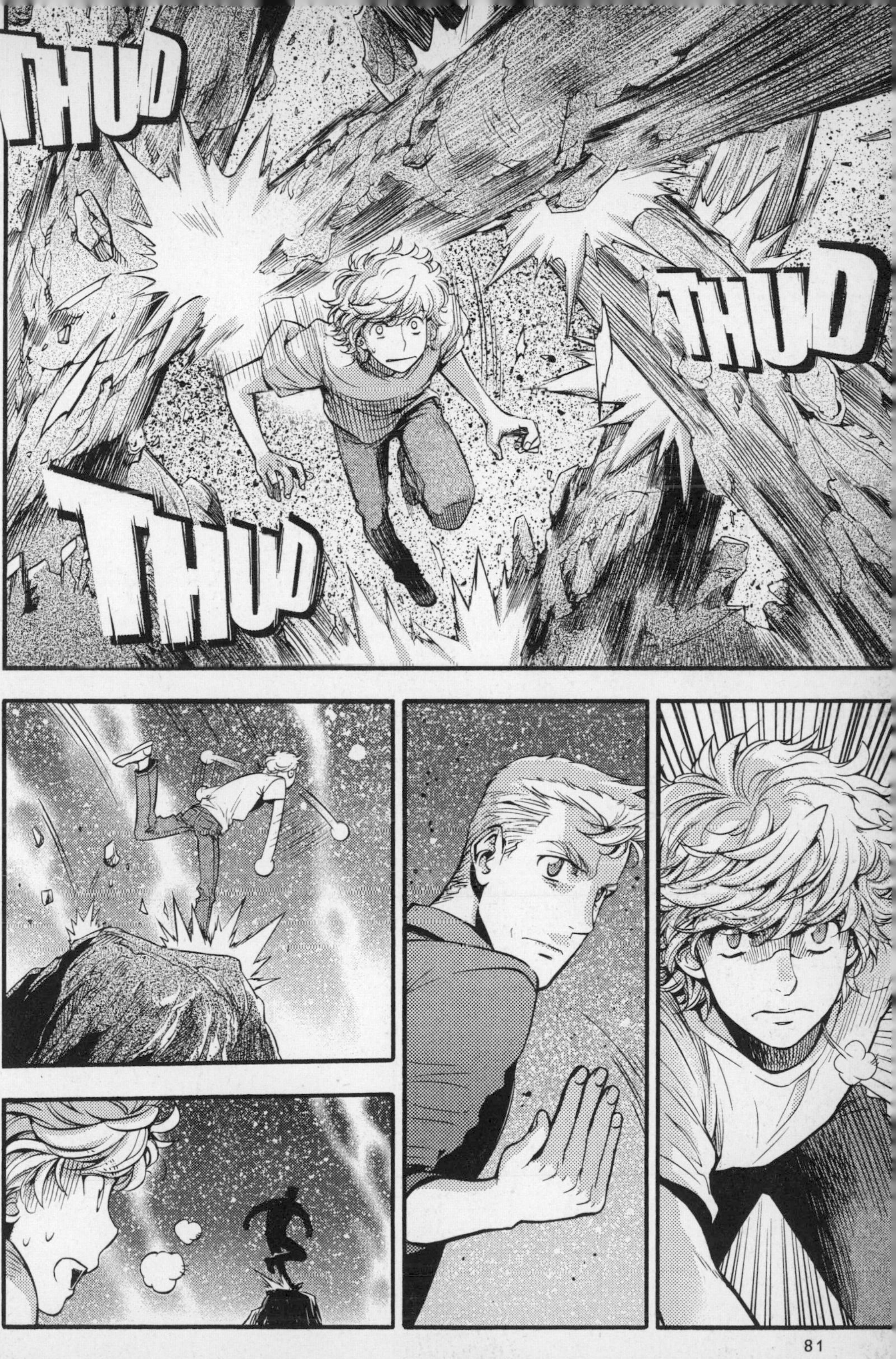
THUD
THUD
THUD

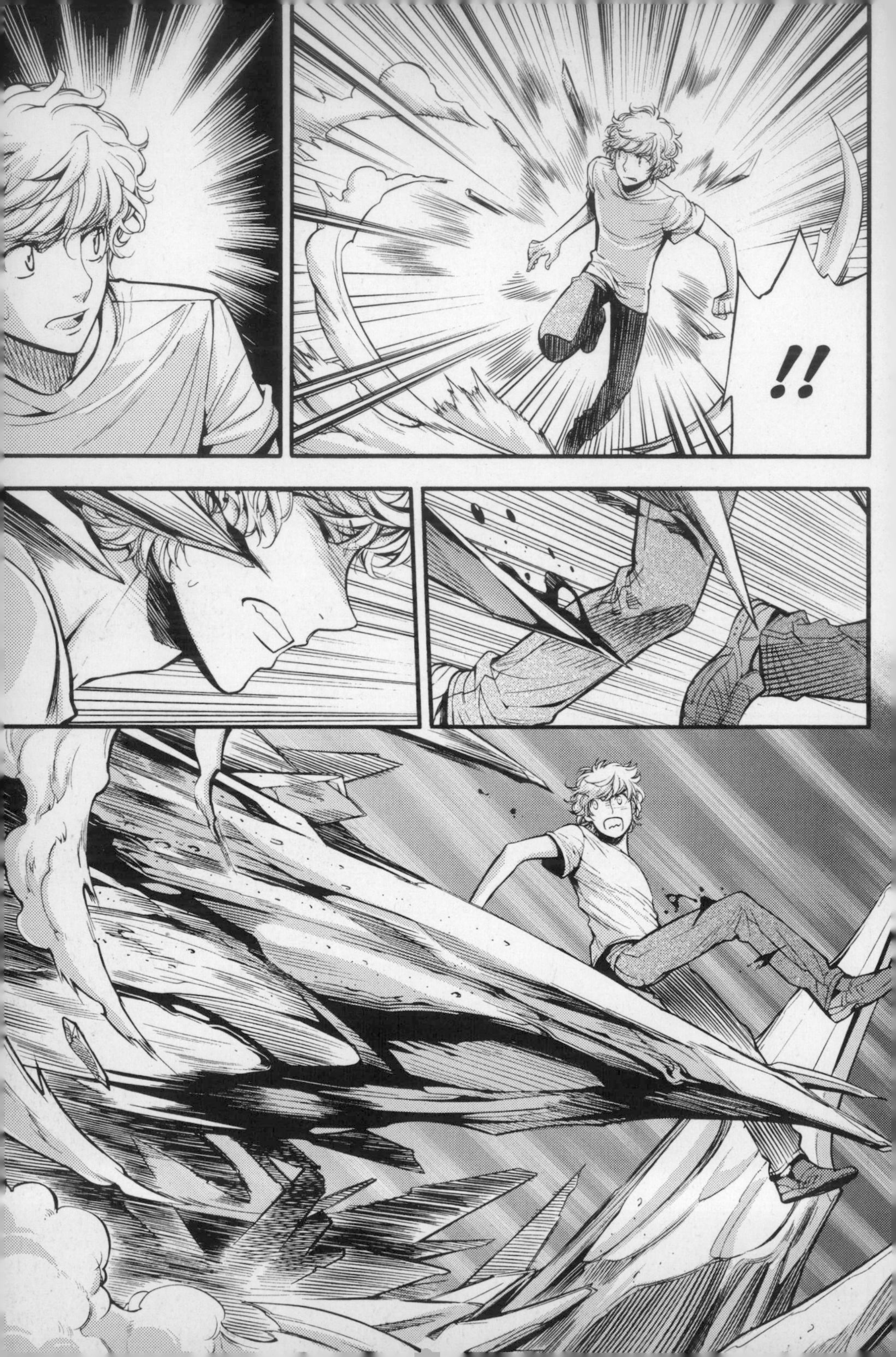
!!

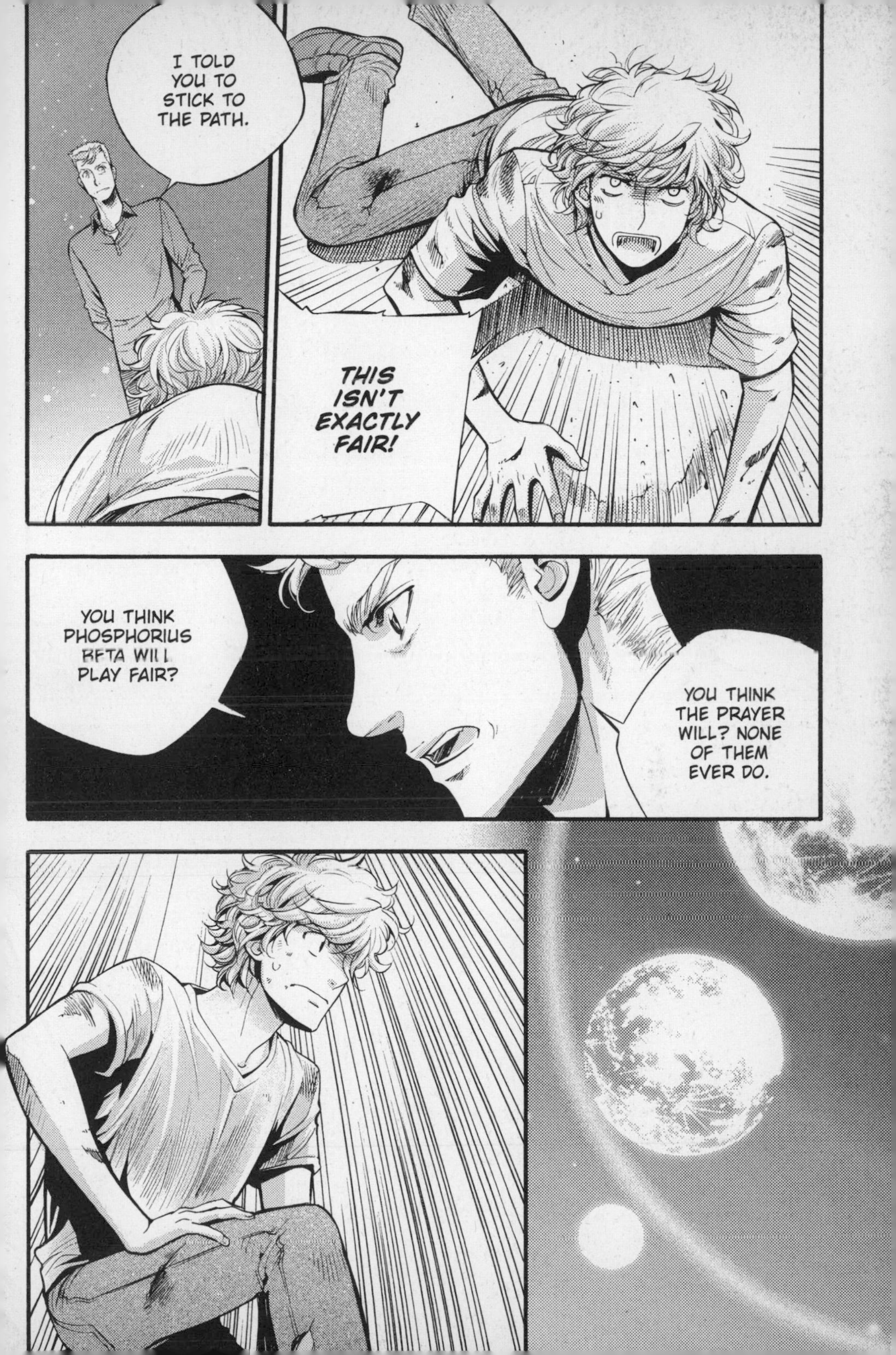
I TOLD YOU TO STICK TO THE PATH.
THIS ISN'T EXACTLY FAIR!
YOU THINK PHOSPHORIUS BETA WILL PLAY FAIR?
YOU THINK THE PRAYER WILL? NONE OF THEM EVER DO.

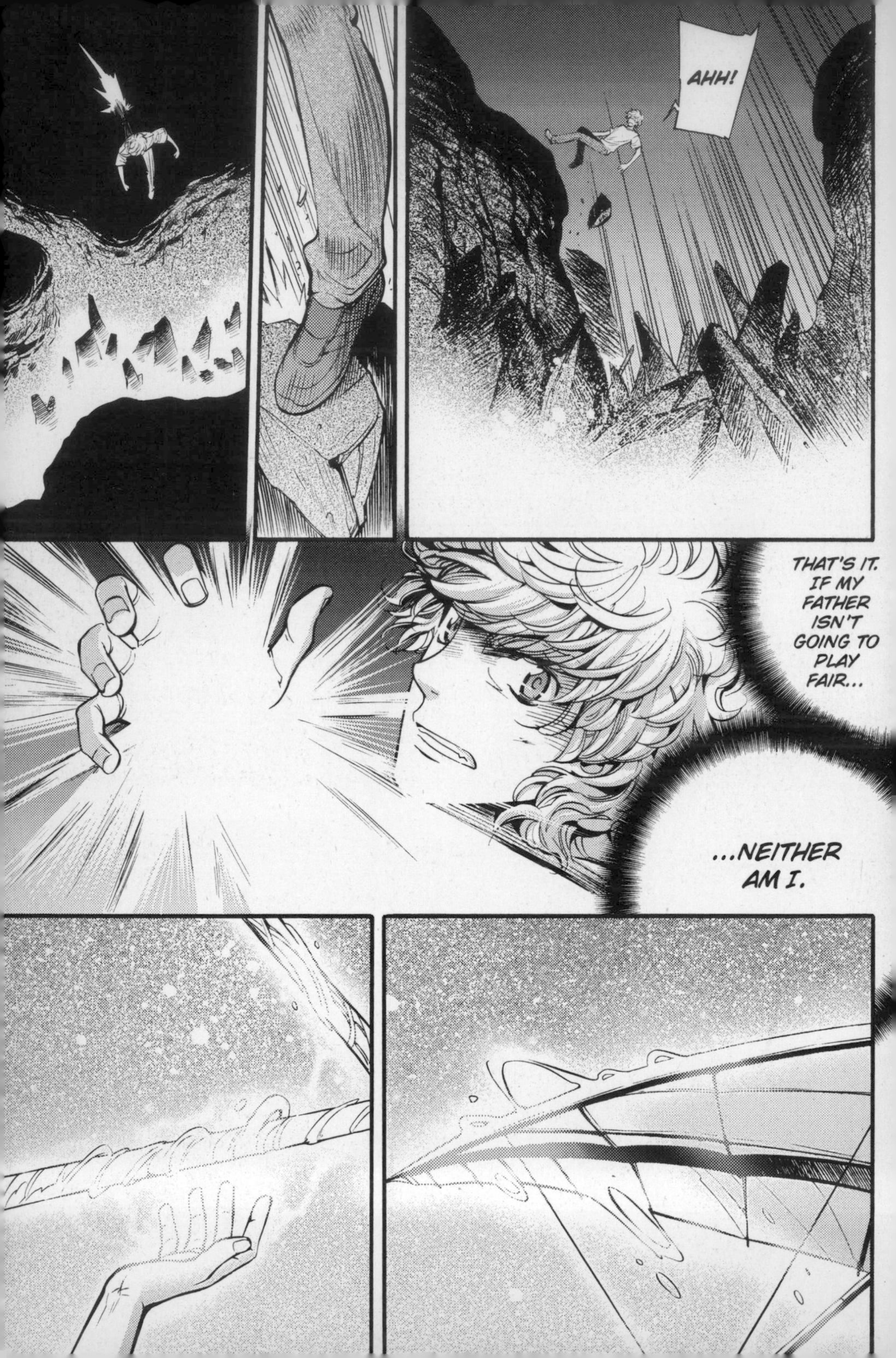
AHH!
THAT'S IT. IF MY FATHER ISN'T GOING TO PLAY FAIR...
...NEITHER AM I.

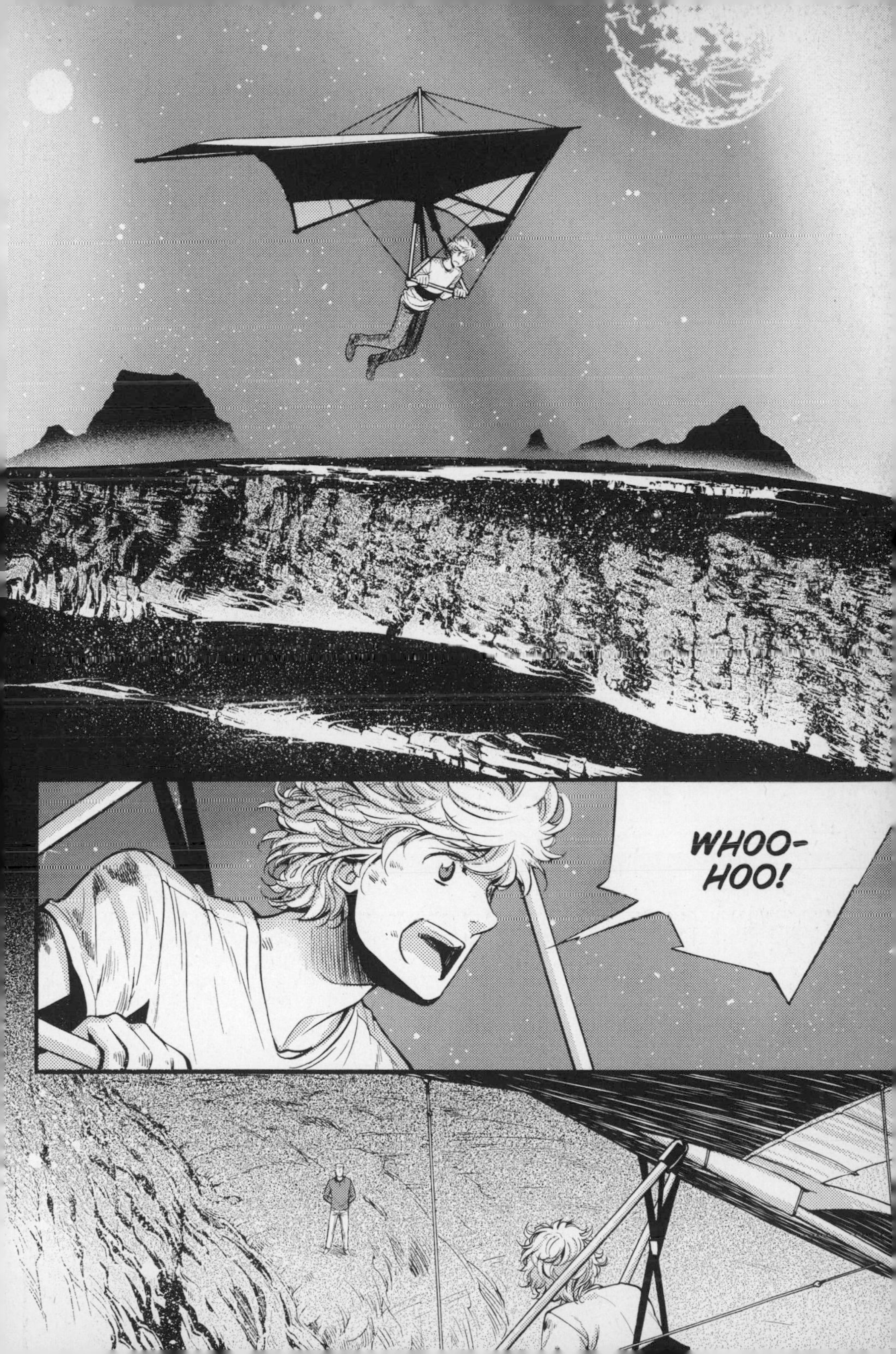
WHOO-HOO!

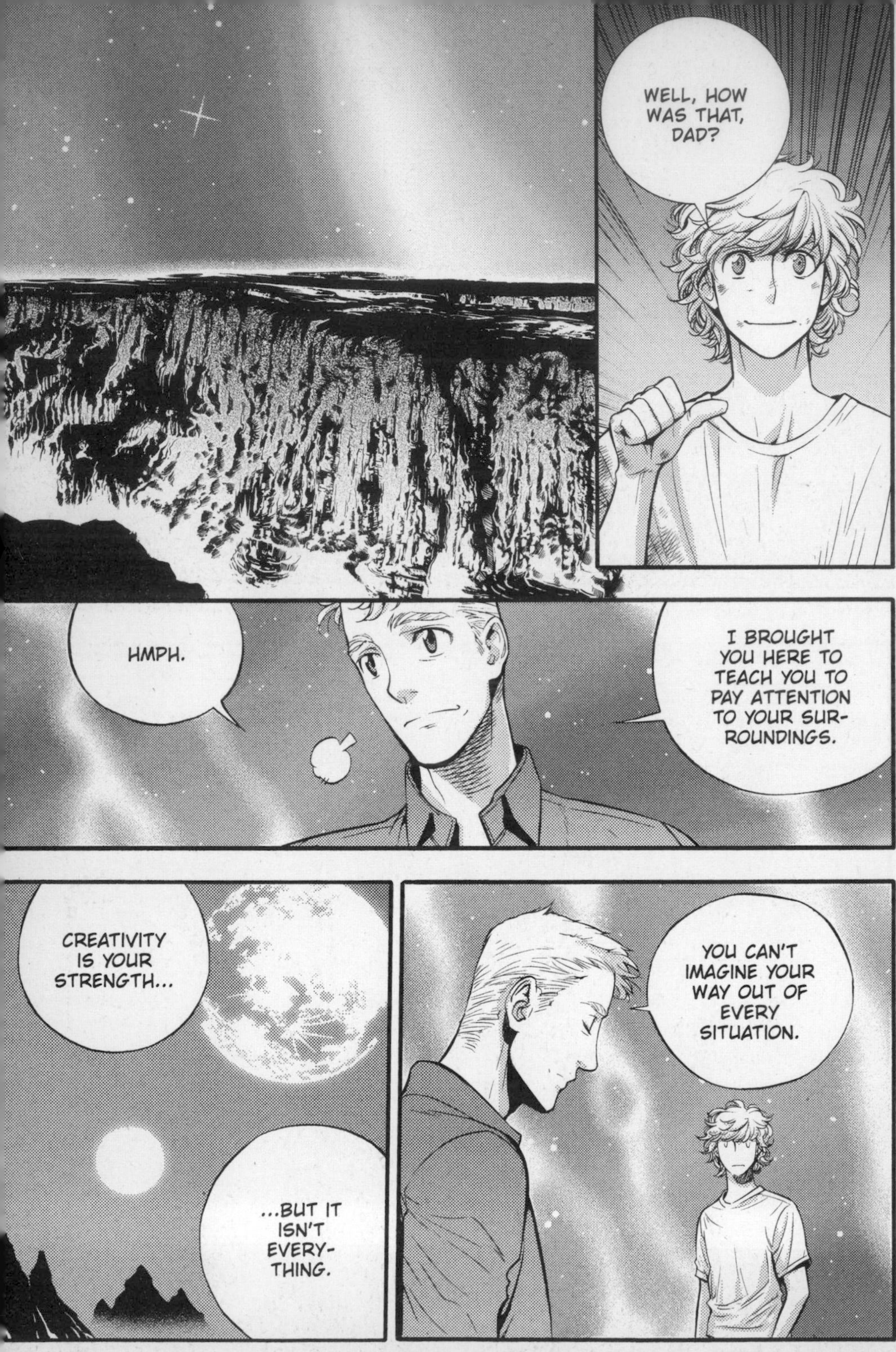
WELL, HOW WAS THAT, DAD?
HMPH.
I BROUGHT YOU HERE TO TEACH YOU TO PAY ATTENTION TO YOUR SUR-ROUNDINGS.
CREATIVITY IS YOUR STRENGTH...
...BUT IT ISN'T EVERY-THING.
YOU CAN'T IMAGINE YOUR WAY OUT OF EVERY SITUATION.

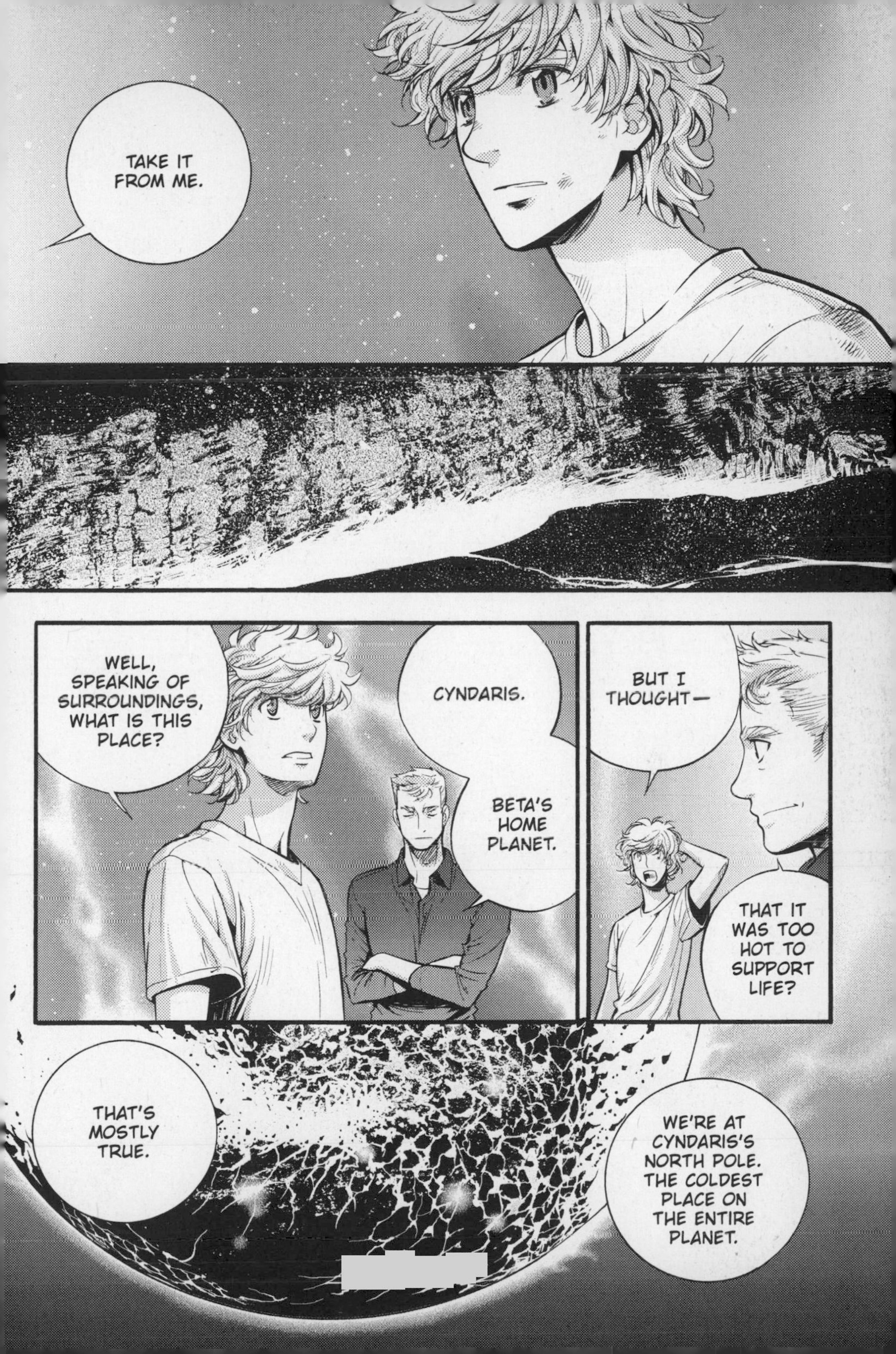
TAKE IT FROM ME.
WELL, SPEAKING OF SURROUNDINGS, WHAT IS THIS PLACE?
CYNDARIS.
BETA'S HOME PLANET.
BUT I THOUGHT—
THAT IT WAS TOO HOT TO SUPPORT LIFE?
THAT'S MOSTLY TRUE.
WE'RE AT CYNDARIS'S NORTH POLE. THE COLDEST PLACE ON THE ENTIRE PLANET.

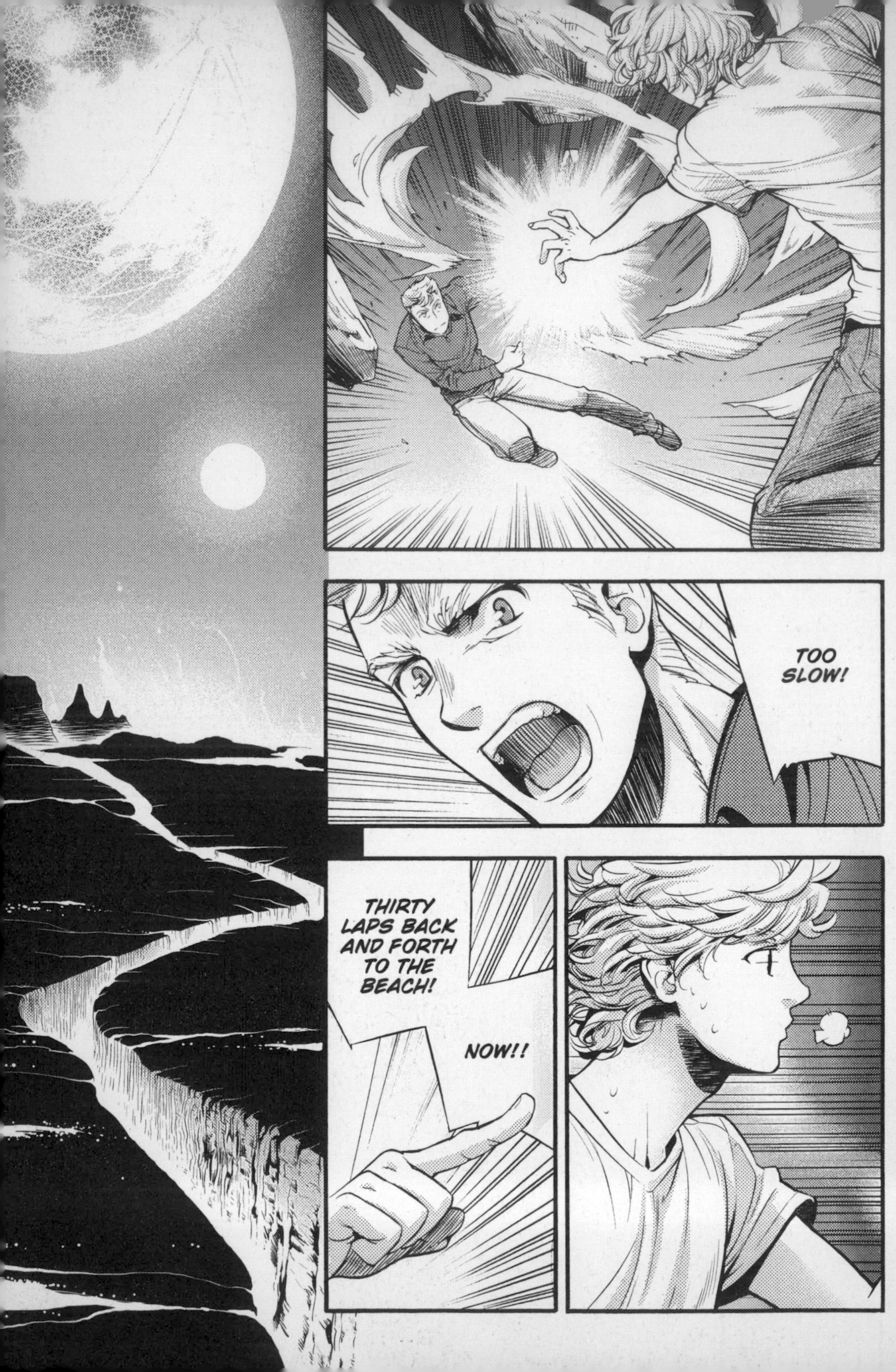
TOO SLOW!
THIRTY LAPS BACK AND FORTH TO THE BEACH!
NOW!!

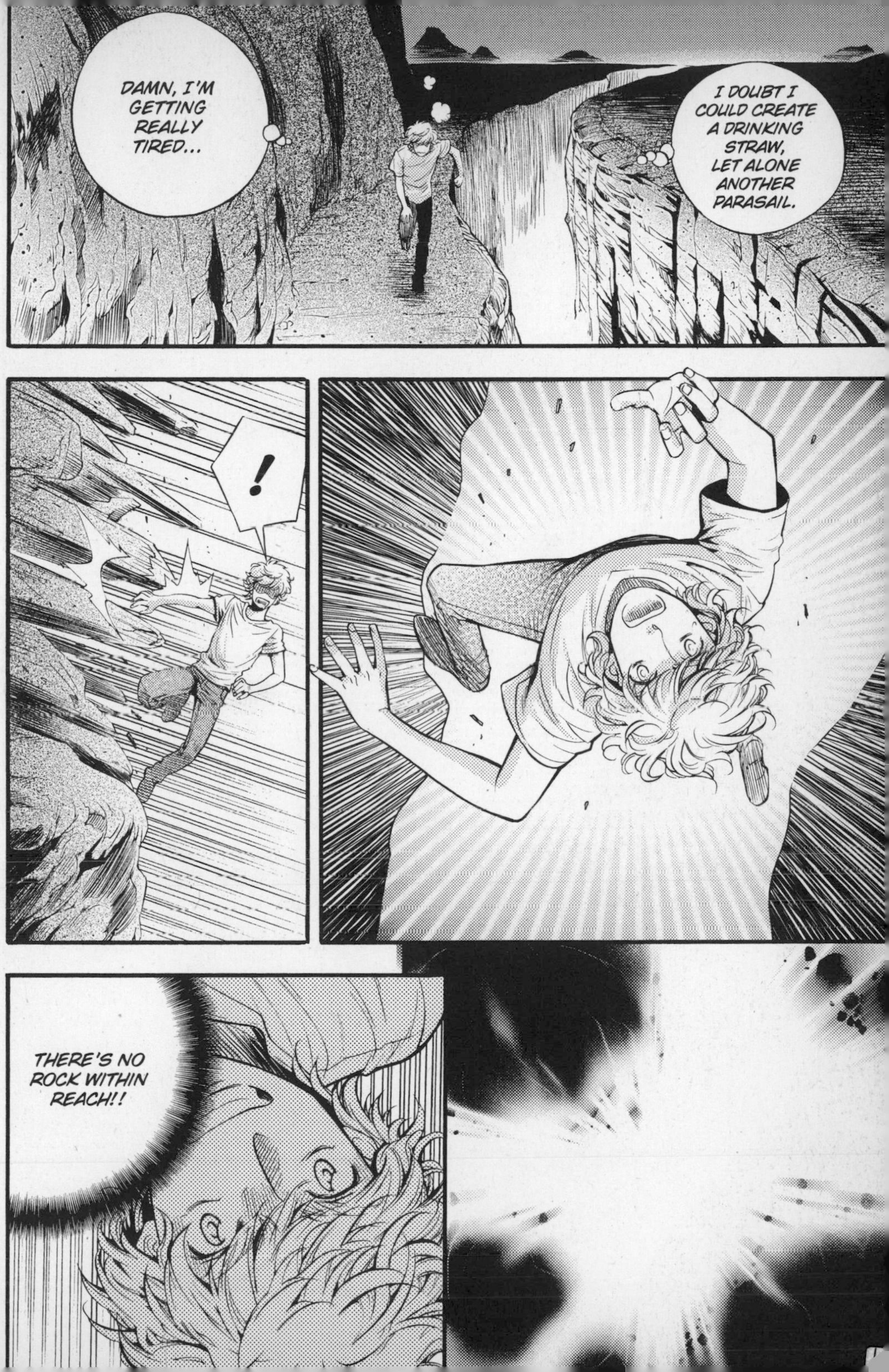
DAMN, I'M GETTING REALLY TIRED...
I DOUBT I COULD CREATE A DRINKING STRAW, LET ALONE ANOTHER PARASAIL.
!
THERE'S NO ROCK WITHIN REACH!!

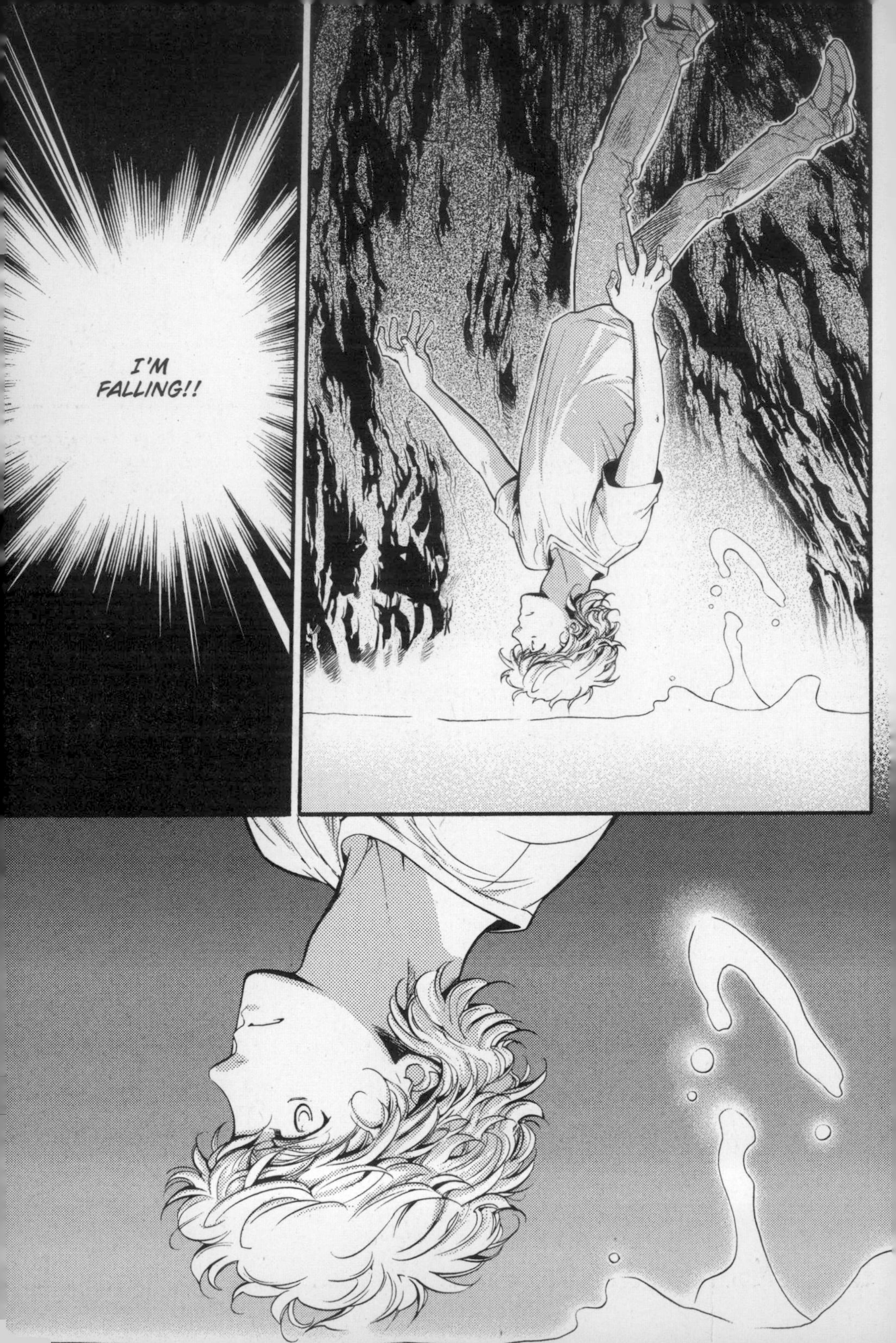
I'M FALLING!!

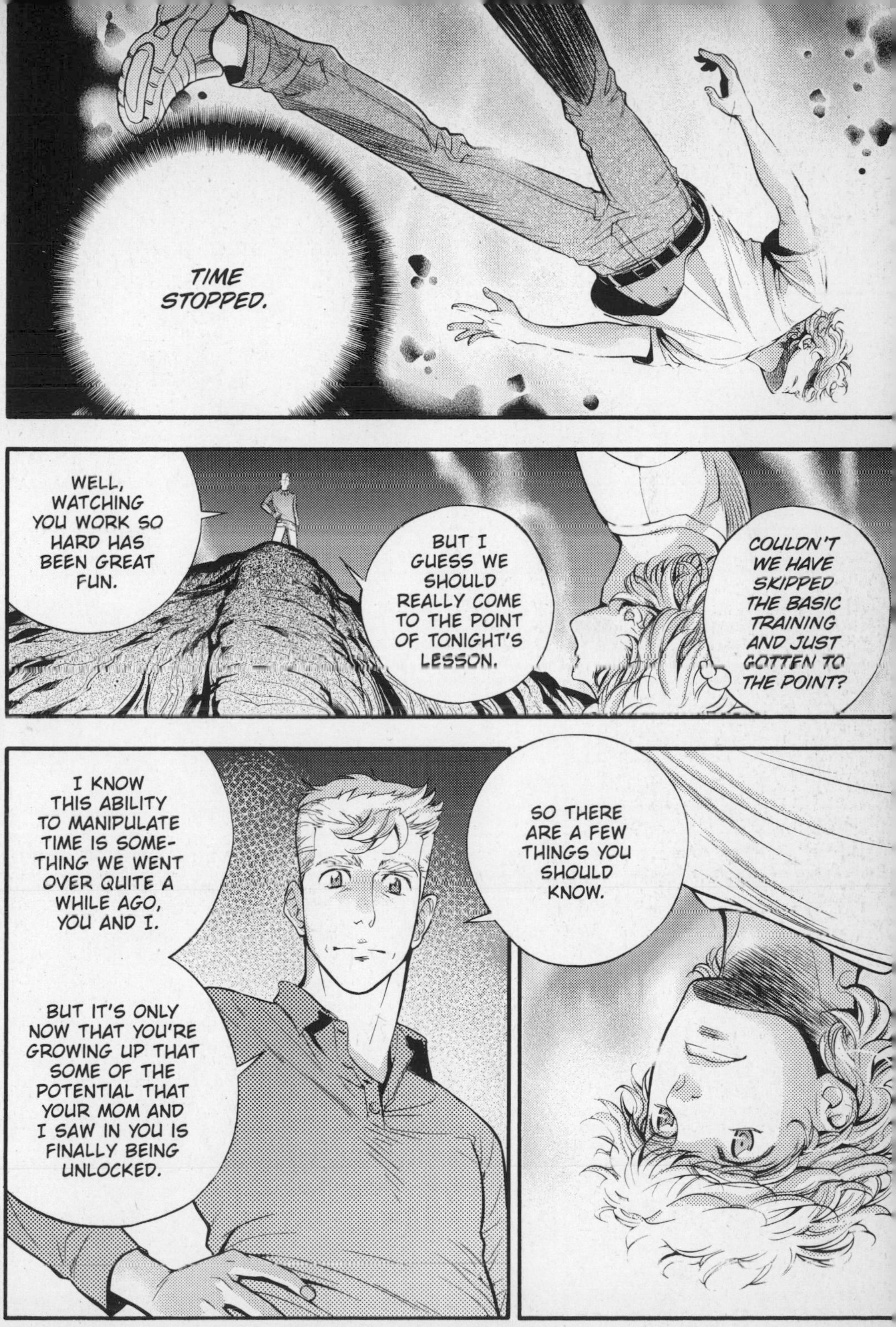
TIME STOPPED.
WELL, WATCHING YOU WORK SO HARD HAS BEEN GREAT FUN.
BUT I GUESS WE SHOULD REALLY COME TO THE POINT OF TONIGHT'S LESSON.
COULDN'T WE HAVE SKIPPED THE BASIC TRAINING AND JUST GOTTEN TO THE POINT?
I KNOW THIS ABILITY TO MANIPULATE TIME IS SOME-THING WE WENT OVER QUITE A WHILE AGO, YOU AND I.
BUT IT'S ONLY NOW THAT YOU'RE GROWING UP THAT SOME OF THE POTENTIAL THAT YOUR MOM AND I SAW IN YOU IS FINALLY BEING UNLOCKED.
SO THERE ARE A FEW THINGS YOU SHOULD KNOW.

NUMBER ONE: BRINGING NEW THINGS INTO THE WORLD IS NOT AN ABILITY YOU SHOULD TAKE LIGHTLY.

BUT BEING ABLE TO GO BACK AND CHANGE THINGS IS AN EVEN GREATER BURDEN.

I WAS NEVER TOO GOOD AT IT.

NONE OF THE FAMILY WAS.

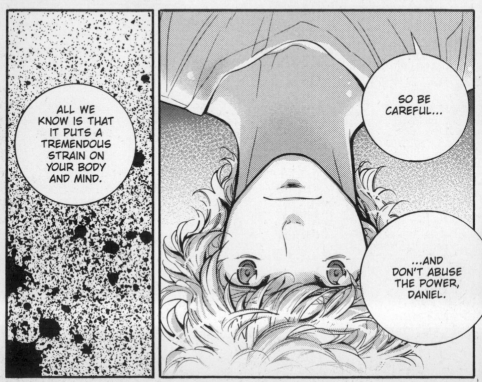

ALL WE KNOW IS THAT IT PUTS A TREMENDOUS STRAIN ON YOUR BODY AND MIND.

SO BE CAREFUL...

...AND DON'T ABUSE THE POWER, DANIEL.

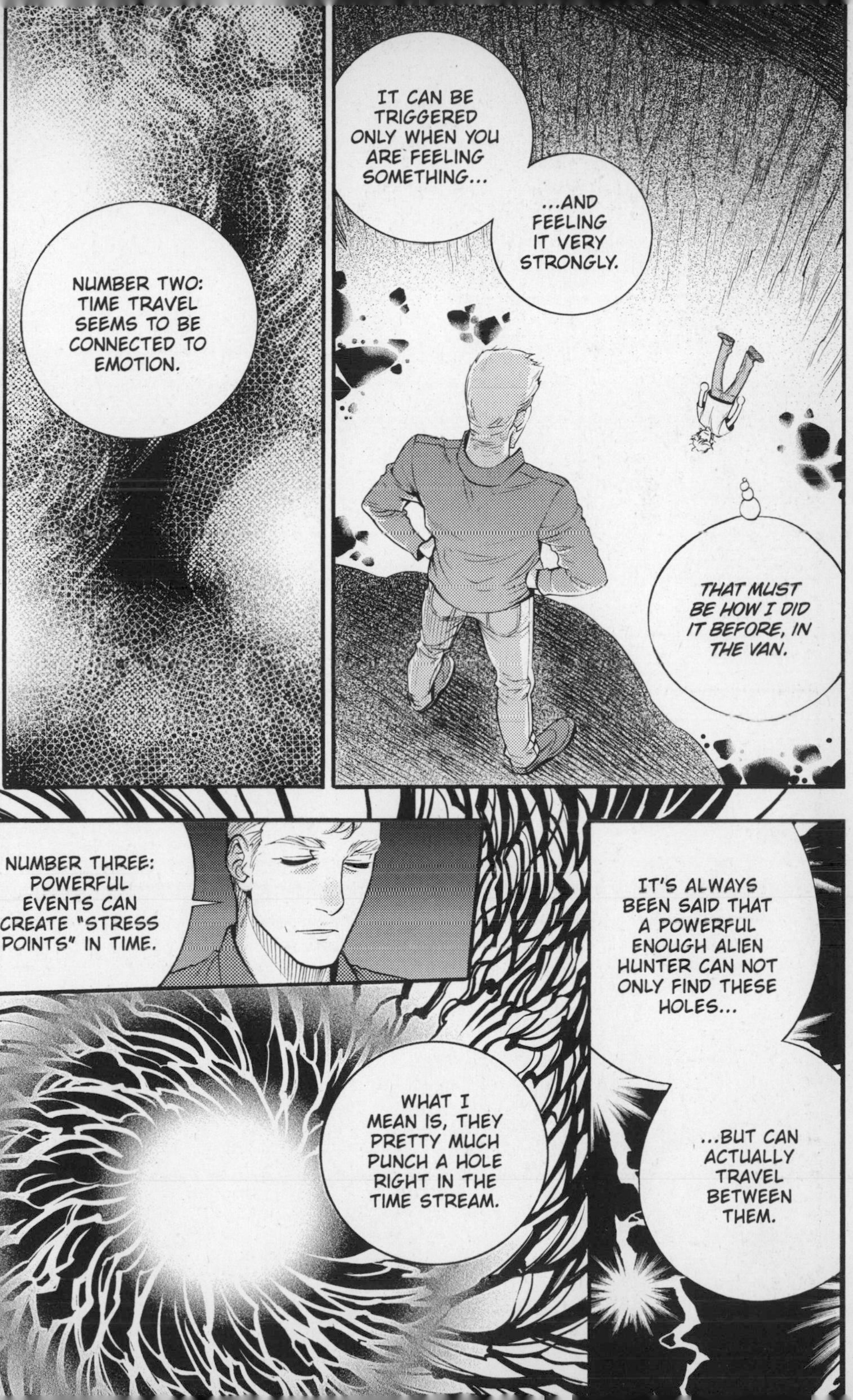
NUMBER TWO: TIME TRAVEL SEEMS TO BE CONNECTED TO EMOTION.
IT CAN BE TRIGGERED ONLY WHEN YOU ARE FEELING SOMETHING...
...AND FEELING IT VERY STRONGLY.
THAT MUST BE HOW I DID IT BEFORE, IN THE VAN.
NUMBER THREE: POWERFUL EVENTS CAN CREATE "STRESS POINTS" IN TIME.
WHAT I MEAN IS, THEY PRETTY MUCH PUNCH A HOLE RIGHT IN THE TIME STREAM.
IT'S ALWAYS BEEN SAID THAT A POWERFUL ENOUGH ALIEN HUNTER CAN NOT ONLY FIND THESE HOLES...
...BUT CAN ACTUALLY TRAVEL BETWEEN THEM.

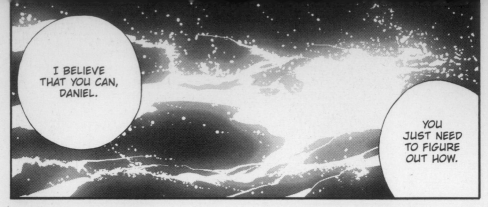

I BELIEVE THAT YOU CAN, DANIEL.

YOU JUST NEED TO FIGURE OUT HOW.

YOU CARRIED YOURSELF WELL TONIGHT.

I'D SAY YOU'RE AT LEAST ONE PERCENT OF THE WAY TO BEING A TRULY EFFECTIVE ALIEN HUNTER.

FANTASTIC.

IF TIME STOPPED...

...HOW COME—

HOW COME I'M NOT FROZEN?

HOW SHOULD I KNOW?

THIS IS YOUR DREAM.

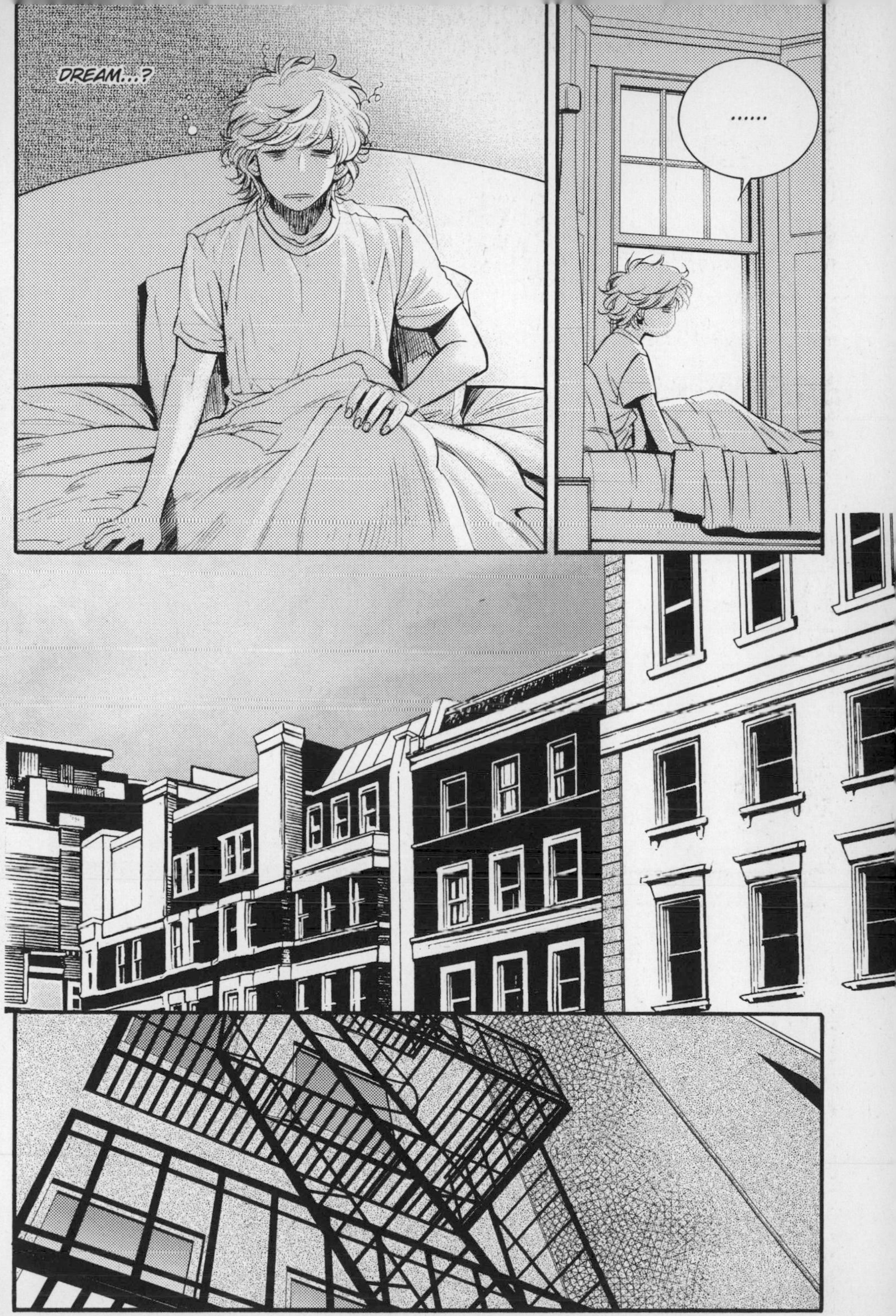
DREAM...?
......

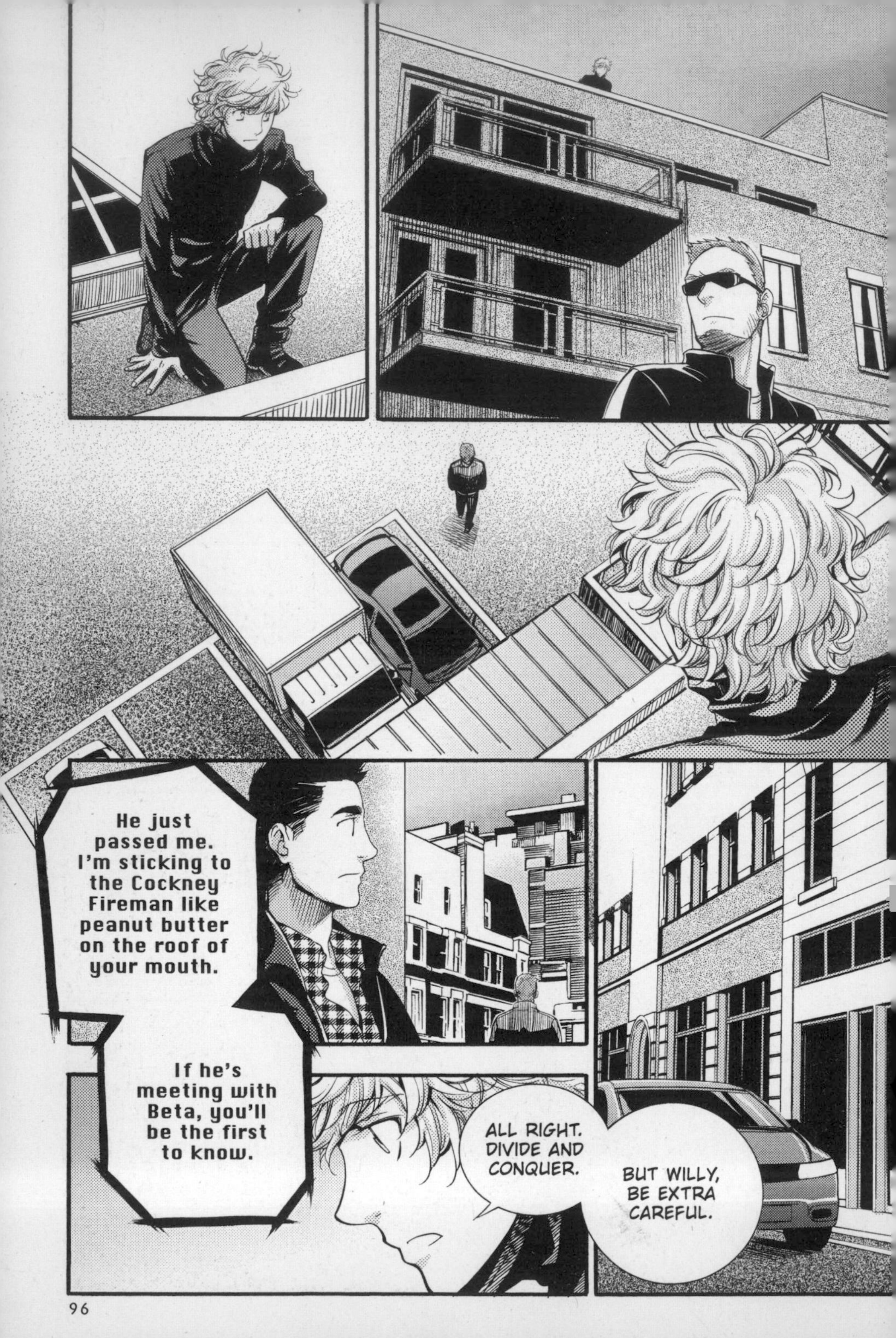
He just passed me. I'm sticking to the Cockney Fireman like peanut butter on the roof of your mouth.
If he's meeting with Beta, you'll be the first to know.
ALL RIGHT. DIVIDE AND CONQUER.
BUT WILLY, BE EXTRA CAREFUL.

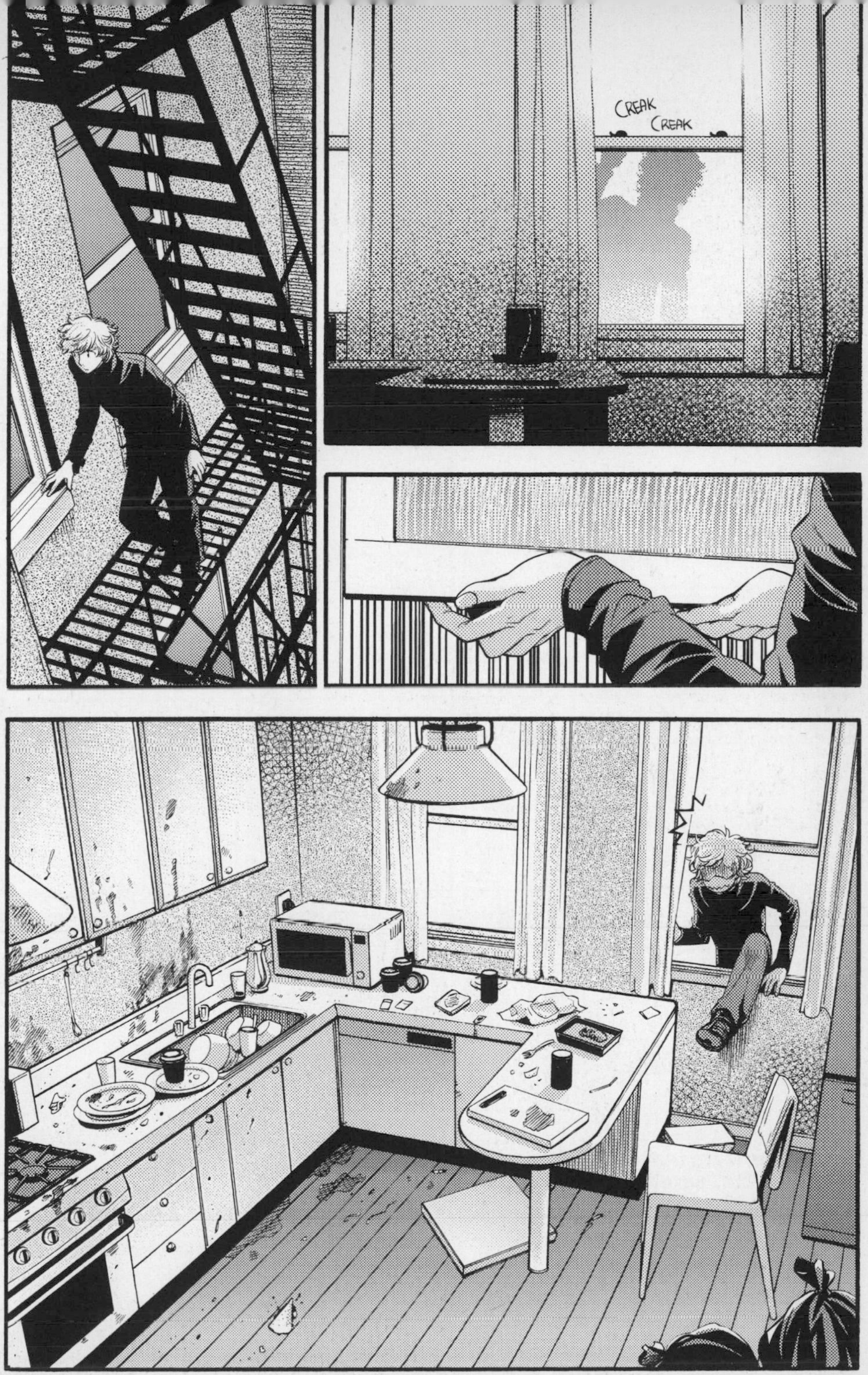
CREAK
CREAK

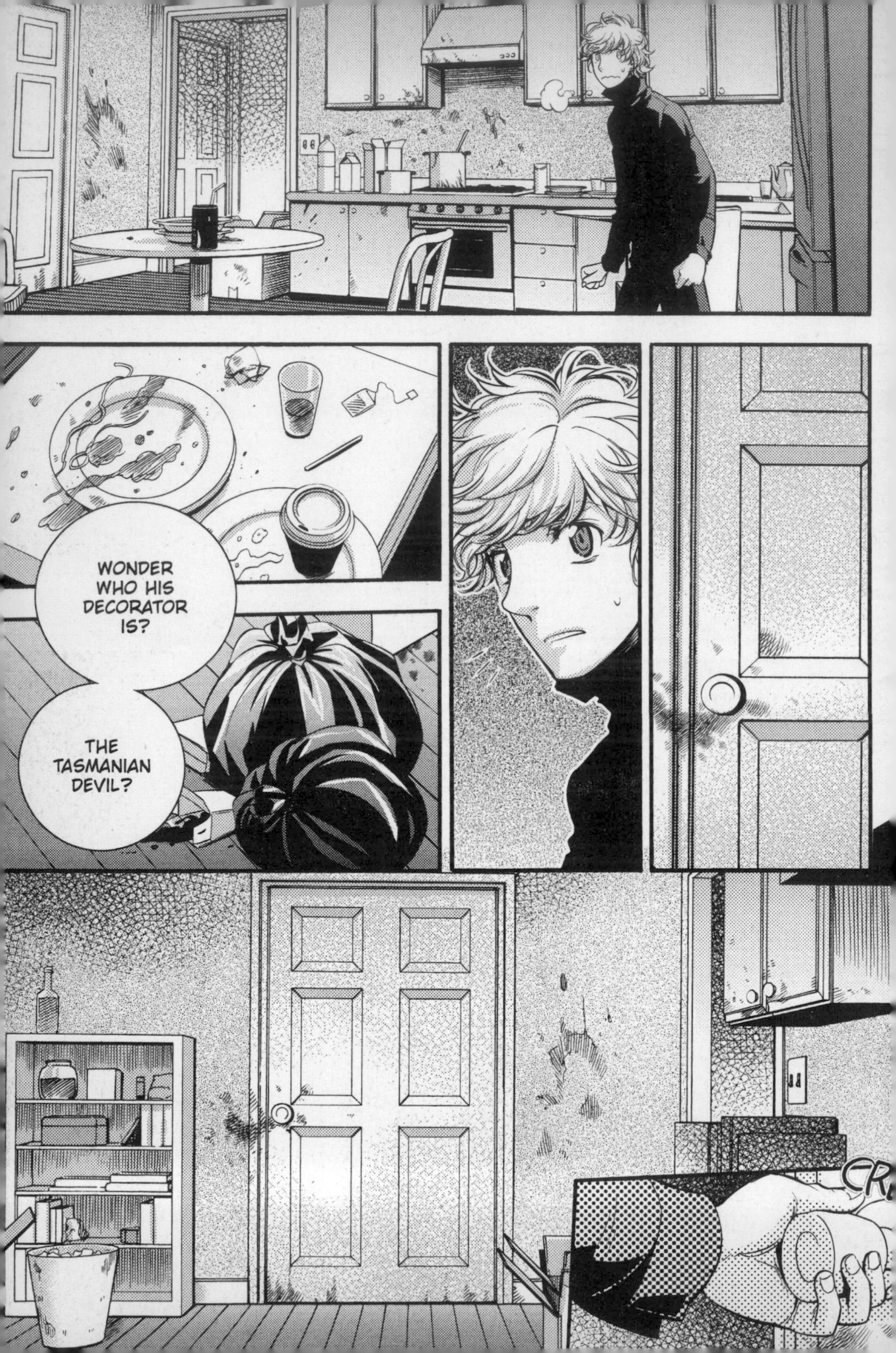
WONDER WHO HIS DECORATOR IS?
THE TASMANIAN DEVIL?

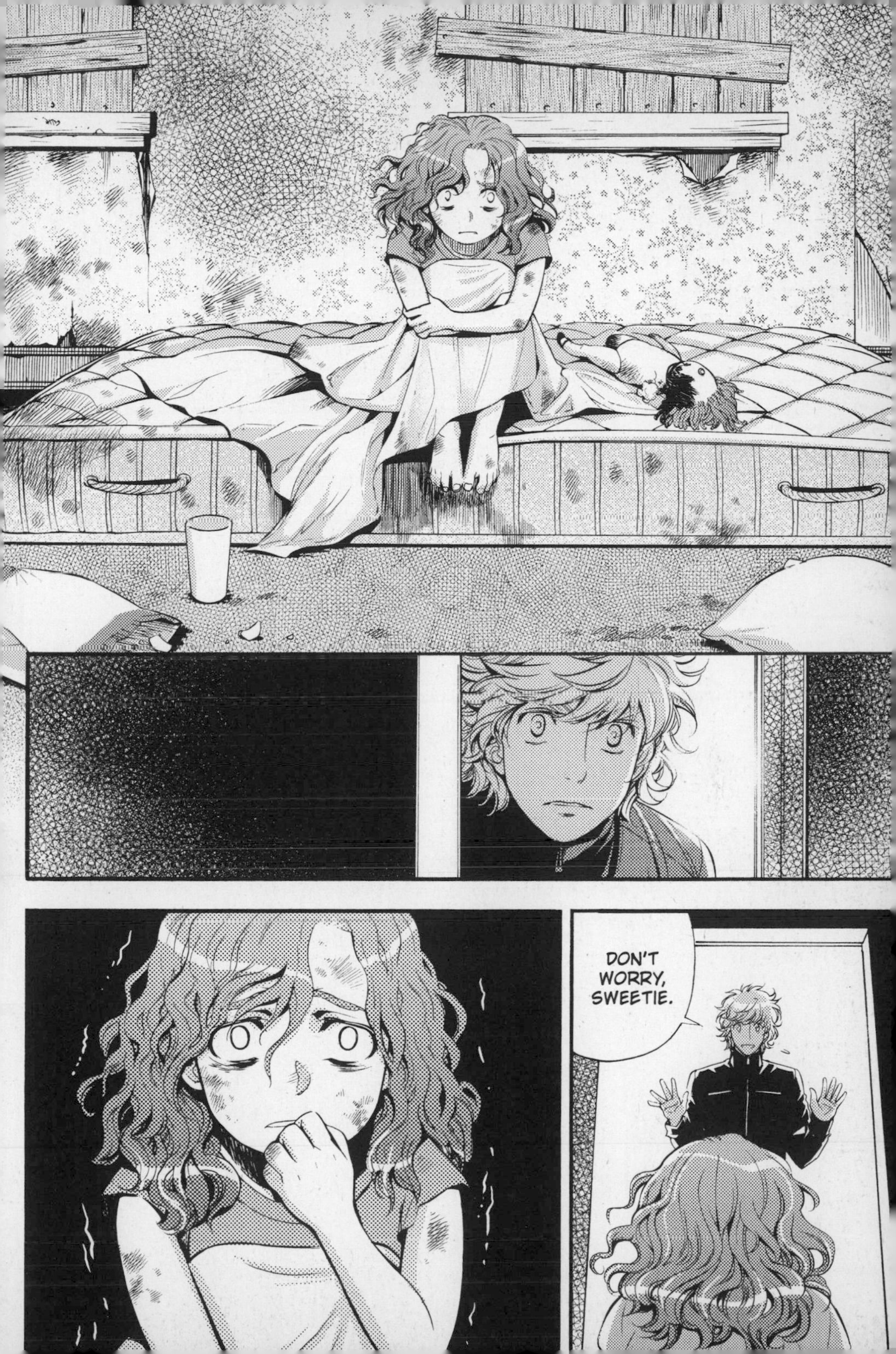
DON'T
WORRY,
SWEETIE.

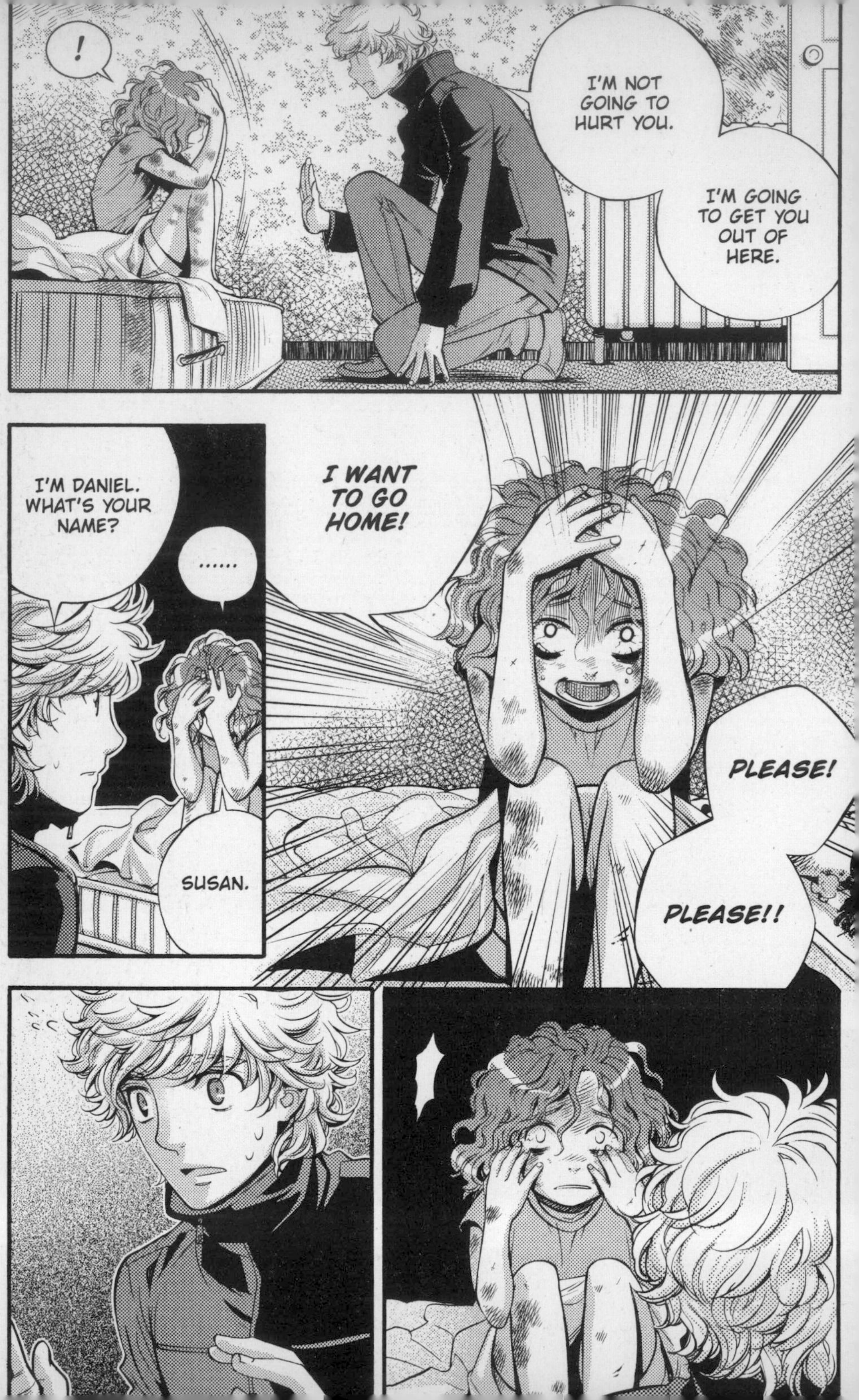
!
I'M NOT GOING TO HURT YOU.
I'M GOING TO GET YOU OUT OF HERE.
I'M DANIEL. WHAT'S YOUR NAME?
......
SUSAN.
I WANT TO GO HOME!
PLEASE!
PLEASE!!

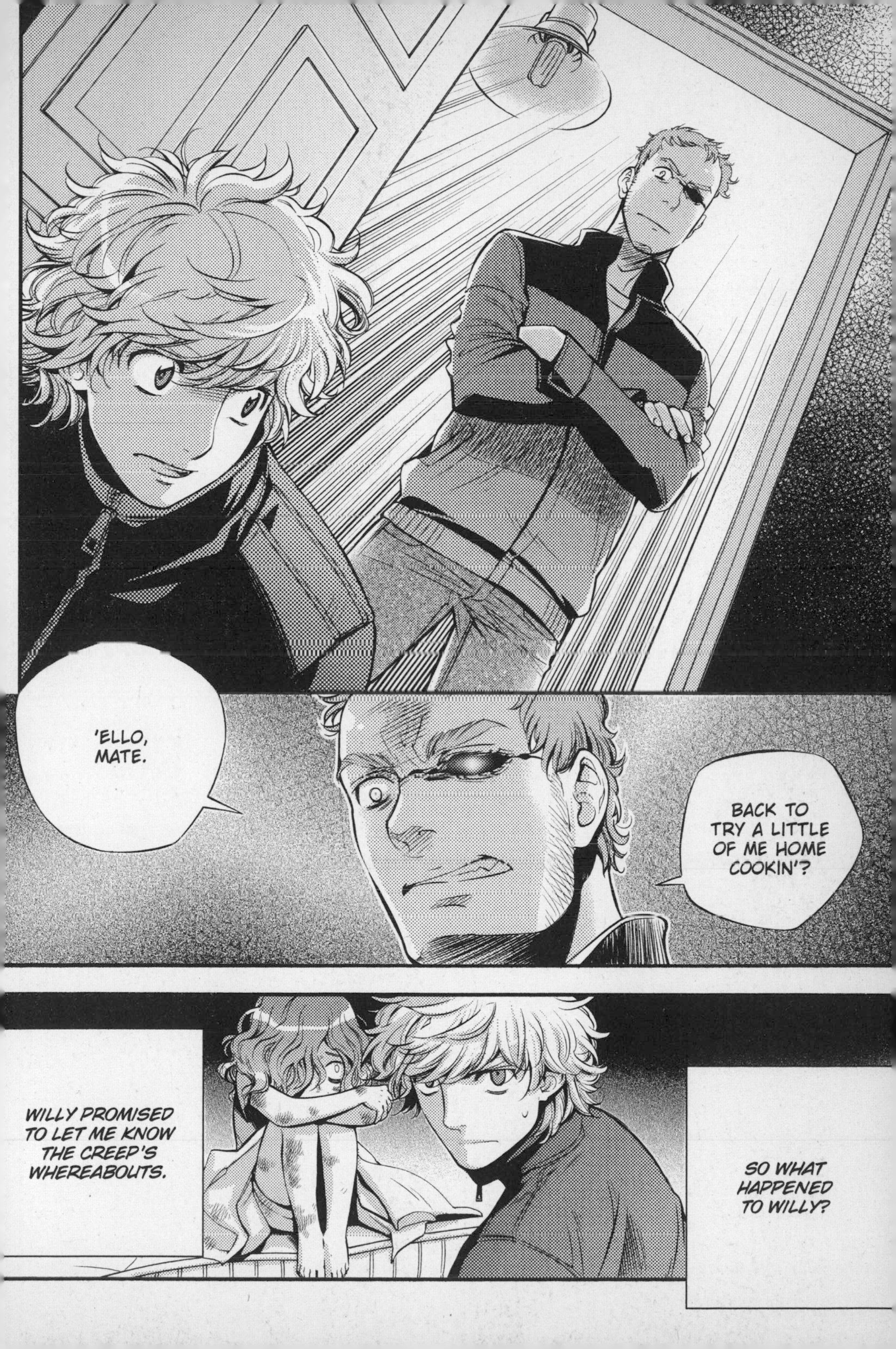
'ELLO, MATE.
BACK TO TRY A LITTLE OF ME HOME COOKIN'?
WILLY PROMISED TO LET ME KNOW THE CREEP'S WHEREABOUTS.
SO WHAT HAPPENED TO WILLY?

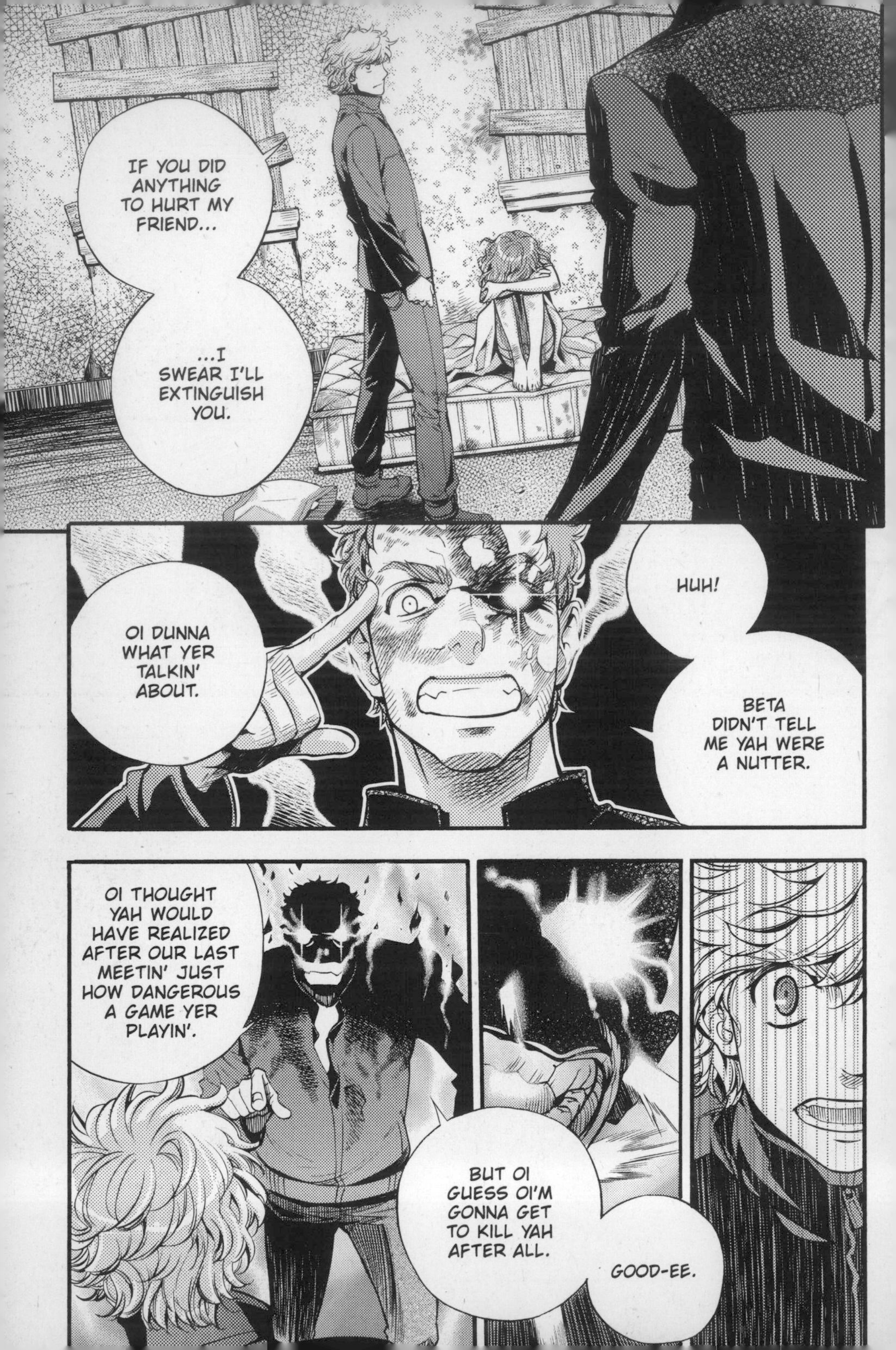
IF YOU DID ANYTHING TO HURT MY FRIEND...
...I SWEAR I'LL EXTINGUISH YOU.
OI DUNNA WHAT YER TALKIN' ABOUT.
HUH!
BETA DIDN'T TELL ME YAH WERE A NUTTER.
OI THOUGHT YAH WOULD HAVE REALIZED AFTER OUR LAST MEETIN' JUST HOW DANGEROUS A GAME YER PLAYIN'.
BUT OI GUESS OI'M GONNA GET TO KILL YAH AFTER ALL.
GOOD-EE.

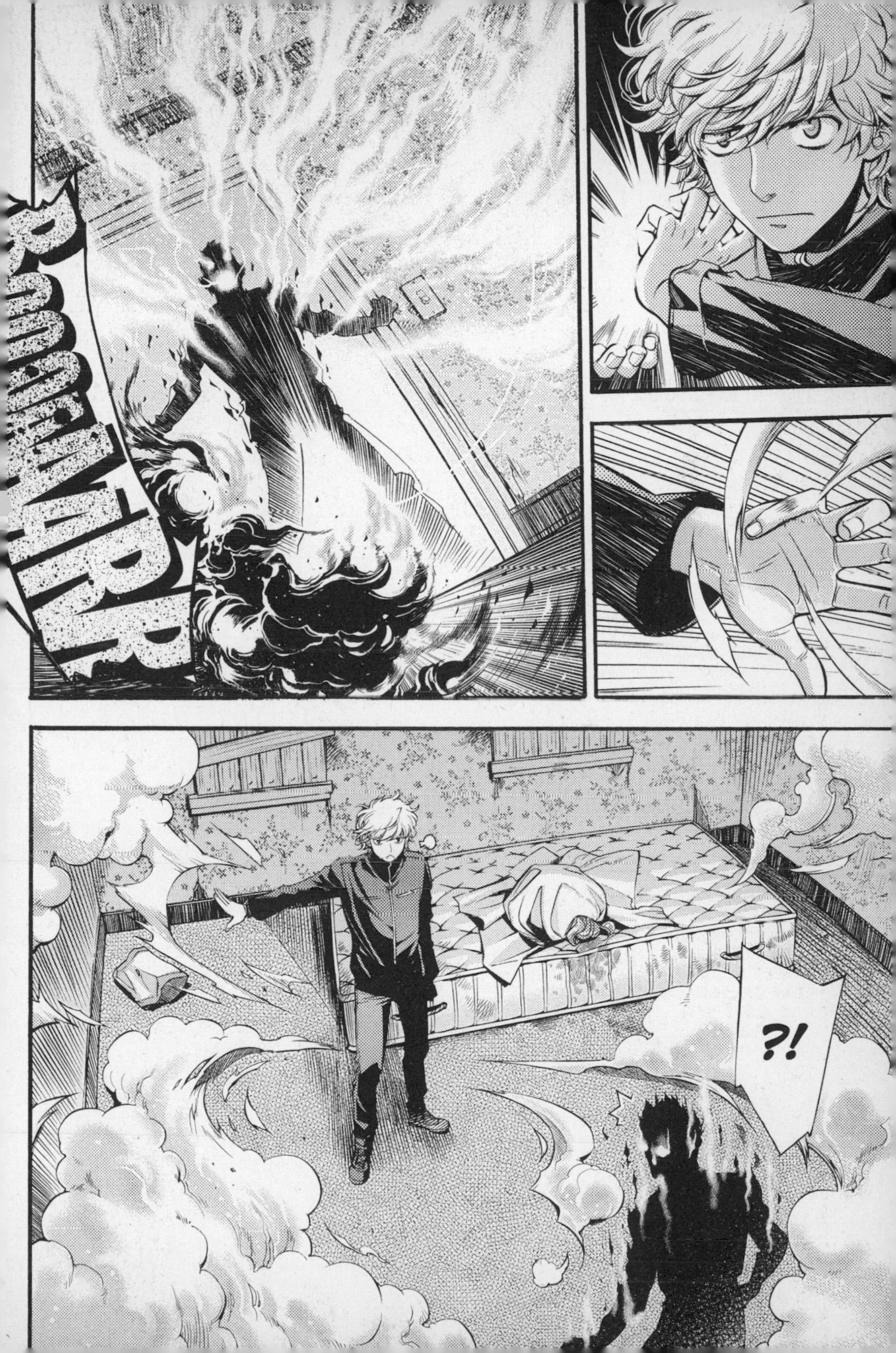
BOOOOFWARR!
?!

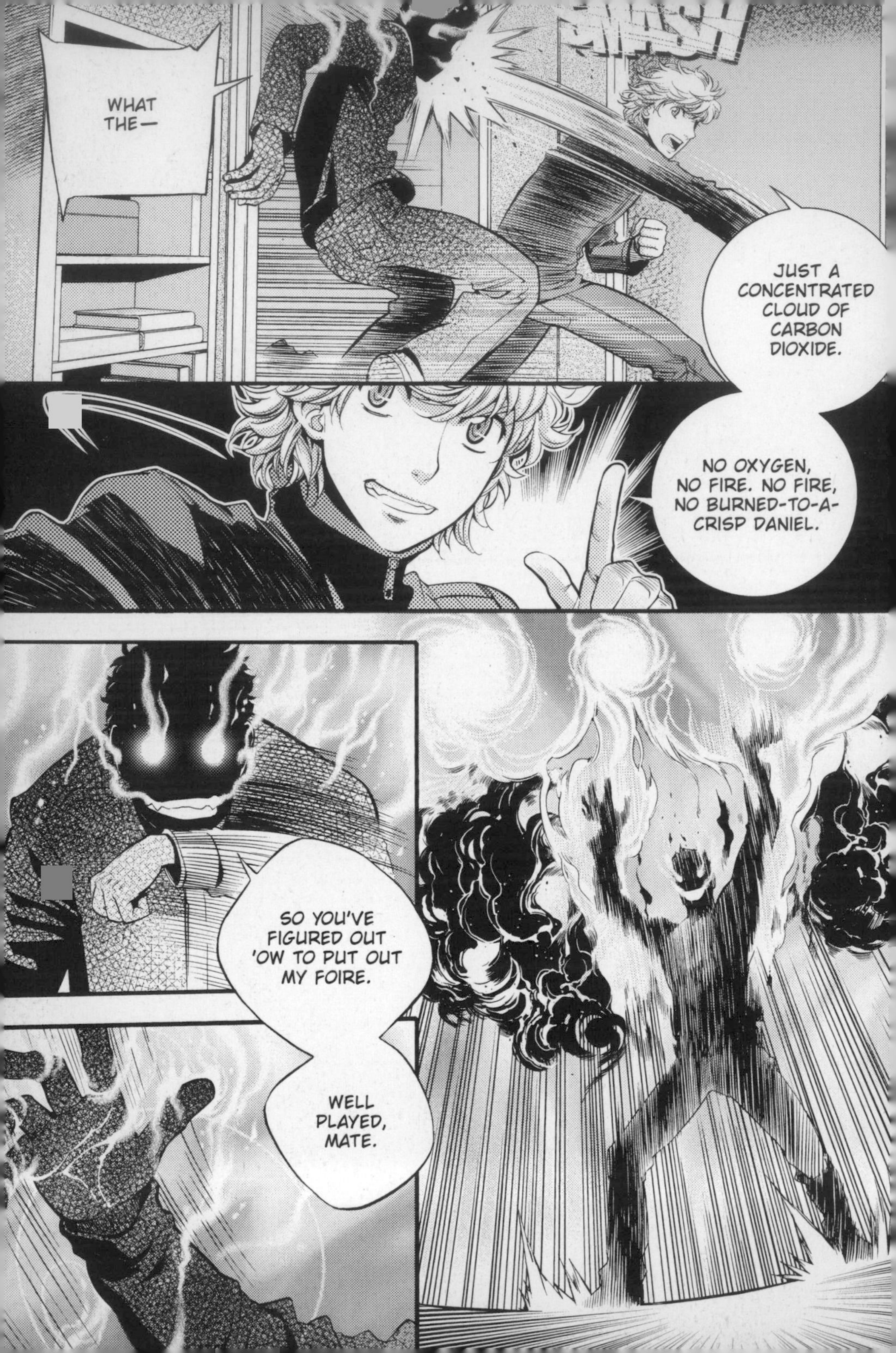
WHAT THE—
JUST A CONCENTRATED CLOUD OF CARBON DIOXIDE.
NO OXYGEN, NO FIRE. NO FIRE, NO BURNED-TO-A-CRISP DANIEL.
SO YOU'VE FIGURED OUT 'OW TO PUT OUT MY FOIRE.
WELL PLAYED, MATE.

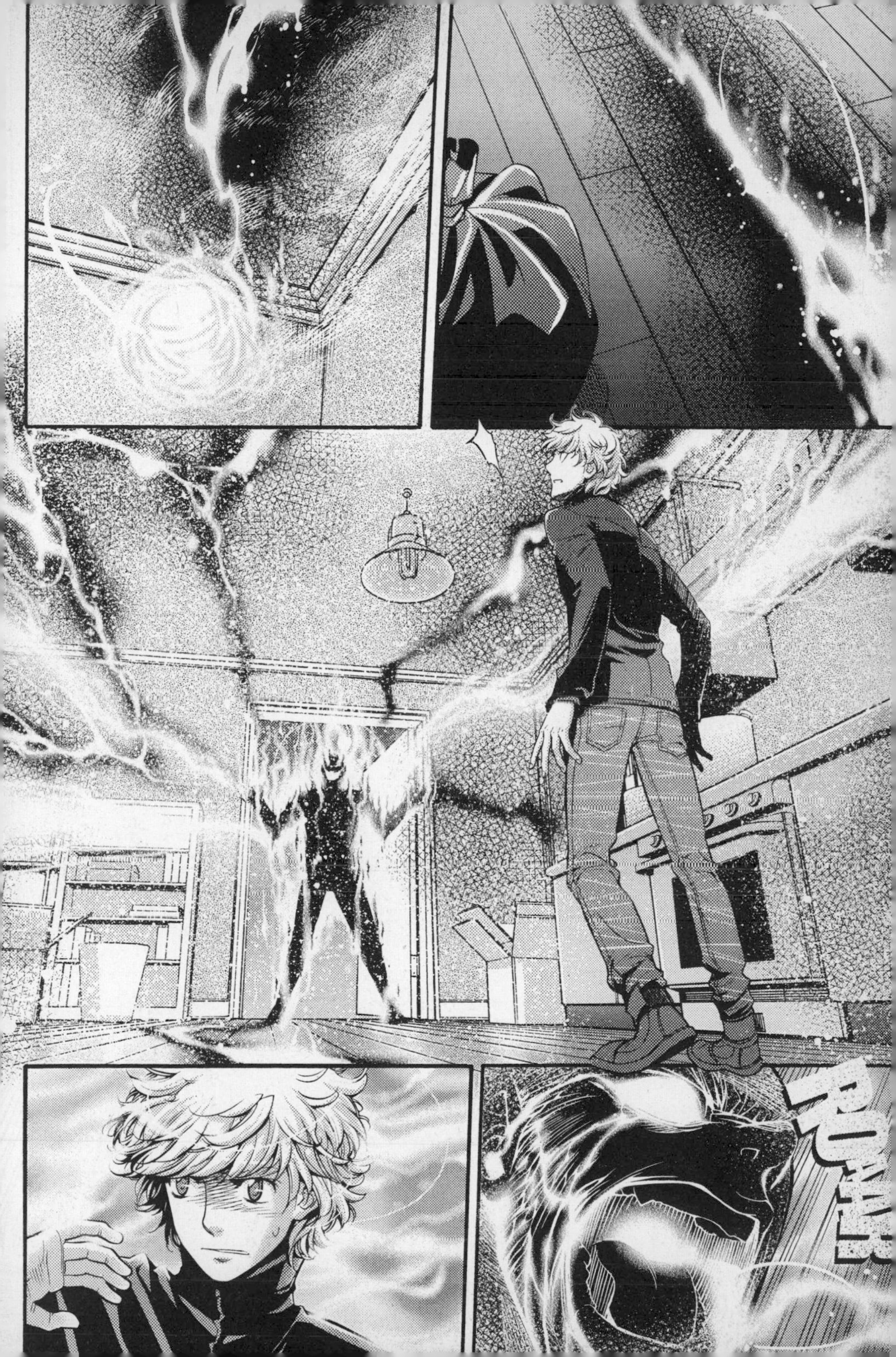

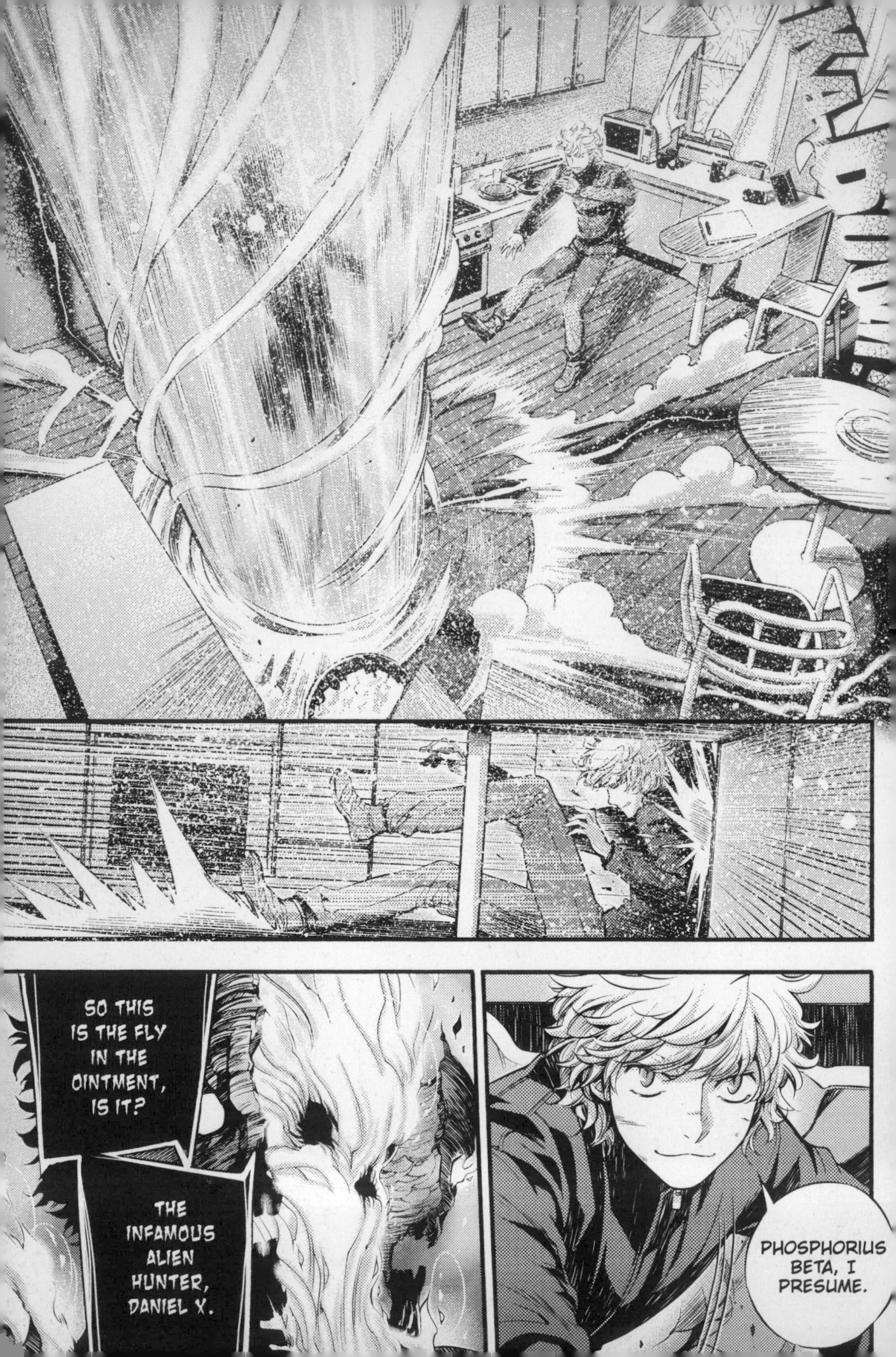
SO THIS IS THE FLY IN THE OINTMENT, IS IT?
THE INFAMOUS ALIEN HUNTER, DANIEL X.
PHOSPHORIUS BETA, I PRESUME.

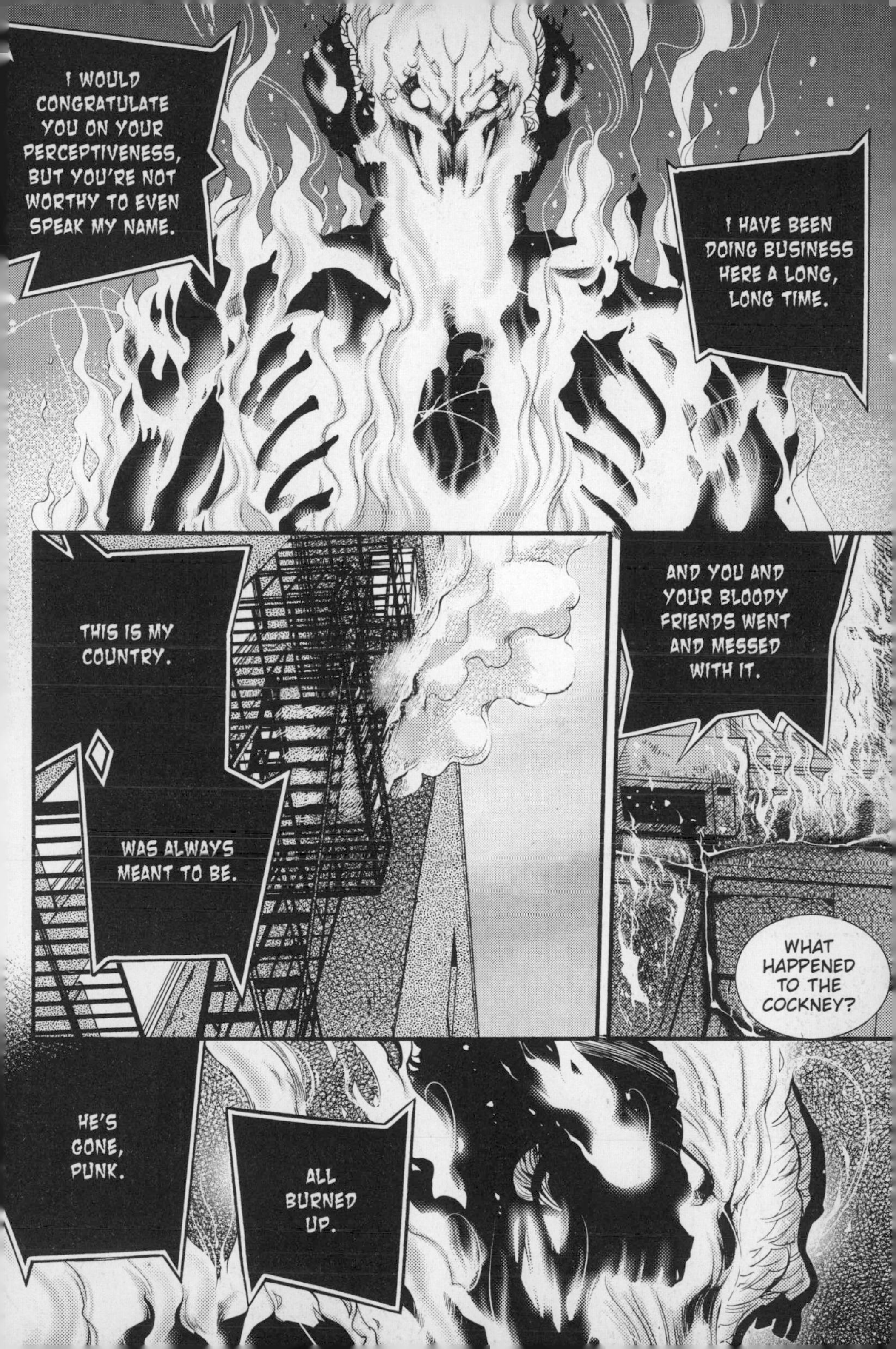
I WOULD CONGRATULATE YOU ON YOUR PERCEPTIVENESS, BUT YOU'RE NOT WORTHY TO EVEN SPEAK MY NAME.
I HAVE BEEN DOING BUSINESS HERE A LONG, LONG TIME.
THIS IS MY COUNTRY.
WAS ALWAYS MEANT TO BE.
AND YOU AND YOUR BLOODY FRIENDS WENT AND MESSED WITH IT.
WHAT HAPPENED TO THE COCKNEY?
HE'S GONE, PUNK.
ALL BURNED UP.

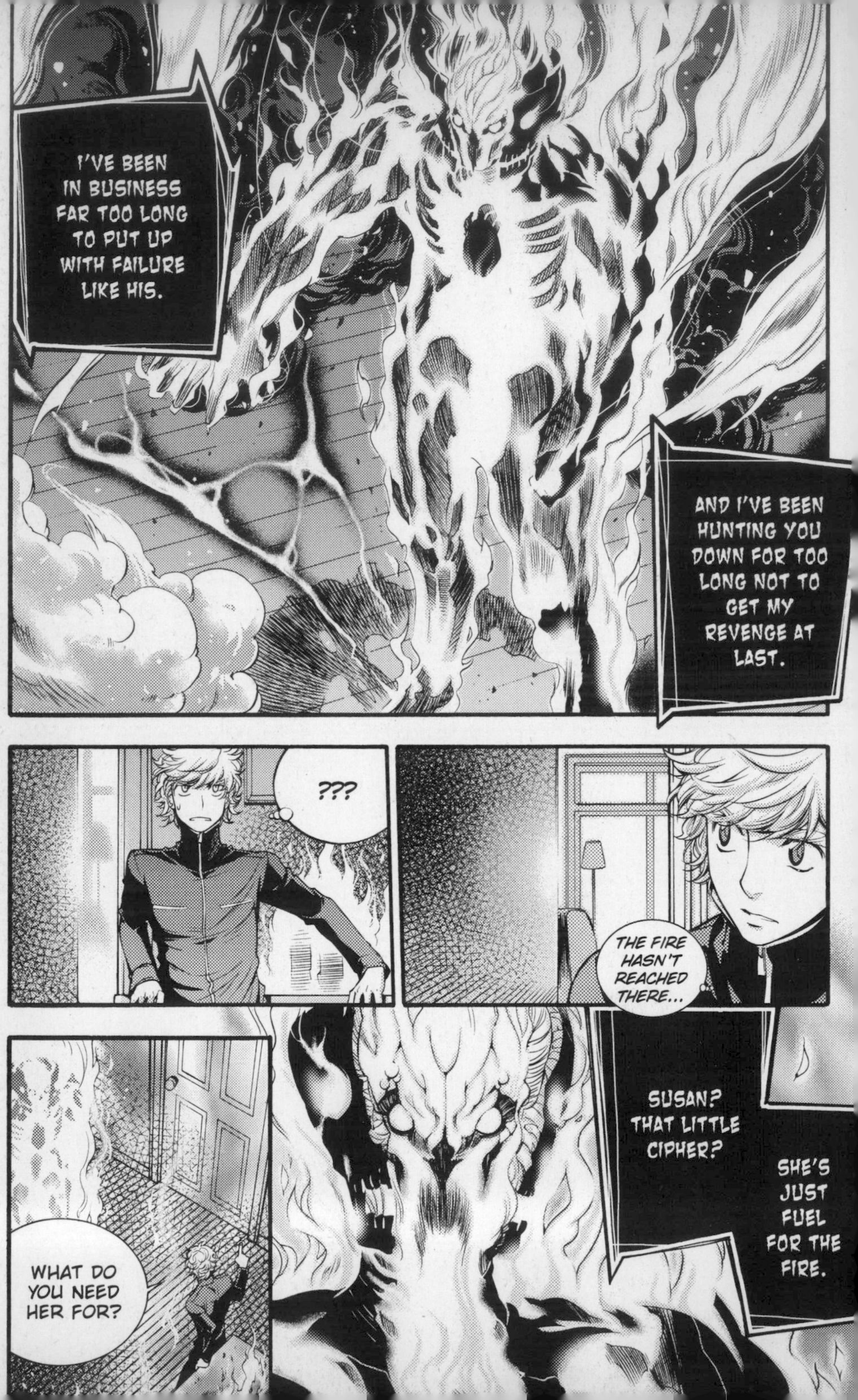
I'VE BEEN IN BUSINESS FAR TOO LONG TO PUT UP WITH FAILURE LIKE HIS.
AND I'VE BEEN HUNTING YOU DOWN FOR TOO LONG NOT TO GET MY REVENGE AT LAST.
???
THE FIRE HASN'T REACHED THERE...
WHAT DO YOU NEED HER FOR?
SUSAN? THAT LITTLE CIPHER?
SHE'S JUST FUEL FOR THE FIRE.

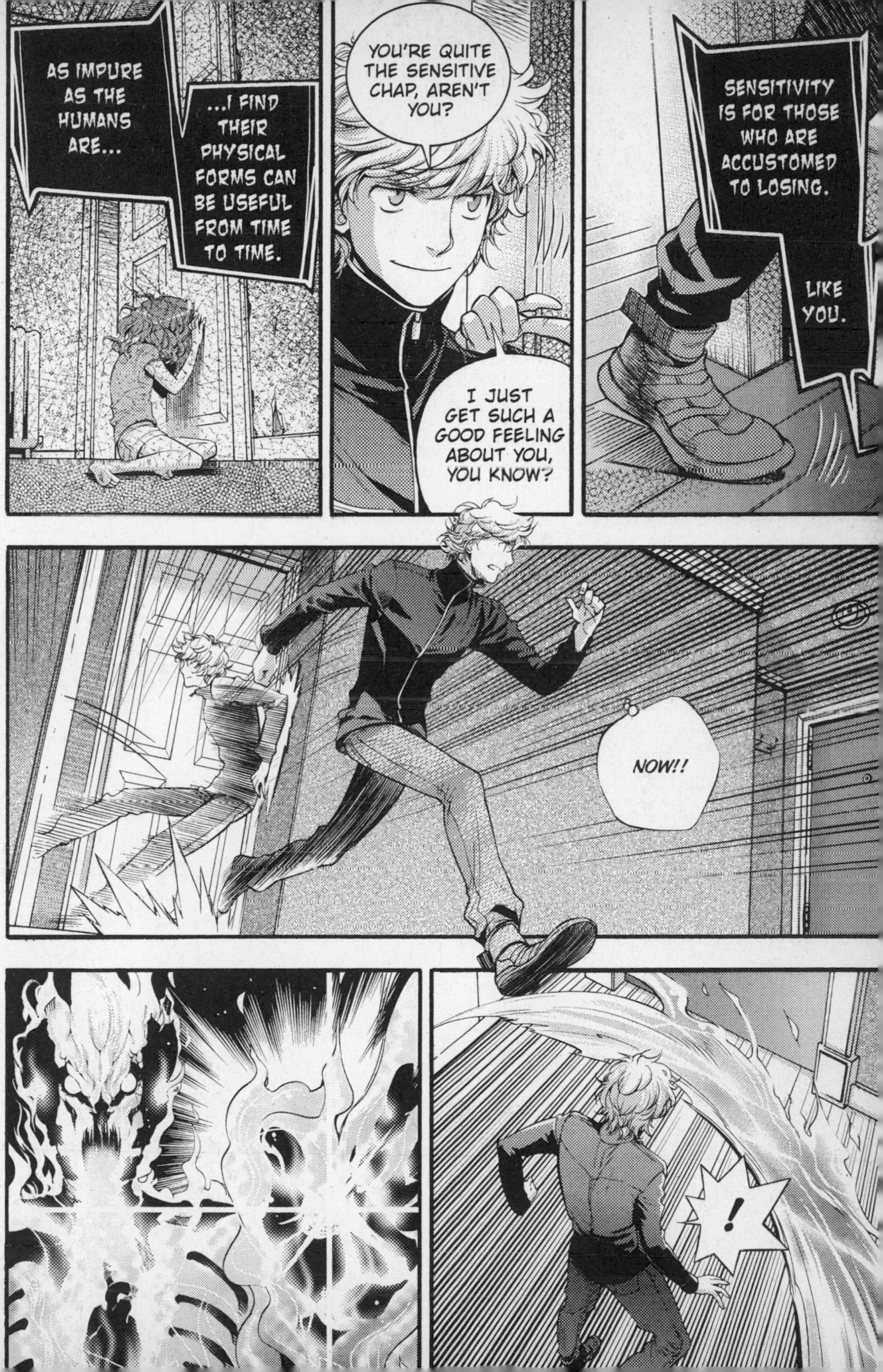
AS IMPURE AS THE HUMANS ARE...
...I FIND THEIR PHYSICAL FORMS CAN BE USEFUL FROM TIME TO TIME.
YOU'RE QUITE THE SENSITIVE CHAP, AREN'T YOU?
I JUST GET SUCH A GOOD FEELING ABOUT YOU, YOU KNOW?
SENSITIVITY IS FOR THOSE WHO ARE ACCUSTOMED TO LOSING.
LIKE YOU.
NOW!!
!

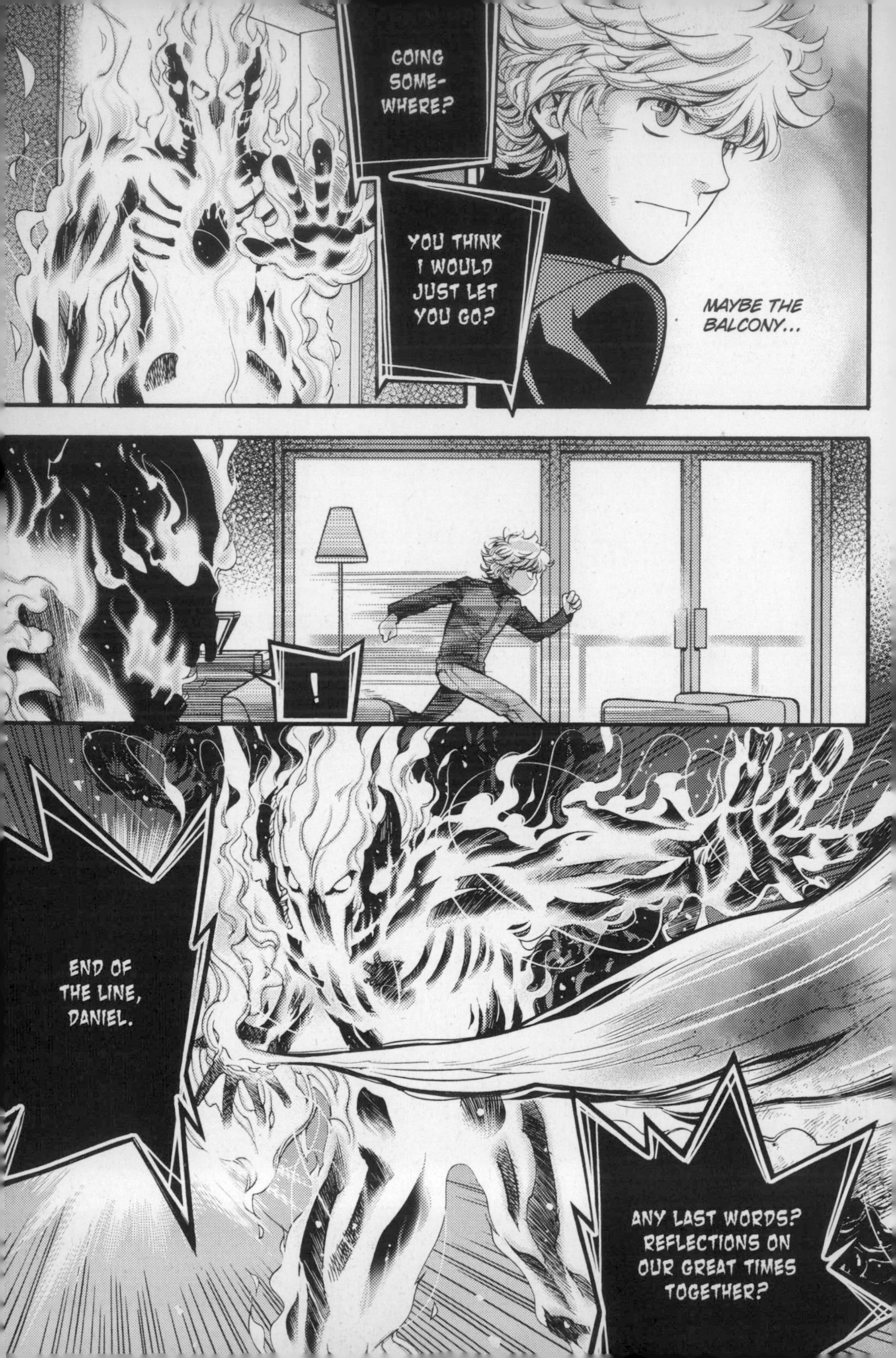
GOING SOME-WHERE?
YOU THINK I WOULD JUST LET YOU GO?
MAYBE THE BALCONY...
!
END OF THE LINE, DANIEL.
ANY LAST WORDS? REFLECTIONS ON OUR GREAT TIMES TOGETHER?

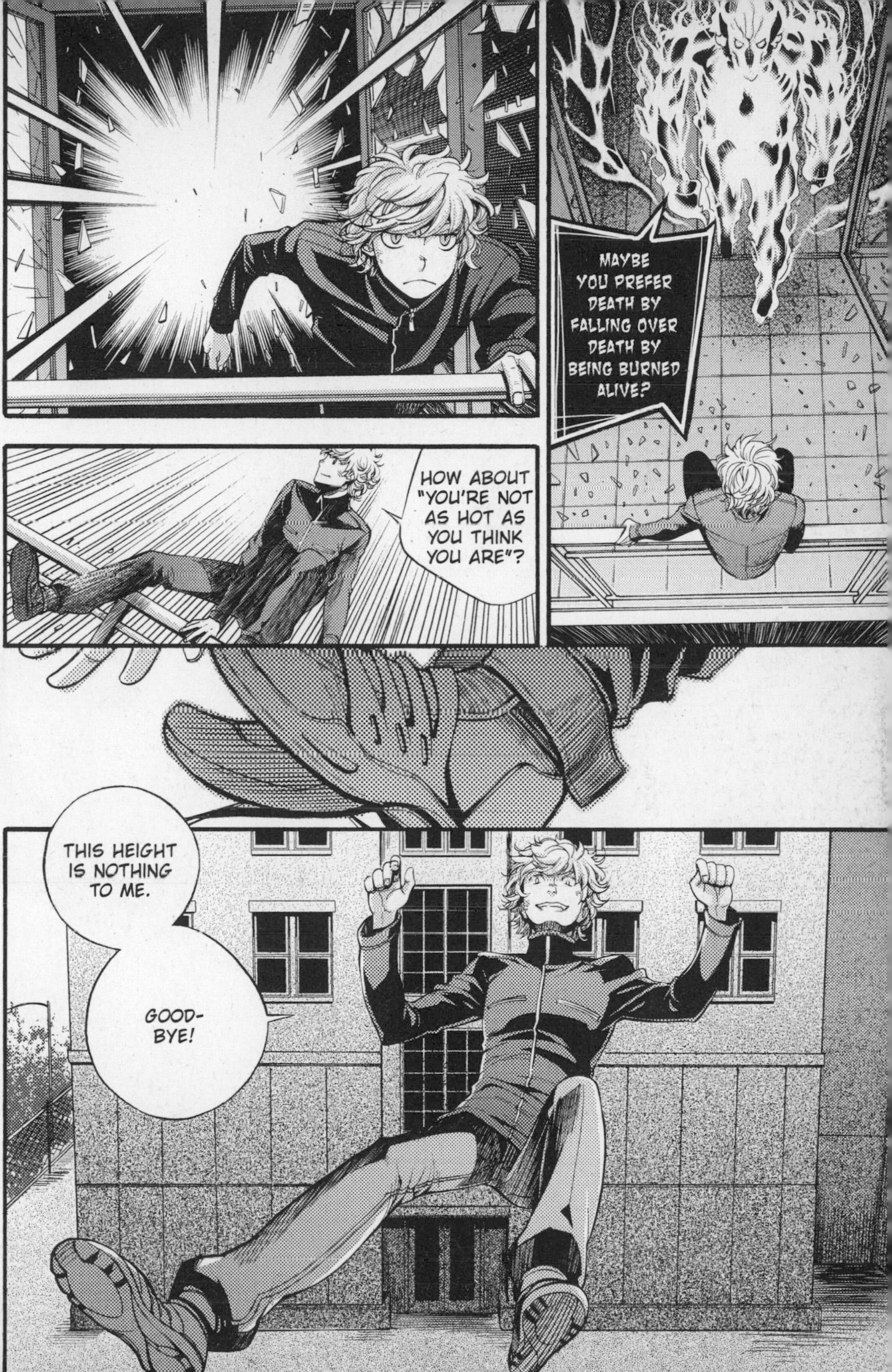
MAYBE YOU PREFER DEATH BY FALLING OVER DEATH BY BEING BURNED ALIVE?
HOW ABOUT "YOU'RE NOT AS HOT AS YOU THINK YOU ARE"?
THIS HEIGHT IS NOTHING TO ME.
GOOD-BYE!

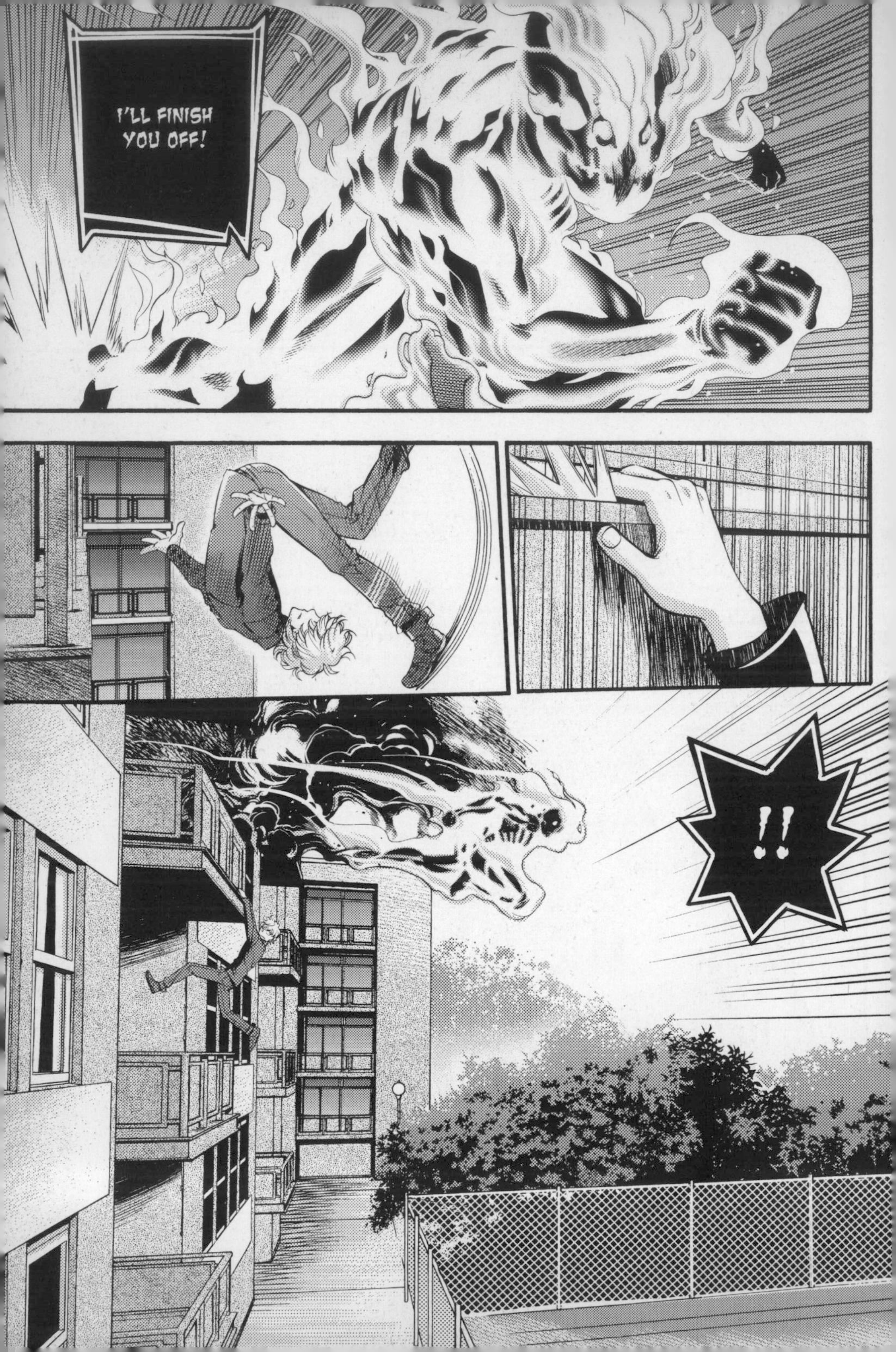
I'LL FINISH YOU OFF!
!!

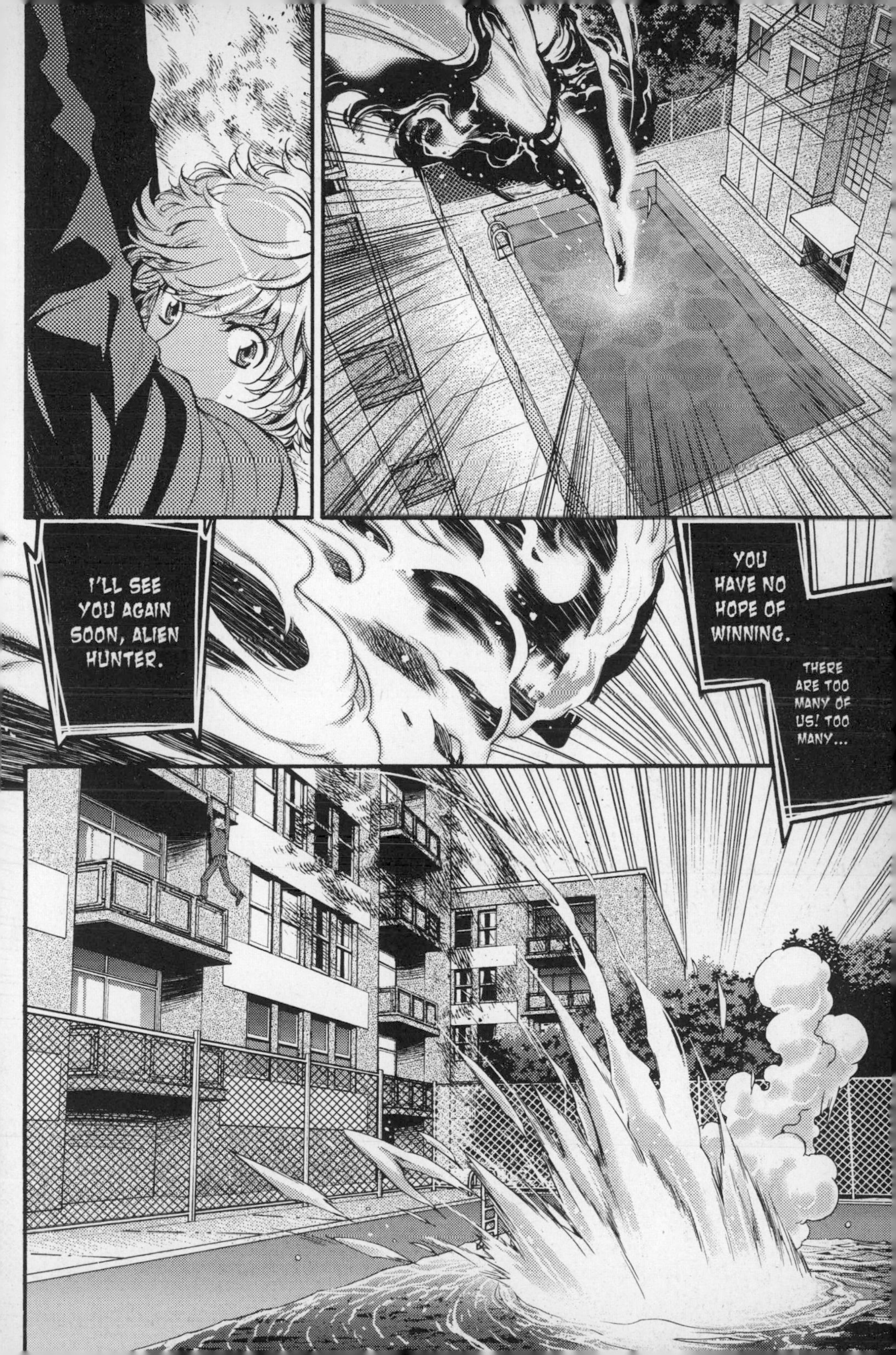
I'LL SEE YOU AGAIN SOON, ALIEN HUNTER.
YOU HAVE NO HOPE OF WINNING.
THERE ARE TOO MANY OF US! TOO MANY...

DANIEL X

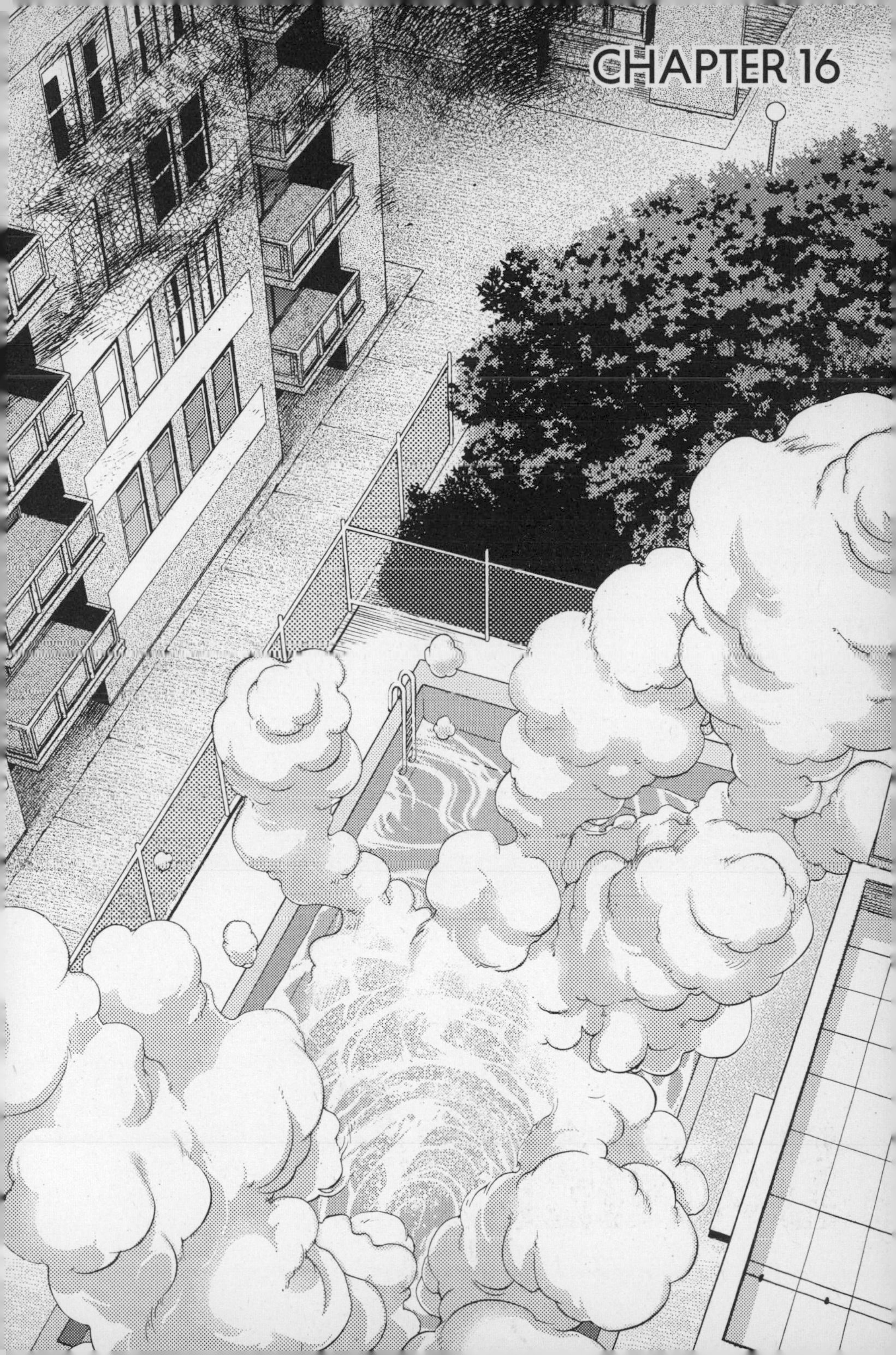
CHAPTER 16

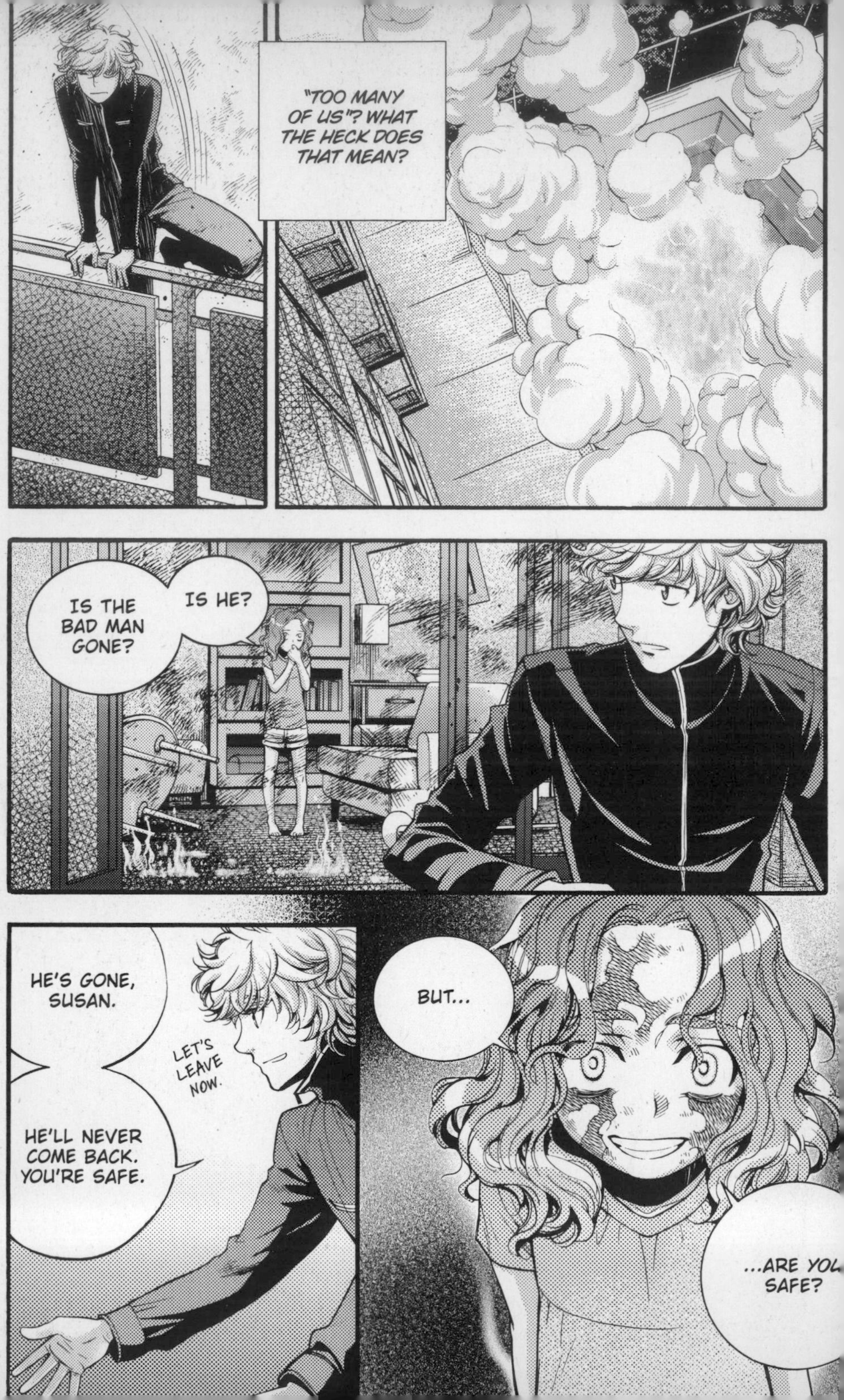
"TOO MANY OF US"? WHAT THE HECK DOES THAT MEAN?
IS THE BAD MAN GONE?
IS HE?
HE'S GONE, SUSAN.
LET'S LEAVE NOW.
HE'LL NEVER COME BACK. YOU'RE SAFE.
BUT...
...ARE YOU SAFE?

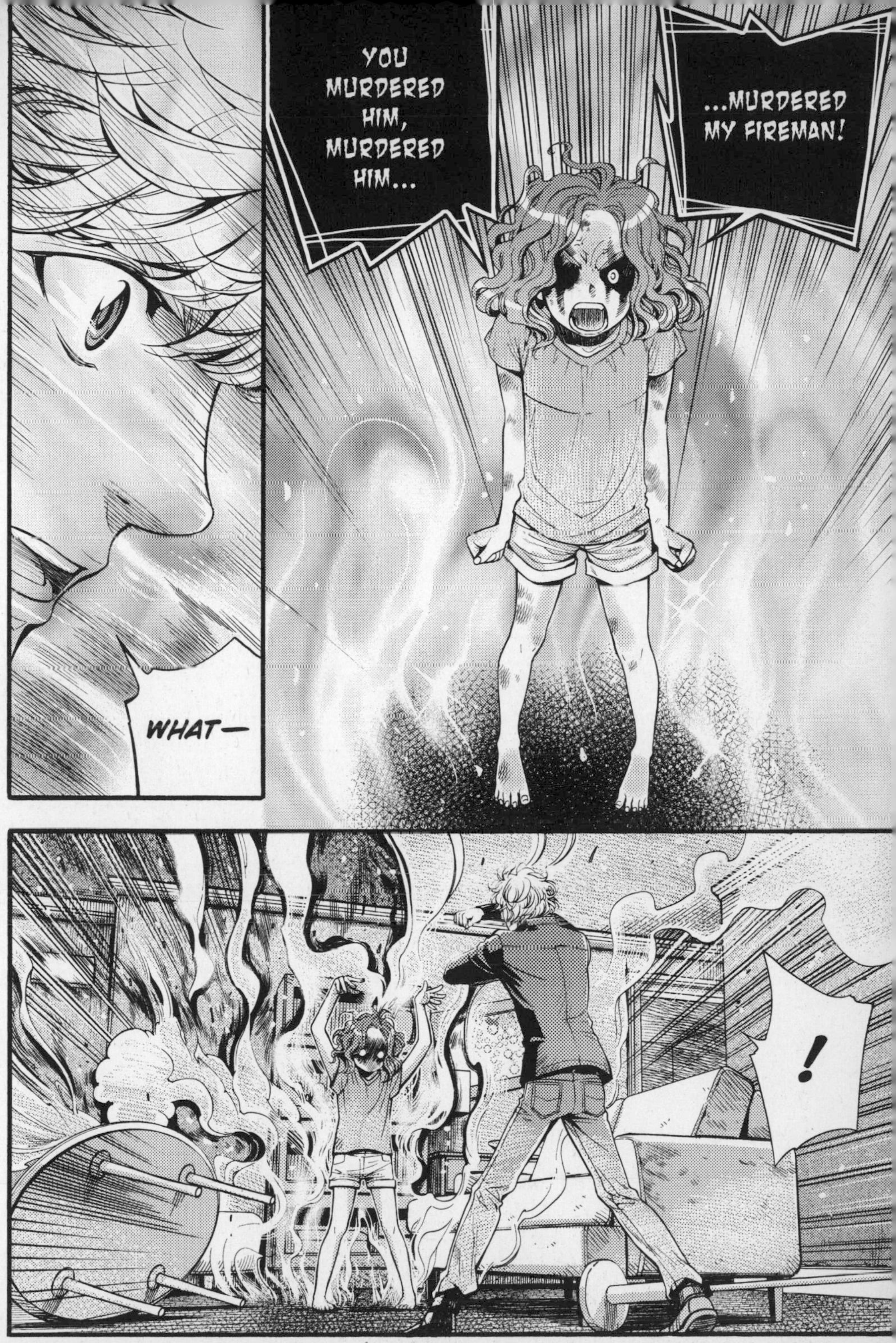
WHAT—
YOU MURDERED HIM, MURDERED HIM...
...MURDERED MY FIREMAN!
!

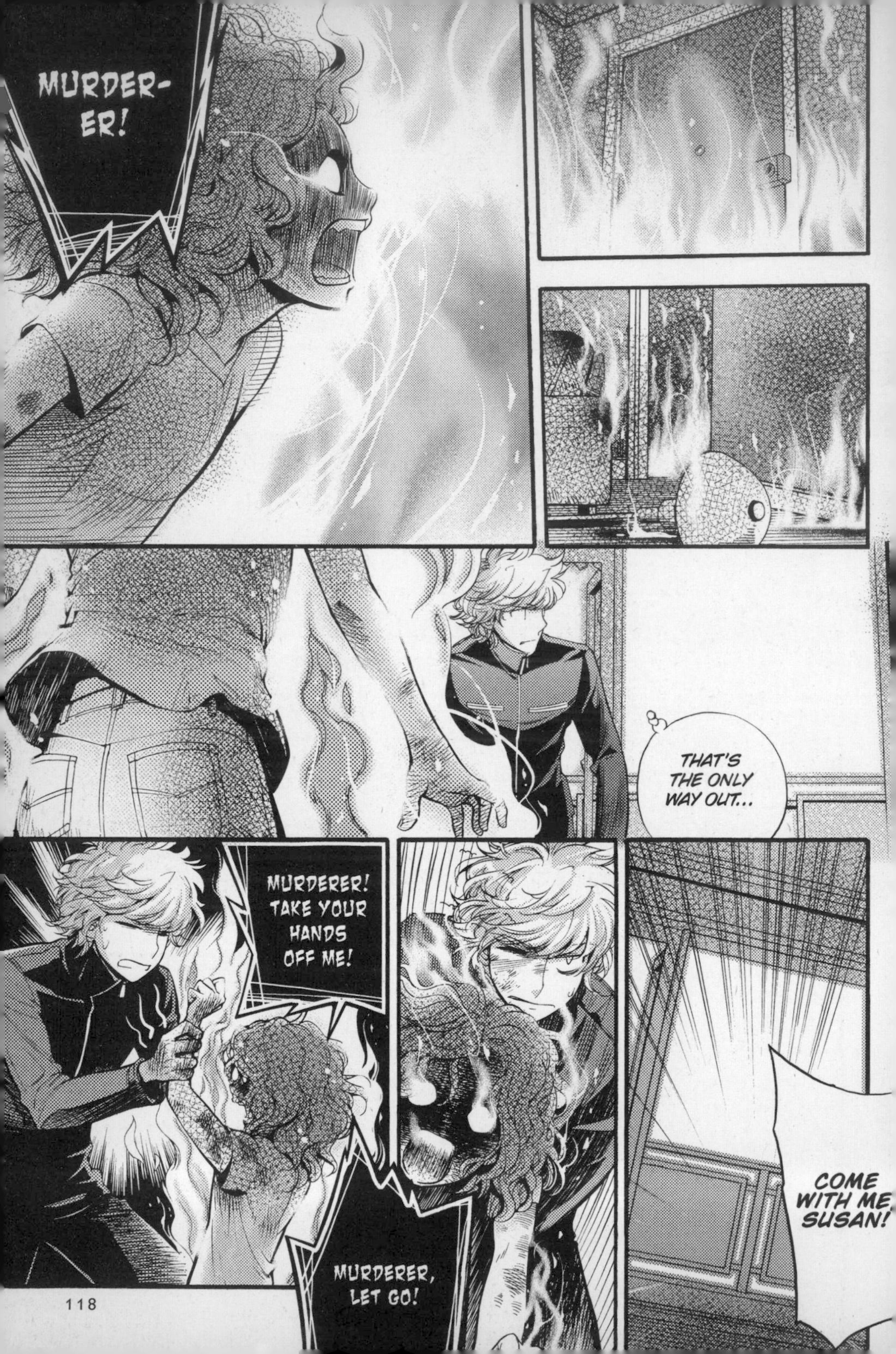
MURDER-
ER!
THAT'S THE ONLY WAY OUT...
MURDERER! TAKE YOUR HANDS OFF ME!
MURDERER, LET GO!
COME WITH ME, SUSAN!

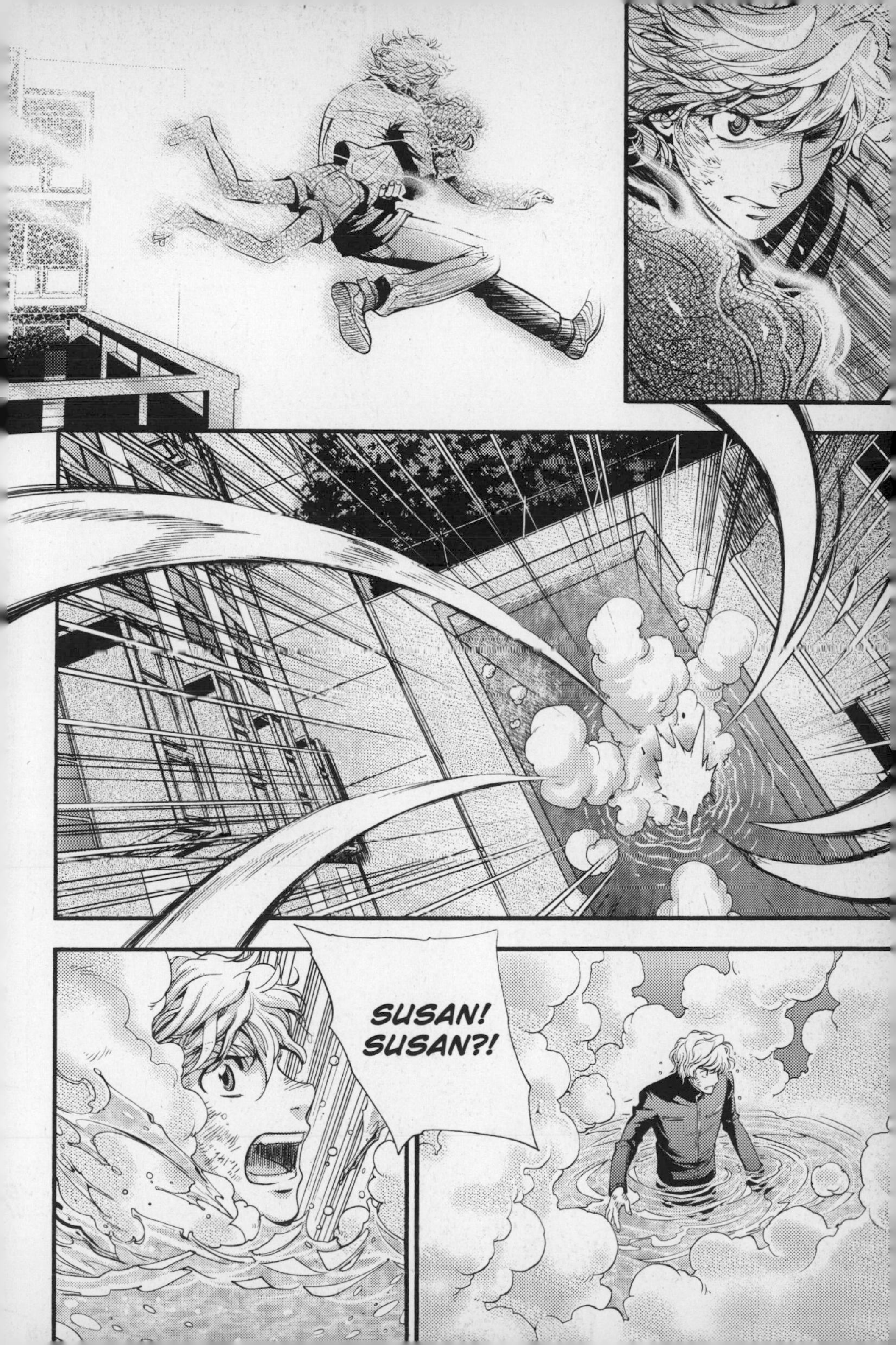
SUSAN!
SUSAN?!

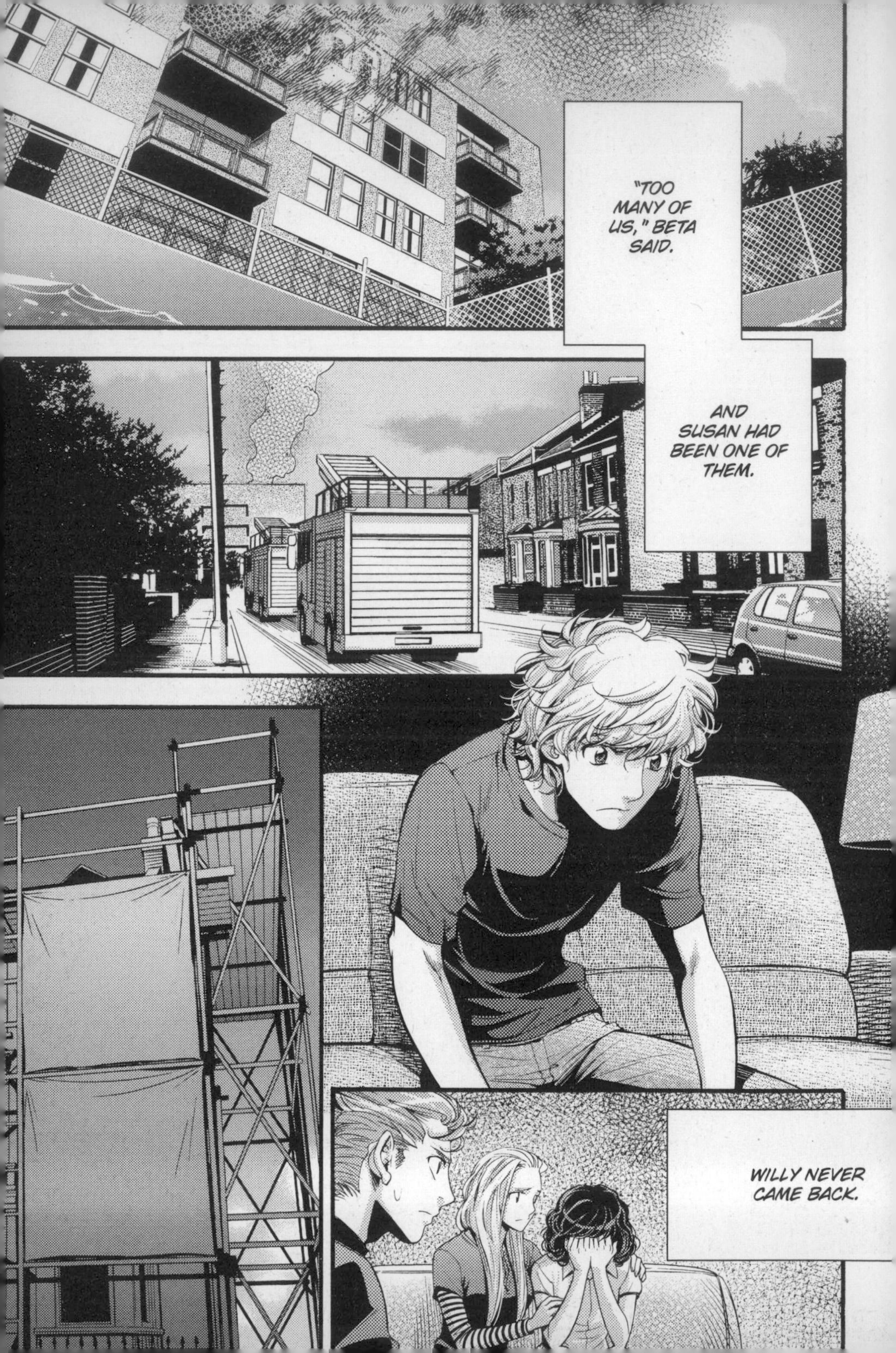
"TOO MANY OF US," BETA SAID.
AND SUSAN HAD BEEN ONE OF THEM.
WILLY NEVER CAME BACK.

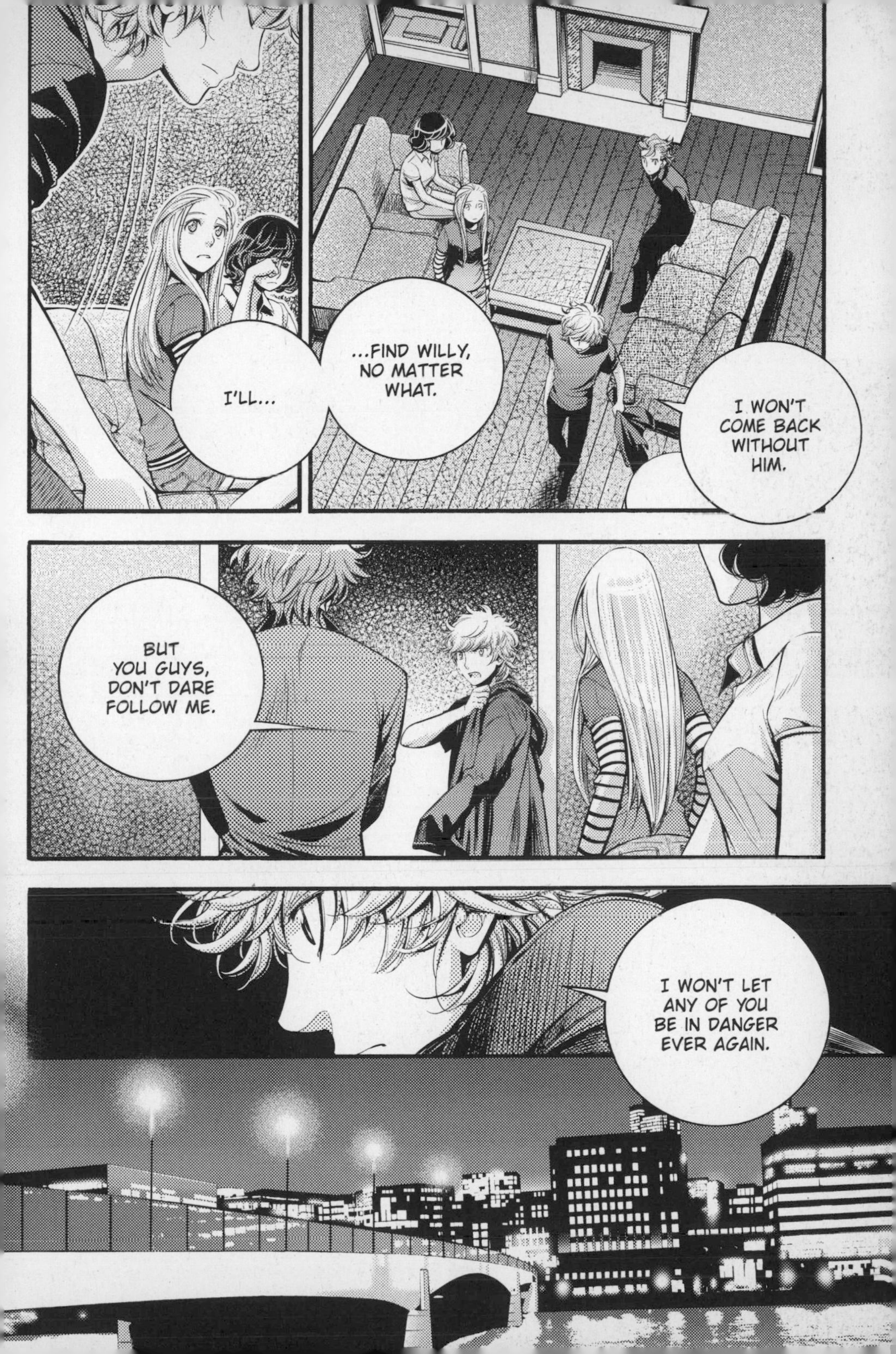
I'LL...
...FIND WILLY, NO MATTER WHAT.
I WON'T COME BACK WITHOUT HIM.
BUT YOU GUYS, DON'T DARE FOLLOW ME.
I WON'T LET ANY OF YOU BE IN DANGER EVER AGAIN.

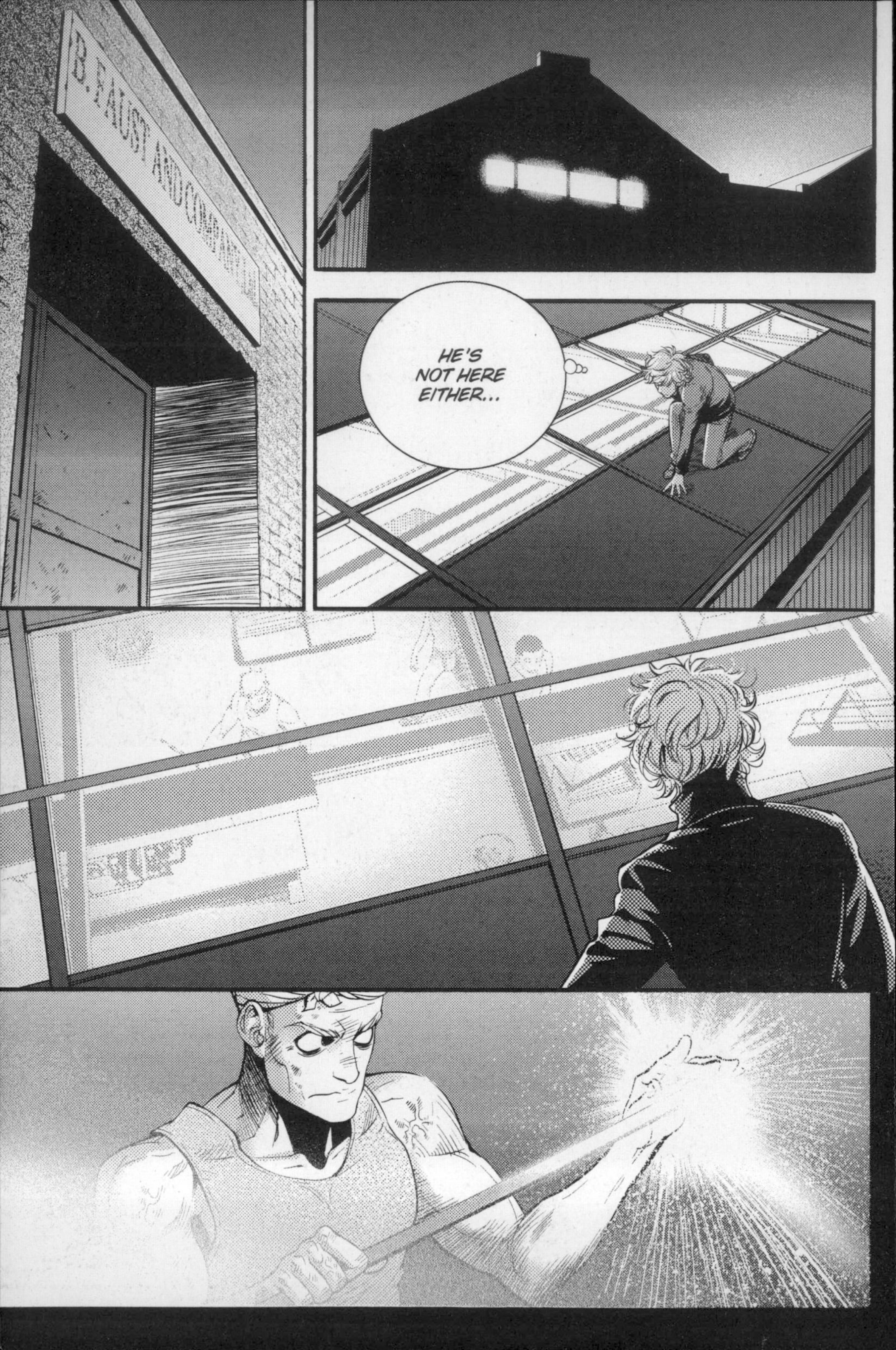
B. FAUST AND COMPANY
HE'S NOT HERE EITHER...

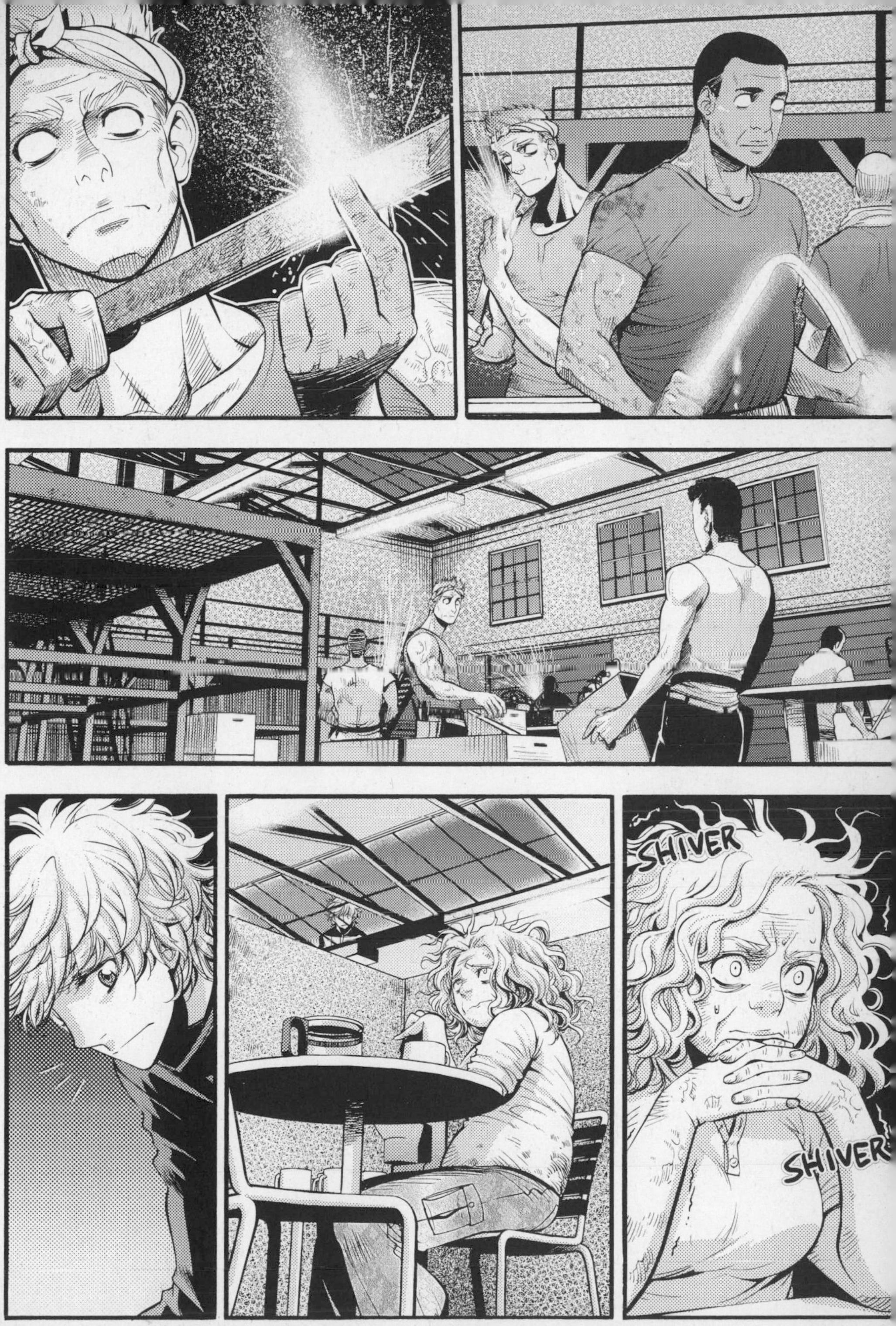
SHIVER
SHIVER

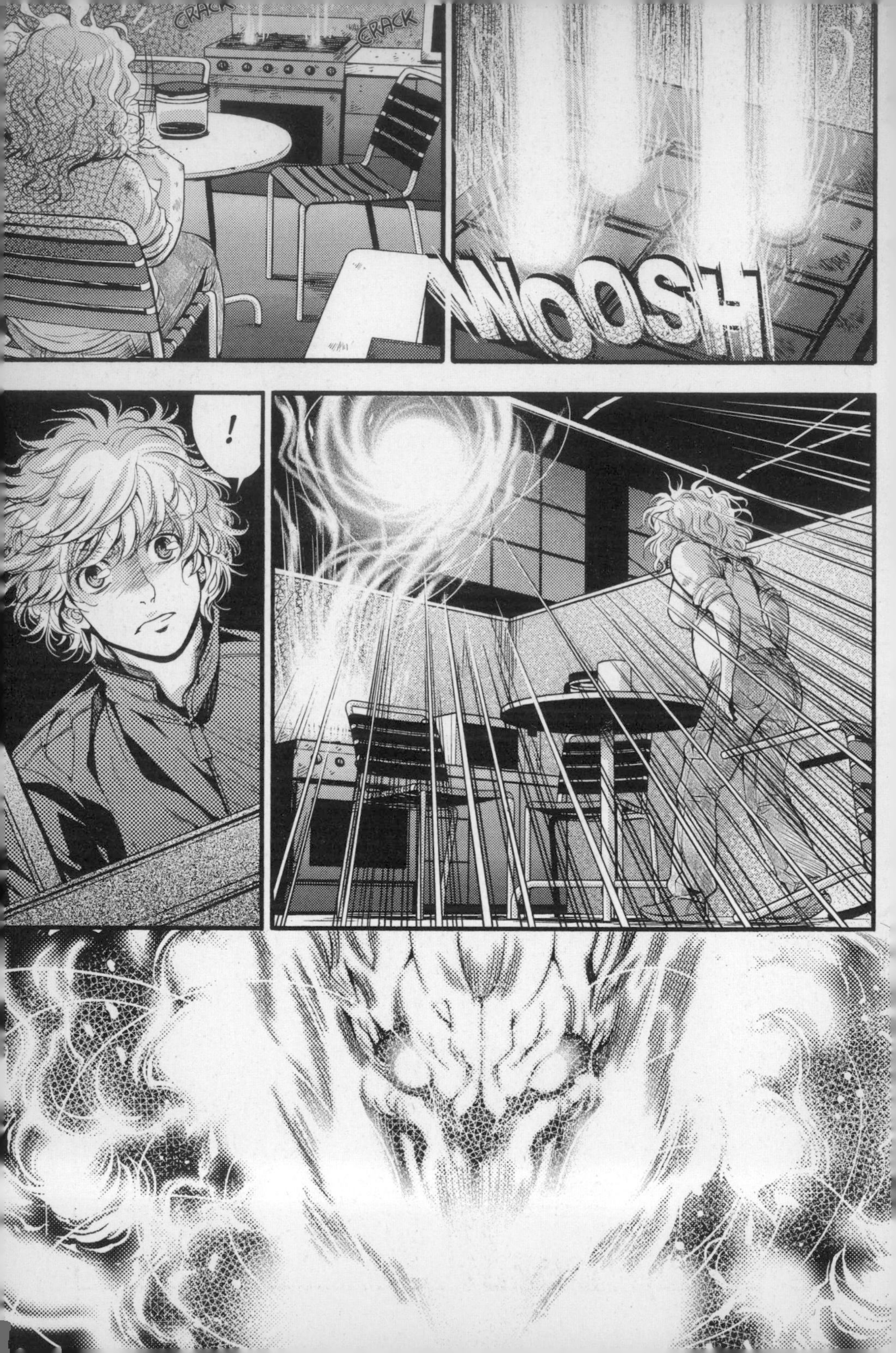
CRACK
CRACK
WOOSH
!

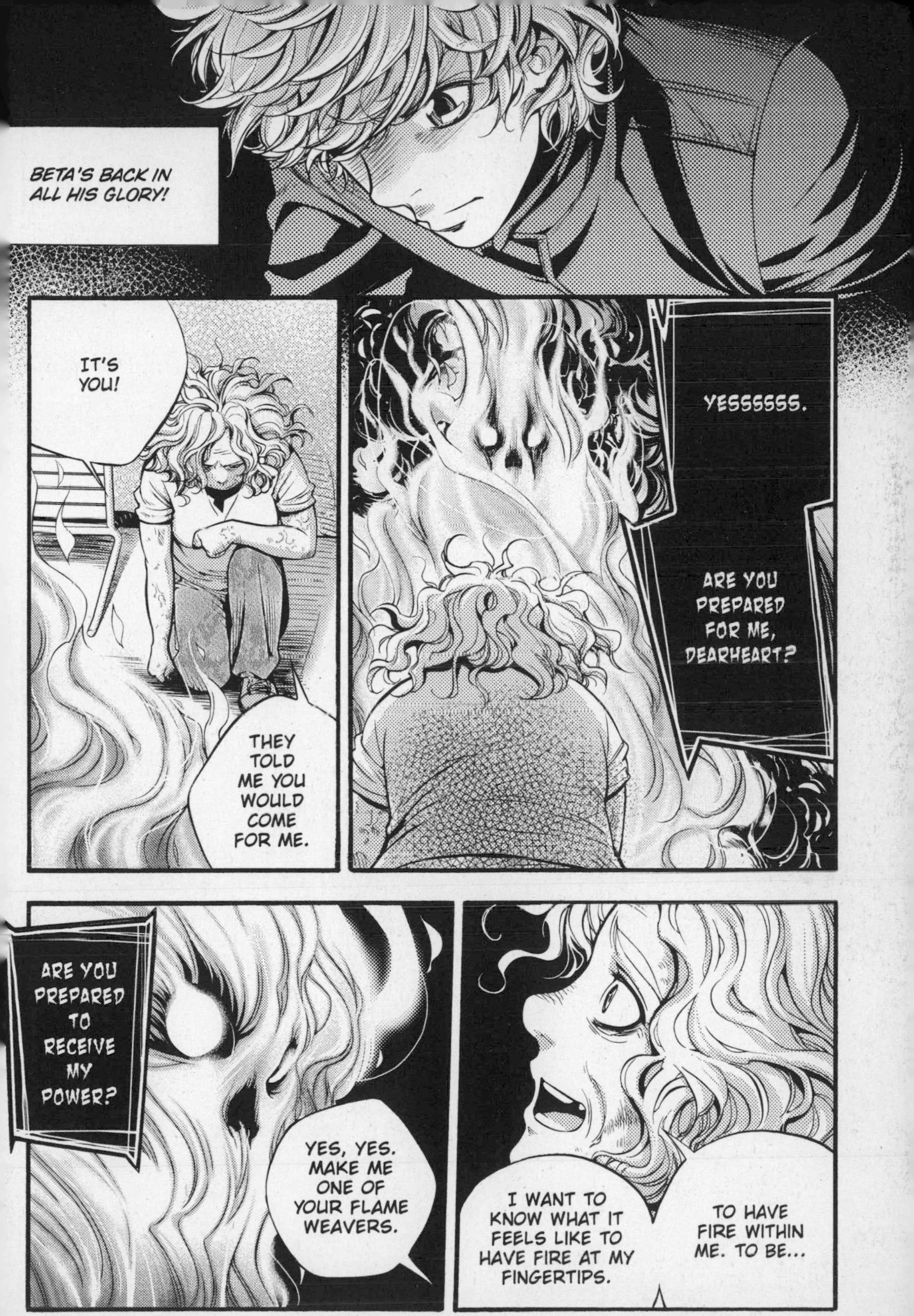

BETA'S BACK IN ALL HIS GLORY!
IT'S YOU!
THEY TOLD ME YOU WOULD COME FOR ME.
YESSSSSS.
ARE YOU PREPARED FOR ME, DEARHEART?
ARE YOU PREPARED TO RECEIVE MY POWER?
YES, YES. MAKE ME ONE OF YOUR FLAME WEAVERS.
I WANT TO KNOW WHAT IT FEELS LIKE TO HAVE FIRE AT MY FINGERTIPS.
TO HAVE FIRE WITHIN ME. TO BE...

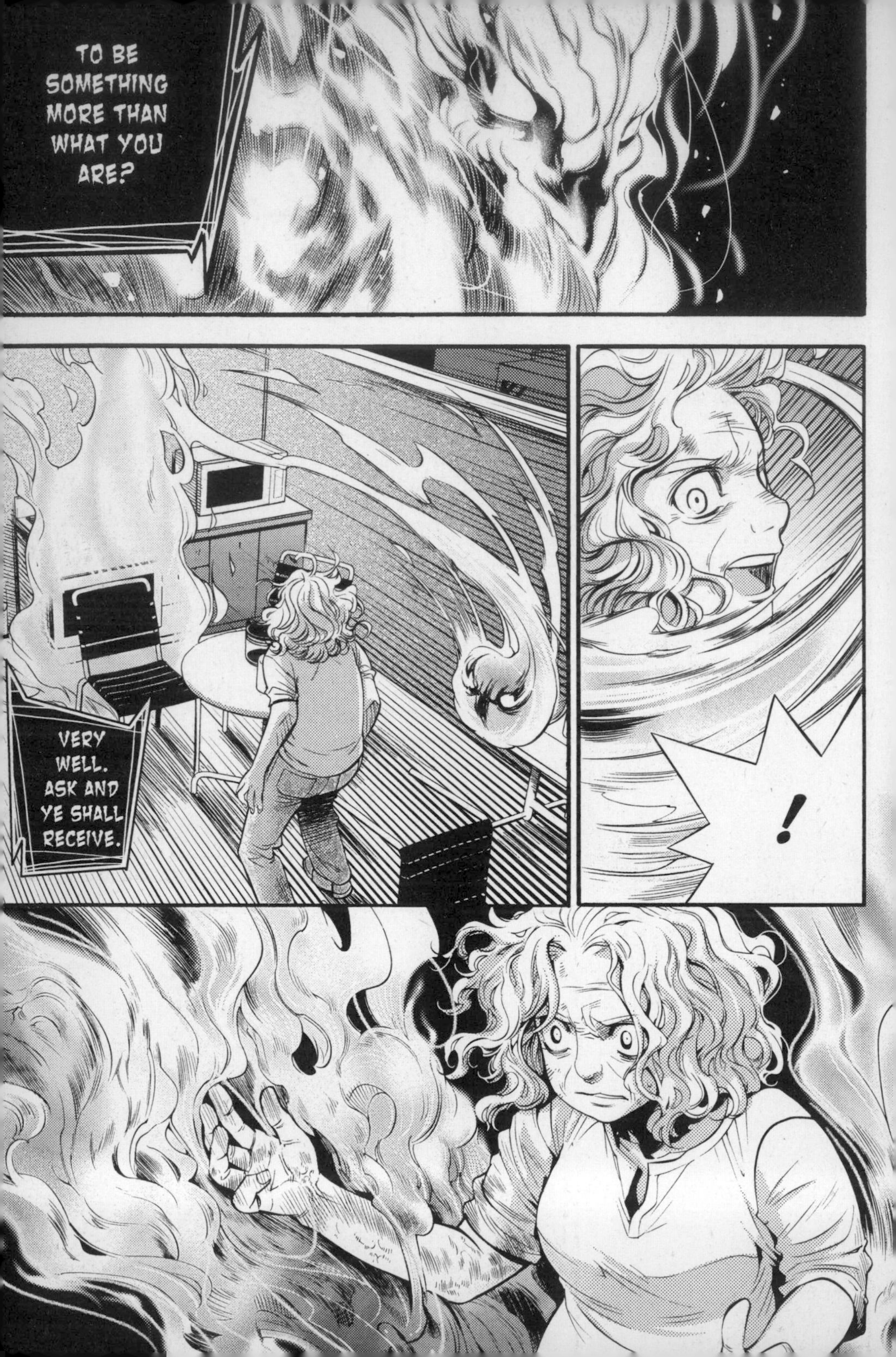
TO BE SOMETHING MORE THAN WHAT YOU ARE?
VERY WELL. ASK AND YE SHALL RECEIVE.
!

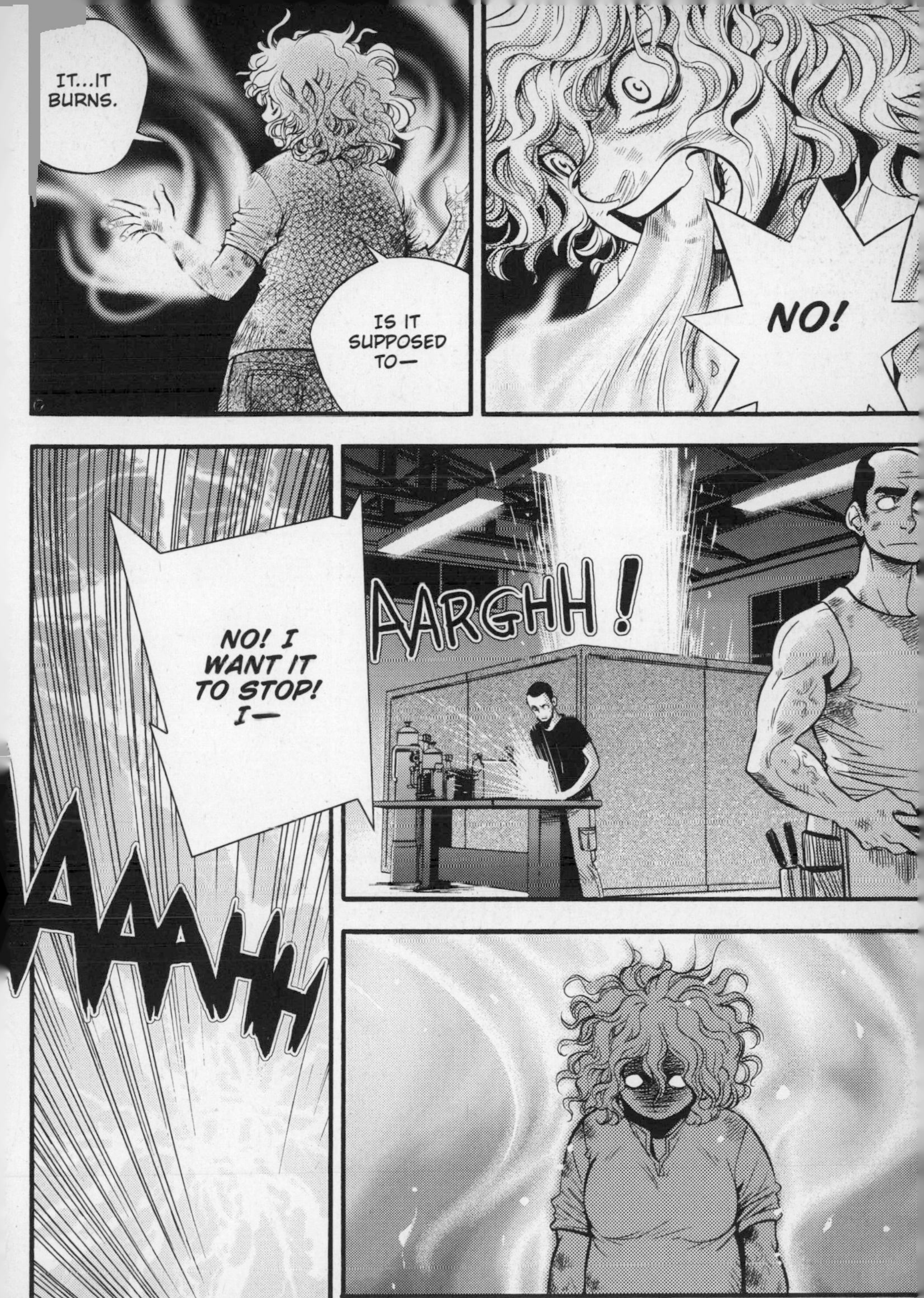

IT...IT BURNS.
IS IT SUPPOSED TO—
NO!
NO! I WANT IT TO STOP! I—
AAAHH
AARGHH!

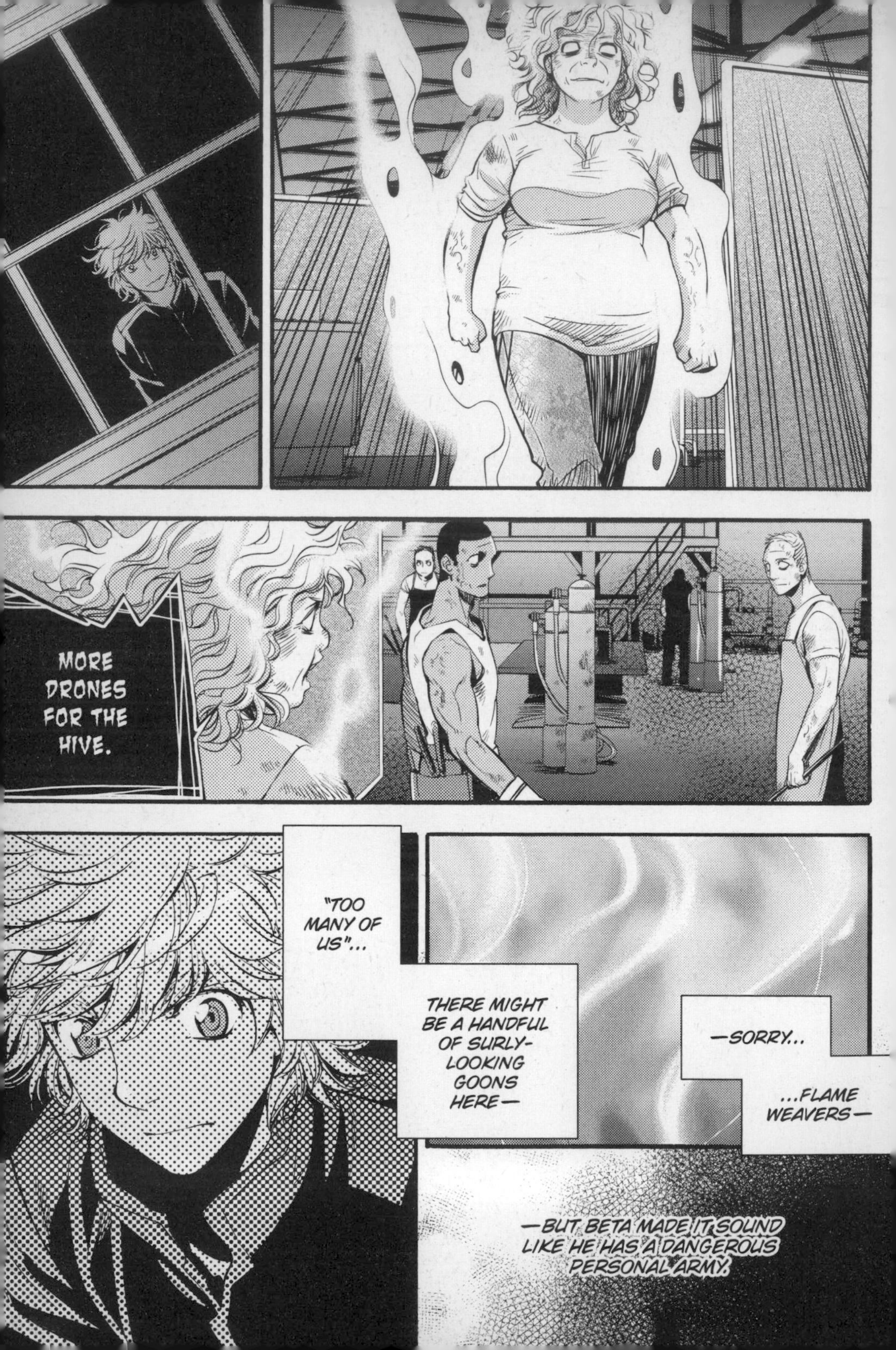
MORE DRONES FOR THE HIVE.
"TOO MANY OF US"...
THERE MIGHT BE A HANDFUL OF SURLY-LOOKING GOONS HERE—
—SORRY...
...FLAME WEAVERS—
—BUT BETA MADE IT SOUND LIKE HE HAS A DANGEROUS PERSONAL ARMY.

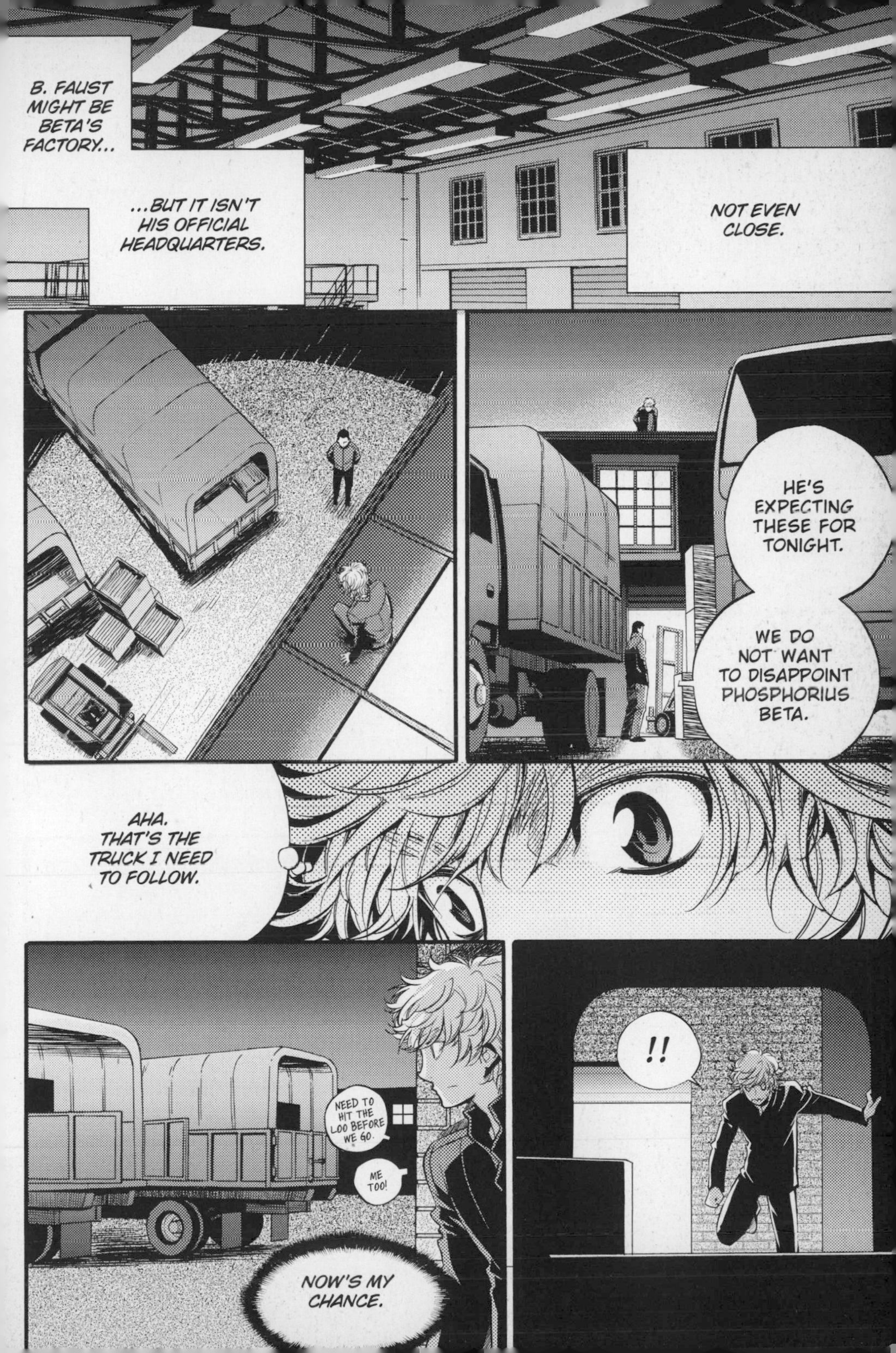
B. FAUST MIGHT BE BETA'S FACTORY...
...BUT IT ISN'T HIS OFFICIAL HEADQUARTERS.
NOT EVEN CLOSE.
HE'S EXPECTING THESE FOR TONIGHT.
WE DO NOT WANT TO DISAPPOINT PHOSPHORIUS BETA.
AHA. THAT'S THE TRUCK I NEED TO FOLLOW.
NEED TO HIT THE LOO BEFORE WE GO.
ME TOO!
NOW'S MY CHANCE.
!!

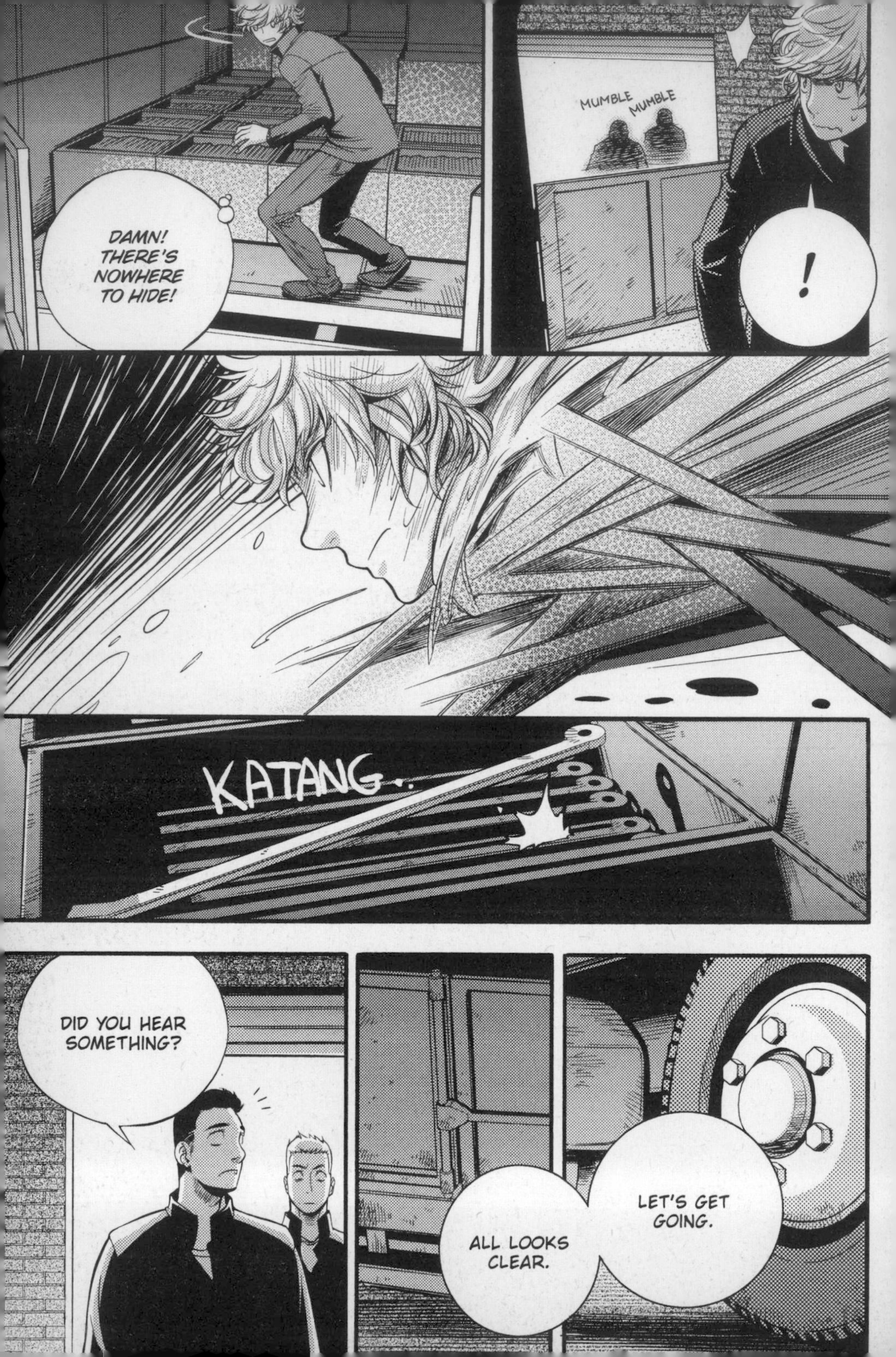
DAMN! THERE'S NOWHERE TO HIDE!
MUMBLE MUMBLE
!
KATANG
DID YOU HEAR SOMETHING?
ALL LOOKS CLEAR.
LET'S GET GOING.

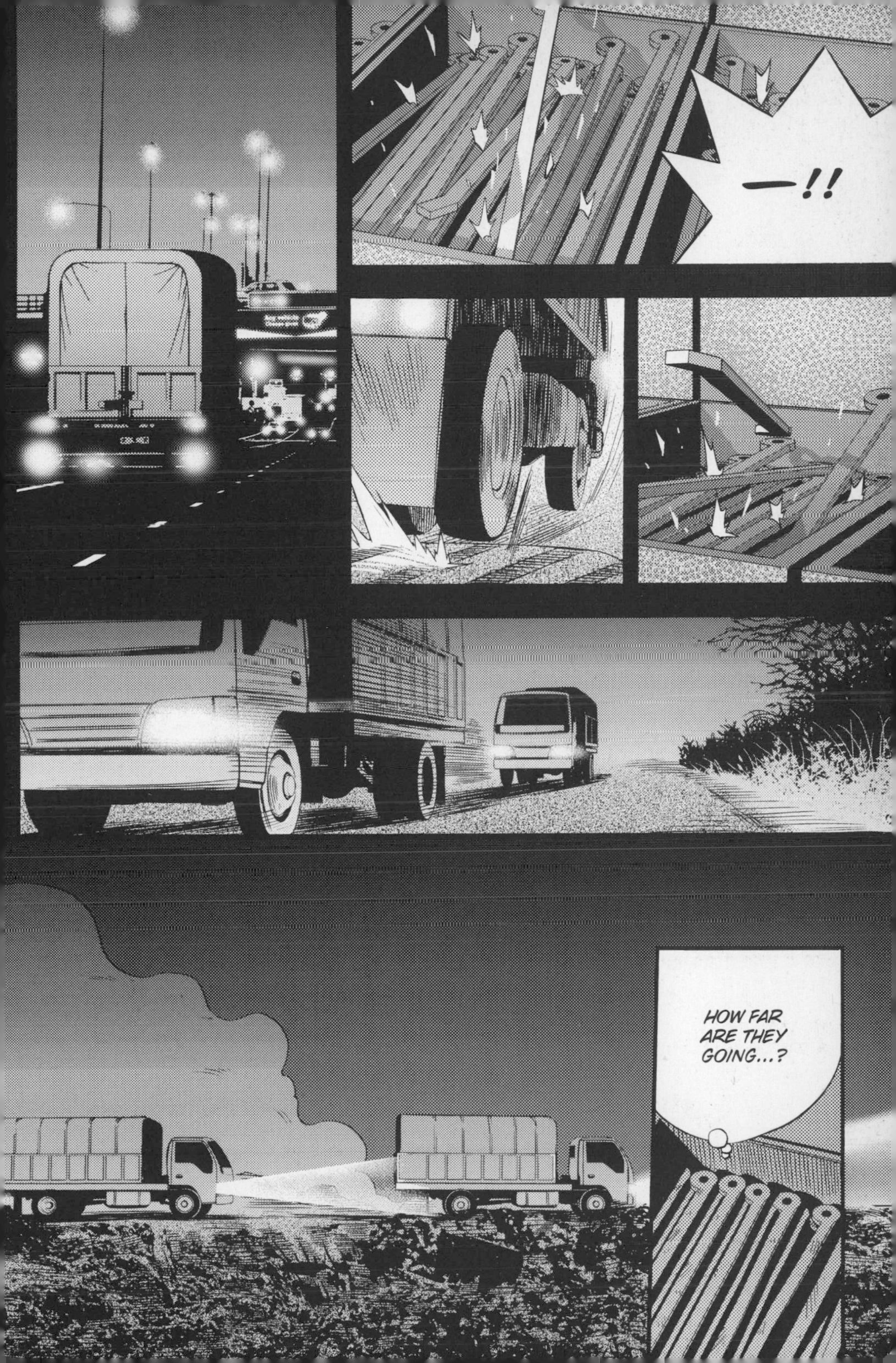

—!!
HOW FAR ARE THEY GOING...?

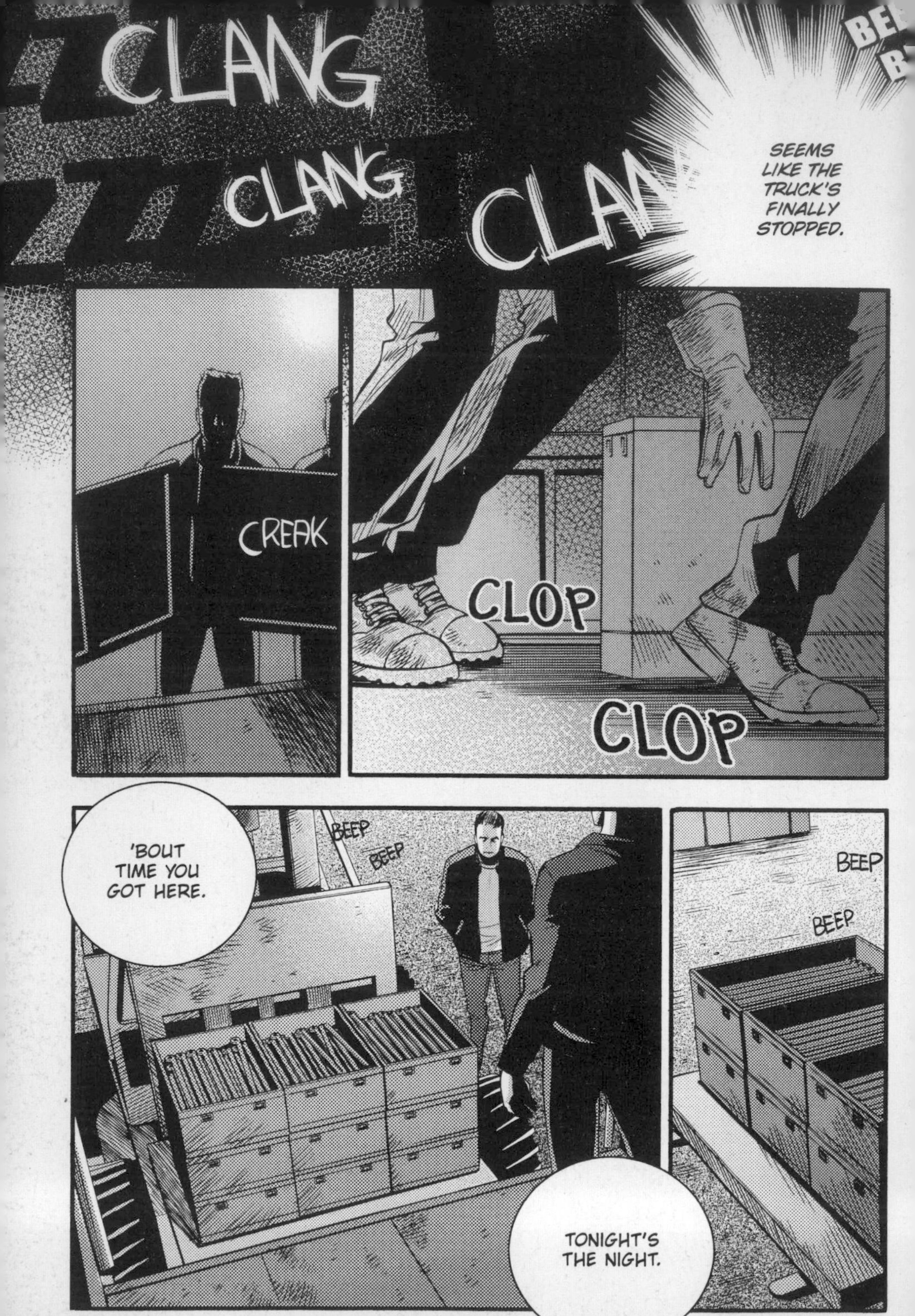
CLANG
CLANG
CLAN
SEEMS LIKE THE TRUCK'S FINALLY STOPPED.
CREAK
CLOP
CLOP
'BOUT TIME YOU GOT HERE.
BEEP
BEEP
TONIGHT'S THE NIGHT.
BEEP
BEEP

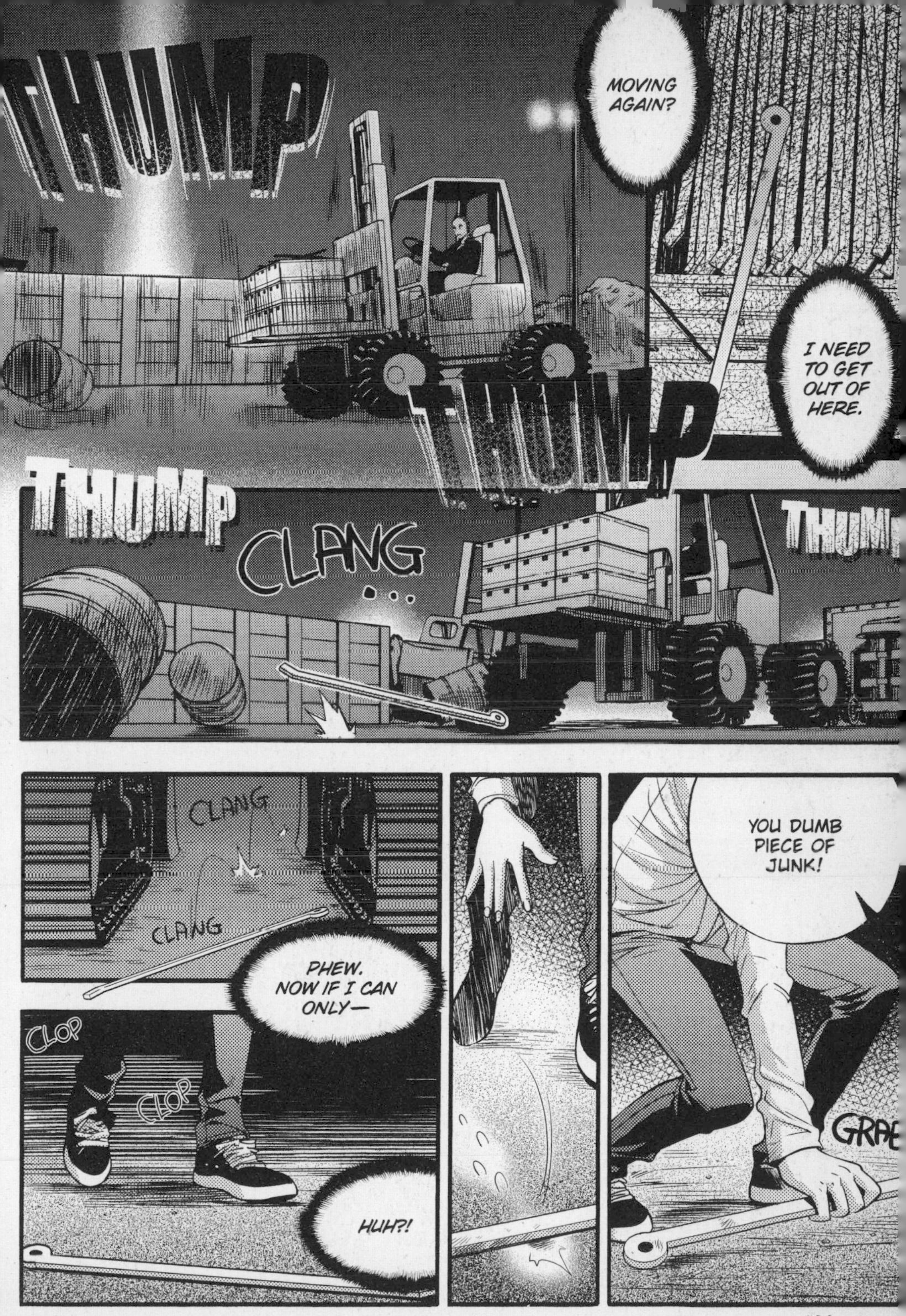
THUMP
MOVING AGAIN?
I NEED TO GET OUT OF HERE.
THUMP
THUMP
CLANG
...
THUMP
CLANG
CLANG
PHEW. NOW IF I CAN ONLY—
CLOP
CLOP
HUH?!
YOU DUMB PIECE OF JUNK!

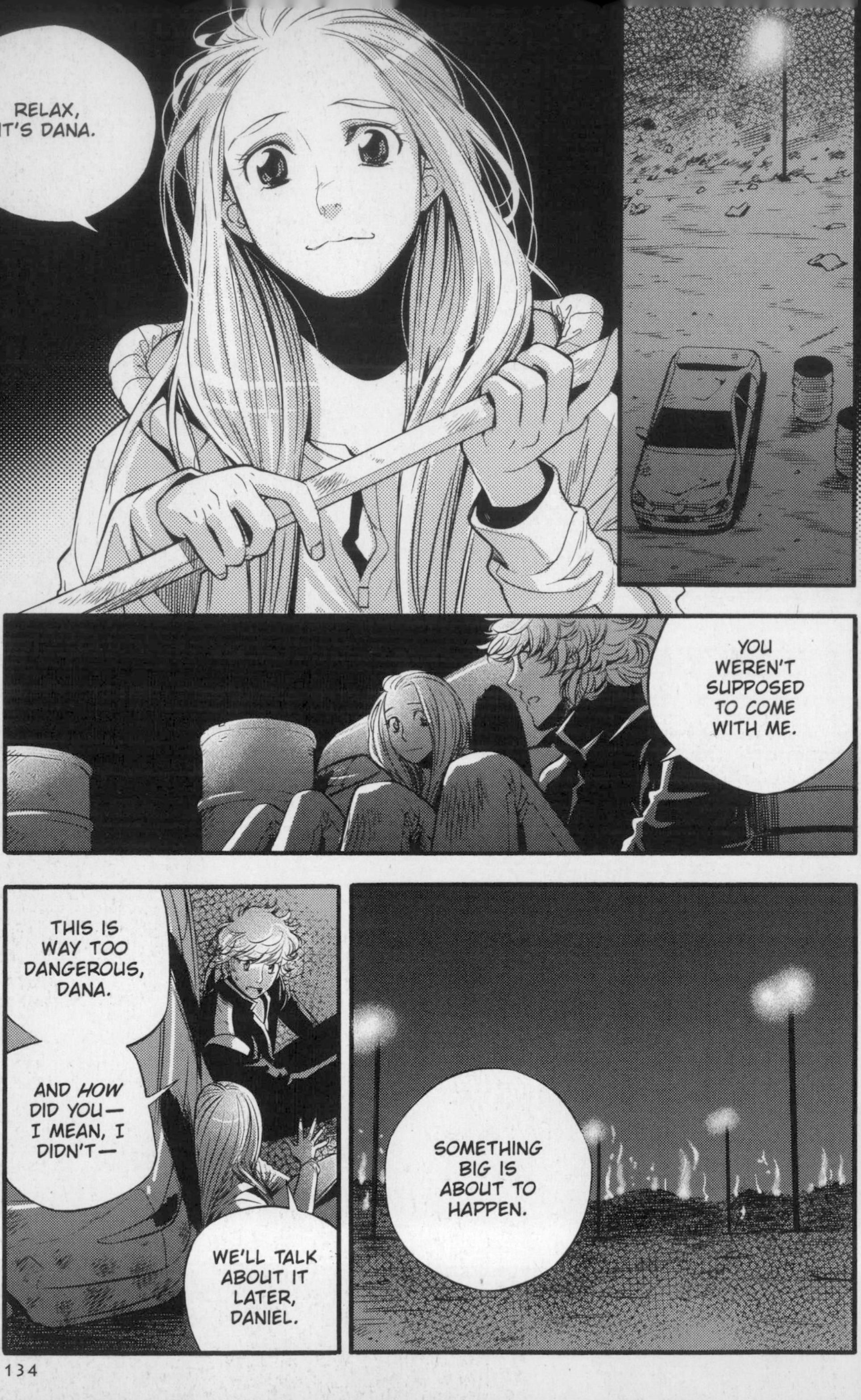
RELAX, IT'S DANA.
YOU WEREN'T SUPPOSED TO COME WITH ME.
THIS IS WAY TOO DANGEROUS, DANA.
AND *HOW* DID YOU— I MEAN, I DIDN'T—
WE'LL TALK ABOUT IT LATER, DANIEL.
SOMETHING BIG IS ABOUT TO HAPPEN.

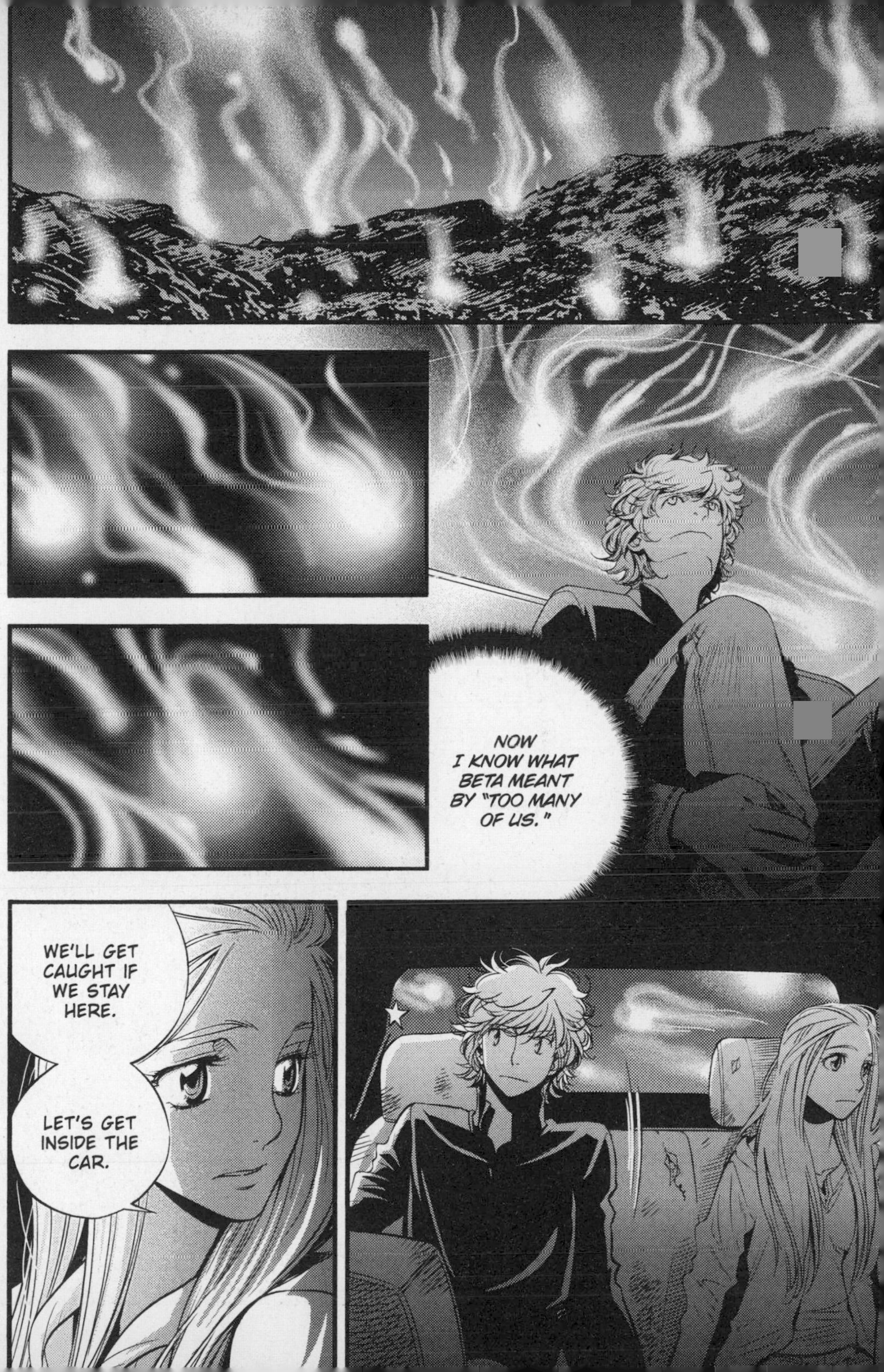
NOW I KNOW WHAT BETA MEANT BY "TOO MANY OF US."
WE'LL GET CAUGHT IF WE STAY HERE.
LET'S GET INSIDE THE CAR.

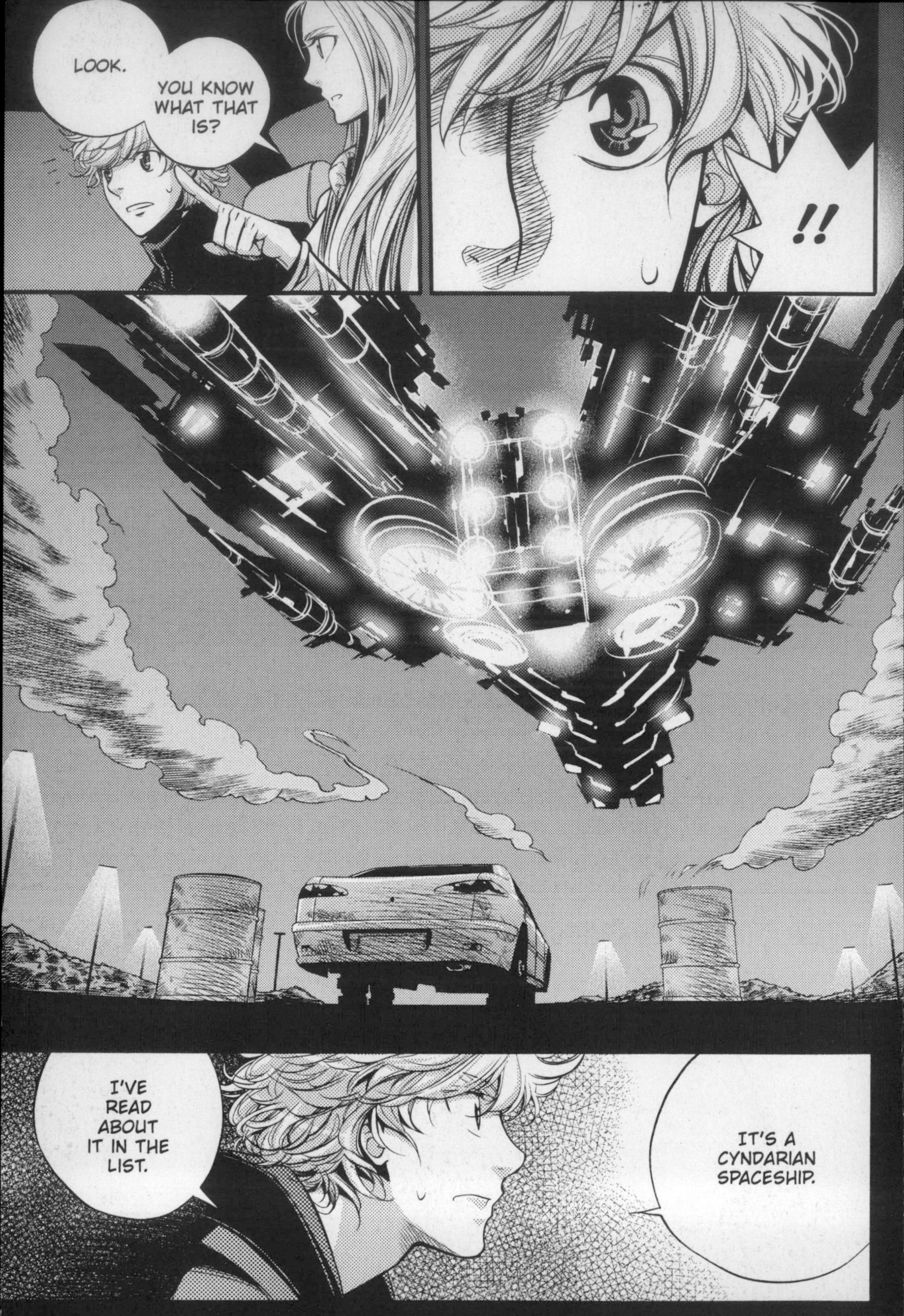
LOOK.
YOU KNOW WHAT THAT IS?
!!
I'VE READ ABOUT IT IN THE LIST.
IT'S A CYNDARIAN SPACESHIP.

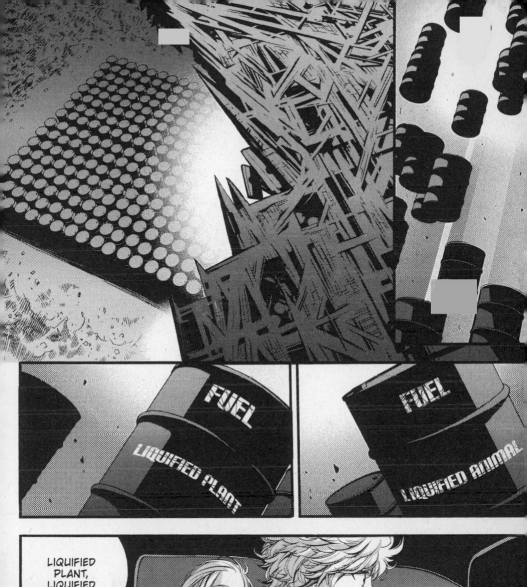

FUEL
LIQUIFIED PLANT

FUEL
LIQUIFIED ANIMAL

LIQUIFIED PLANT, LIQUIFIED ANIMAL...?

DOES THAT MEAN WITHIN THAT SPACE-SHIP IS—

ALL THE WONDERFUL LIFE THAT EARTH HAS TO OFFER IS NOTHING MORE THAN FUEL TO HIM.

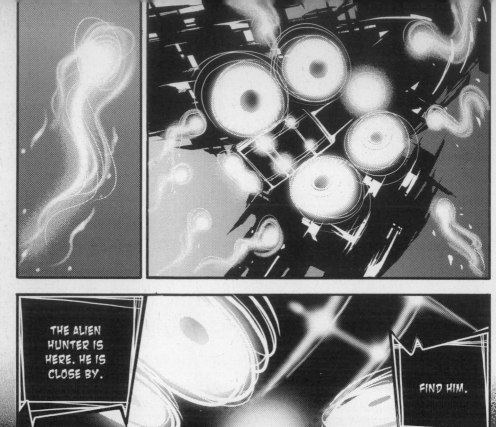

THE ALIEN HUNTER IS HERE. HE IS CLOSE BY.

FIND HIM.

NOW! BRING HIM TO ME DEAD OR ALIVE!

WHOEVER BRINGS ME DANIEL X WILL GLOW FOR ETERNITY!

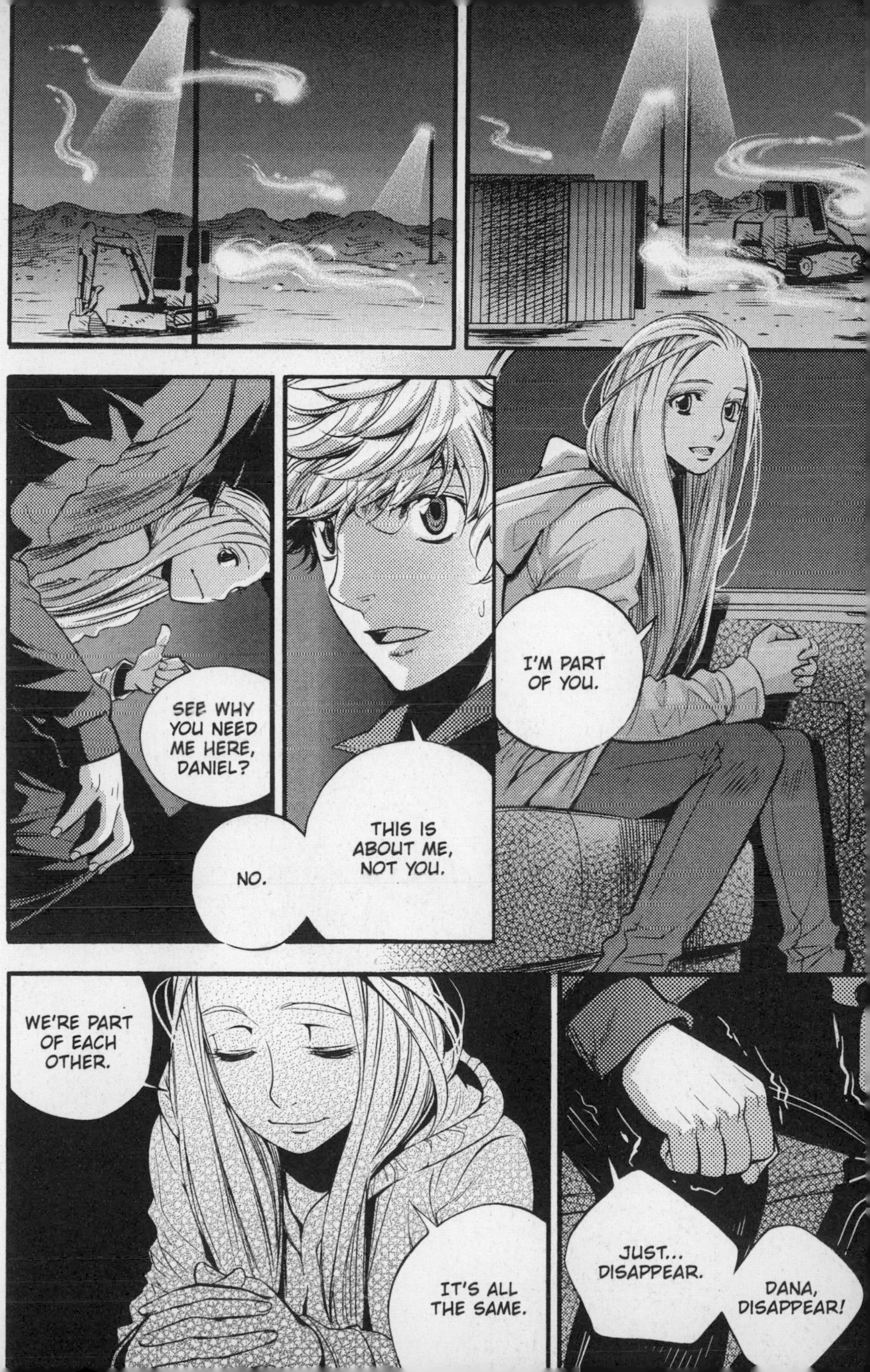
SEE WHY YOU NEED ME HERE, DANIEL?
NO.
THIS IS ABOUT ME, NOT YOU.
I'M PART OF YOU.
WE'RE PART OF EACH OTHER.
IT'S ALL THE SAME.
JUST... DISAPPEAR.
DANA, DISAPPEAR!

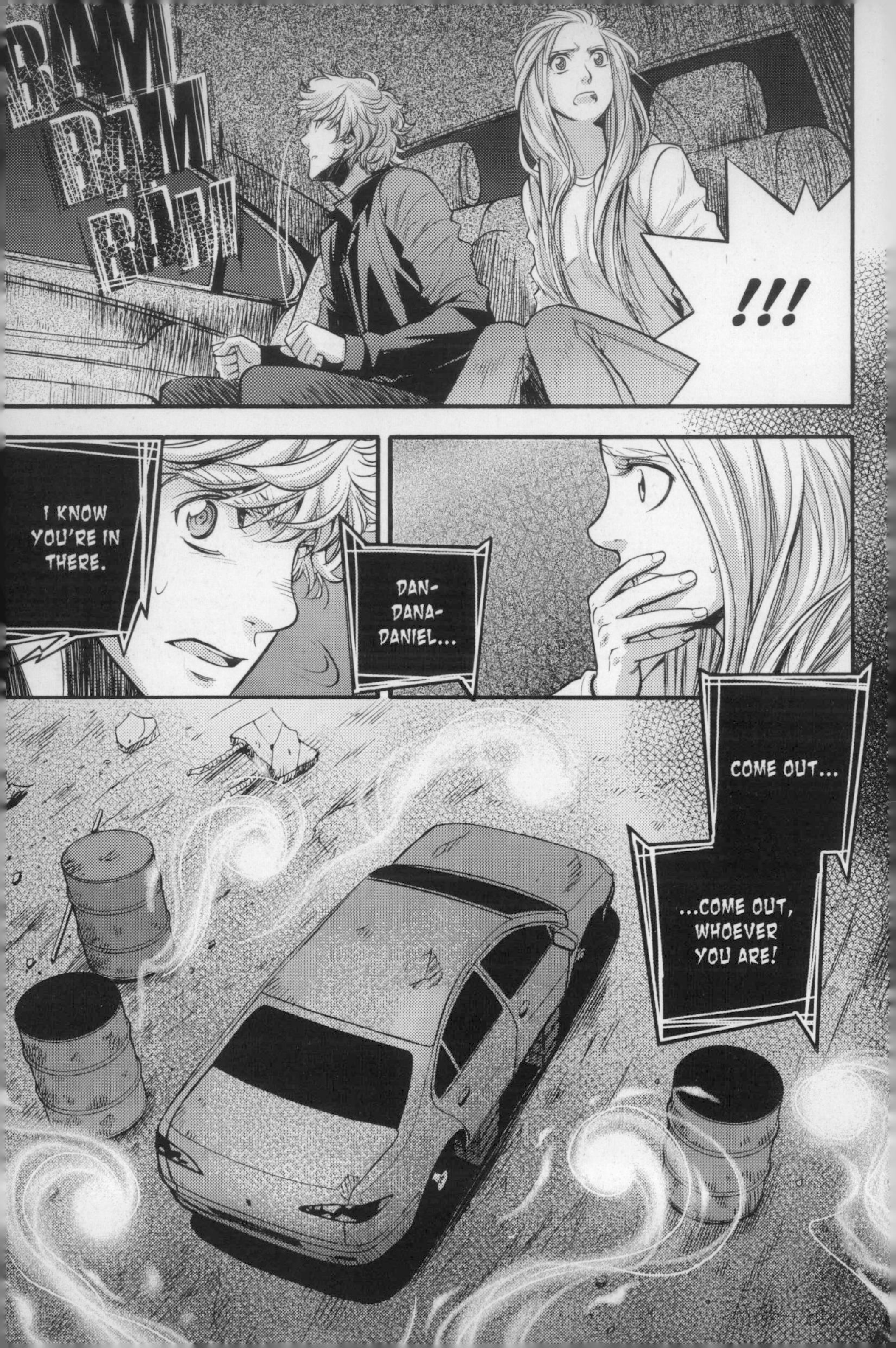
BAM BAM BAM
!!!
I KNOW YOU'RE IN THERE.
DAN-DANA-DANIEL...
COME OUT...
...COME OUT, WHOEVER YOU ARE!

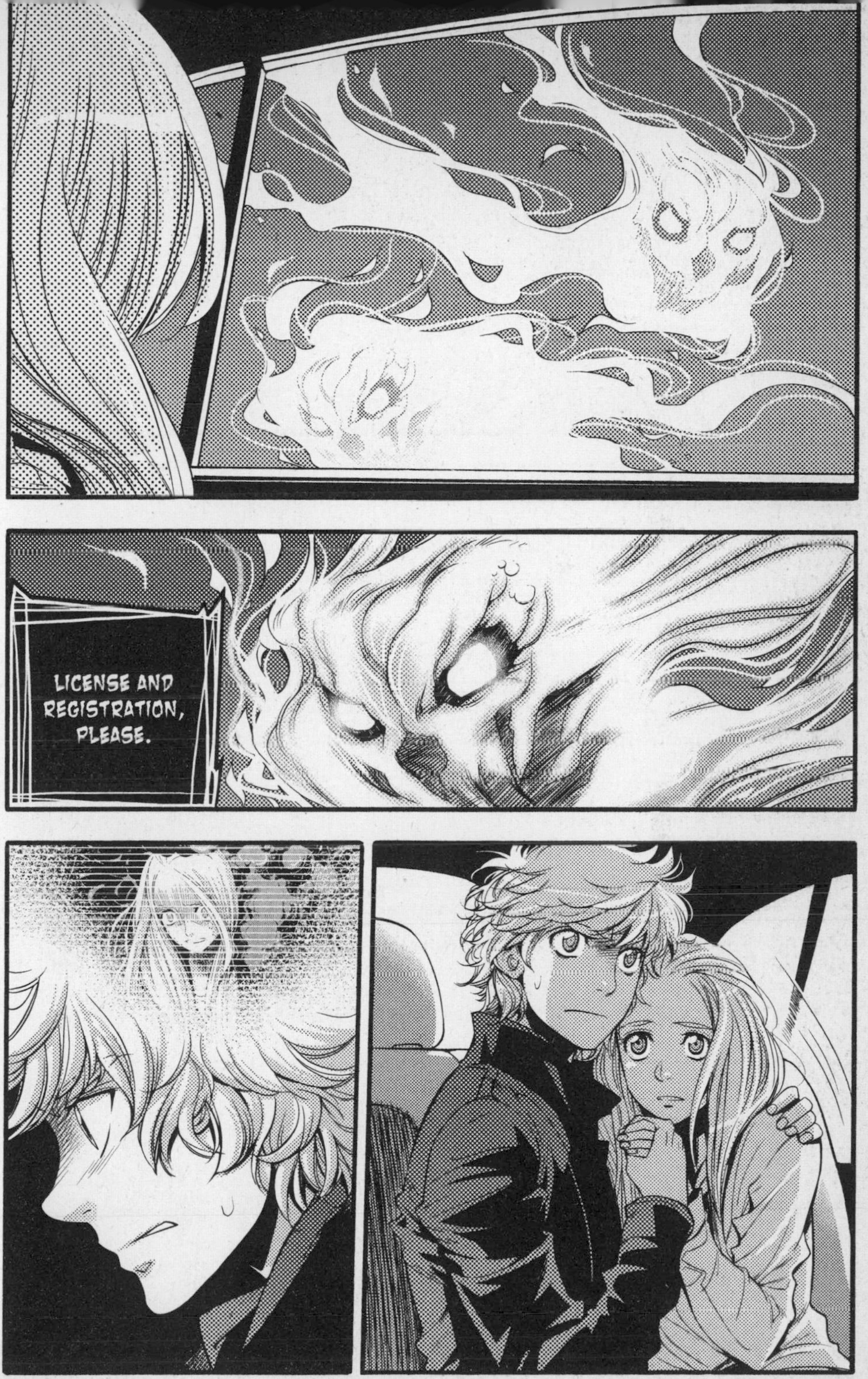
LICENSE AND
REGISTRATION,
PLEASE.

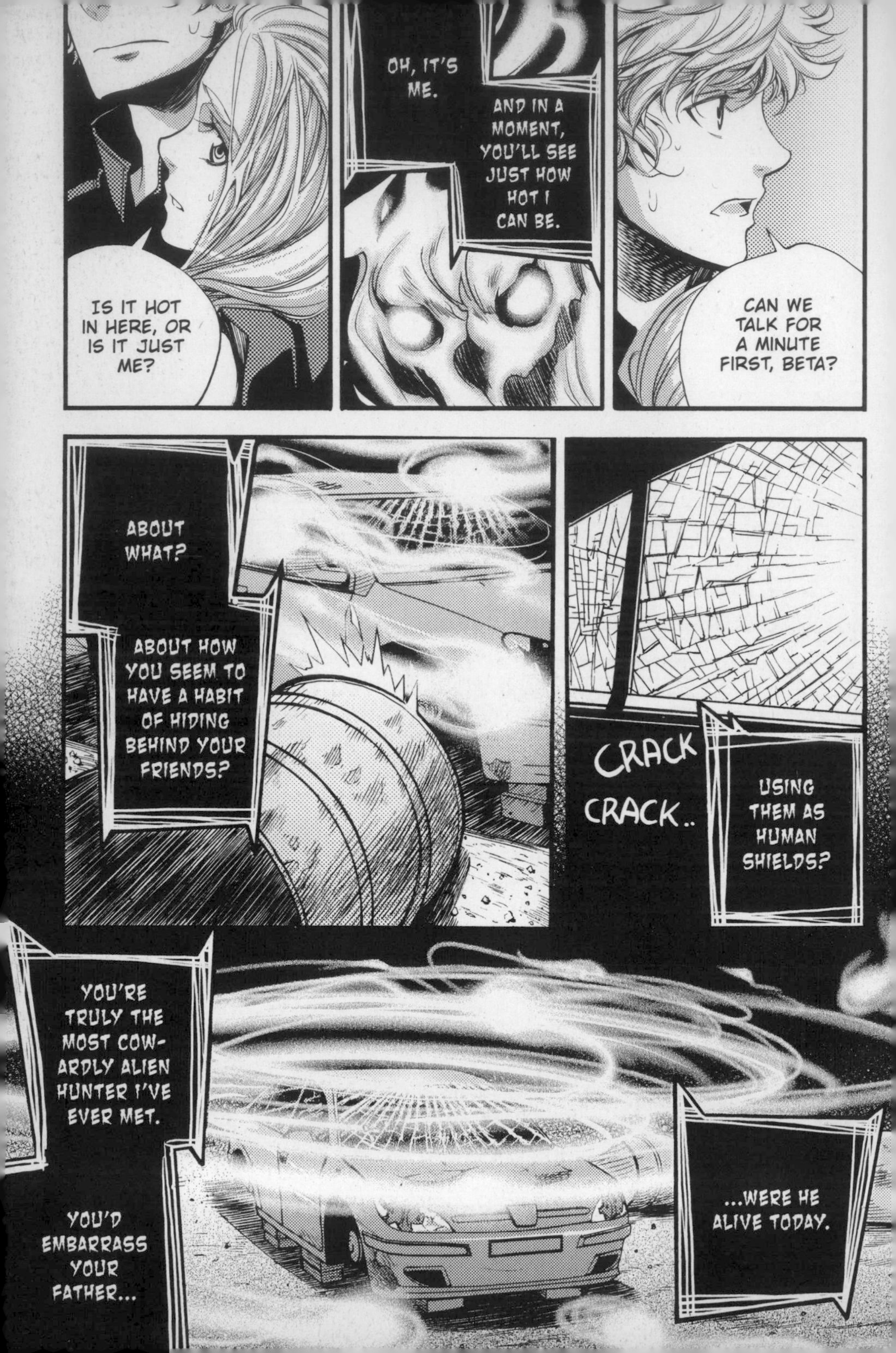
IS IT HOT IN HERE, OR IS IT JUST ME?
OH, IT'S ME.
AND IN A MOMENT, YOU'LL SEE JUST HOW HOT I CAN BE.
CAN WE TALK FOR A MINUTE FIRST, BETA?
ABOUT WHAT?
ABOUT HOW YOU SEEM TO HAVE A HABIT OF HIDING BEHIND YOUR FRIENDS?
CRACK
CRACK..
USING THEM AS HUMAN SHIELDS?
YOU'RE TRULY THE MOST COW-ARDLY ALIEN HUNTER I'VE EVER MET.
YOU'D EMBARRASS YOUR FATHER...
...WERE HE ALIVE TODAY.

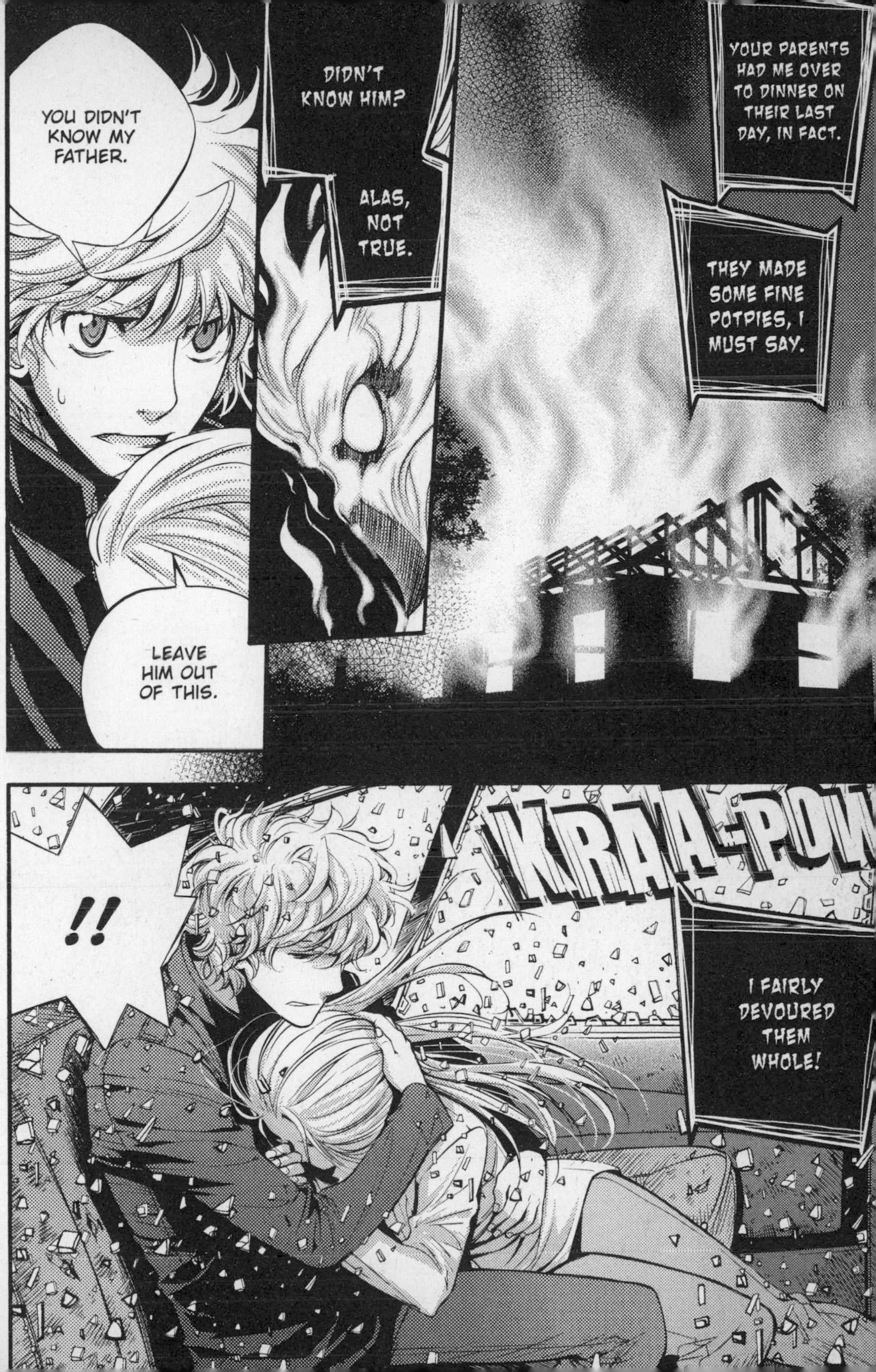
YOU DIDN'T KNOW MY FATHER.
LEAVE HIM OUT OF THIS.
DIDN'T KNOW HIM?
ALAS, NOT TRUE.
YOUR PARENTS HAD ME OVER TO DINNER ON THEIR LAST DAY, IN FACT.
THEY MADE SOME FINE POTPIES, I MUST SAY.
!!
KRAA-POW
I FAIRLY DEVOURED THEM WHOLE!

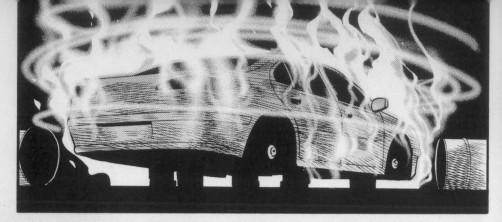

NOWHERE FOR YOU TO GO NOW, DANIEL.

I HOPE YOU PREFER CREMATION OVER BURIAL.

I CAN'T REALLY OFFER YOU THE LATTER OPTION.

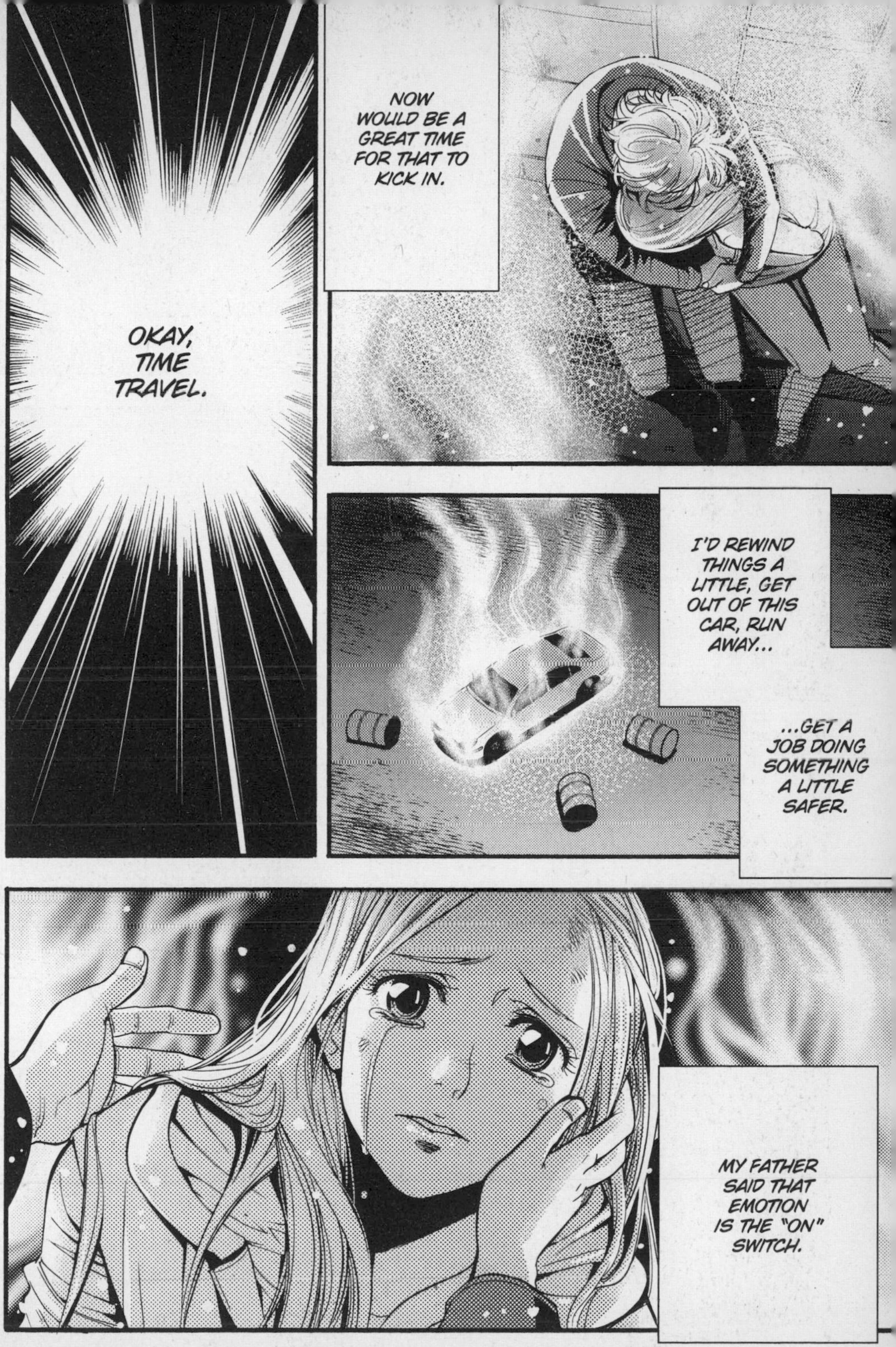
OKAY, TIME TRAVEL.
NOW WOULD BE A GREAT TIME FOR THAT TO KICK IN.
I'D REWIND THINGS A LITTLE, GET OUT OF THIS CAR, RUN AWAY...
...GET A JOB DOING SOMETHING A LITTLE SAFER.
MY FATHER SAID THAT EMOTION IS THE "ON" SWITCH.

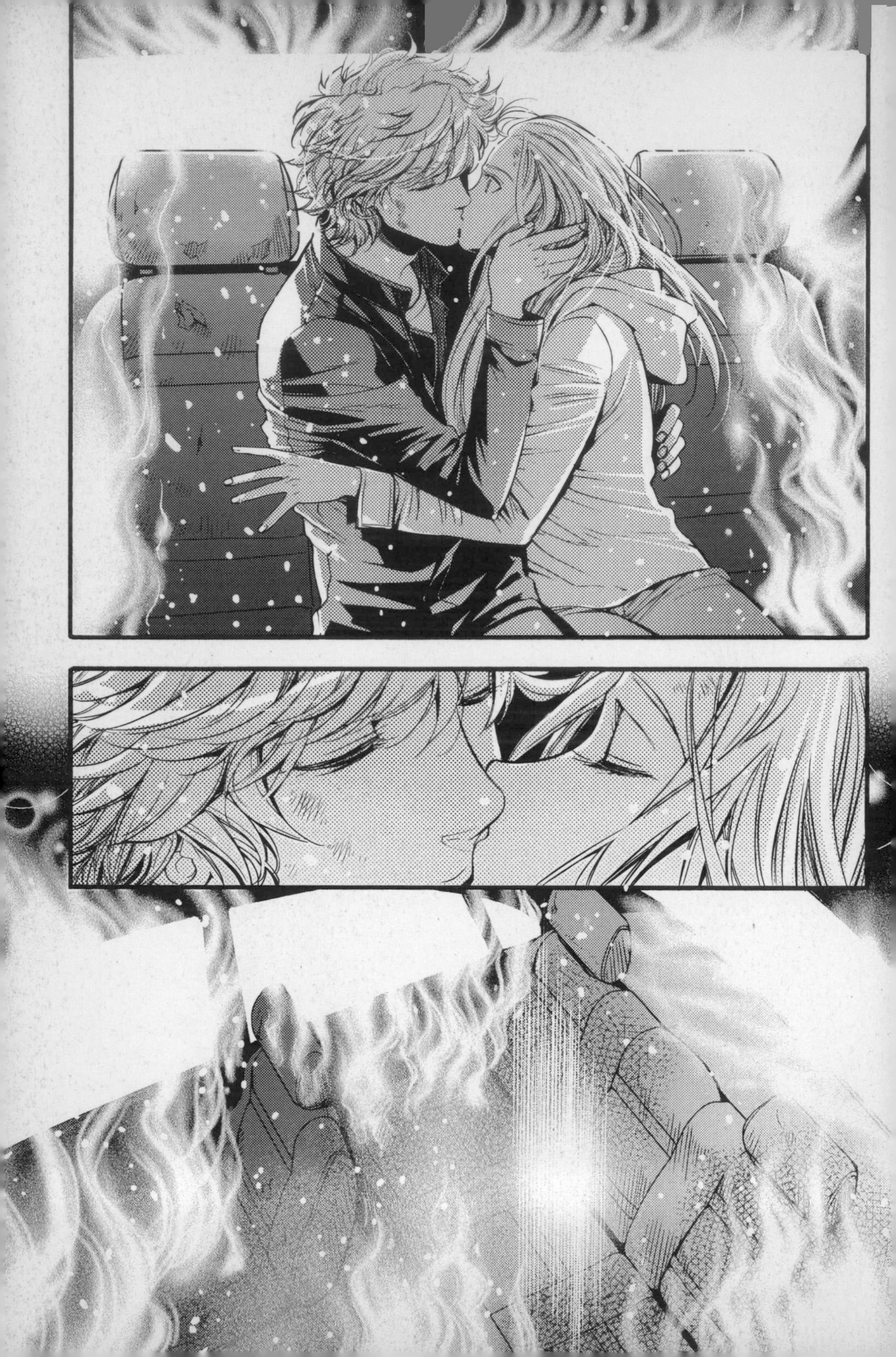

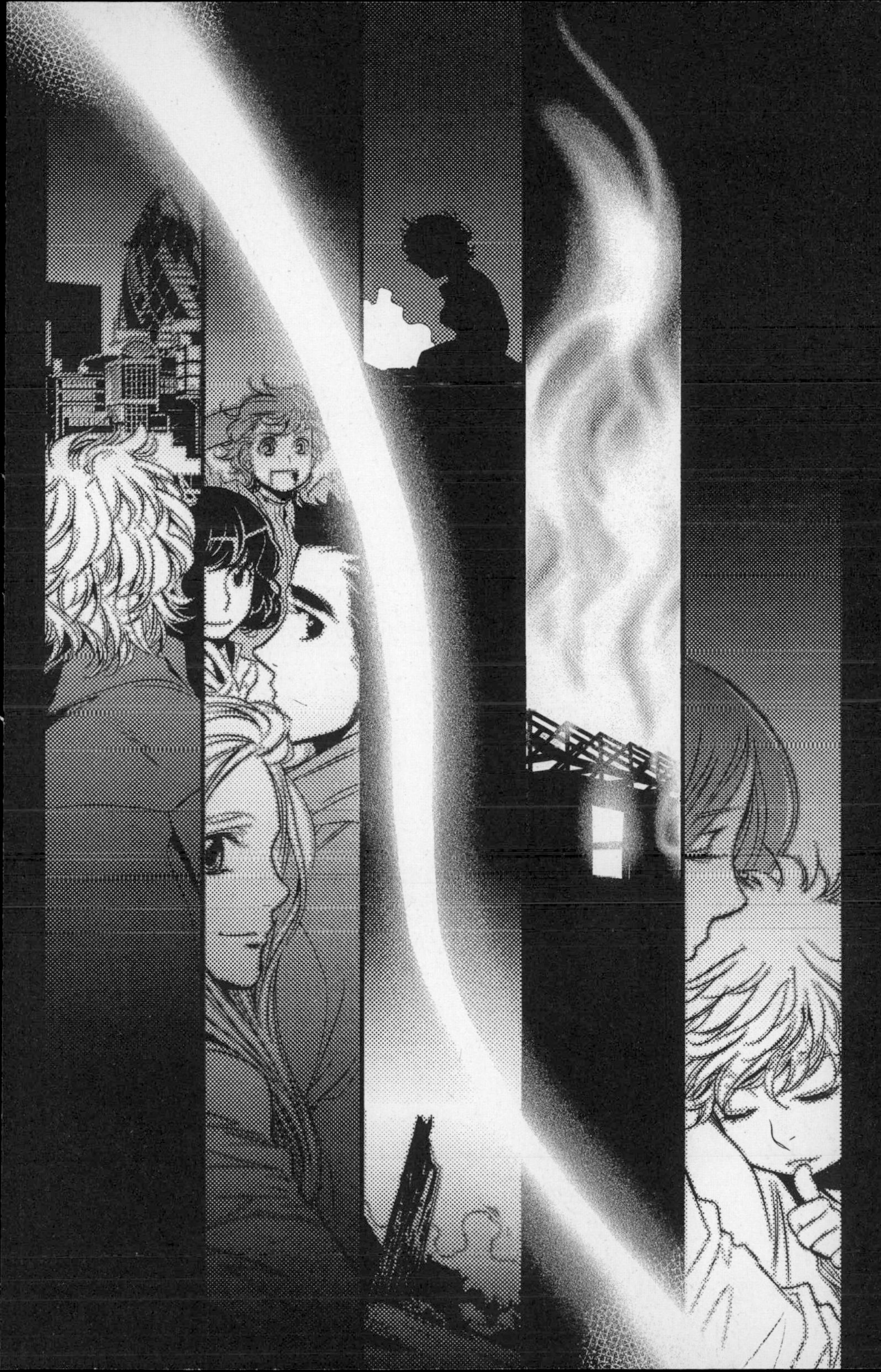

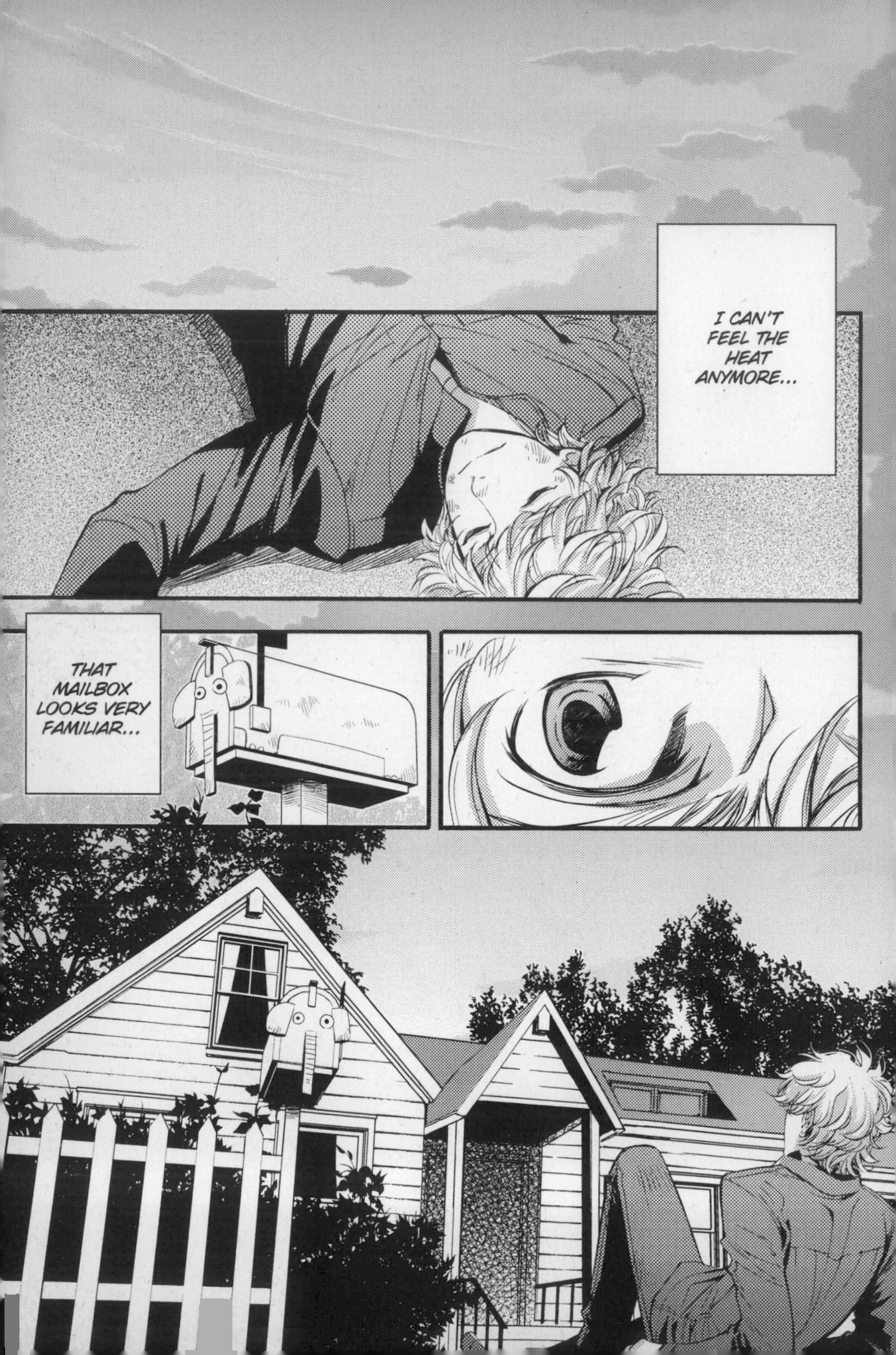
I CAN'T FEEL THE HEAT ANYMORE...
THAT MAILBOX LOOKS VERY FAMILIAR...

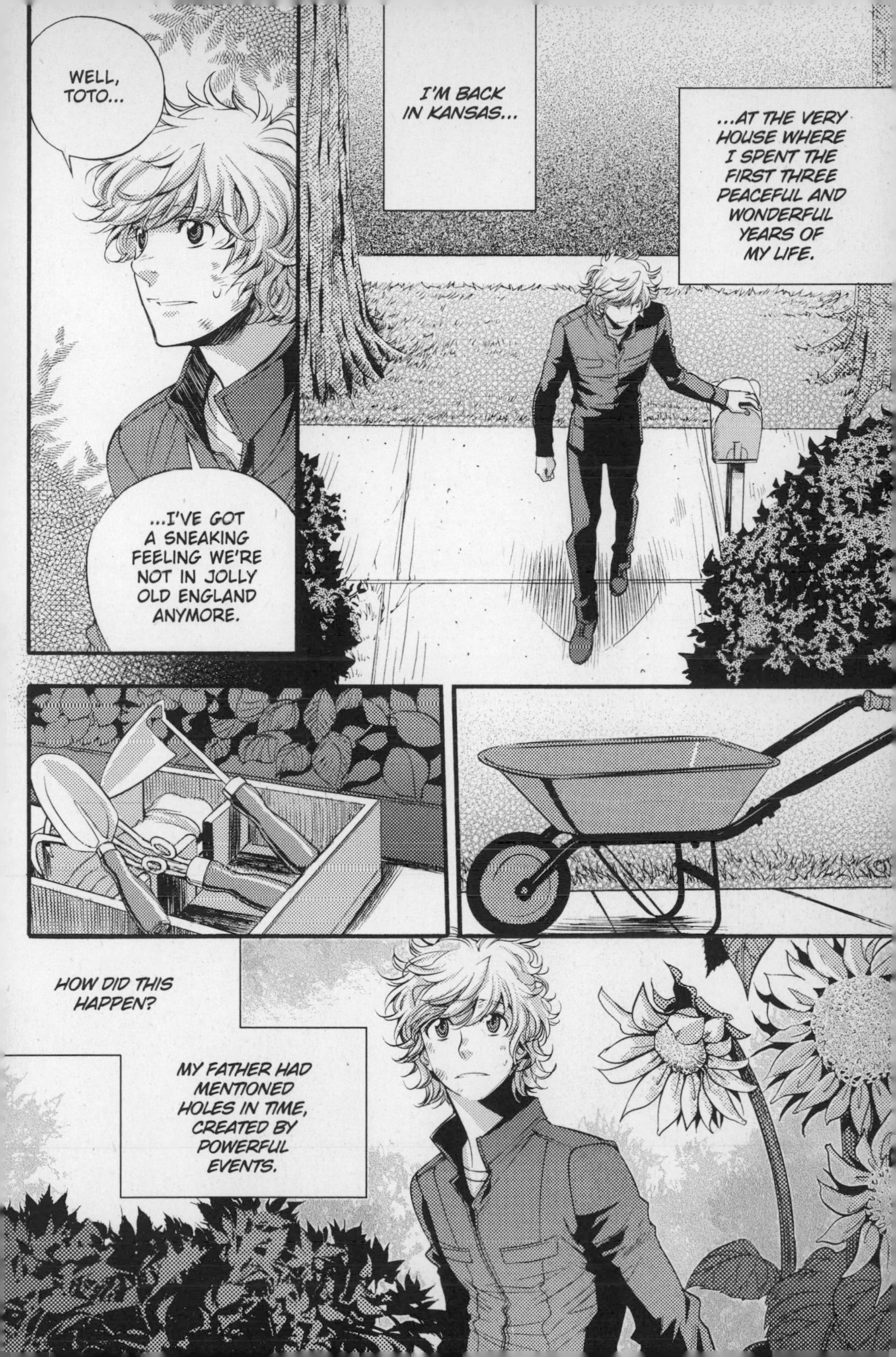
WELL, TOTO...
...I'VE GOT A SNEAKING FEELING WE'RE NOT IN JOLLY OLD ENGLAND ANYMORE.
I'M BACK IN KANSAS...
...AT THE VERY HOUSE WHERE I SPENT THE FIRST THREE PEACEFUL AND WONDERFUL YEARS OF MY LIFE.
HOW DID THIS HAPPEN?
MY FATHER HAD MENTIONED HOLES IN TIME, CREATED BY POWERFUL EVENTS.

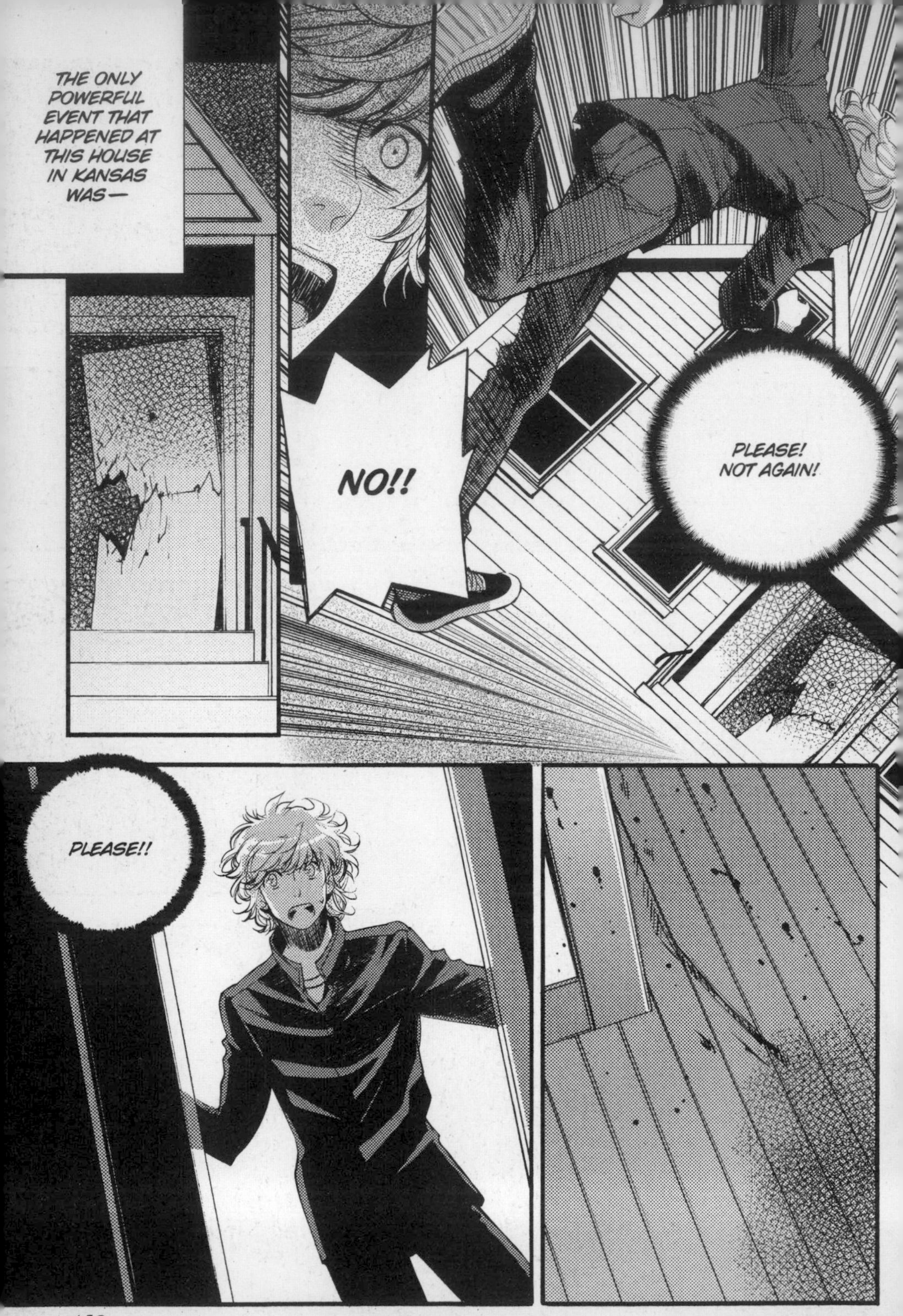
THE ONLY POWERFUL EVENT THAT HAPPENED AT THIS HOUSE IN KANSAS WAS—
NO!!
PLEASE! NOT AGAIN!
PLEASE!!

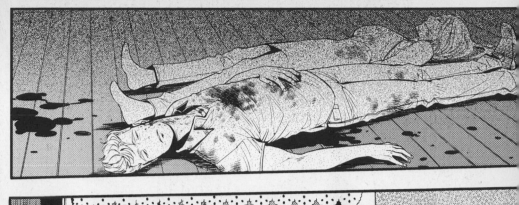

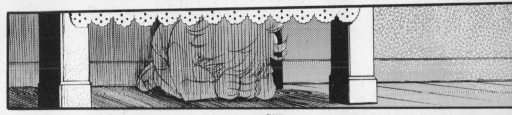

DANIEL, DON'T COME ANY CLOSER.
YOU CAN'T HELP US NOW.
I HEARD THE PORTAL OPEN.
IT COULD ONLY BE YOU, SON.
YOU SHOULDN'T BE HERE, THOUGH.

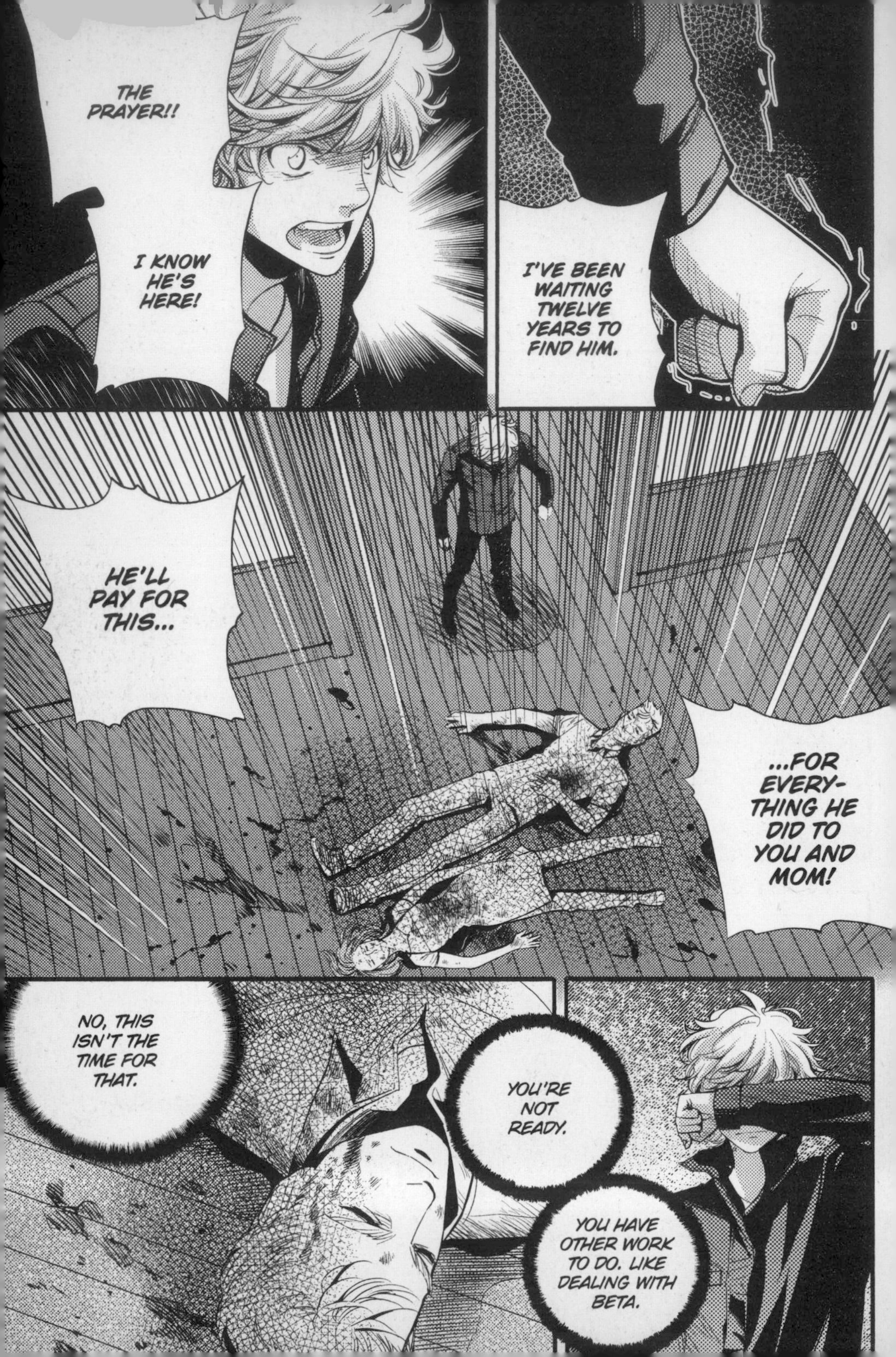
THE PRAYER!!
I KNOW HE'S HERE!
I'VE BEEN WAITING TWELVE YEARS TO FIND HIM.
HE'LL PAY FOR THIS...
...FOR EVERY-THING HE DID TO YOU AND MOM!
NO, THIS ISN'T THE TIME FOR THAT.
YOU'RE NOT READY.
YOU HAVE OTHER WORK TO DO. LIKE DEALING WITH BETA.

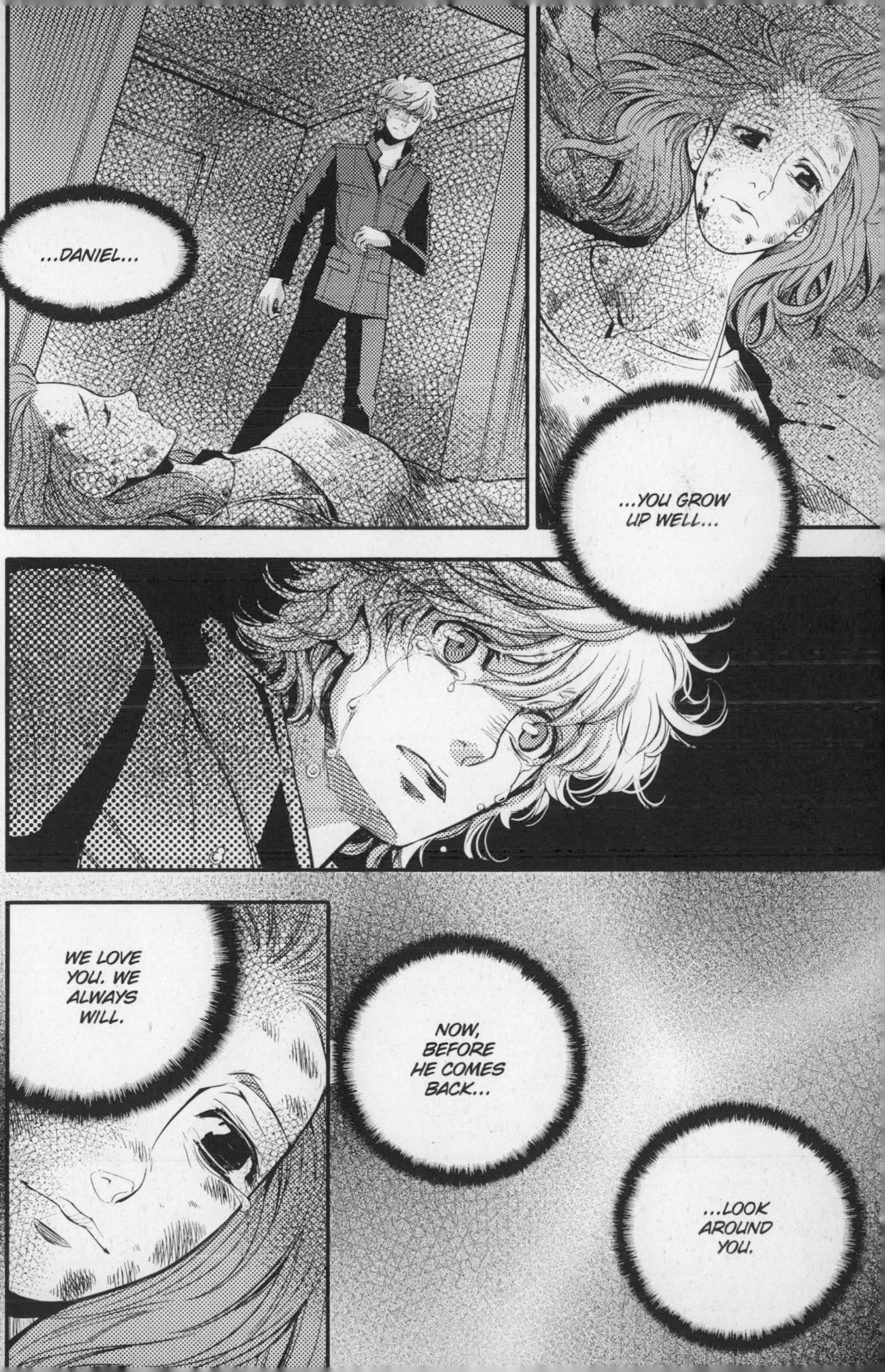
...DANIEL...
...YOU GROW UP WELL...
WE LOVE YOU. WE ALWAYS WILL.
NOW, BEFORE HE COMES BACK...
...LOOK AROUND YOU.

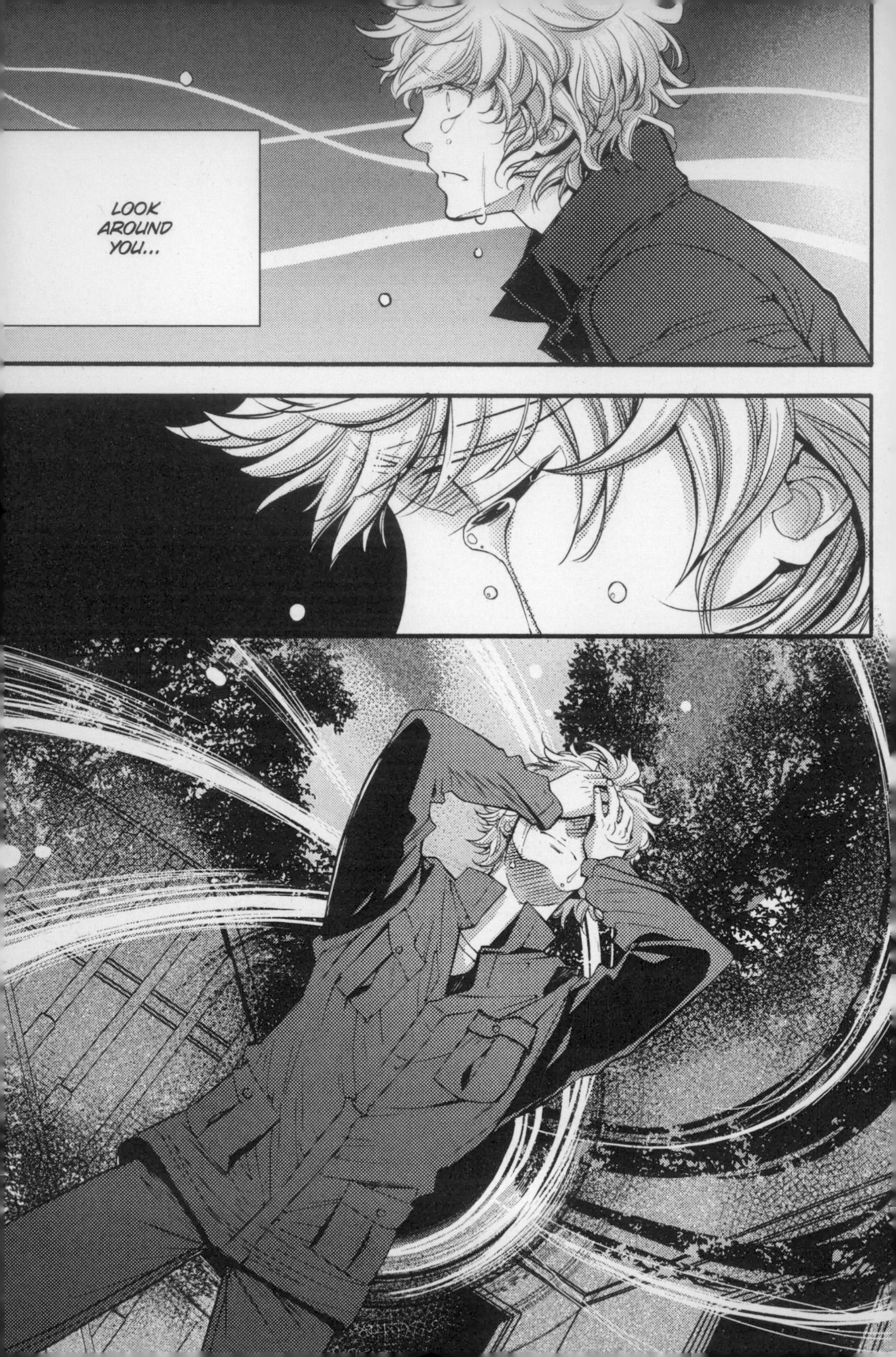
LOOK AROUND YOU...

DANIEL X

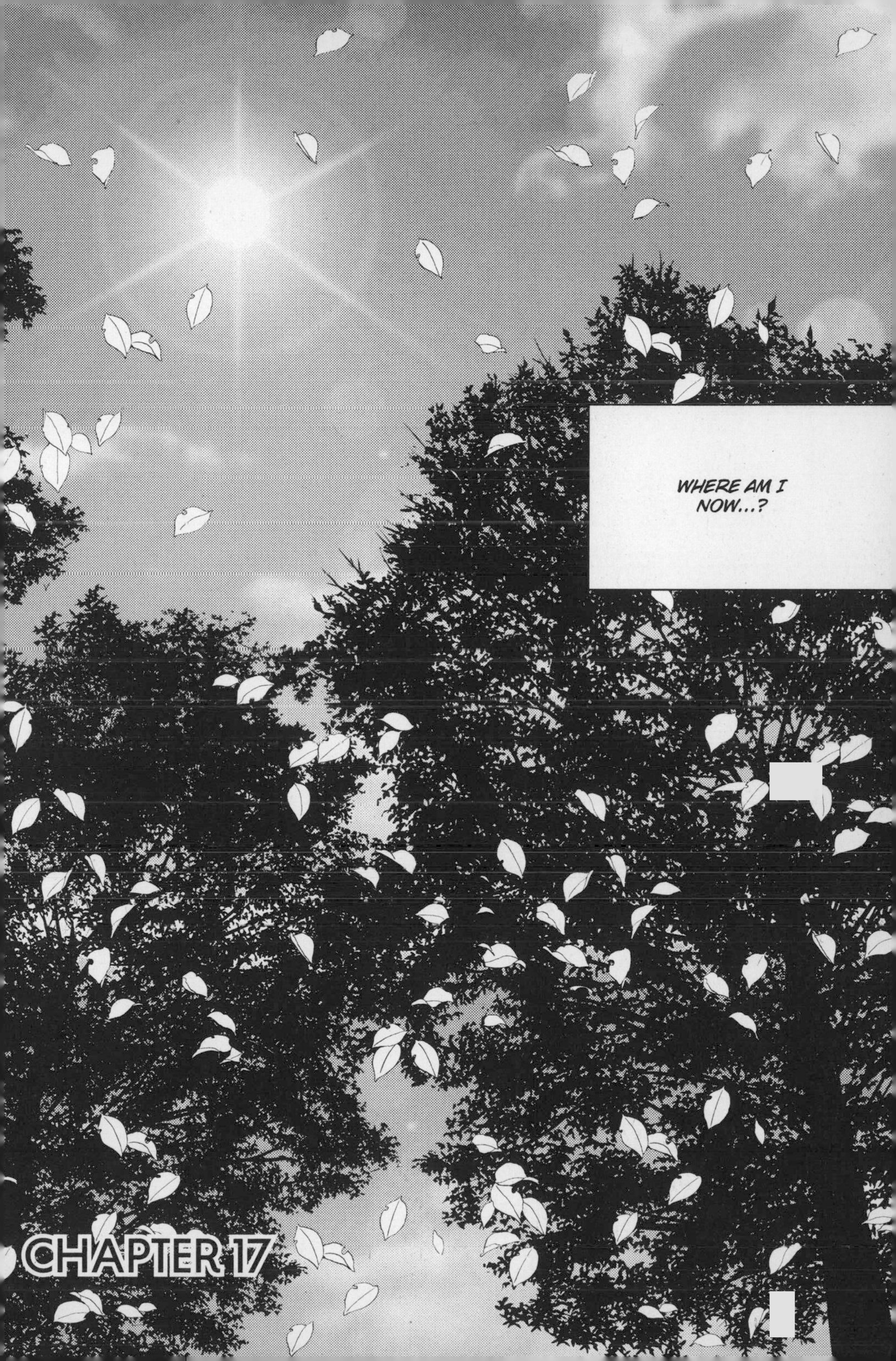
WHERE AM I NOW...?
CHAPTER 17

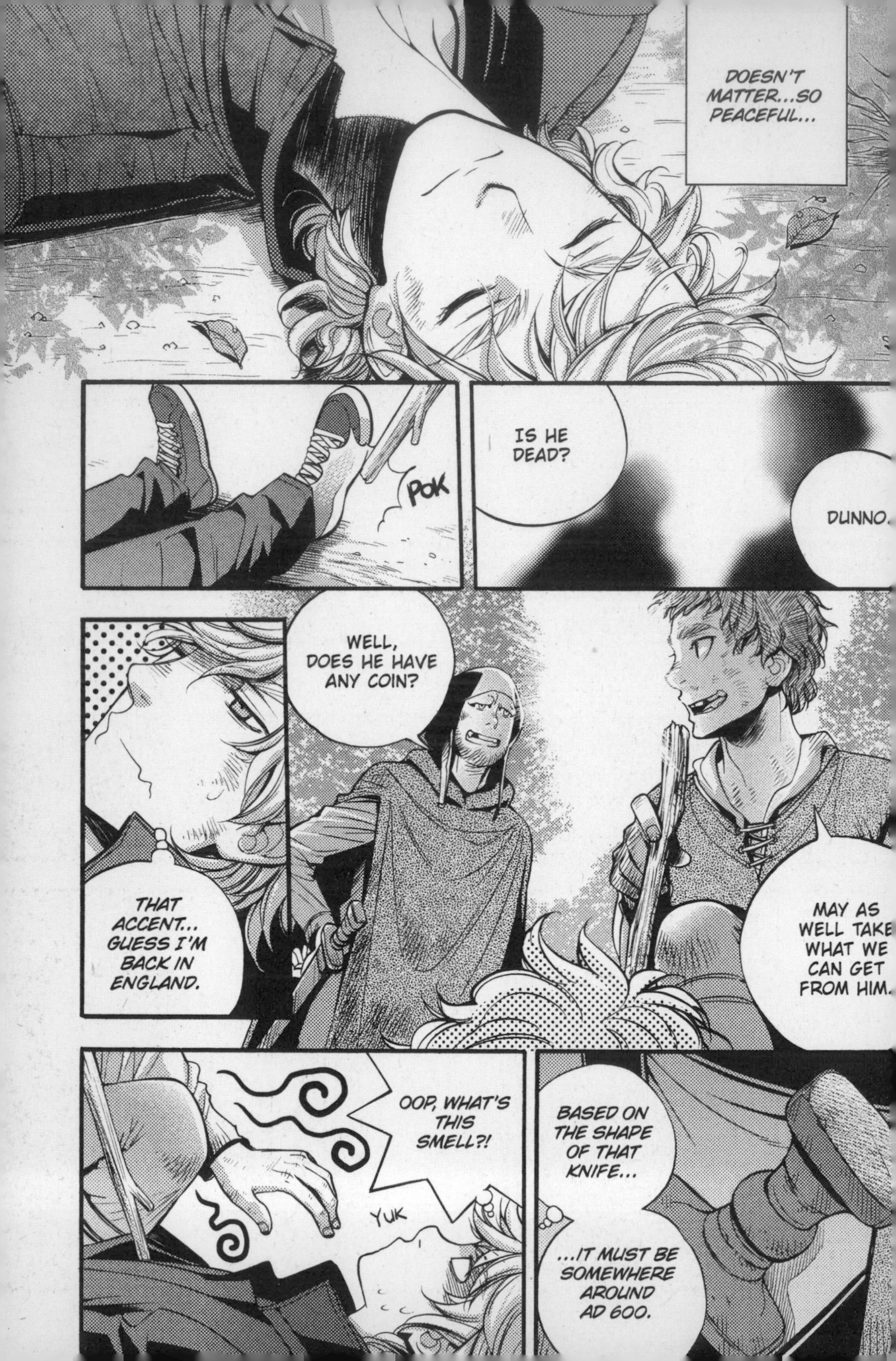
DOESN'T MATTER...SO PEACEFUL...
POK
IS HE DEAD?
DUNNO.
THAT ACCENT... GUESS I'M BACK IN ENGLAND.
WELL, DOES HE HAVE ANY COIN?
MAY AS WELL TAKE WHAT WE CAN GET FROM HIM.
OOP, WHAT'S THIS SMELL?!
YUK
BASED ON THE SHAPE OF THAT KNIFE...
...IT MUST BE SOMEWHERE AROUND AD 600.

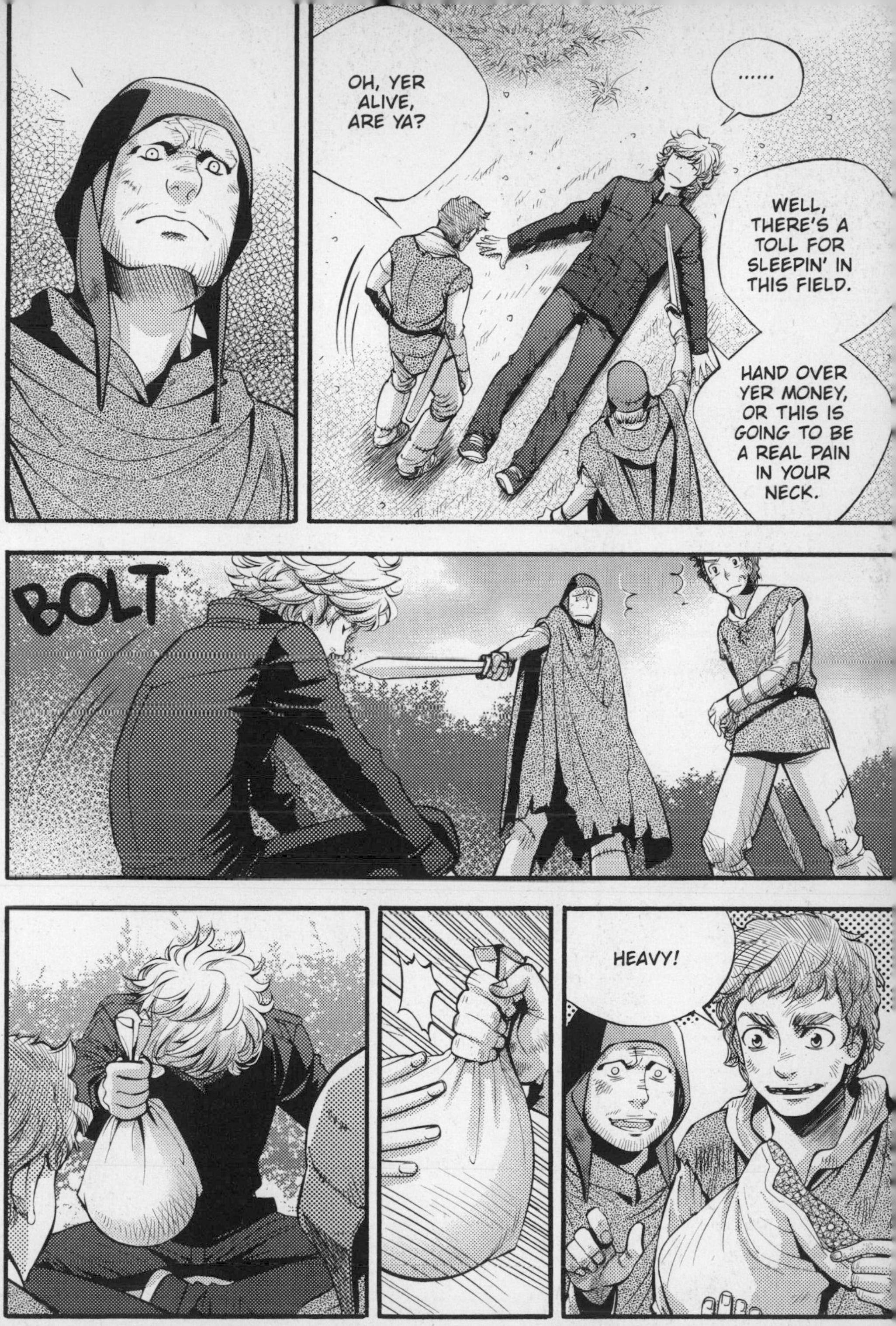
OH, YER ALIVE, ARE YA?
......
WELL, THERE'S A TOLL FOR SLEEPIN' IN THIS FIELD.
HAND OVER YER MONEY, OR THIS IS GOING TO BE A REAL PAIN IN YOUR NECK.
BOLT
HEAVY!

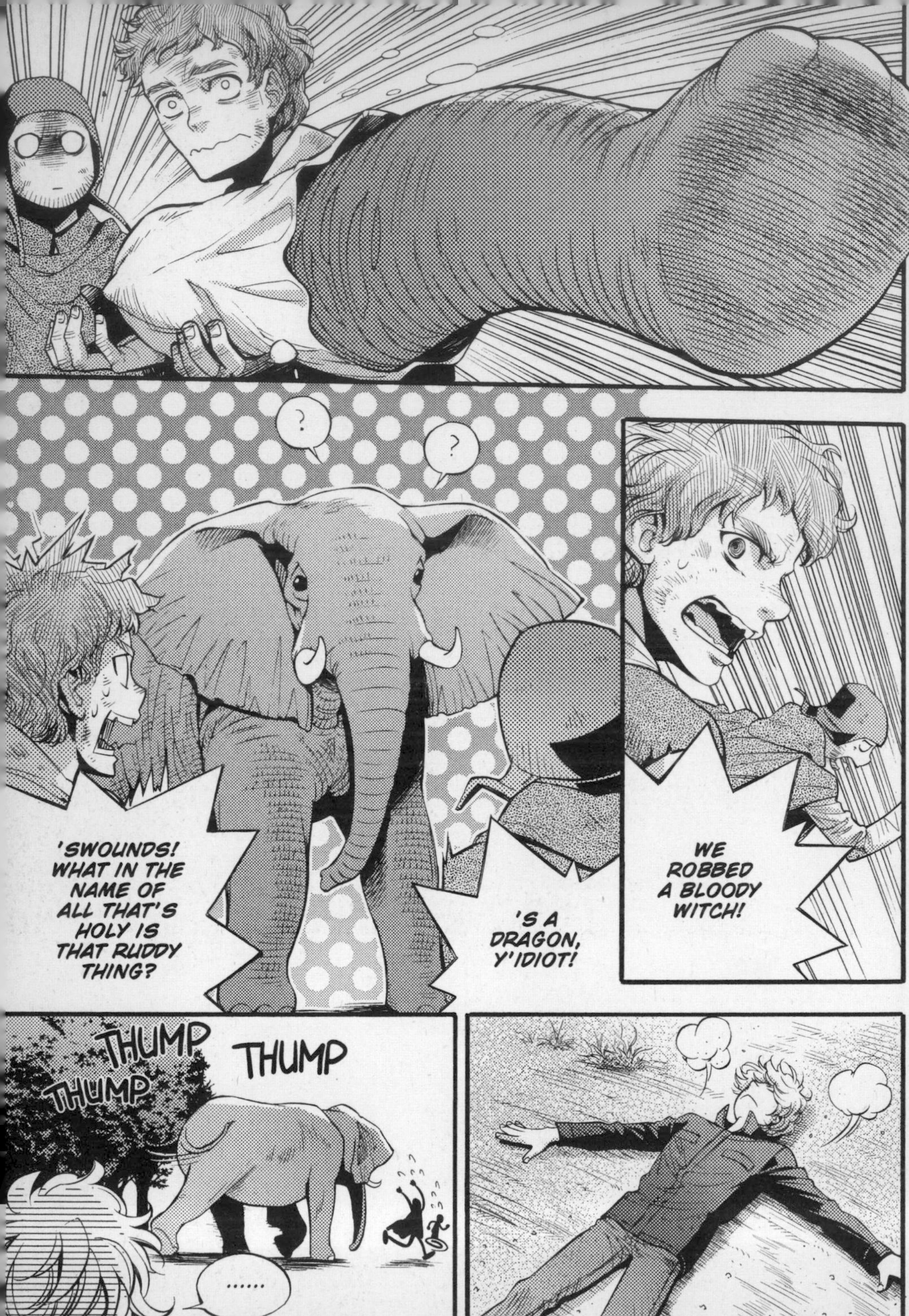
?
?
'SWOUNDS! WHAT IN THE NAME OF ALL THAT'S HOLY IS THAT RUDDY THING?
'S A DRAGON, Y'IDIOT!
WE ROBBED A BLOODY WITCH!
THUMP
THUMP
THUMP
......

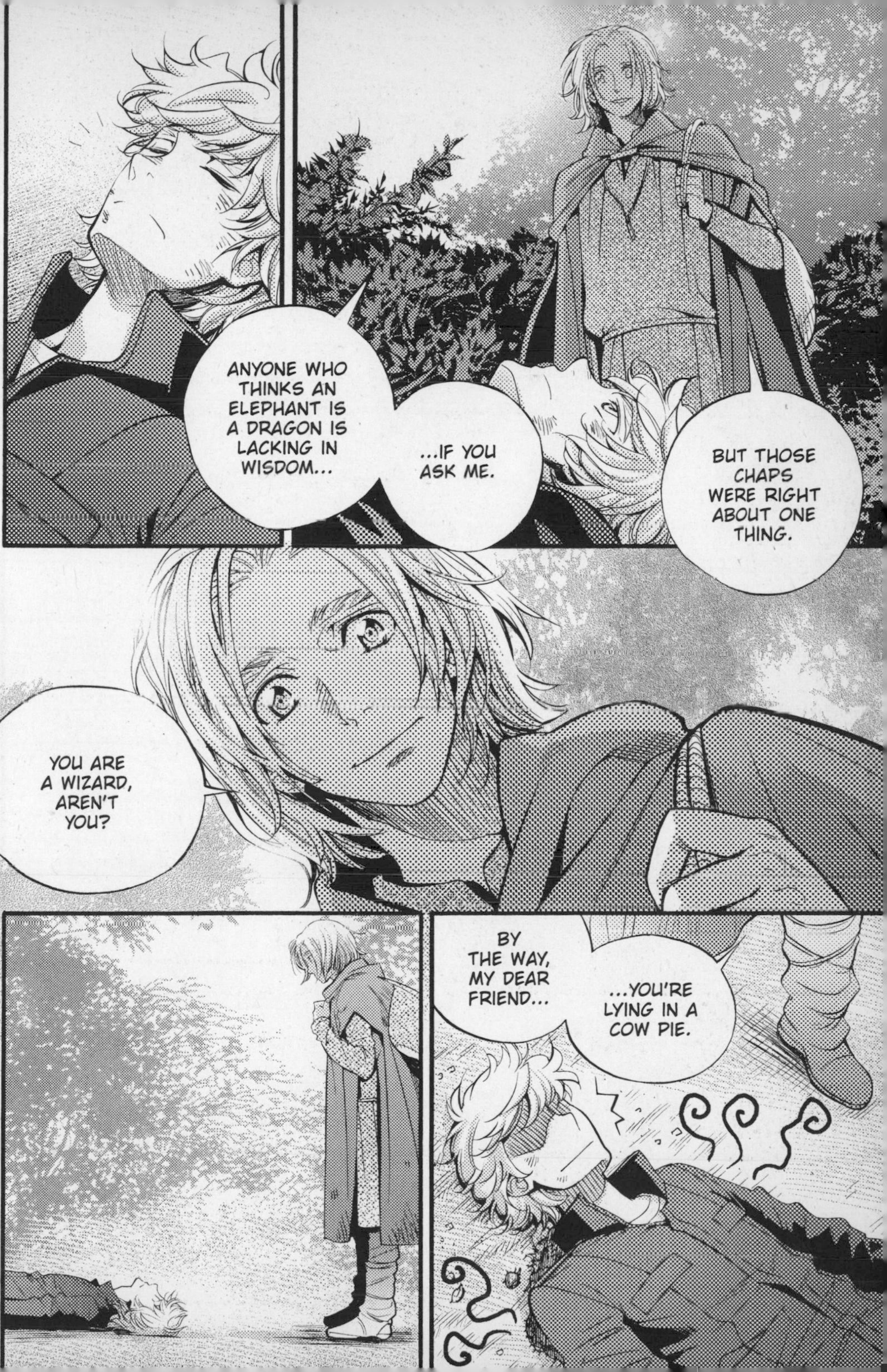
ANYONE WHO THINKS AN ELEPHANT IS A DRAGON IS LACKING IN WISDOM...
...IF YOU ASK ME.
BUT THOSE CHAPS WERE RIGHT ABOUT ONE THING.
YOU ARE A WIZARD, AREN'T YOU?
BY THE WAY, MY DEAR FRIEND...
...YOU'RE LYING IN A COW PIE.

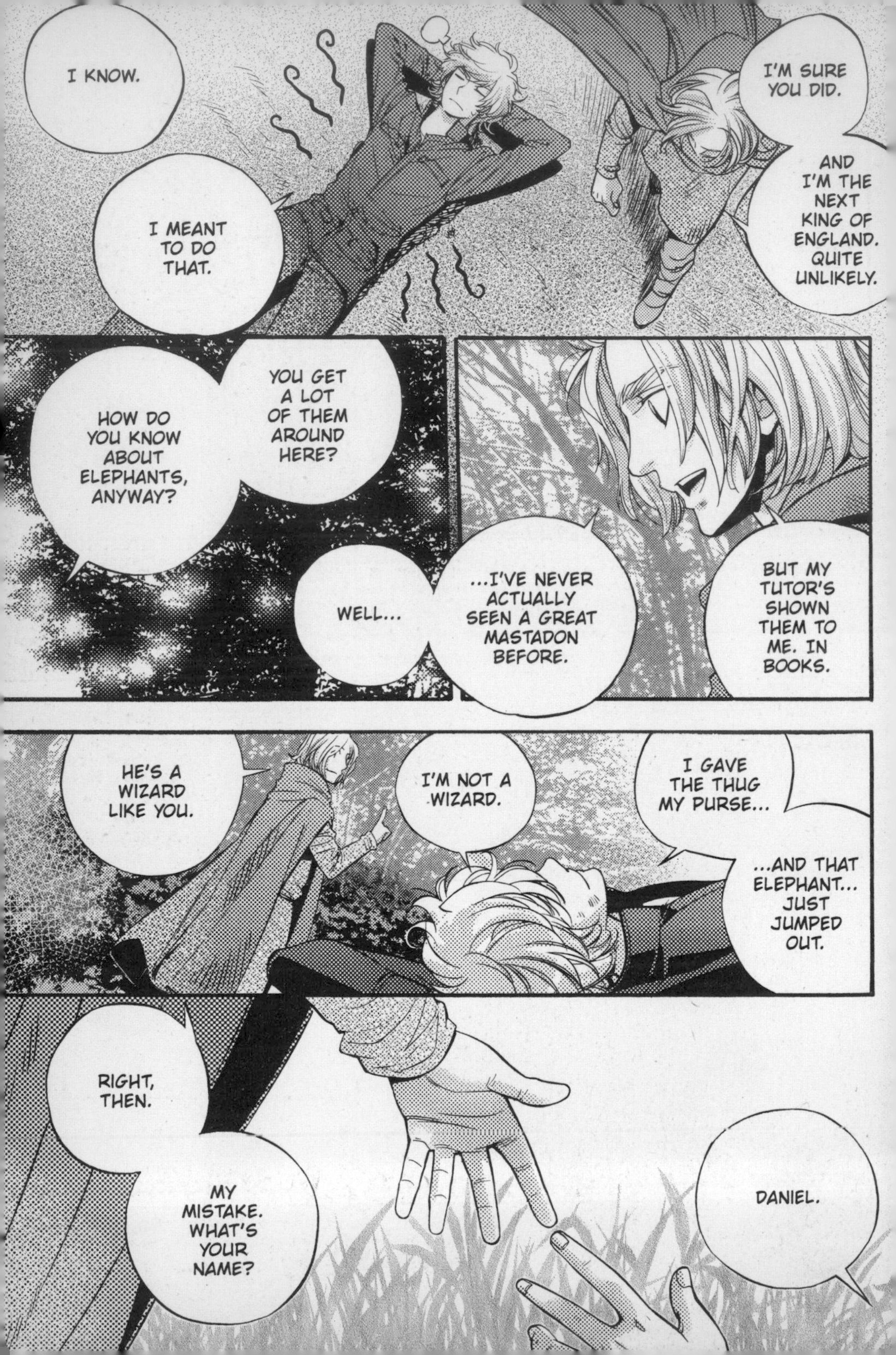
I KNOW.
I'M SURE YOU DID.
I MEANT TO DO THAT.
AND I'M THE NEXT KING OF ENGLAND. QUITE UNLIKELY.
HOW DO YOU KNOW ABOUT ELEPHANTS, ANYWAY?
YOU GET A LOT OF THEM AROUND HERE?
WELL...
...I'VE NEVER ACTUALLY SEEN A GREAT MASTADON BEFORE.
BUT MY TUTOR'S SHOWN THEM TO ME. IN BOOKS.
HE'S A WIZARD LIKE YOU.
I'M NOT A WIZARD.
I GAVE THE THUG MY PURSE...
...AND THAT ELEPHANT... JUST JUMPED OUT.
RIGHT, THEN.
MY MISTAKE. WHAT'S YOUR NAME?
DANIEL.

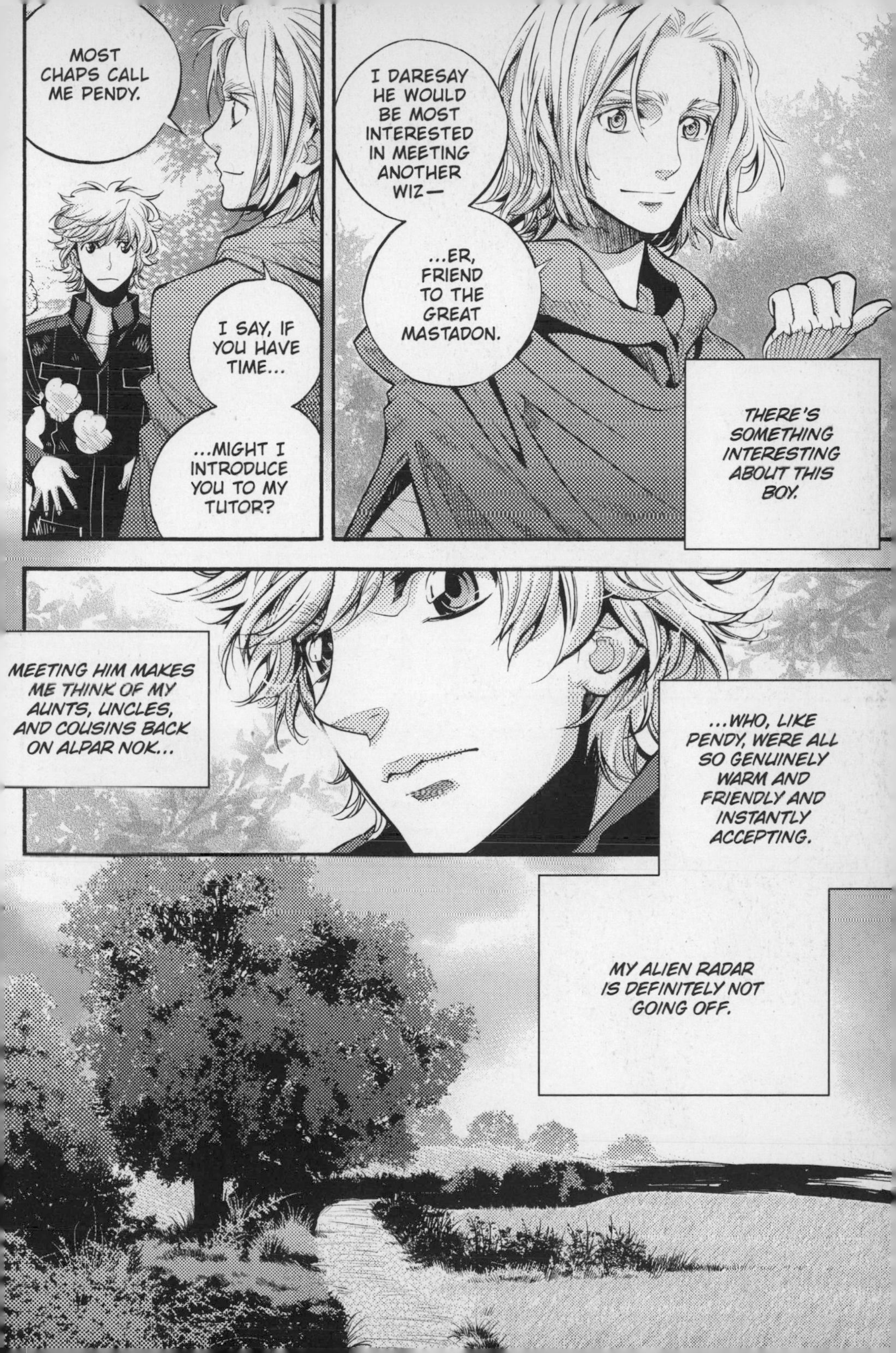
MOST CHAPS CALL ME PENDY.
I SAY, IF YOU HAVE TIME...
...MIGHT I INTRODUCE YOU TO MY TUTOR?
I DARESAY HE WOULD BE MOST INTERESTED IN MEETING ANOTHER WIZ—
...ER, FRIEND TO THE GREAT MASTADON.
THERE'S SOMETHING INTERESTING ABOUT THIS BOY.
MEETING HIM MAKES ME THINK OF MY AUNTS, UNCLES, AND COUSINS BACK ON ALPAR NOK...
...WHO, LIKE PENDY, WERE ALL SO GENUINELY WARM AND FRIENDLY AND INSTANTLY ACCEPTING.
MY ALIEN RADAR IS DEFINITELY NOT GOING OFF.

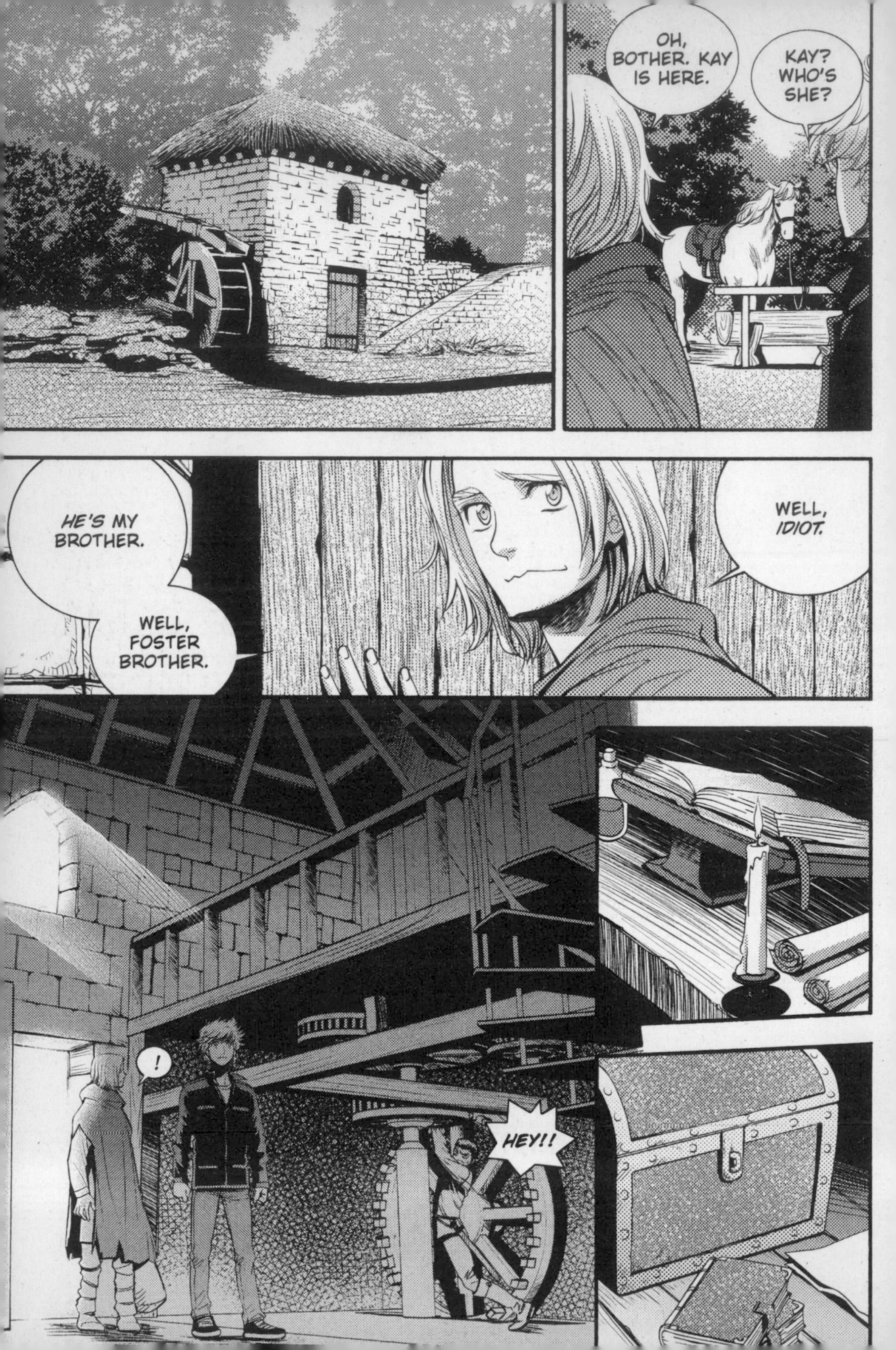
OH, BOTHER. KAY IS HERE.
KAY? WHO'S SHE?
HE'S MY BROTHER.
WELL, FOSTER BROTHER.
WELL, *IDIOT.*
!
HEY!!

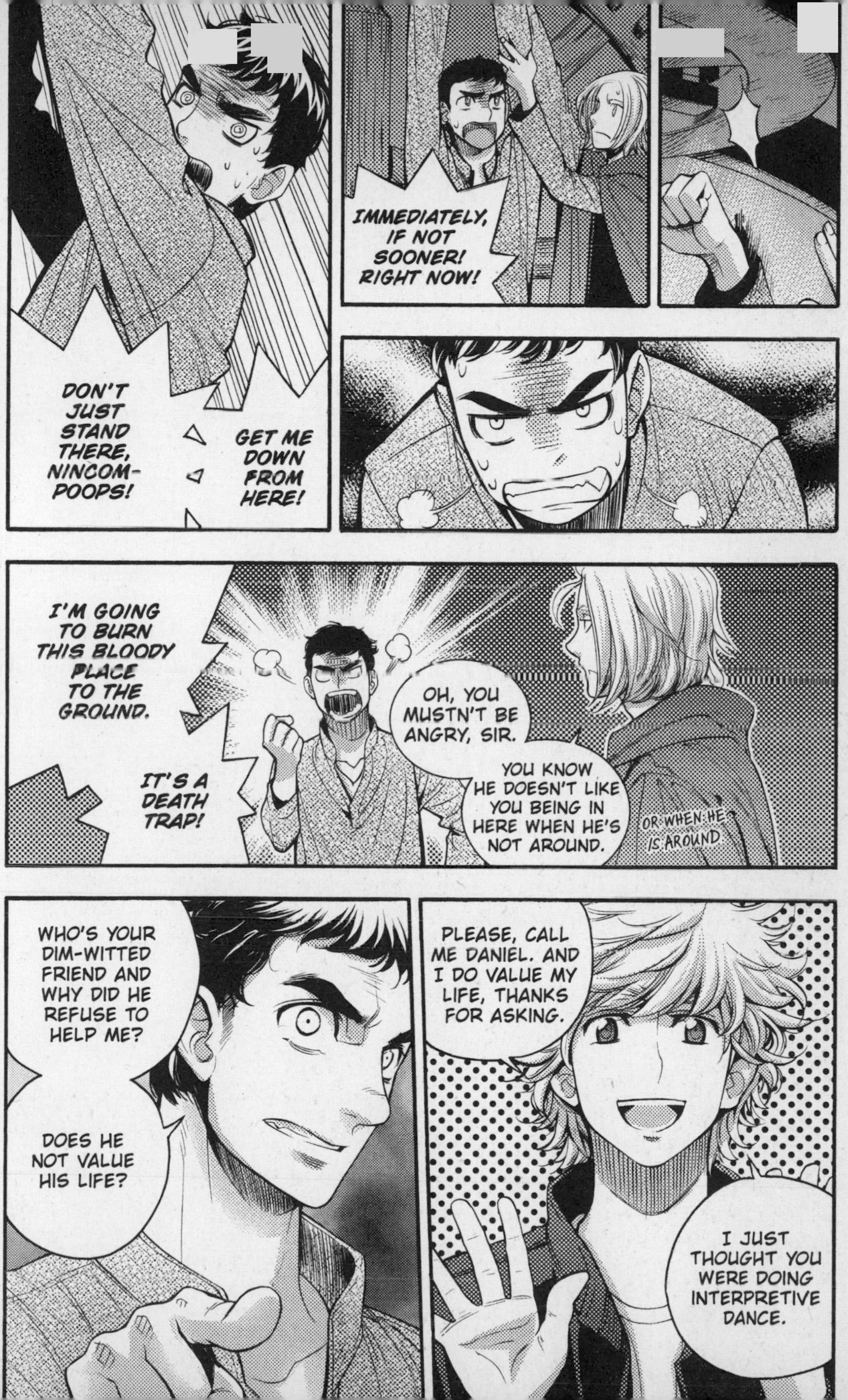
DON'T JUST STAND THERE, NINCOM-POOPS!
GET ME DOWN FROM HERE!
IMMEDIATELY, IF NOT SOONER! RIGHT NOW!
I'M GOING TO BURN THIS BLOODY PLACE TO THE GROUND.
IT'S A DEATH TRAP!
OH, YOU MUSTN'T BE ANGRY, SIR.
YOU KNOW HE DOESN'T LIKE YOU BEING IN HERE WHEN HE'S NOT AROUND.
OR WHEN HE IS AROUND.
WHO'S YOUR DIM-WITTED FRIEND AND WHY DID HE REFUSE TO HELP ME?
DOES HE NOT VALUE HIS LIFE?
PLEASE, CALL ME DANIEL. AND I DO VALUE MY LIFE, THANKS FOR ASKING.
I JUST THOUGHT YOU WERE DOING INTERPRETIVE DANCE.

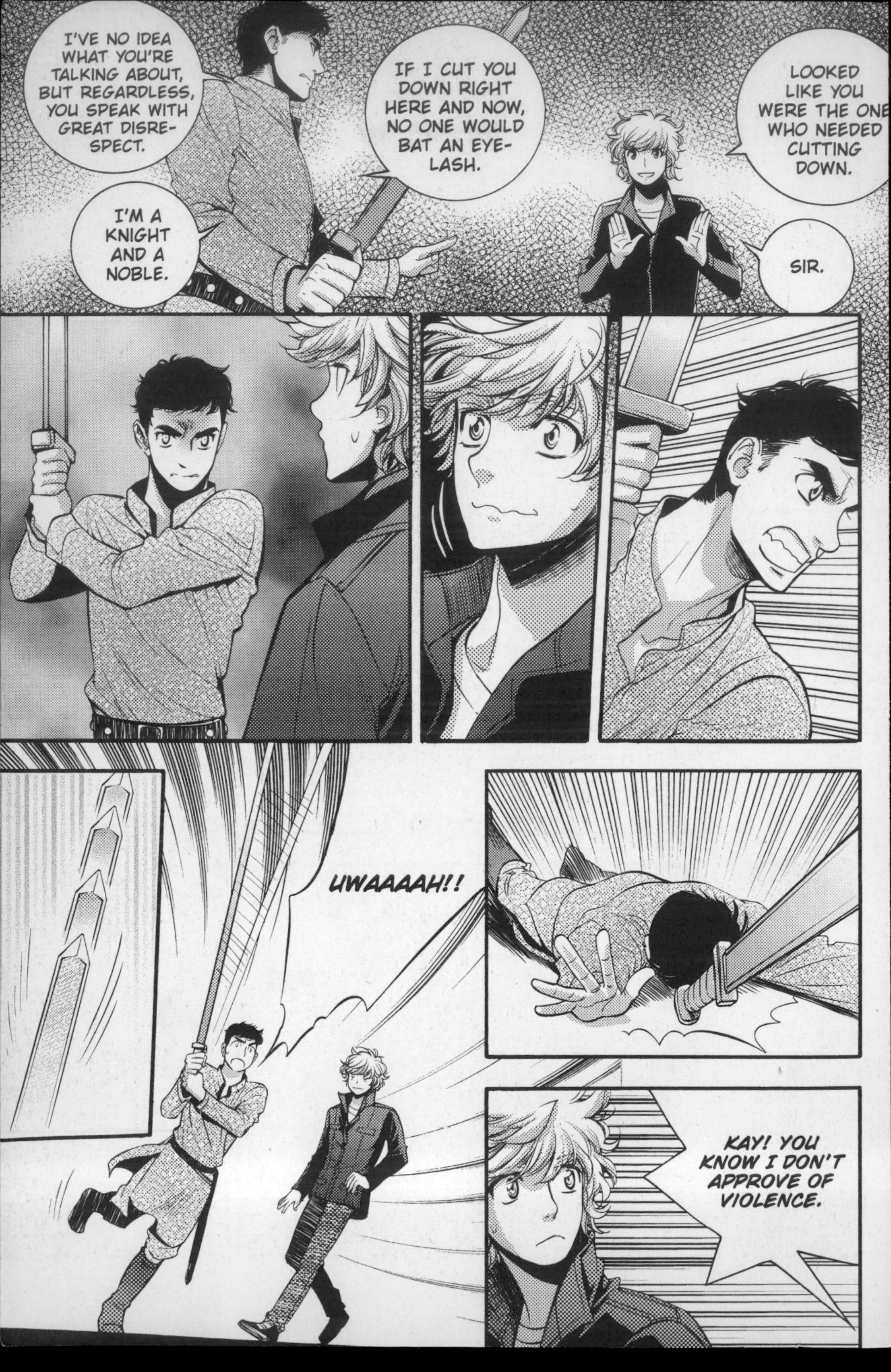
I'VE NO IDEA WHAT YOU'RE TALKING ABOUT, BUT REGARDLESS, YOU SPEAK WITH GREAT DISRE-SPECT.
I'M A KNIGHT AND A NOBLE.
IF I CUT YOU DOWN RIGHT HERE AND NOW, NO ONE WOULD BAT AN EYE-LASH.
LOOKED LIKE YOU WERE THE ONE WHO NEEDED CUTTING DOWN.
SIR.
UWAAAAH!!
KAY! YOU KNOW I DON'T APPROVE OF VIOLENCE.

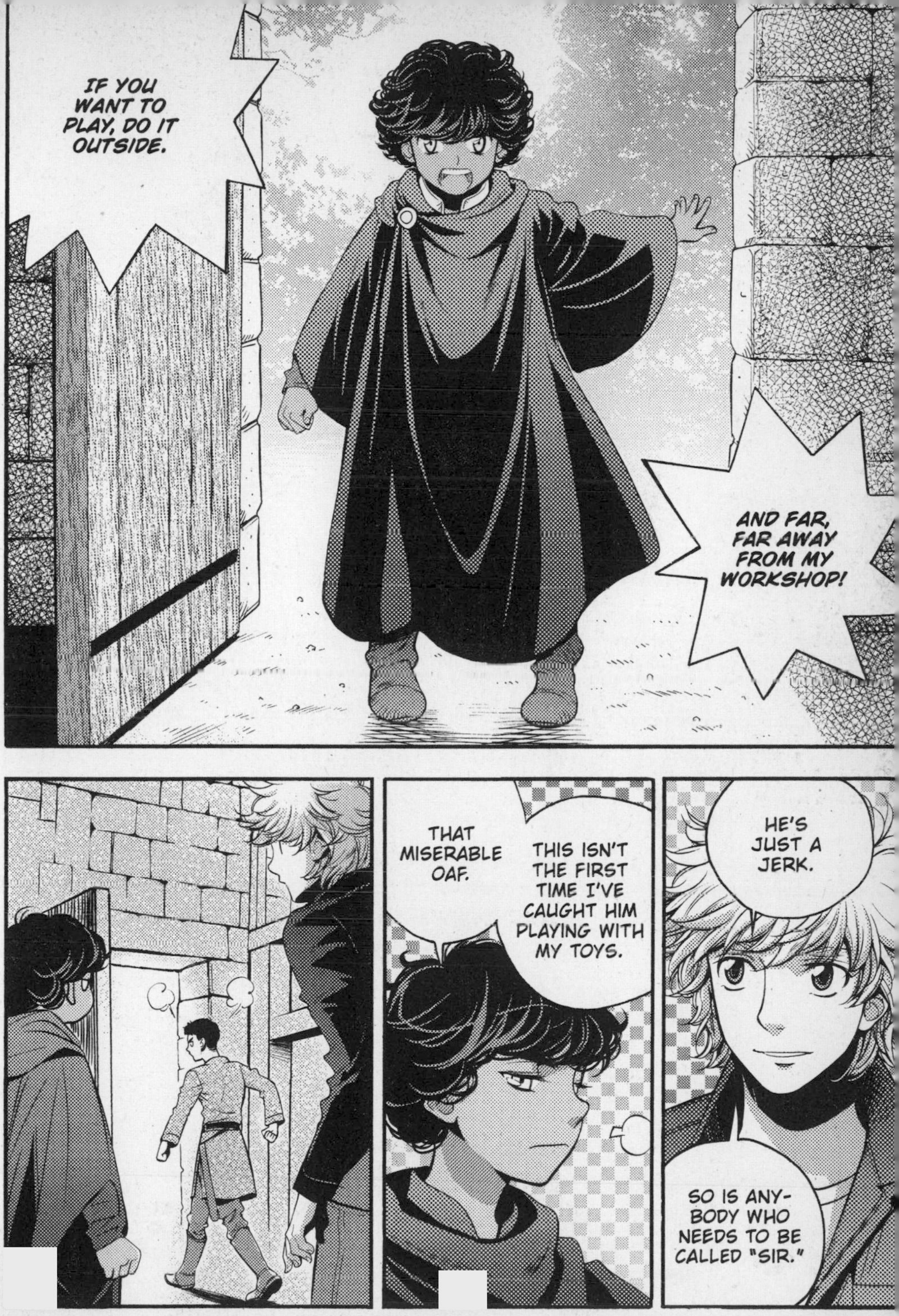
IF YOU WANT TO PLAY, DO IT OUTSIDE.
AND FAR, FAR AWAY FROM MY WORKSHOP!
THAT MISERABLE OAF.
THIS ISN'T THE FIRST TIME I'VE CAUGHT HIM PLAYING WITH MY TOYS.
HE'S JUST A JERK.
SO IS ANY-BODY WHO NEEDS TO BE CALLED "SIR."

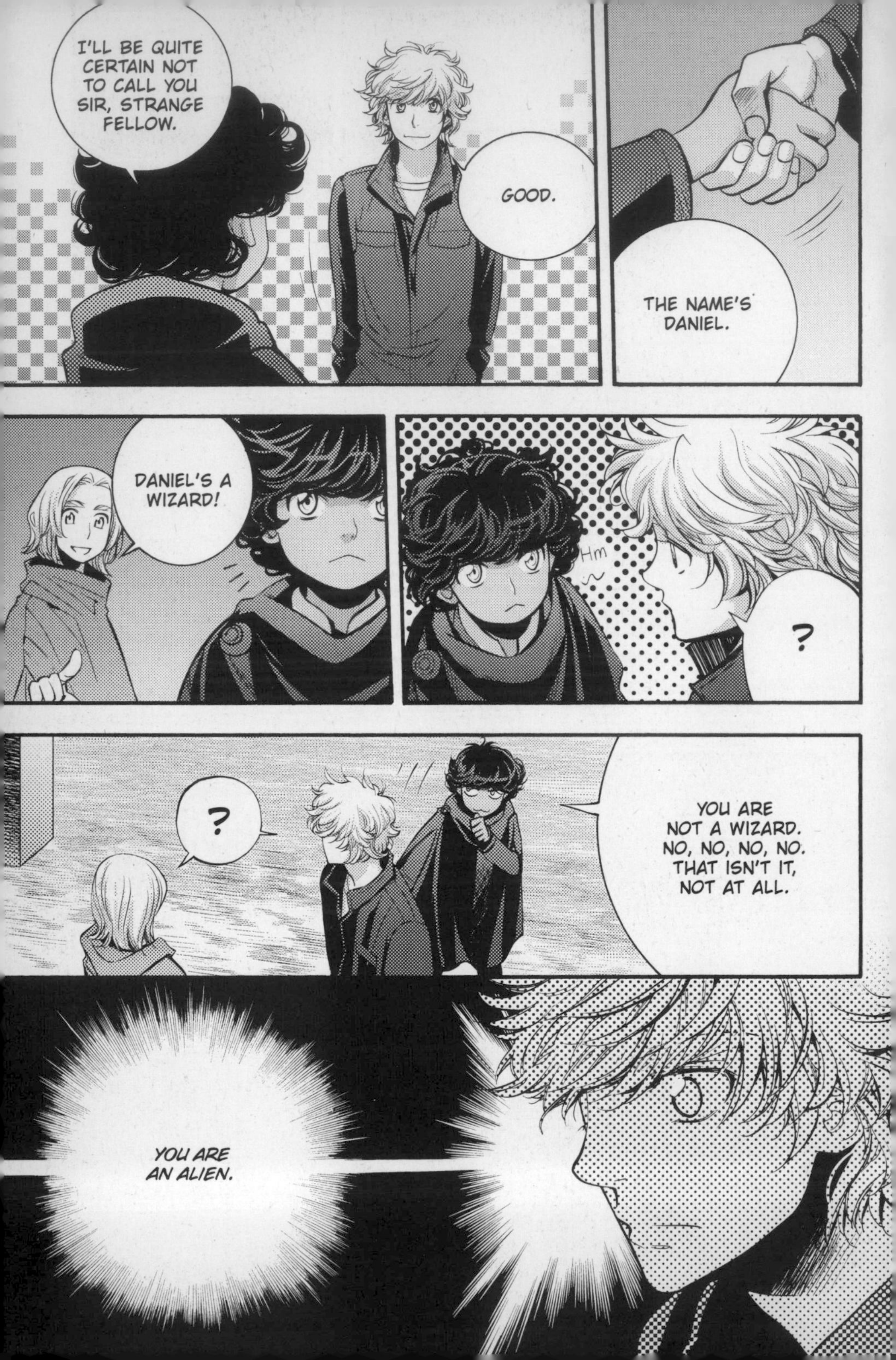
I'LL BE QUITE CERTAIN NOT TO CALL YOU SIR, STRANGE FELLOW.
GOOD.
THE NAME'S DANIEL.
DANIEL'S A WIZARD!
Hm
?
?
YOU ARE NOT A WIZARD. NO, NO, NO, NO. THAT ISN'T IT, NOT AT ALL.
YOU ARE AN ALIEN.

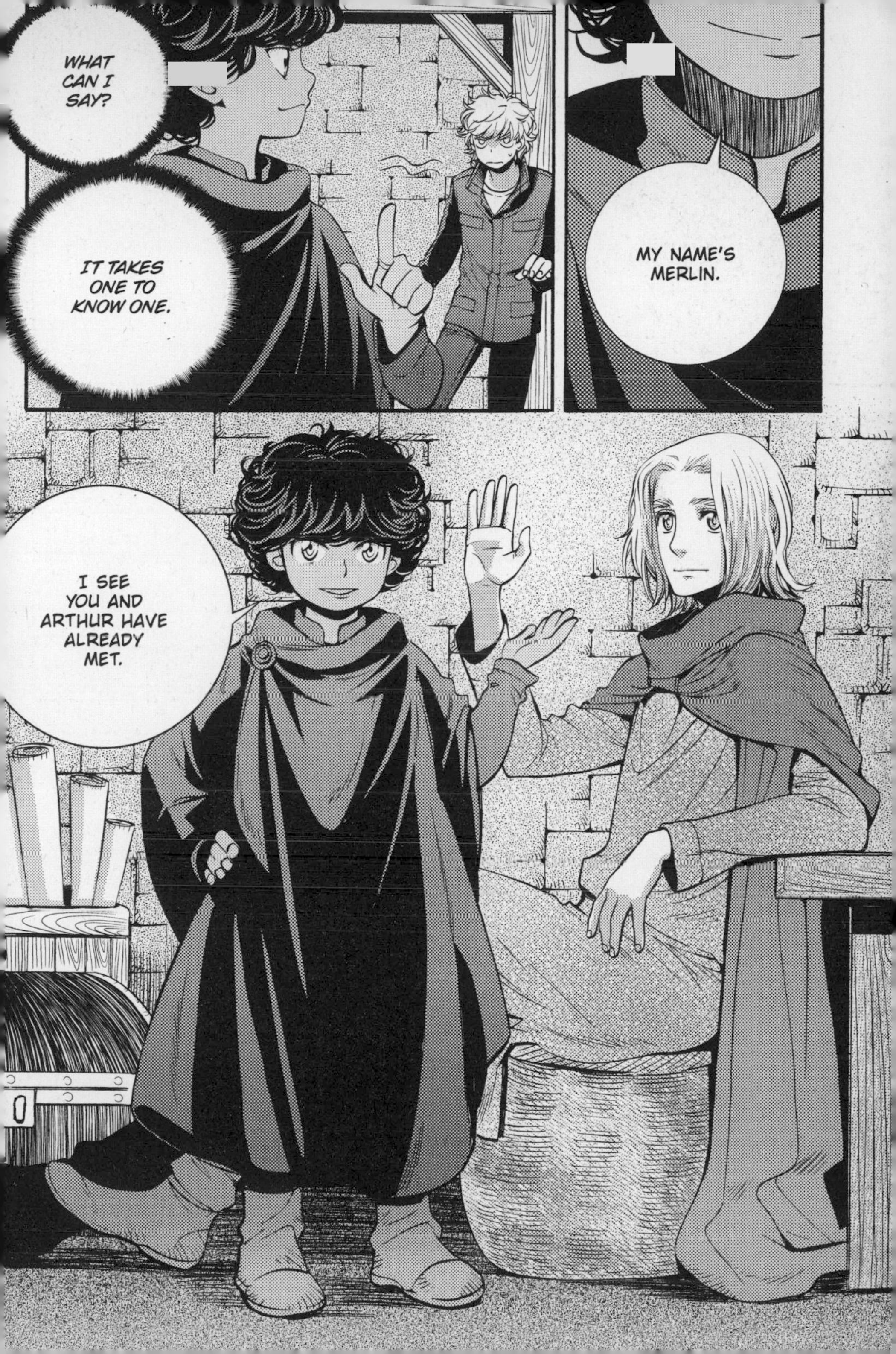

WHAT CAN I SAY?
IT TAKES ONE TO KNOW ONE.
MY NAME'S MERLIN.
I SEE YOU AND ARTHUR HAVE ALREADY MET.

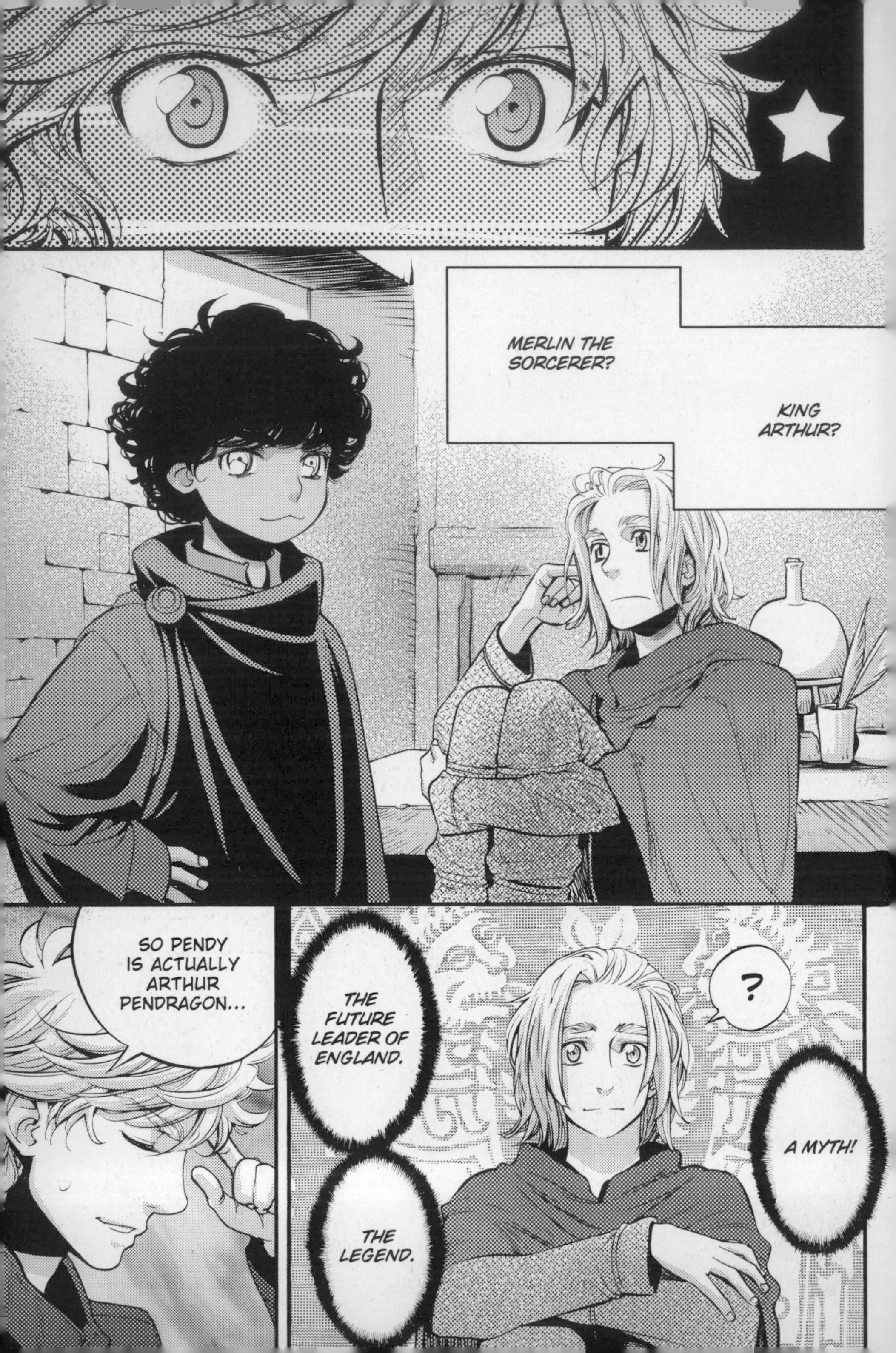
MERLIN THE SORCERER?
KING ARTHUR?
SO PENDY IS ACTUALLY ARTHUR PENDRAGON...
THE FUTURE LEADER OF ENGLAND.
THE LEGEND.
?
A MYTH!

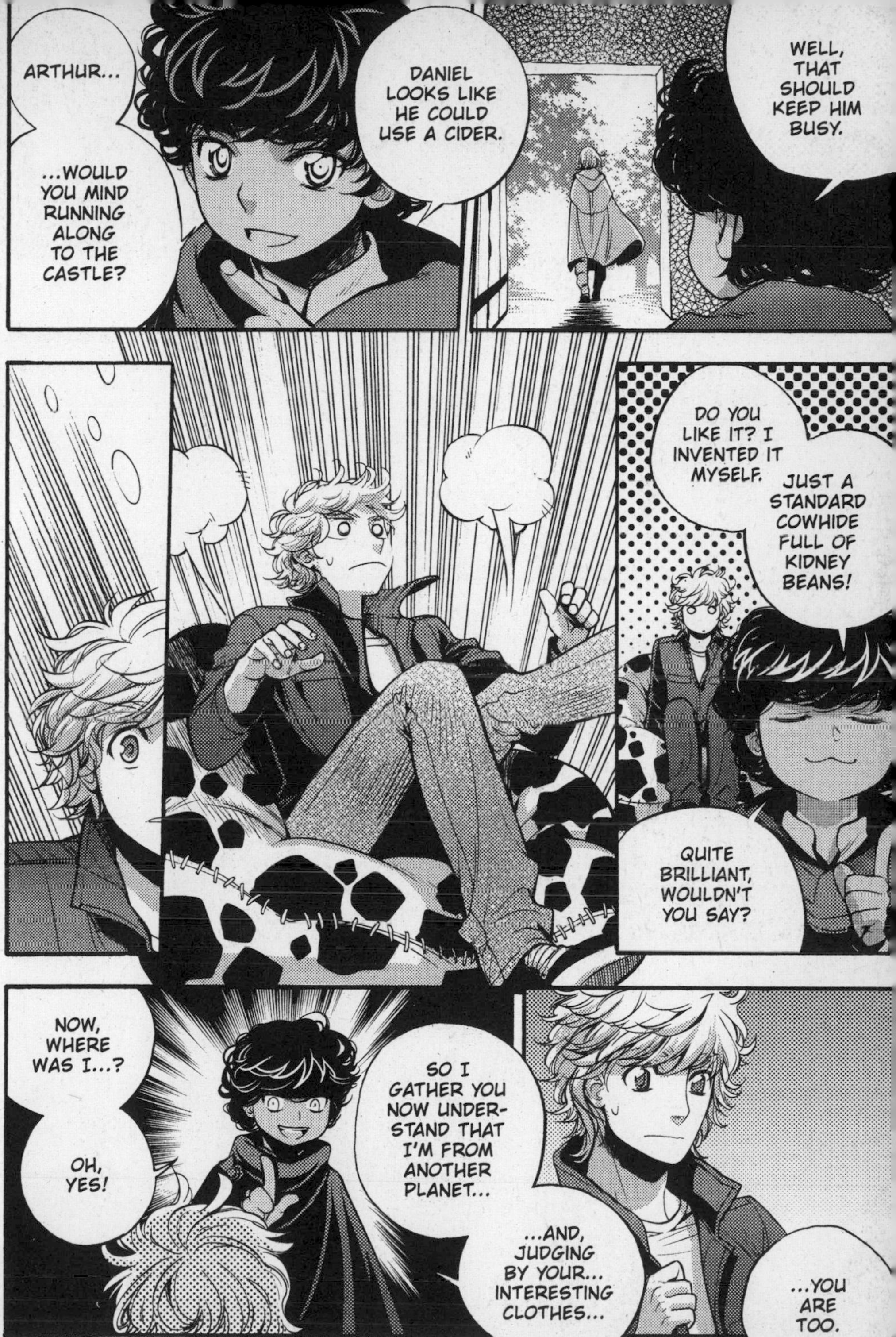
ARTHUR...
...WOULD YOU MIND RUNNING ALONG TO THE CASTLE?
DANIEL LOOKS LIKE HE COULD USE A CIDER.
WELL, THAT SHOULD KEEP HIM BUSY.
DO YOU LIKE IT? I INVENTED IT MYSELF.
JUST A STANDARD COWHIDE FULL OF KIDNEY BEANS!
QUITE BRILLIANT, WOULDN'T YOU SAY?
NOW, WHERE WAS I...?
OH, YES!
SO I GATHER YOU NOW UNDER-STAND THAT I'M FROM ANOTHER PLANET...
...AND, JUDGING BY YOUR... INTERESTING CLOTHES...
...YOU ARE TOO.

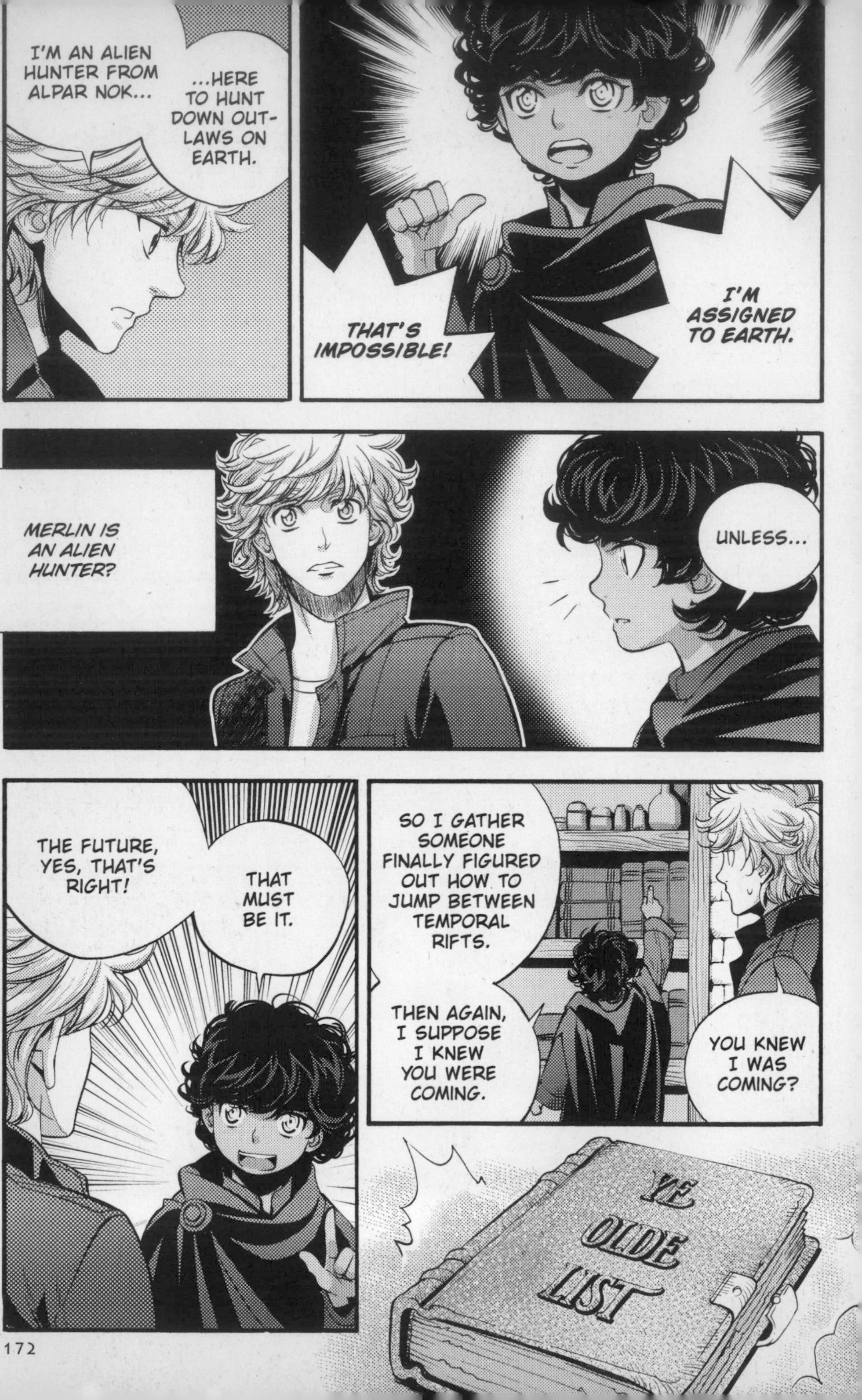
I'M AN ALIEN HUNTER FROM ALPAR NOK...
...HERE TO HUNT DOWN OUT-LAWS ON EARTH.
THAT'S IMPOSSIBLE!
I'M ASSIGNED TO EARTH.
MERLIN IS AN ALIEN HUNTER?
UNLESS...
THE FUTURE, YES, THAT'S RIGHT!
THAT MUST BE IT.
SO I GATHER SOMEONE FINALLY FIGURED OUT HOW TO JUMP BETWEEN TEMPORAL RIFTS.
THEN AGAIN, I SUPPOSE I KNEW YOU WERE COMING.
YOU KNEW I WAS COMING?
YE OLDE LIST

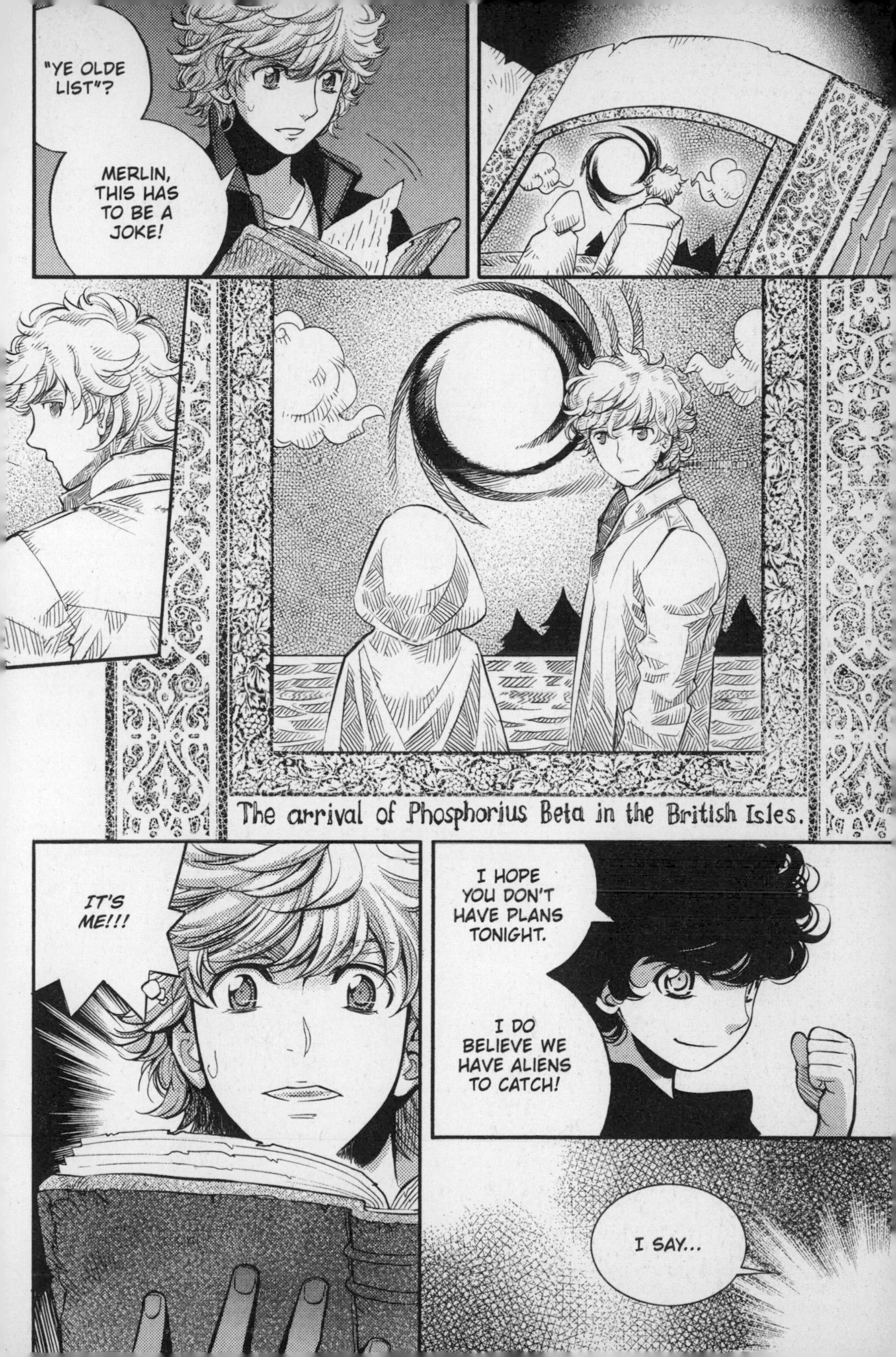
"YE OLDE LIST"?
MERLIN, THIS HAS TO BE A JOKE!
The arrival of Phosphorius Beta in the British Isles.
IT'S ME!!!
I HOPE YOU DON'T HAVE PLANS TONIGHT.
I DO BELIEVE WE HAVE ALIENS TO CATCH!
I SAY...

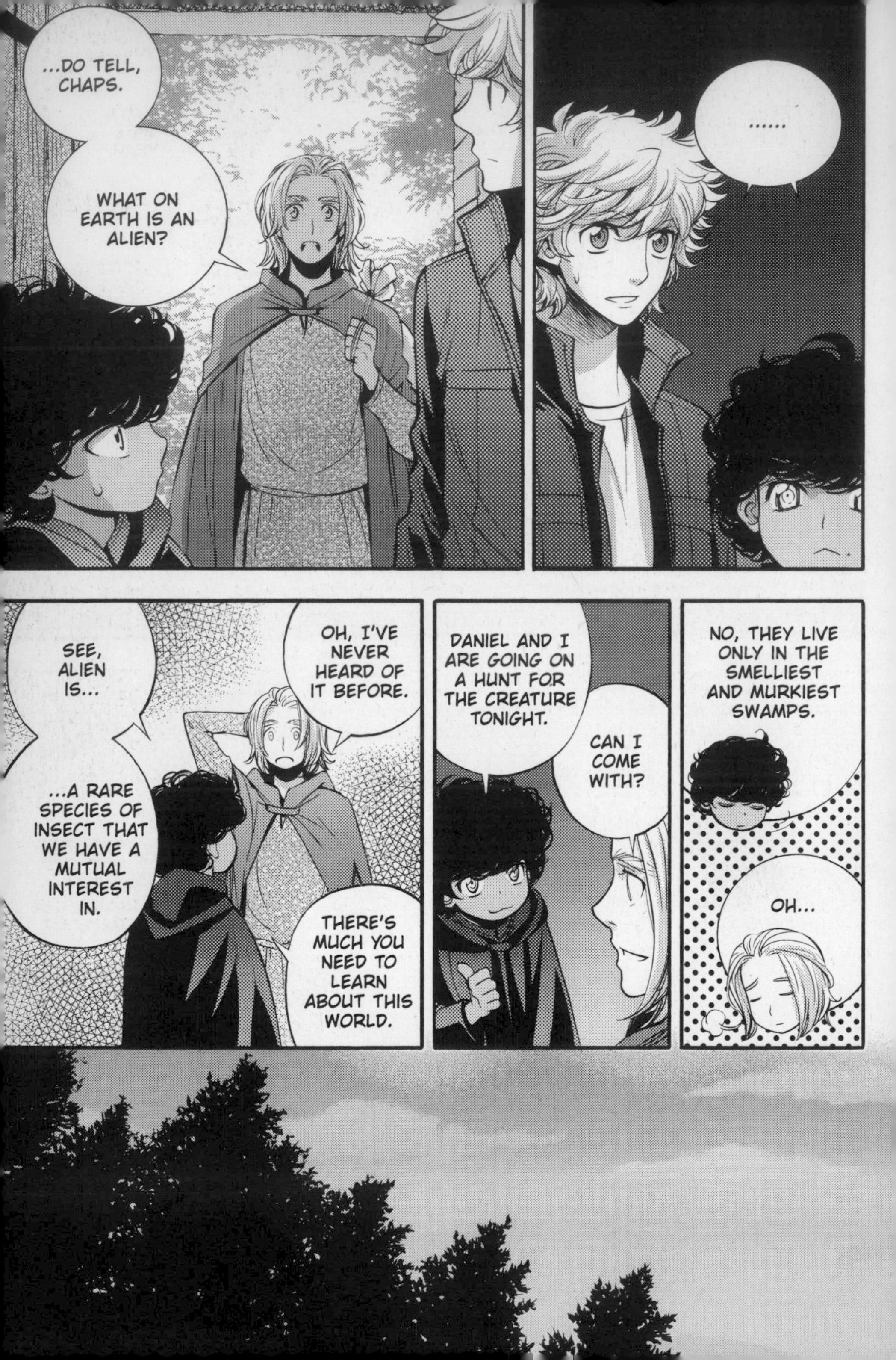
...DO TELL, CHAPS.
WHAT ON EARTH IS AN ALIEN?
......
SEE, ALIEN IS...
...A RARE SPECIES OF INSECT THAT WE HAVE A MUTUAL INTEREST IN.
OH, I'VE NEVER HEARD OF IT BEFORE.
THERE'S MUCH YOU NEED TO LEARN ABOUT THIS WORLD.
DANIEL AND I ARE GOING ON A HUNT FOR THE CREATURE TONIGHT.
CAN I COME WITH?
NO, THEY LIVE ONLY IN THE SMELLIEST AND MURKIEST SWAMPS.
OH...

NOW, THEN. YOU MUST KNOW A GREAT DEAL ABOUT BETA.

YOU CAME ALL THE WAY HERE TO HELP ME, DID YOU NOT?

WE'VE MET, YEAH.

ACTUALLY, I CAME BACK IN TIME TO HELP ME.

RIGHT, THEN. I PRESUME YOU KNOW BETA'S HISTORY?

I KNOW THAT HE'LL BE HERE IN ENGLAND FOR ANOTHER FOURTEEN HUNDRED YEARS.

AND THAT HE WON'T BE FINISHED UNTIL EVERYTHING ON EARTH IS ASH.

YOU MEAN THERE'S MORE?

AH, THAT'S NOT THE HALF OF IT, DANIEL THE TRAVELER.

IT SOUNDS LIKE THEY SENT YOU UN-PREPARED...

...WITH NO CHEAT SHEET.

THIS ISN'T GOOD, NOT GOOD AT ALL.

BUT THE LESSON WILL HAVE TO WAIT. WE'RE HERE.

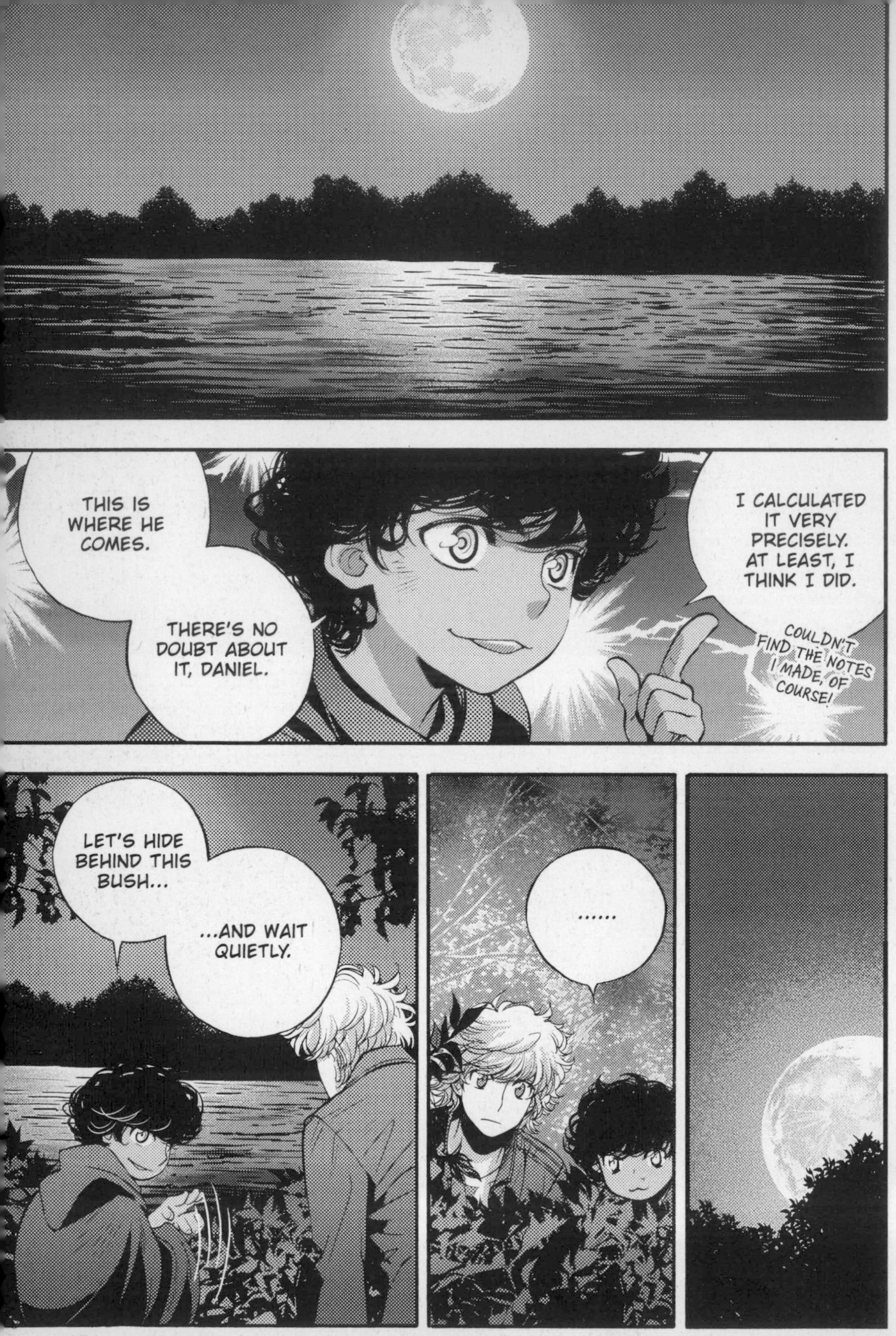
THIS IS WHERE HE COMES.
THERE'S NO DOUBT ABOUT IT, DANIEL.
I CALCULATED IT VERY PRECISELY. AT LEAST, I THINK I DID.
COULDN'T FIND THE NOTES I MADE, OF COURSE!
LET'S HIDE BEHIND THIS BUSH...
...AND WAIT QUIETLY.
......

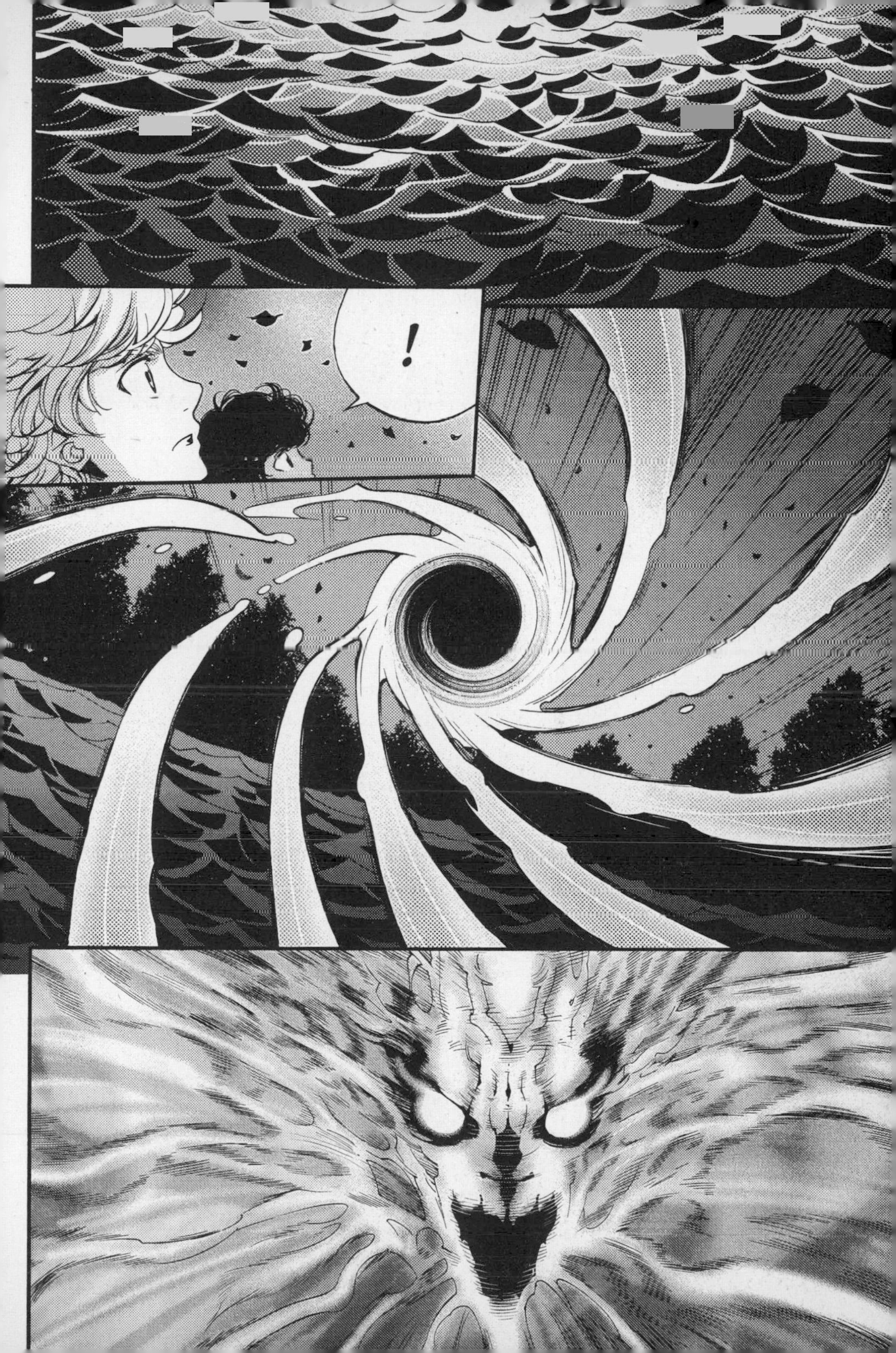
!

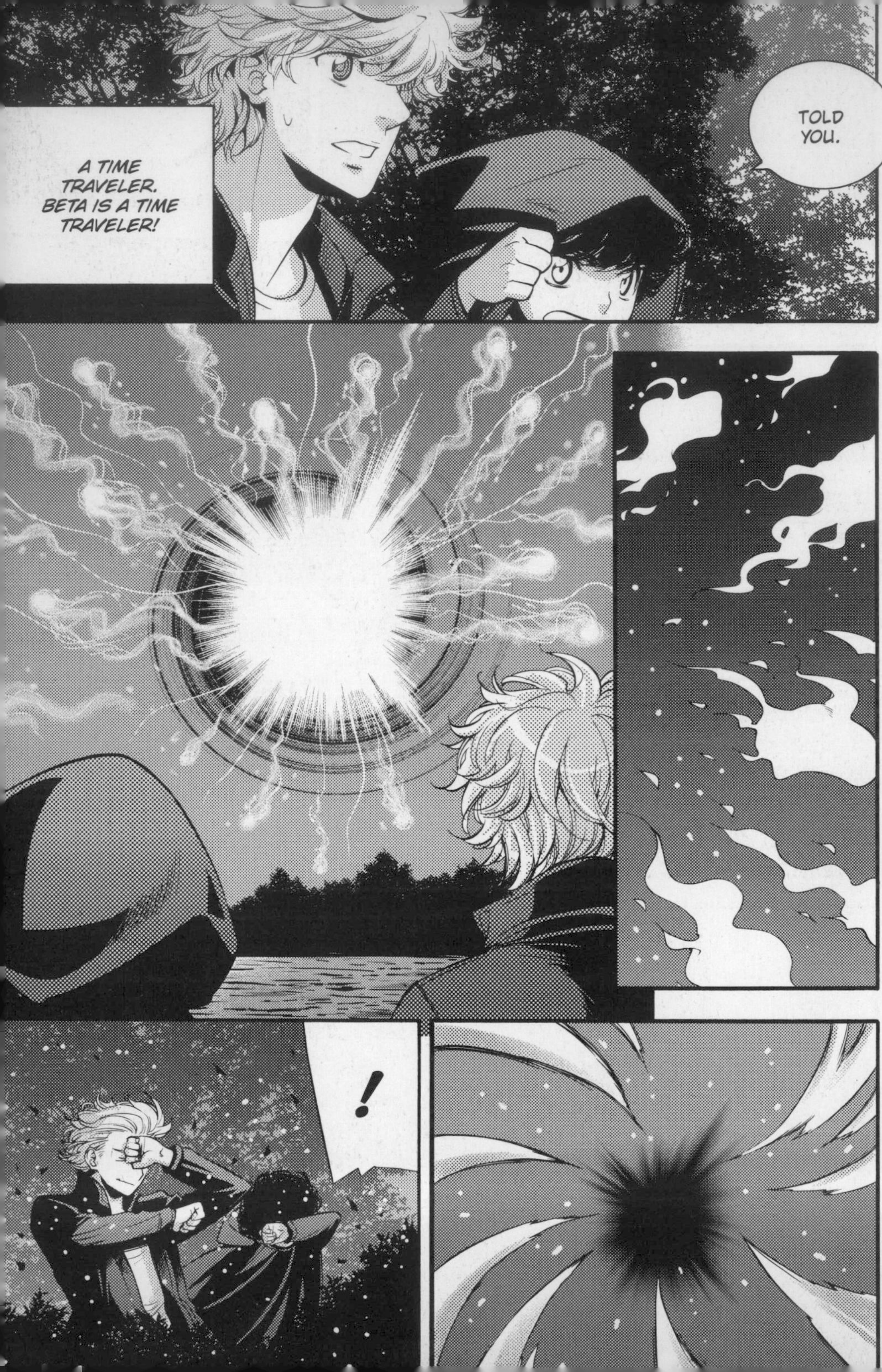
A TIME TRAVELER. BETA IS A TIME TRAVELER!
TOLD YOU.
!

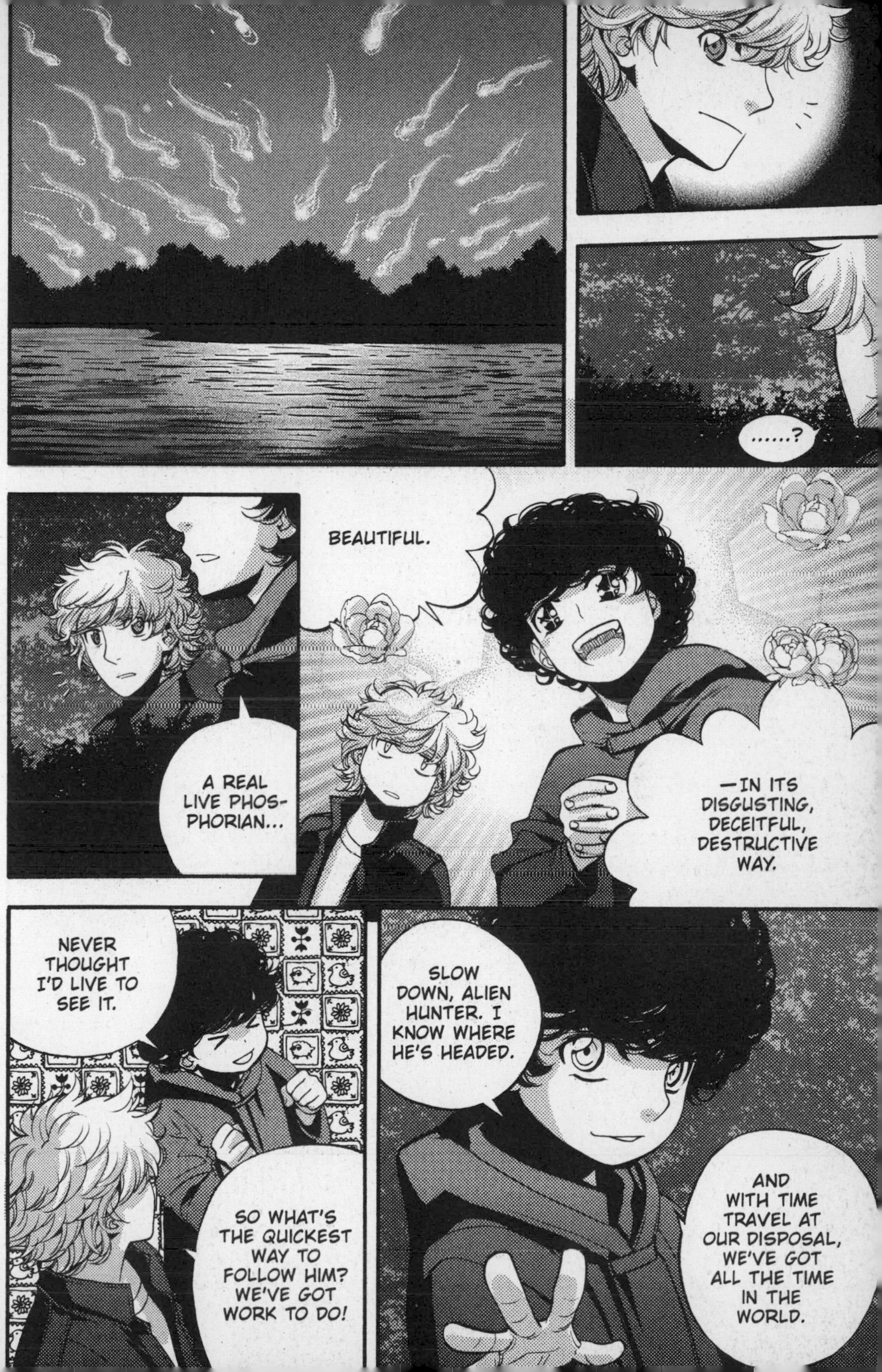
......?
A REAL LIVE PHOS- PHORIAN...
BEAUTIFUL.
—IN ITS DISGUSTING, DECEITFUL, DESTRUCTIVE WAY.
NEVER THOUGHT I'D LIVE TO SEE IT.
SO WHAT'S THE QUICKEST WAY TO FOLLOW HIM? WE'VE GOT WORK TO DO!
SLOW DOWN, ALIEN HUNTER. I KNOW WHERE HE'S HEADED.
AND WITH TIME TRAVEL AT OUR DISPOSAL, WE'VE GOT ALL THE TIME IN THE WORLD.

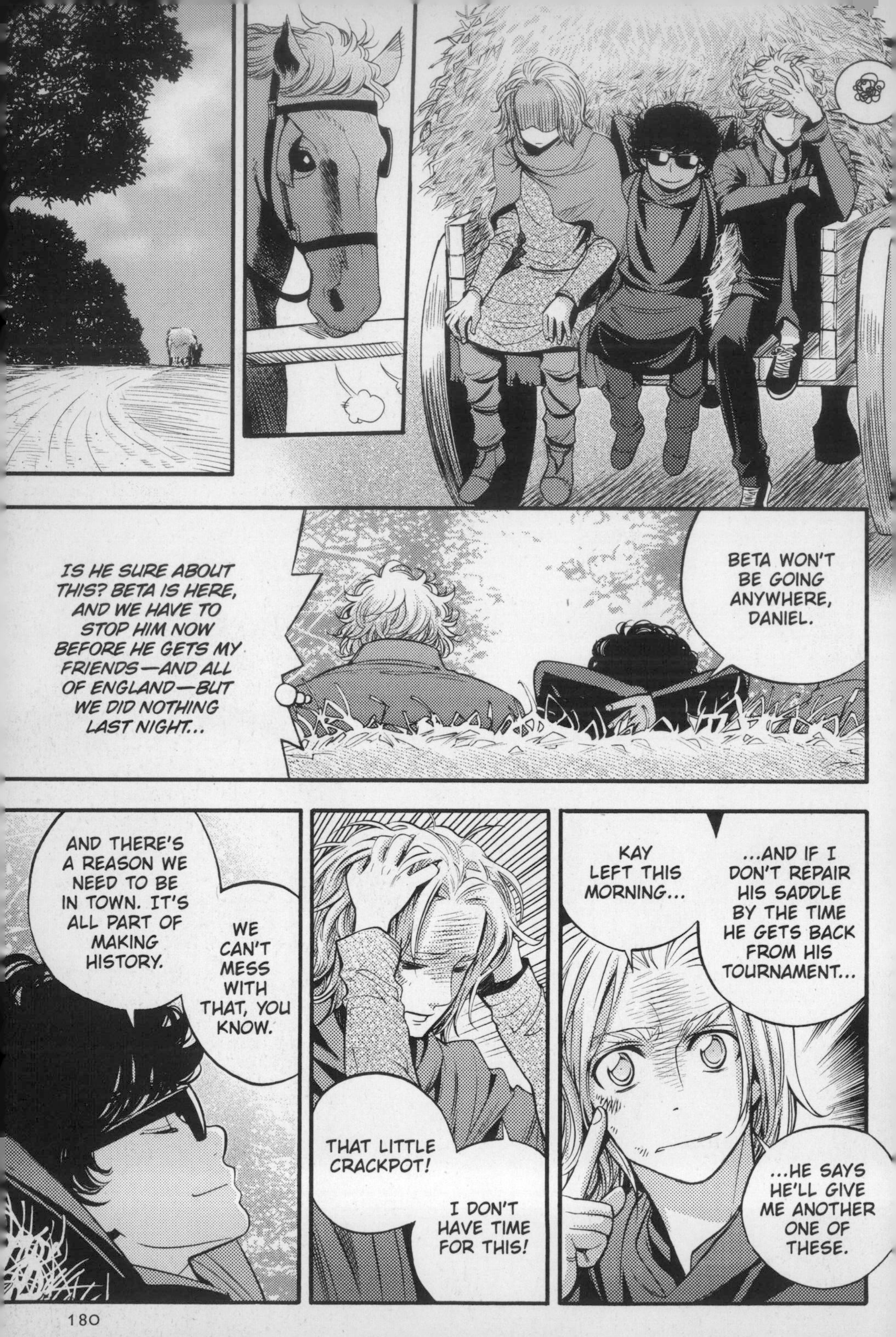

IS HE SURE ABOUT THIS? BETA IS HERE, AND WE HAVE TO STOP HIM NOW BEFORE HE GETS MY FRIENDS—AND ALL OF ENGLAND—BUT WE DID NOTHING LAST NIGHT...
BETA WON'T BE GOING ANYWHERE, DANIEL.
AND THERE'S A REASON WE NEED TO BE IN TOWN. IT'S ALL PART OF MAKING HISTORY.
WE CAN'T MESS WITH THAT, YOU KNOW.
THAT LITTLE CRACKPOT!
I DON'T HAVE TIME FOR THIS!
KAY LEFT THIS MORNING...
...AND IF I DON'T REPAIR HIS SADDLE BY THE TIME HE GETS BACK FROM HIS TOURNAMENT...
...HE SAYS HE'LL GIVE ME ANOTHER ONE OF THESE.

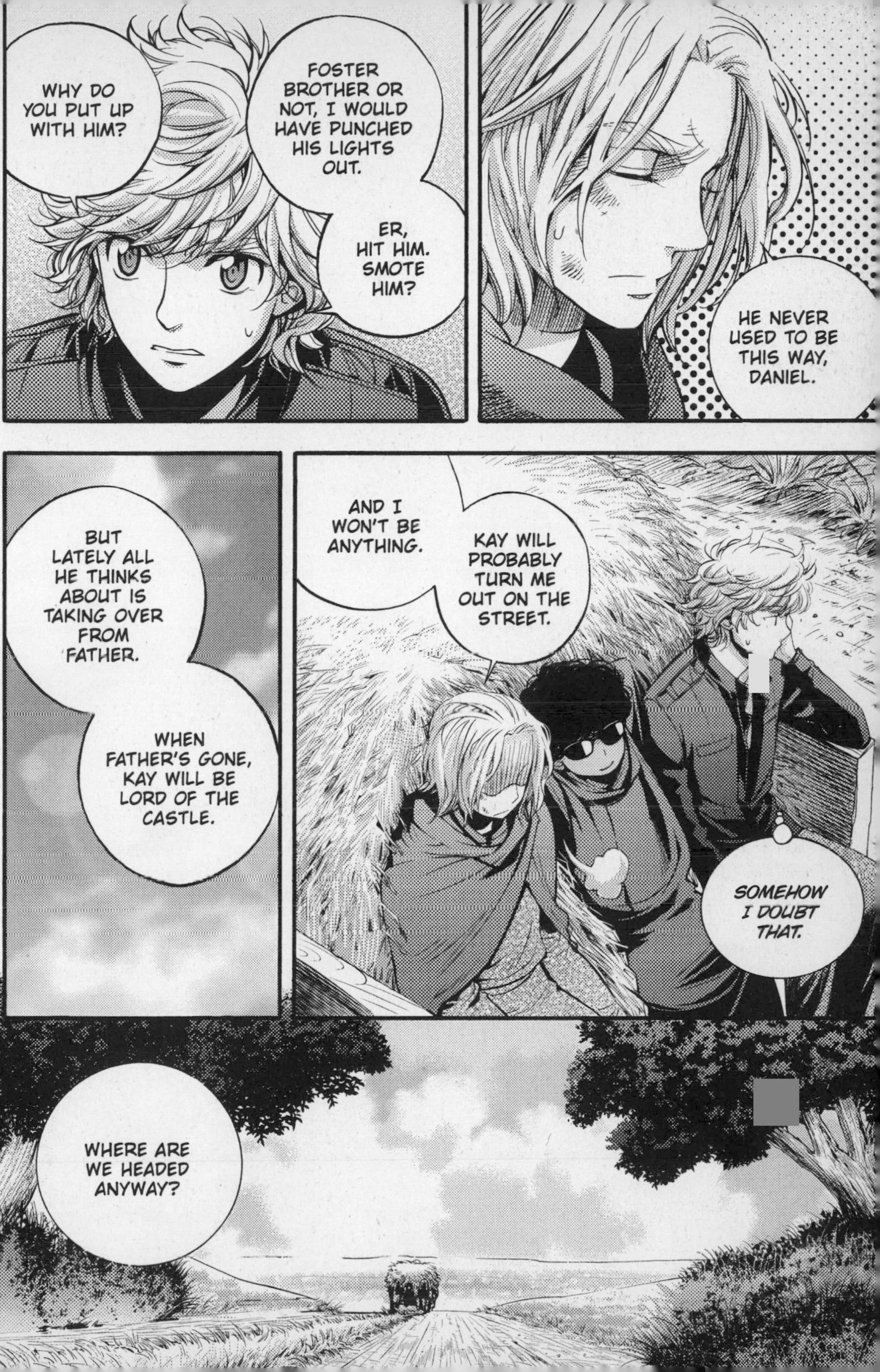
WHY DO YOU PUT UP WITH HIM?
FOSTER BROTHER OR NOT, I WOULD HAVE PUNCHED HIS LIGHTS OUT.
ER, HIT HIM. SMOTE HIM?
HE NEVER USED TO BE THIS WAY, DANIEL.
BUT LATELY ALL HE THINKS ABOUT IS TAKING OVER FROM FATHER.
WHEN FATHER'S GONE, KAY WILL BE LORD OF THE CASTLE.
AND I WON'T BE ANYTHING.
KAY WILL PROBABLY TURN ME OUT ON THE STREET.
SOMEHOW I DOUBT THAT.
WHERE ARE WE HEADED ANYWAY?

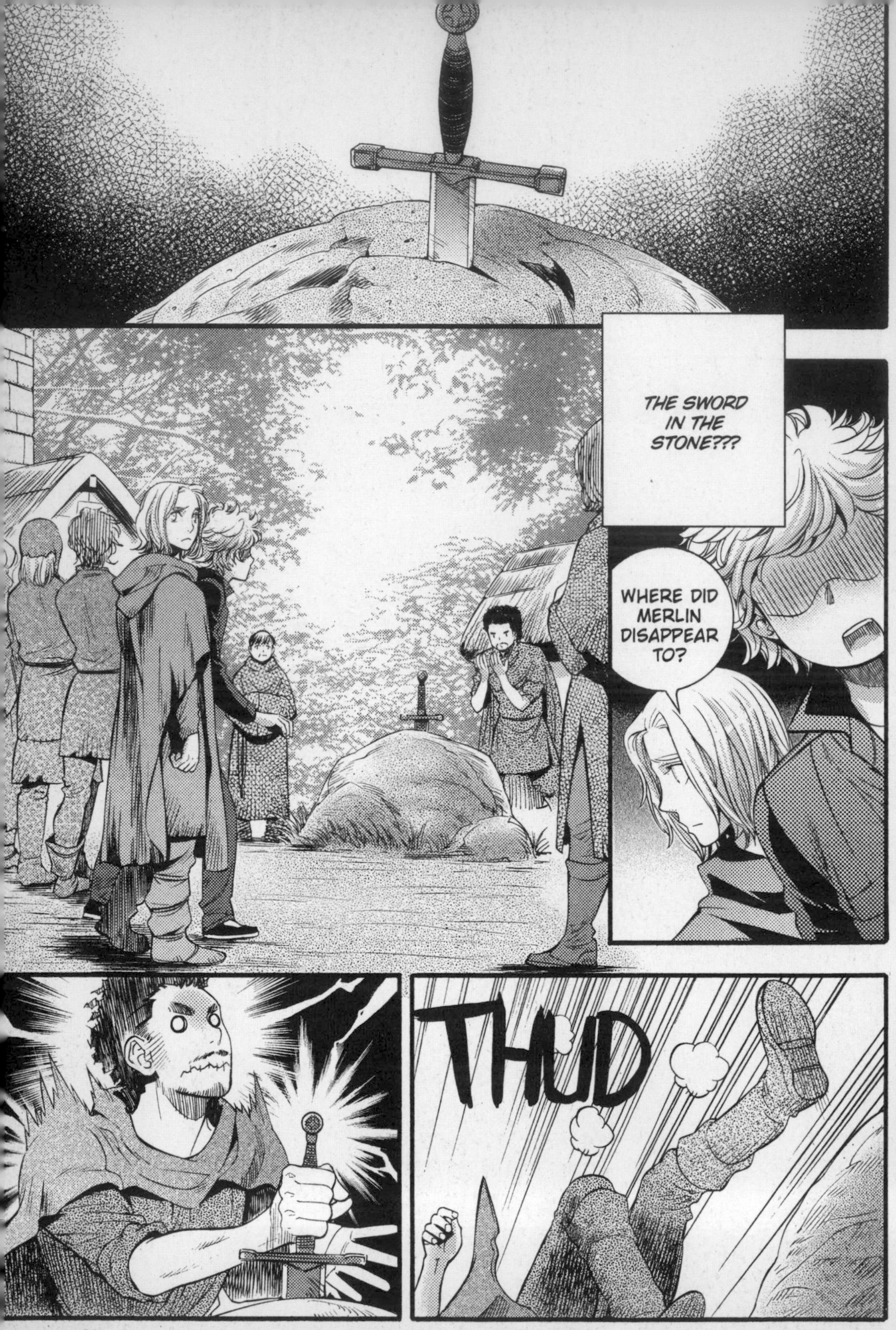
THE SWORD IN THE STONE???
WHERE DID MERLIN DISAPPEAR TO?
THUD

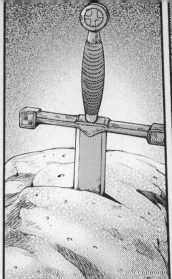

THIS IS NO
SWORD.

MERLIN?

IS THAT
YOU?

HEH
HEH.

GUILTY AS
CHARGED.

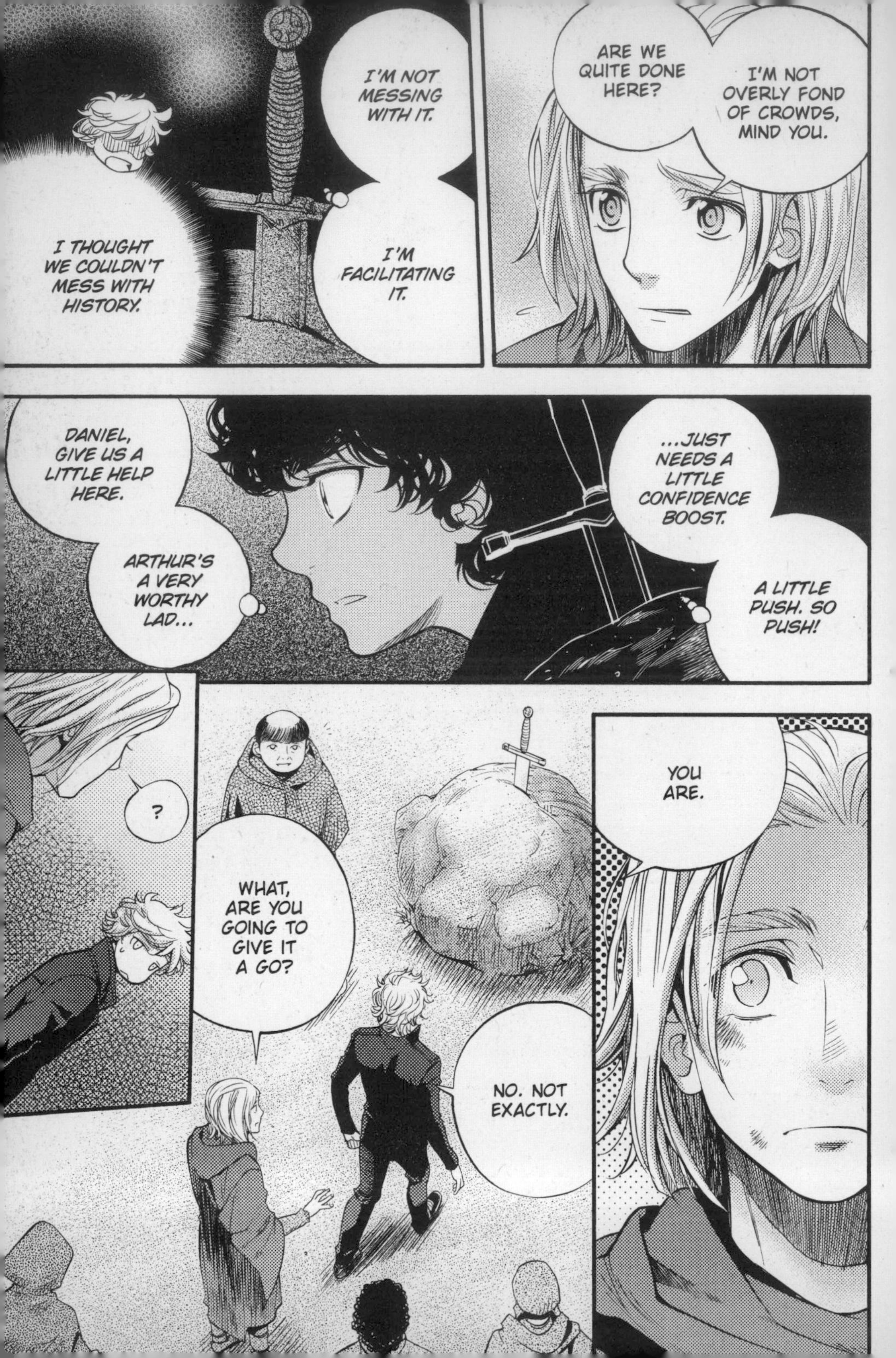

I THOUGHT WE COULDN'T MESS WITH HISTORY.
I'M NOT MESSING WITH IT.
I'M FACILITATING IT.
ARE WE QUITE DONE HERE?
I'M NOT OVERLY FOND OF CROWDS, MIND YOU.
DANIEL, GIVE US A LITTLE HELP HERE.
ARTHUR'S A VERY WORTHY LAD...
...JUST NEEDS A LITTLE CONFIDENCE BOOST.
A LITTLE PUSH. SO PUSH!
?
WHAT, ARE YOU GOING TO GIVE IT A GO?
NO. NOT EXACTLY.
YOU ARE.

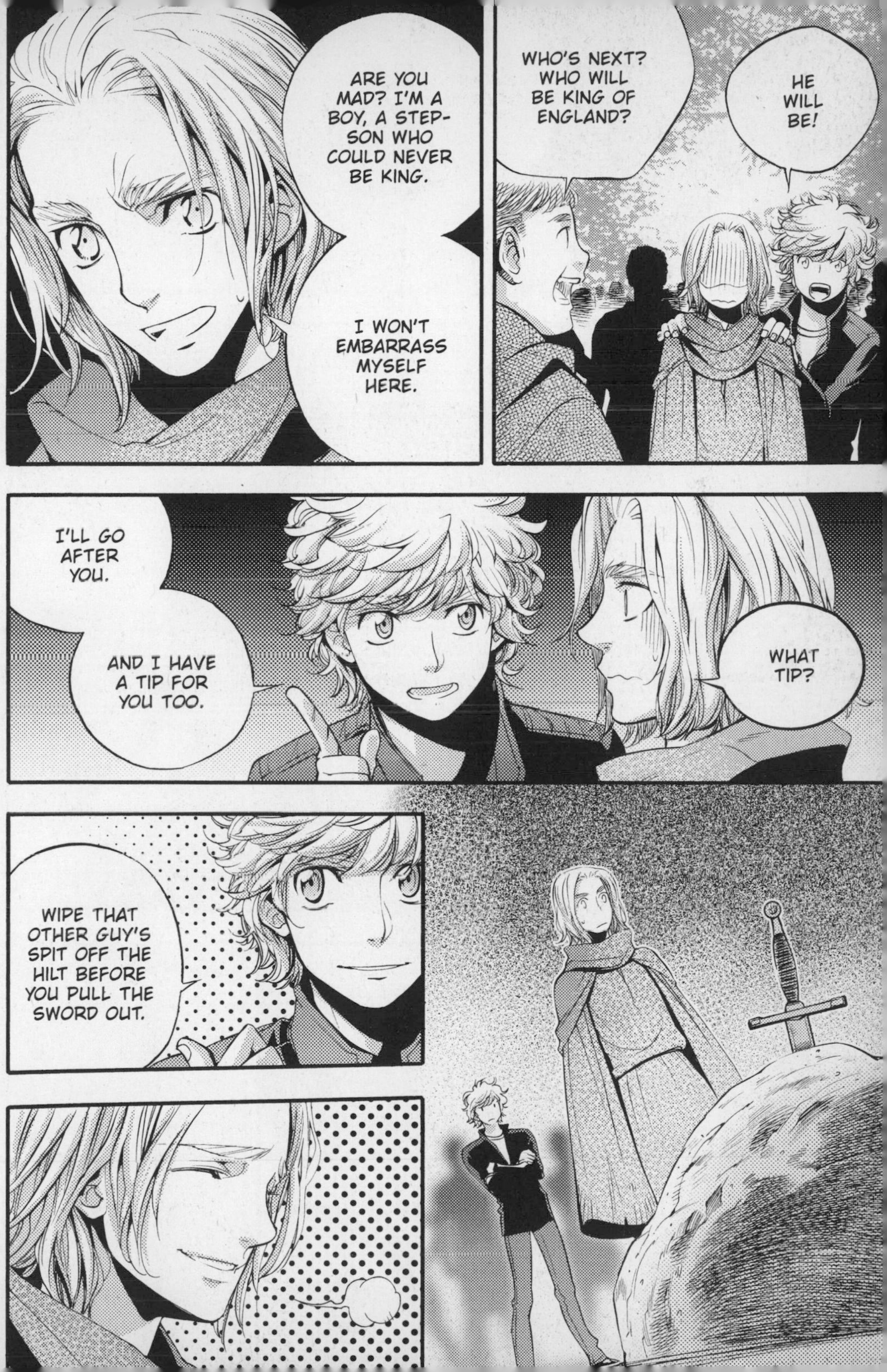
ARE YOU MAD? I'M A BOY, A STEP-SON WHO COULD NEVER BE KING.
I WON'T EMBARRASS MYSELF HERE.
WHO'S NEXT? WHO WILL BE KING OF ENGLAND?
HE WILL BE!
I'LL GO AFTER YOU.
AND I HAVE A TIP FOR YOU TOO.
WHAT TIP?
WIPE THAT OTHER GUY'S SPIT OFF THE HILT BEFORE YOU PULL THE SWORD OUT.

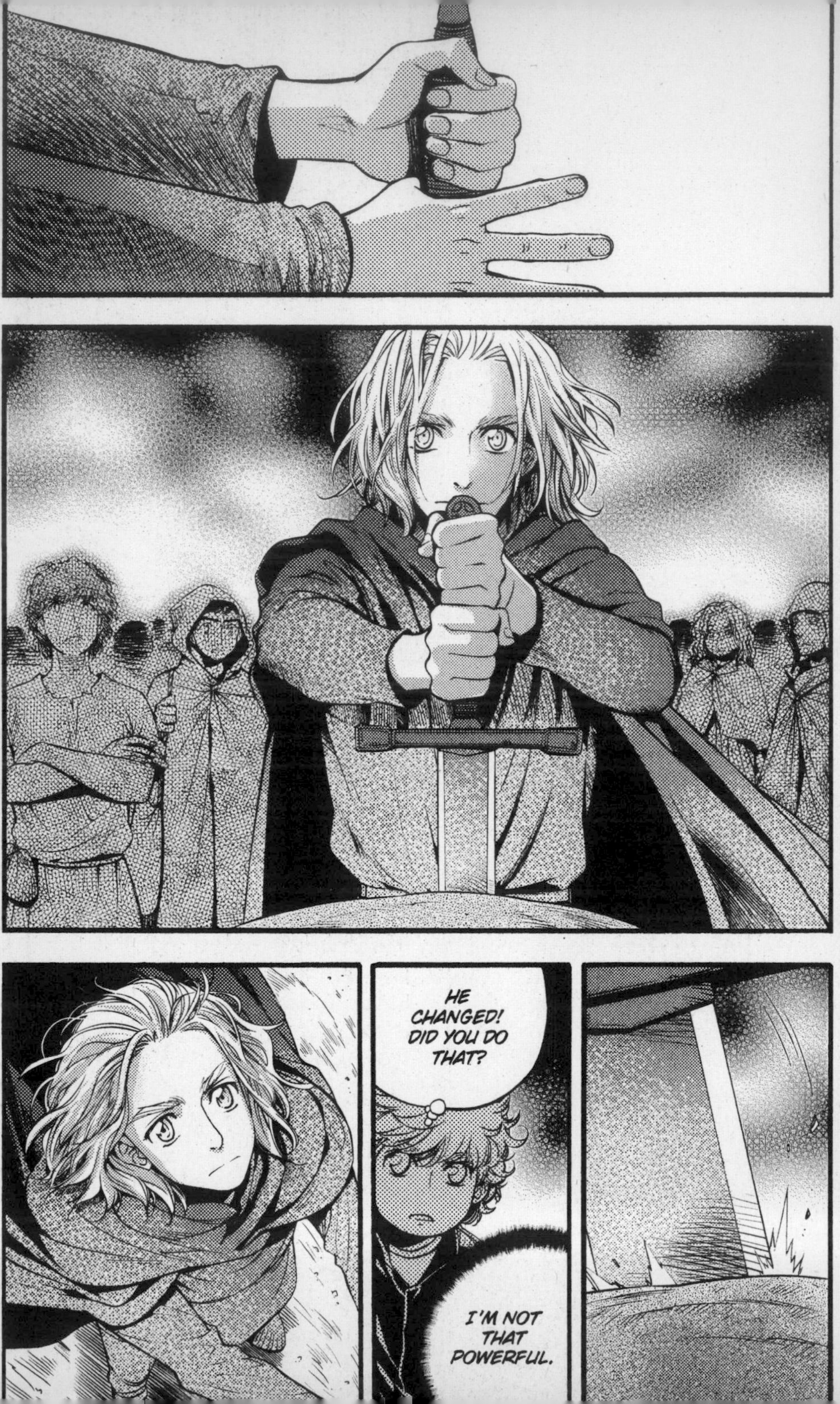
HE CHANGED! DID YOU DO THAT?
I'M NOT THAT POWERFUL.

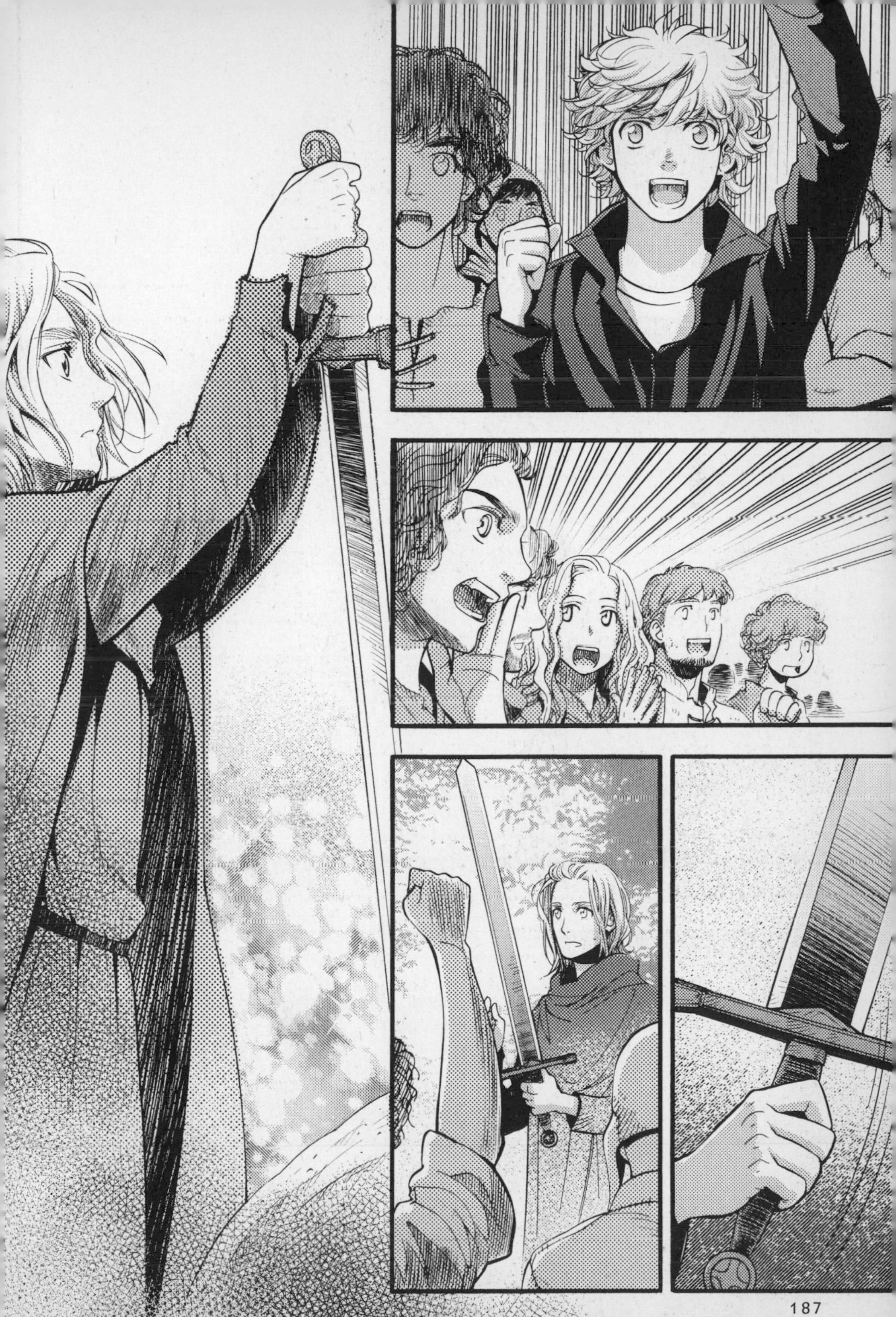

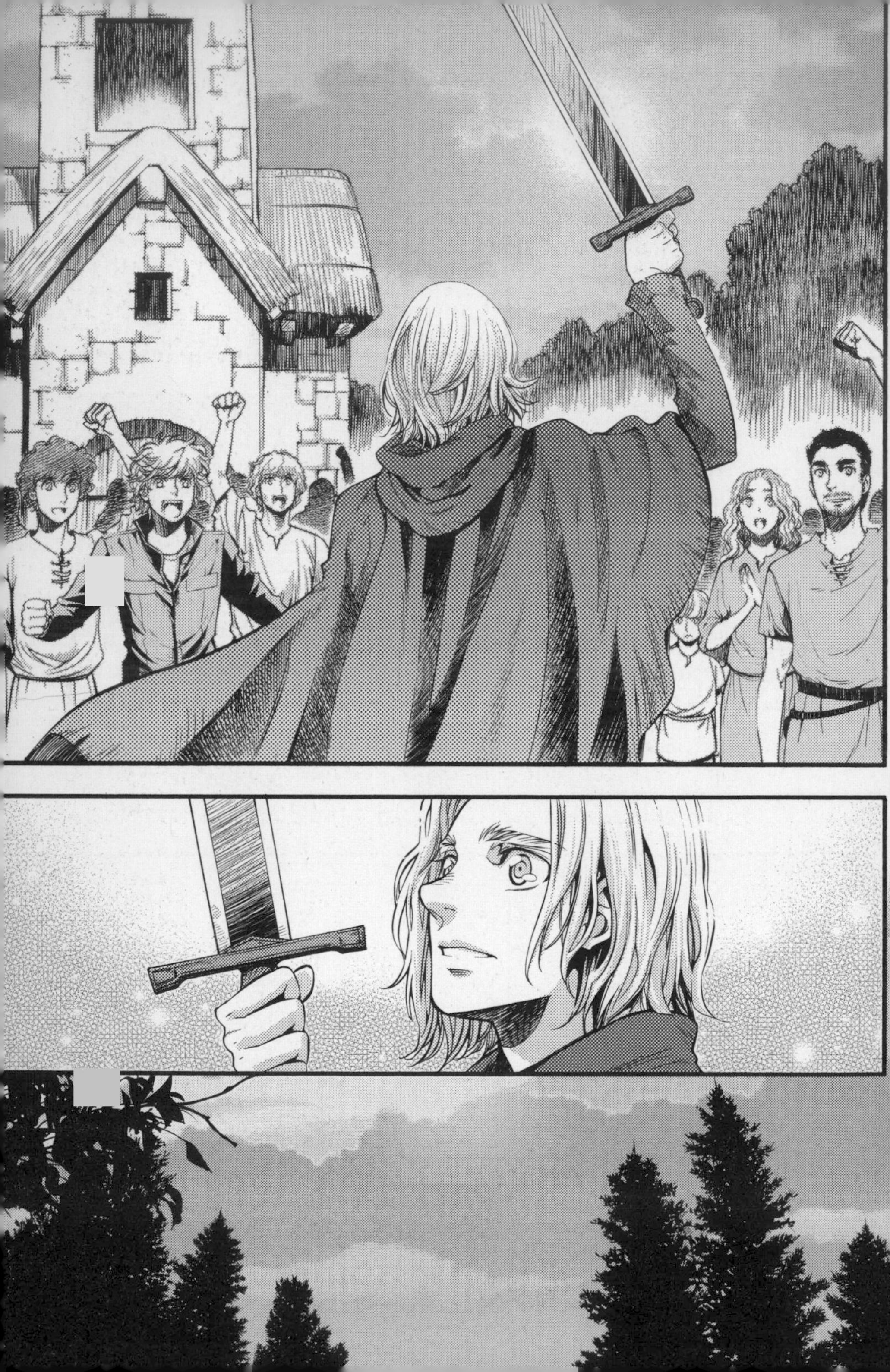

YOU NEEDN'T CALL ME THAT, DANIEL.

MY LORD.

189

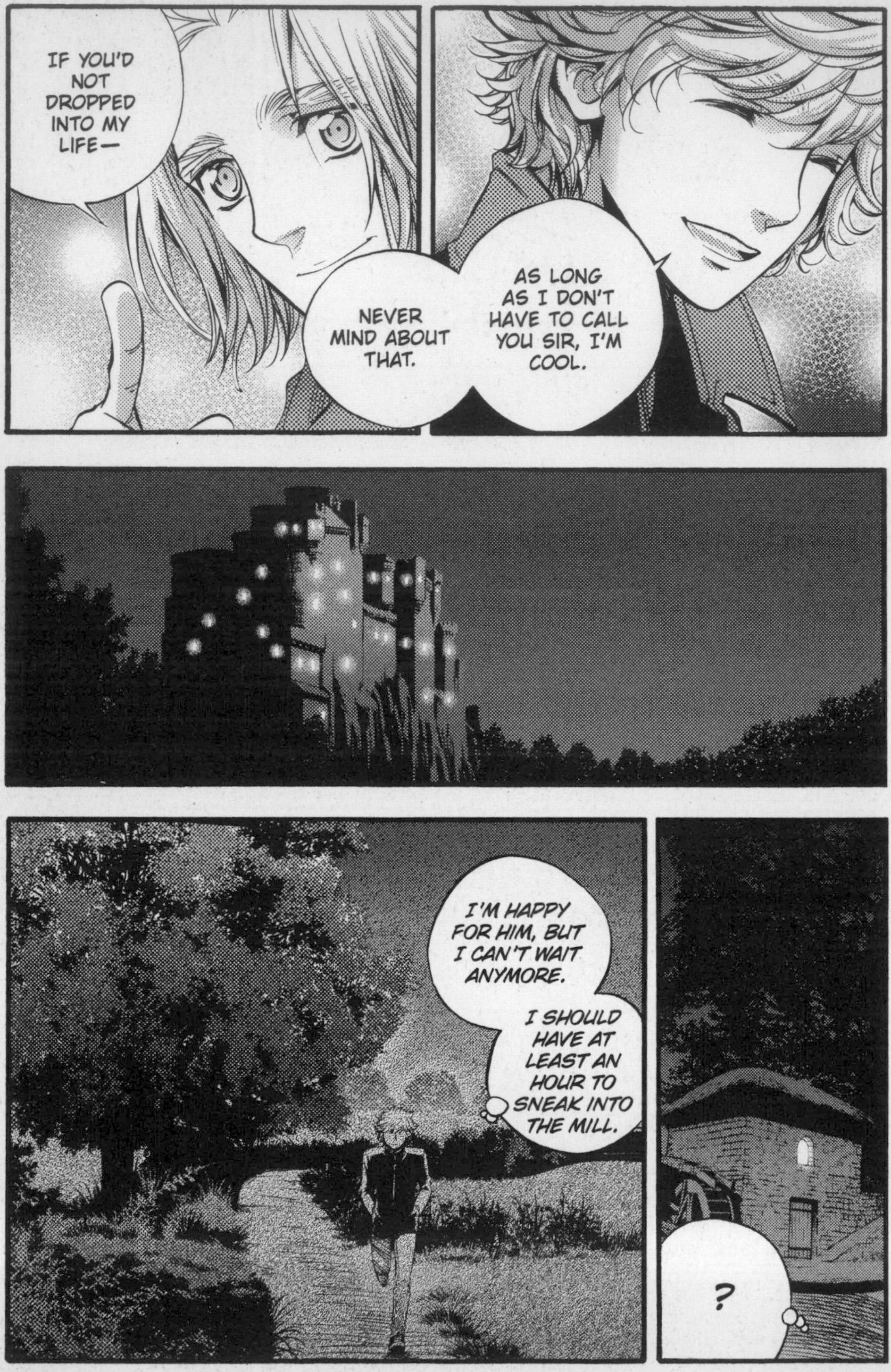
IF YOU'D NOT DROPPED INTO MY LIFE—
NEVER MIND ABOUT THAT.
AS LONG AS I DON'T HAVE TO CALL YOU SIR, I'M COOL.
I'M HAPPY FOR HIM, BUT I CAN'T WAIT ANYMORE.
I SHOULD HAVE AT LEAST AN HOUR TO SNEAK INTO THE MILL.
?

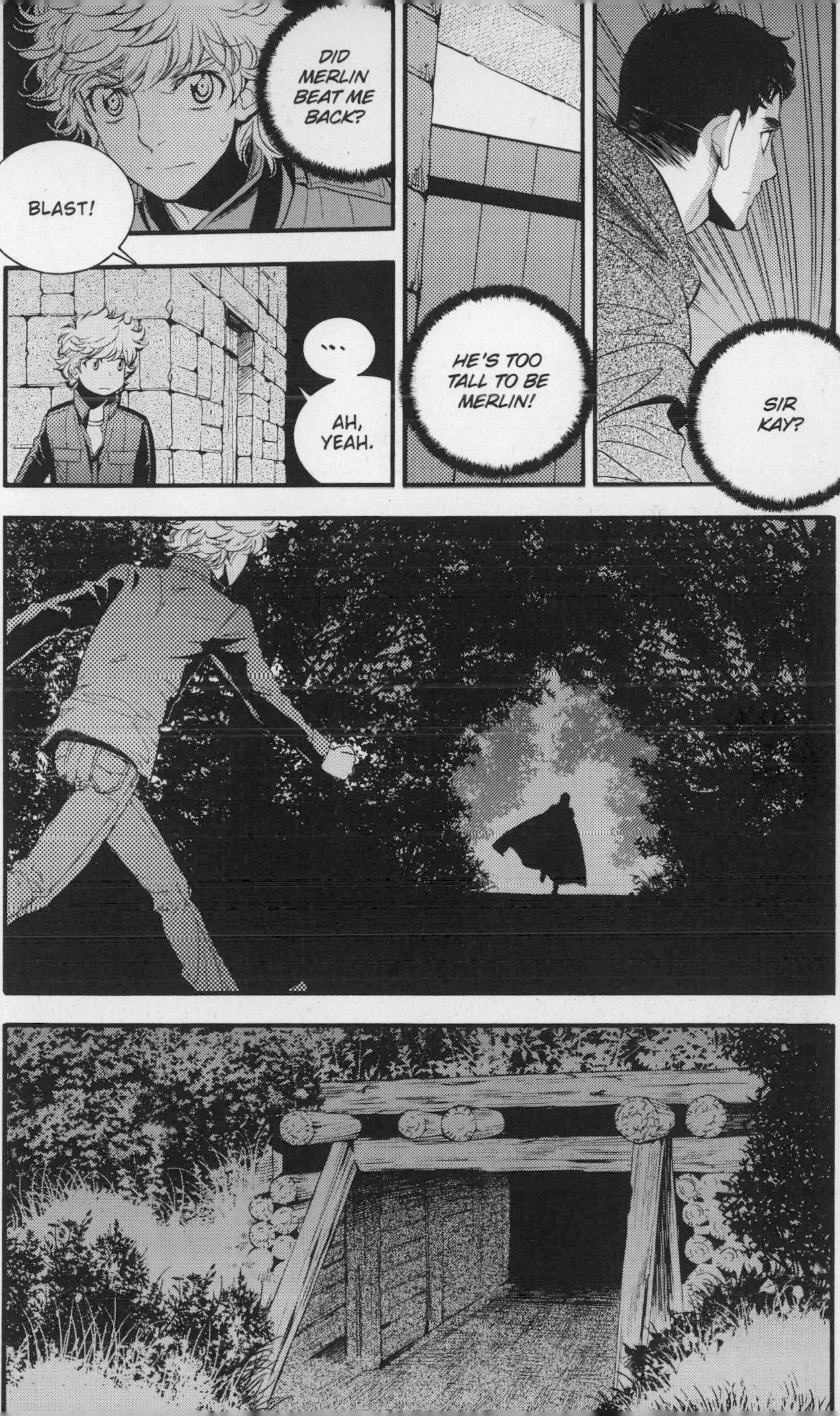
DID MERLIN BEAT ME BACK?
BLAST!
...
AH, YEAH.
HE'S TOO TALL TO BE MERLIN!
SIR KAY?

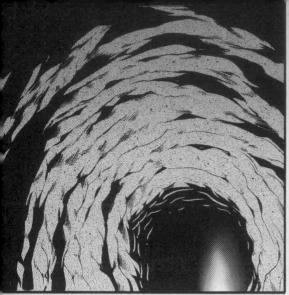

FIGURES IT WOULD BE UNDERGROUND, DUSTY, AND FOUL SMELLING.

MORE ALIENS NEED TO STAY AT THE RITZ.

!

I FEEL VIBRATIONS... AND IT'S GETTING LOUDER...

AM I READY FOR HIM?

HOW LONG WOULD IT TAKE TO RUN OUT OF THIS PLACE IN THE DARK?

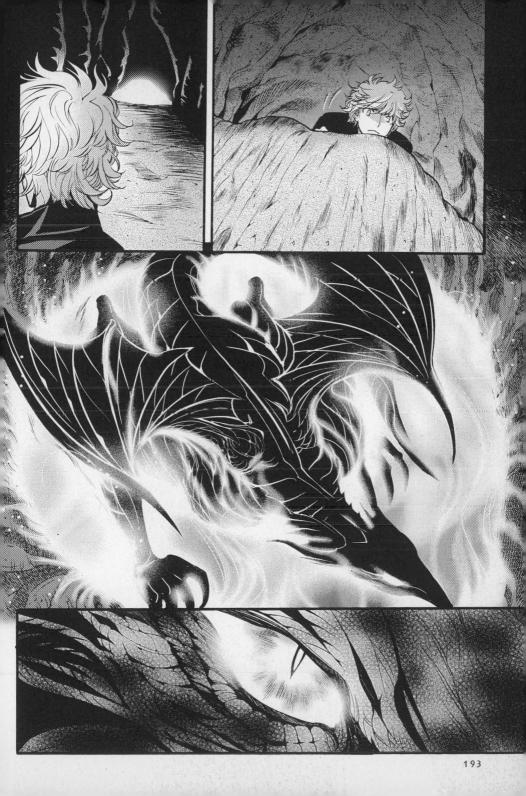

193

DANIEL X

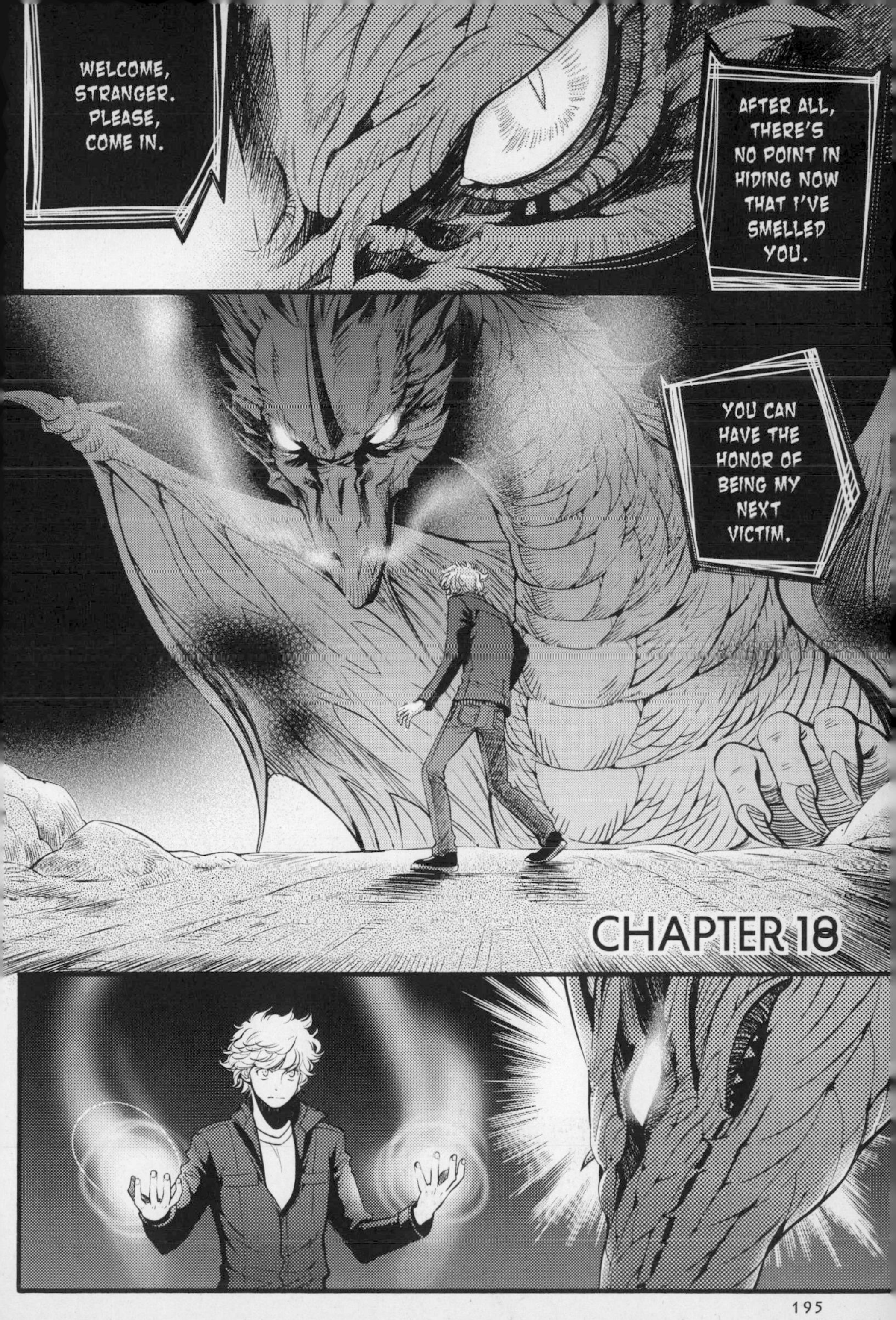
WELCOME, STRANGER. PLEASE, COME IN.
AFTER ALL, THERE'S NO POINT IN HIDING NOW THAT I'VE SMELLED YOU.
YOU CAN HAVE THE HONOR OF BEING MY NEXT VICTIM.
CHAPTER 18

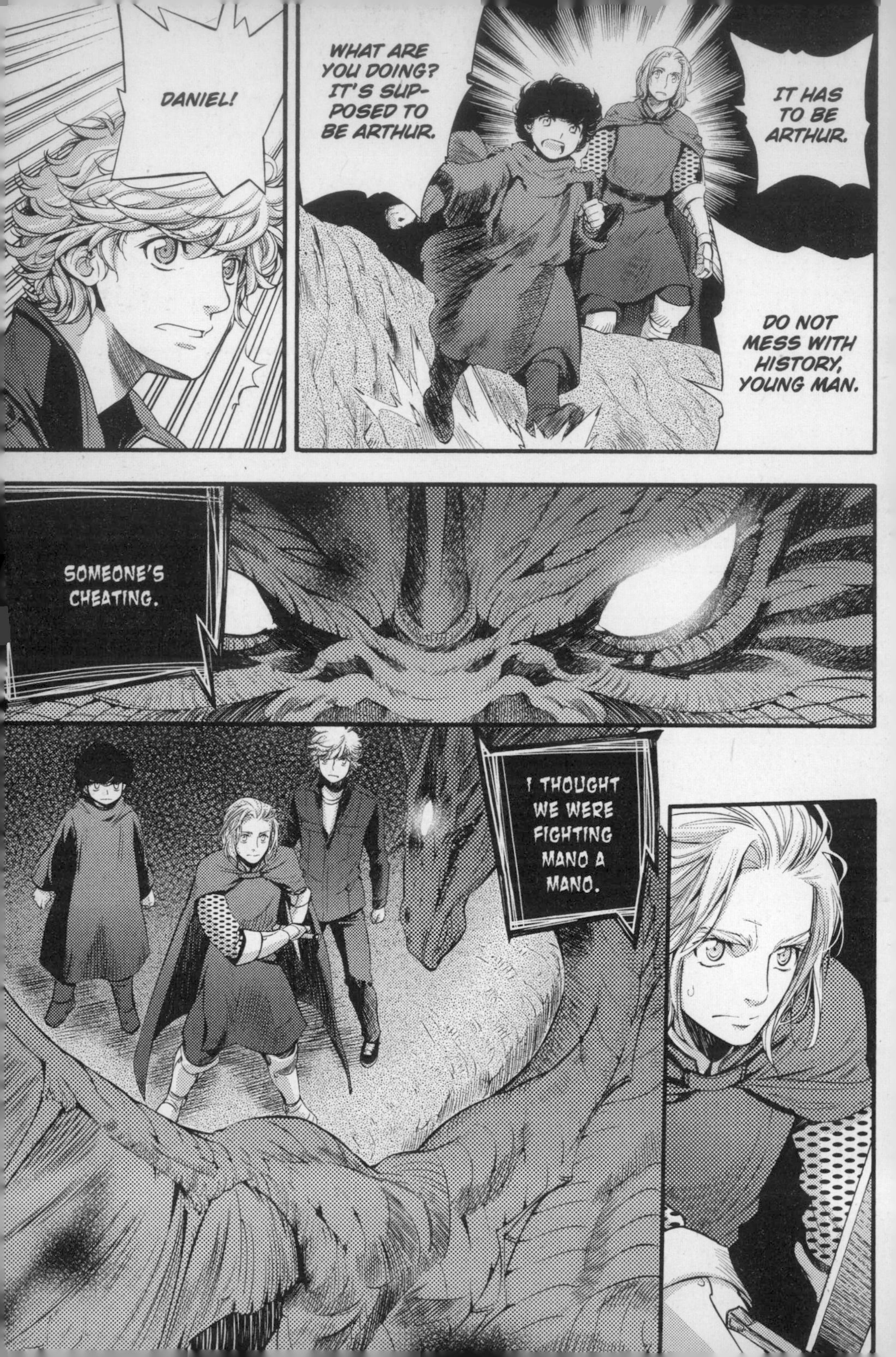
DANIEL!
WHAT ARE YOU DOING? IT'S SUP-POSED TO BE ARTHUR.
IT HAS TO BE ARTHUR.
DO NOT MESS WITH HISTORY, YOUNG MAN.
SOMEONE'S CHEATING.
I THOUGHT WE WERE FIGHTING MANO A MANO.

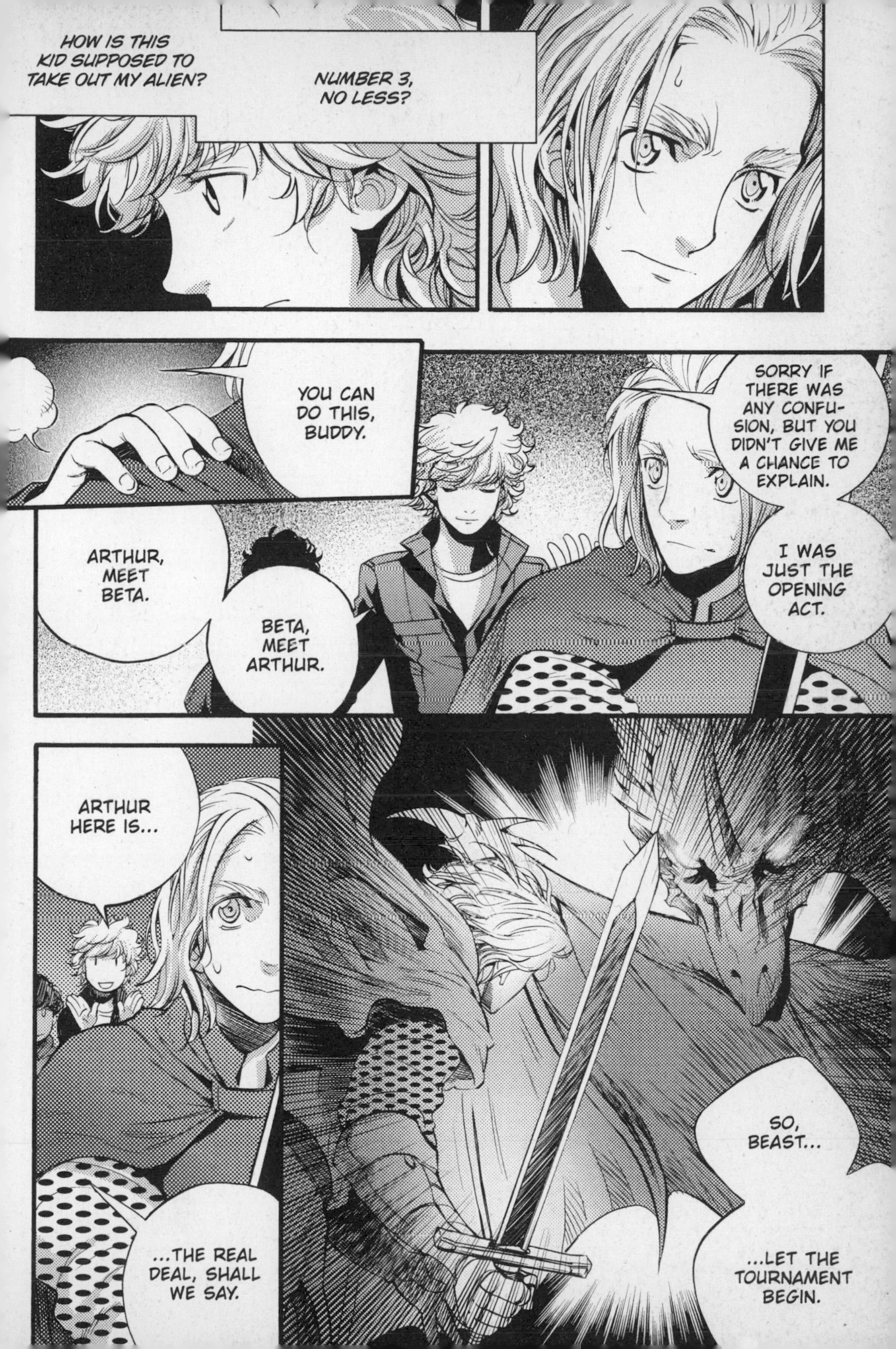
HOW IS THIS KID SUPPOSED TO TAKE OUT MY ALIEN?
NUMBER 3, NO LESS?
YOU CAN DO THIS, BUDDY.
ARTHUR, MEET BETA.
BETA, MEET ARTHUR.
SORRY IF THERE WAS ANY CONFUSION, BUT YOU DIDN'T GIVE ME A CHANCE TO EXPLAIN.
I WAS JUST THE OPENING ACT.
ARTHUR HERE IS...
...THE REAL DEAL, SHALL WE SAY.
SO, BEAST...
...LET THE TOURNAMENT BEGIN.

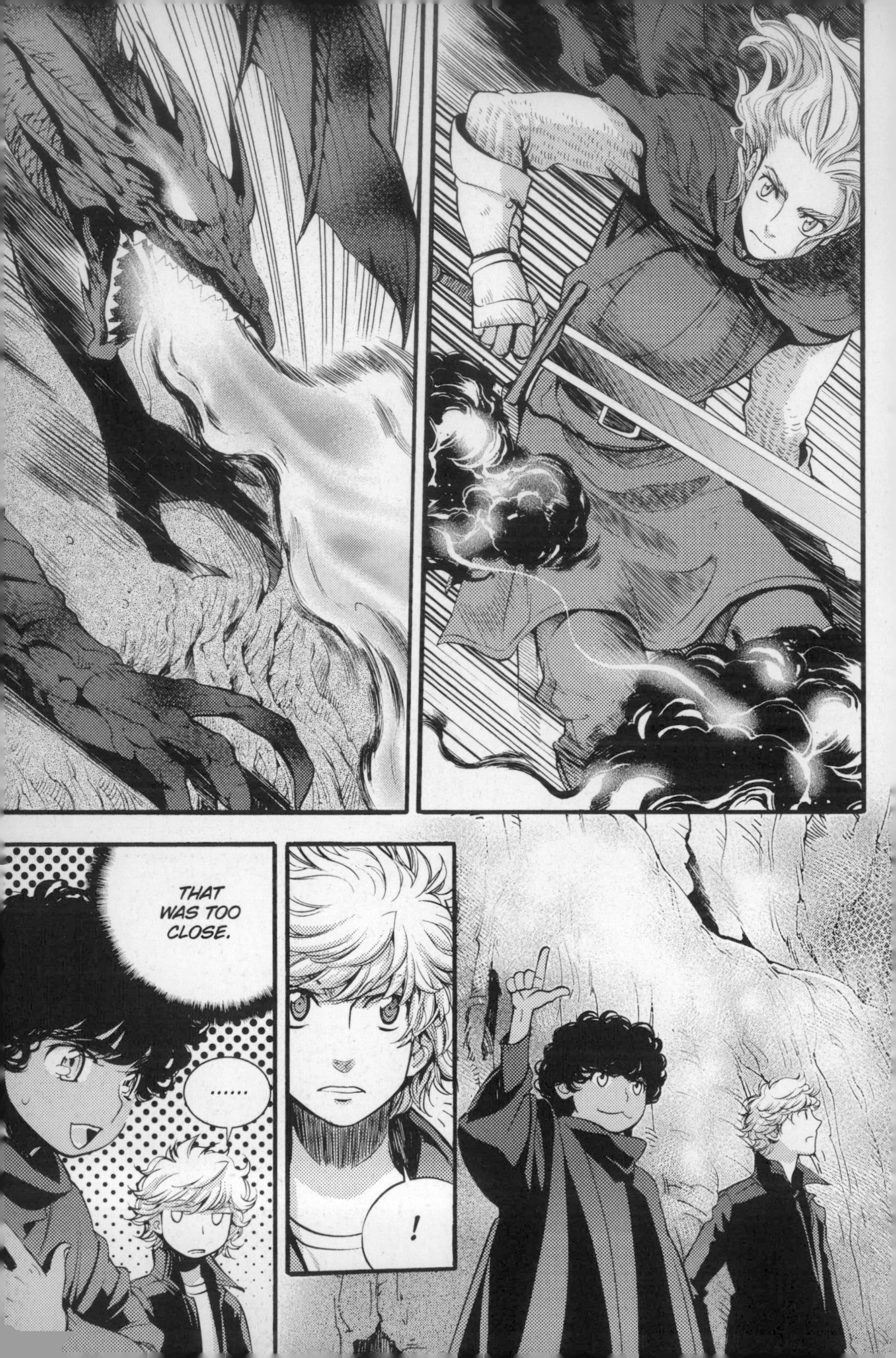
THAT WAS TOO CLOSE.
......
!

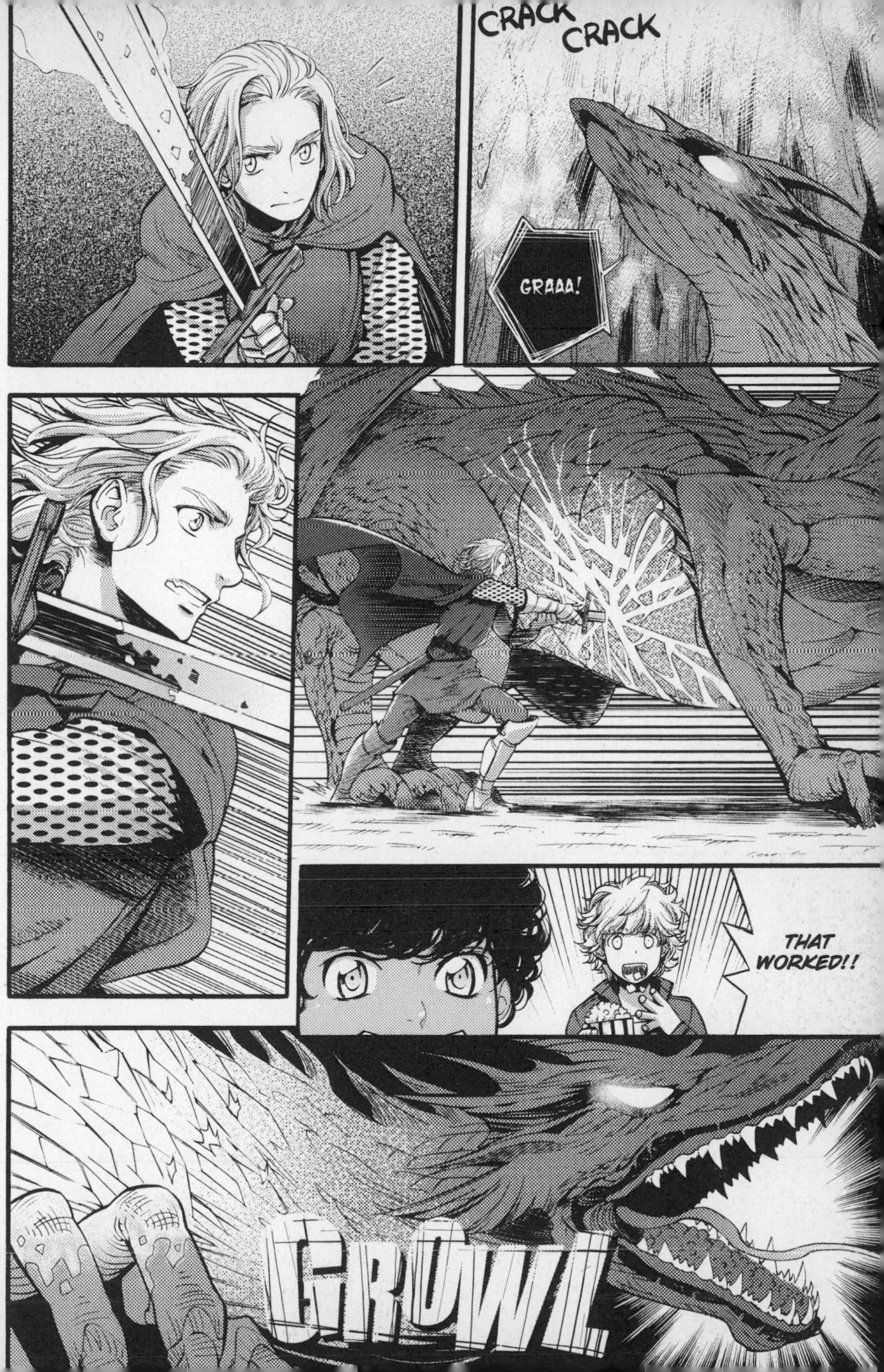
CRACK
CRACK
GRAAA!
THAT WORKED!!
GROWL

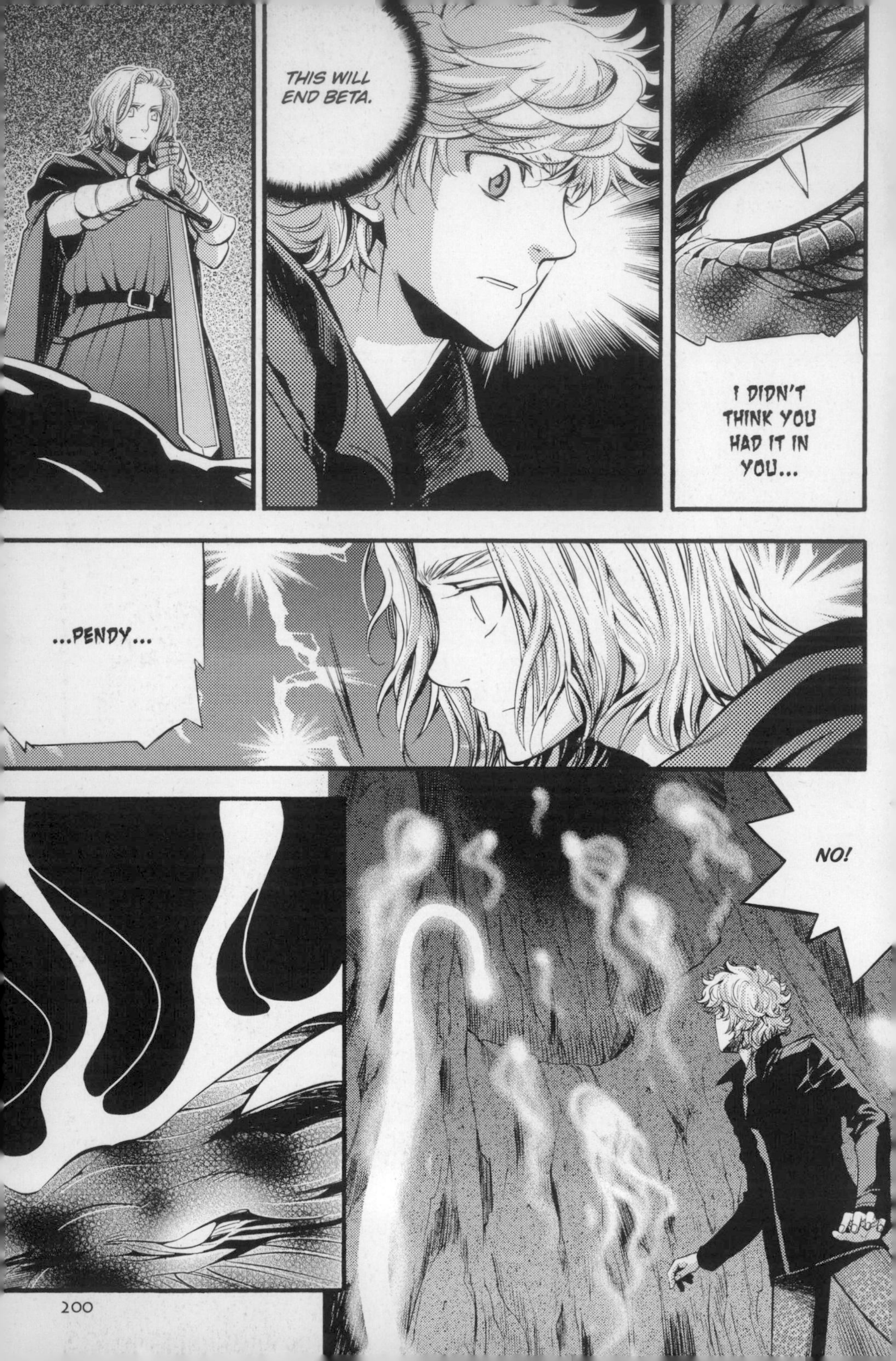
THIS WILL END BETA.
I DIDN'T THINK YOU HAD IT IN YOU...
...PENDY...
NO!

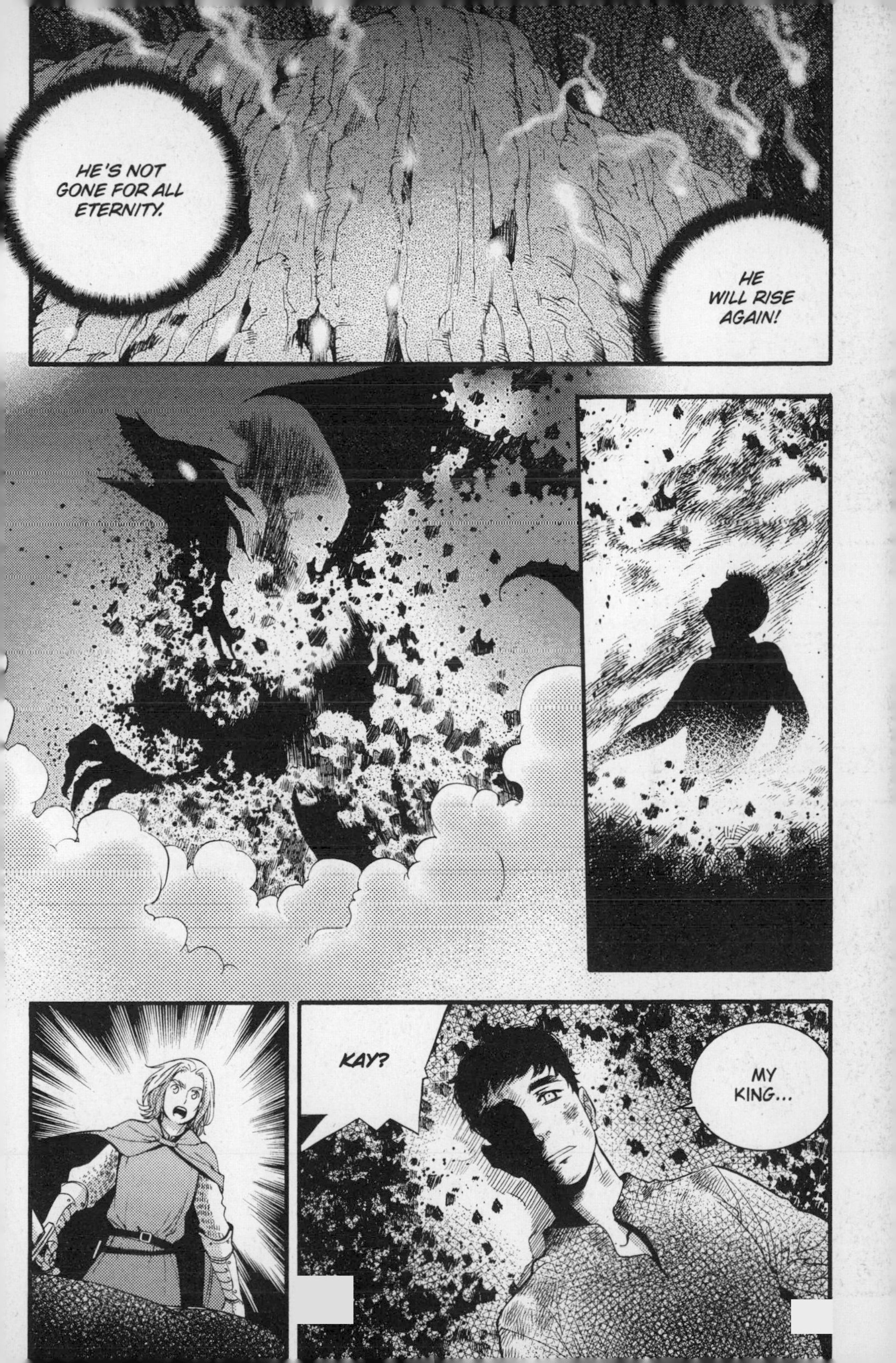
HE'S NOT GONE FOR ALL ETERNITY.
HE WILL RISE AGAIN!
KAY?
MY KING...

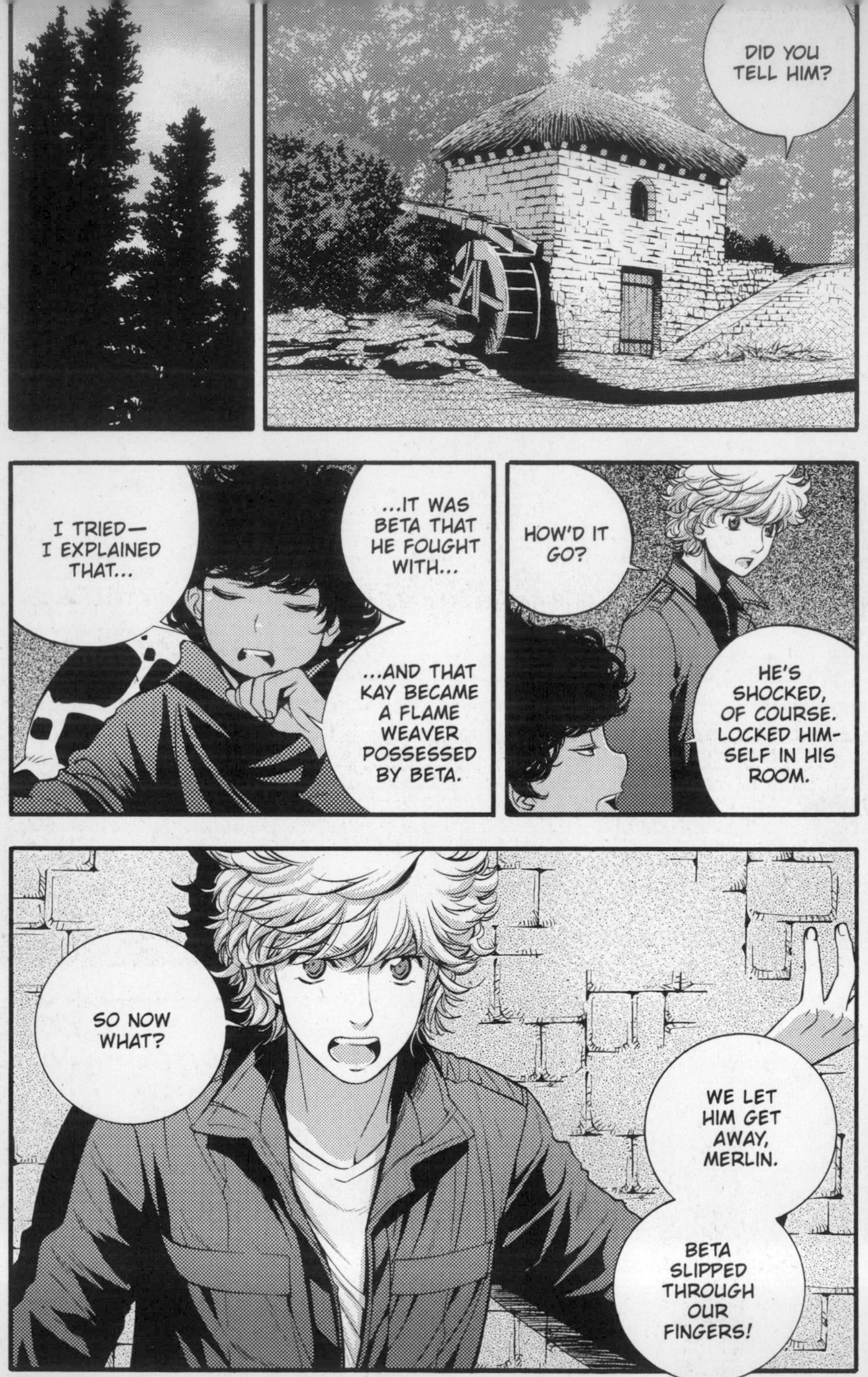
DID YOU TELL HIM?
I TRIED— I EXPLAINED THAT...
...IT WAS BETA THAT HE FOUGHT WITH...
...AND THAT KAY BECAME A FLAME WEAVER POSSESSED BY BETA.
HOW'D IT GO?
HE'S SHOCKED, OF COURSE. LOCKED HIMSELF IN HIS ROOM.
SO NOW WHAT?
WE LET HIM GET AWAY, MERLIN.
BETA SLIPPED THROUGH OUR FINGERS!

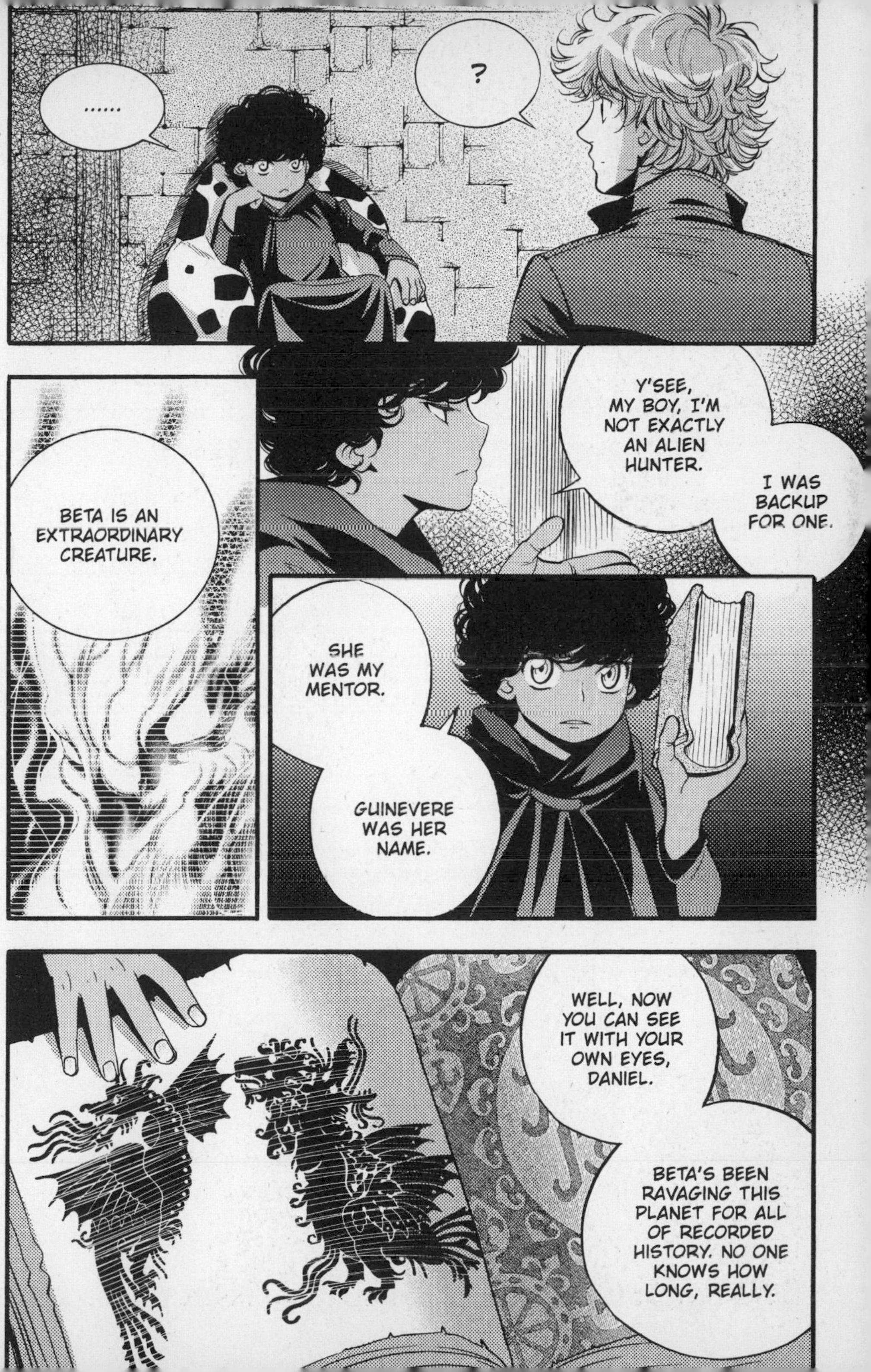
......
?
BETA IS AN EXTRAORDINARY CREATURE.
Y'SEE, MY BOY, I'M NOT EXACTLY AN ALIEN HUNTER.
I WAS BACKUP FOR ONE.
SHE WAS MY MENTOR.
GUINEVERE WAS HER NAME.
WELL, NOW YOU CAN SEE IT WITH YOUR OWN EYES, DANIEL.
BETA'S BEEN RAVAGING THIS PLANET FOR ALL OF RECORDED HISTORY. NO ONE KNOWS HOW LONG, REALLY.

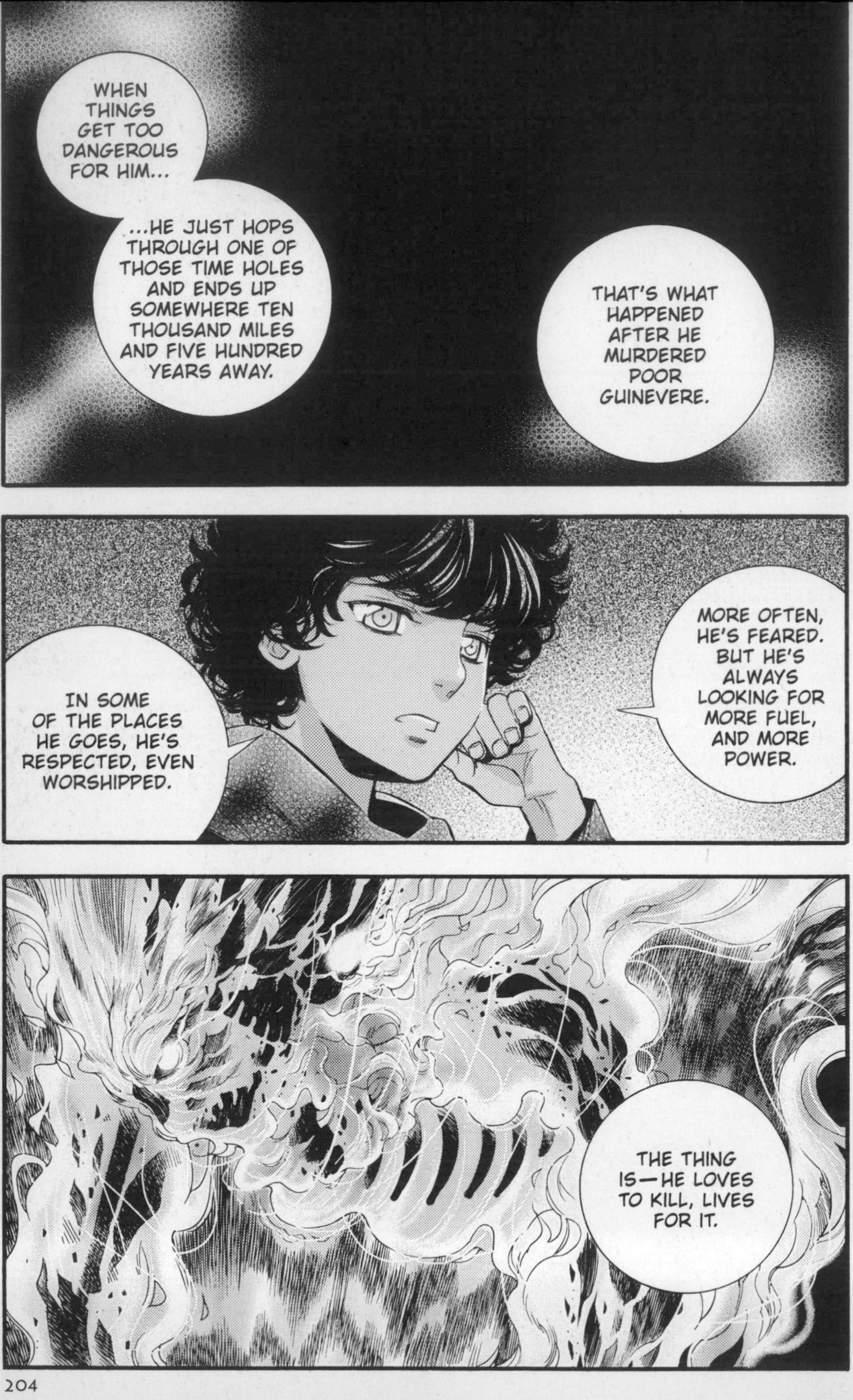
WHEN THINGS GET TOO DANGEROUS FOR HIM...
...HE JUST HOPS THROUGH ONE OF THOSE TIME HOLES AND ENDS UP SOMEWHERE TEN THOUSAND MILES AND FIVE HUNDRED YEARS AWAY.
THAT'S WHAT HAPPENED AFTER HE MURDERED POOR GUINEVERE.
IN SOME OF THE PLACES HE GOES, HE'S RESPECTED, EVEN WORSHIPPED.
MORE OFTEN, HE'S FEARED. BUT HE'S ALWAYS LOOKING FOR MORE FUEL, AND MORE POWER.
THE THING IS—HE LOVES TO KILL, LIVES FOR IT.

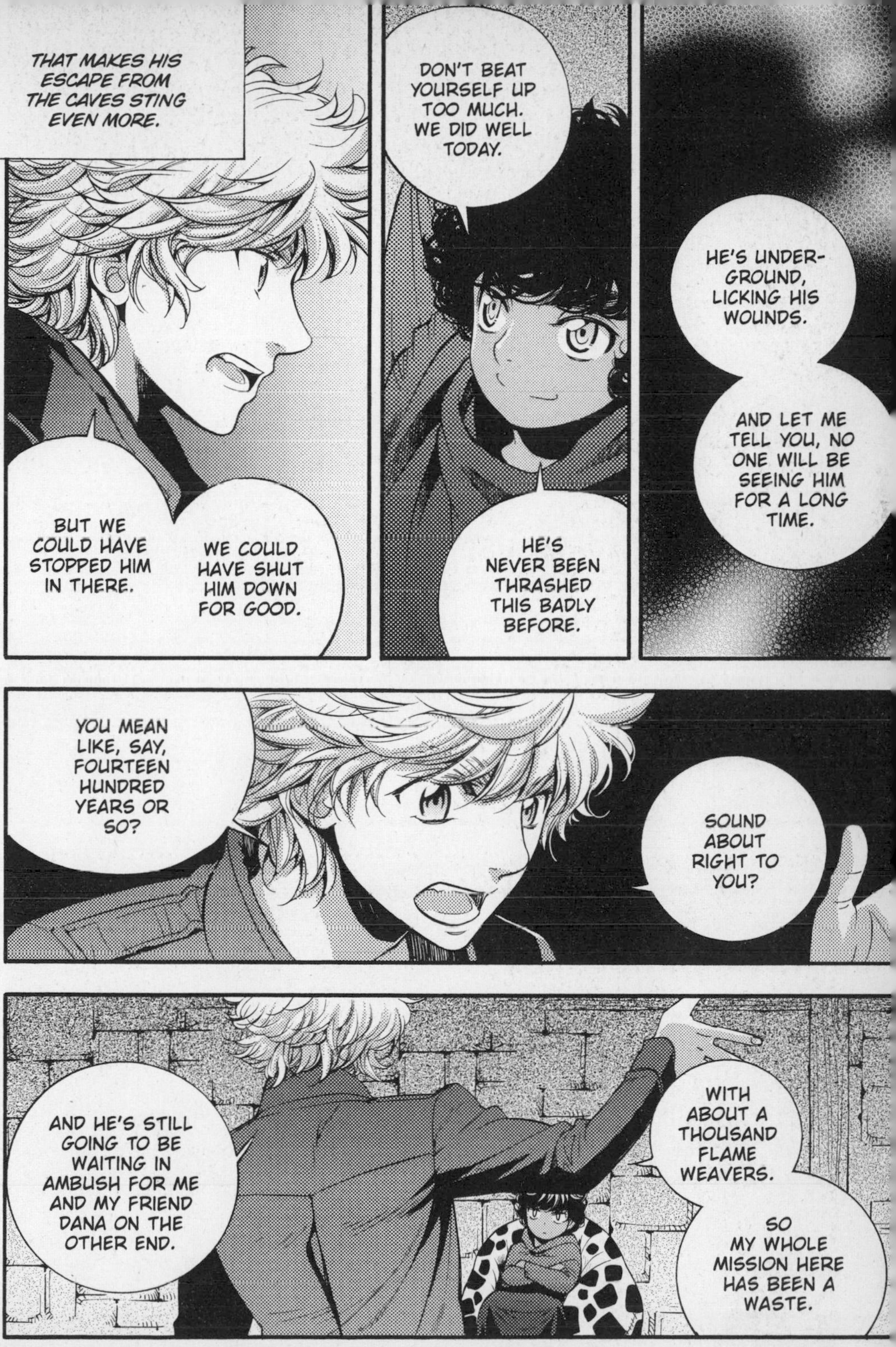
THAT MAKES HIS ESCAPE FROM THE CAVES STING EVEN MORE.
BUT WE COULD HAVE STOPPED HIM IN THERE.
WE COULD HAVE SHUT HIM DOWN FOR GOOD.
DON'T BEAT YOURSELF UP TOO MUCH. WE DID WELL TODAY.
HE'S NEVER BEEN THRASHED THIS BADLY BEFORE.
HE'S UNDER-GROUND, LICKING HIS WOUNDS.
AND LET ME TELL YOU, NO ONE WILL BE SEEING HIM FOR A LONG TIME.
YOU MEAN LIKE, SAY, FOURTEEN HUNDRED YEARS OR SO?
SOUND ABOUT RIGHT TO YOU?
AND HE'S STILL GOING TO BE WAITING IN AMBUSH FOR ME AND MY FRIEND DANA ON THE OTHER END.
WITH ABOUT A THOUSAND FLAME WEAVERS.
SO MY WHOLE MISSION HERE HAS BEEN A WASTE.

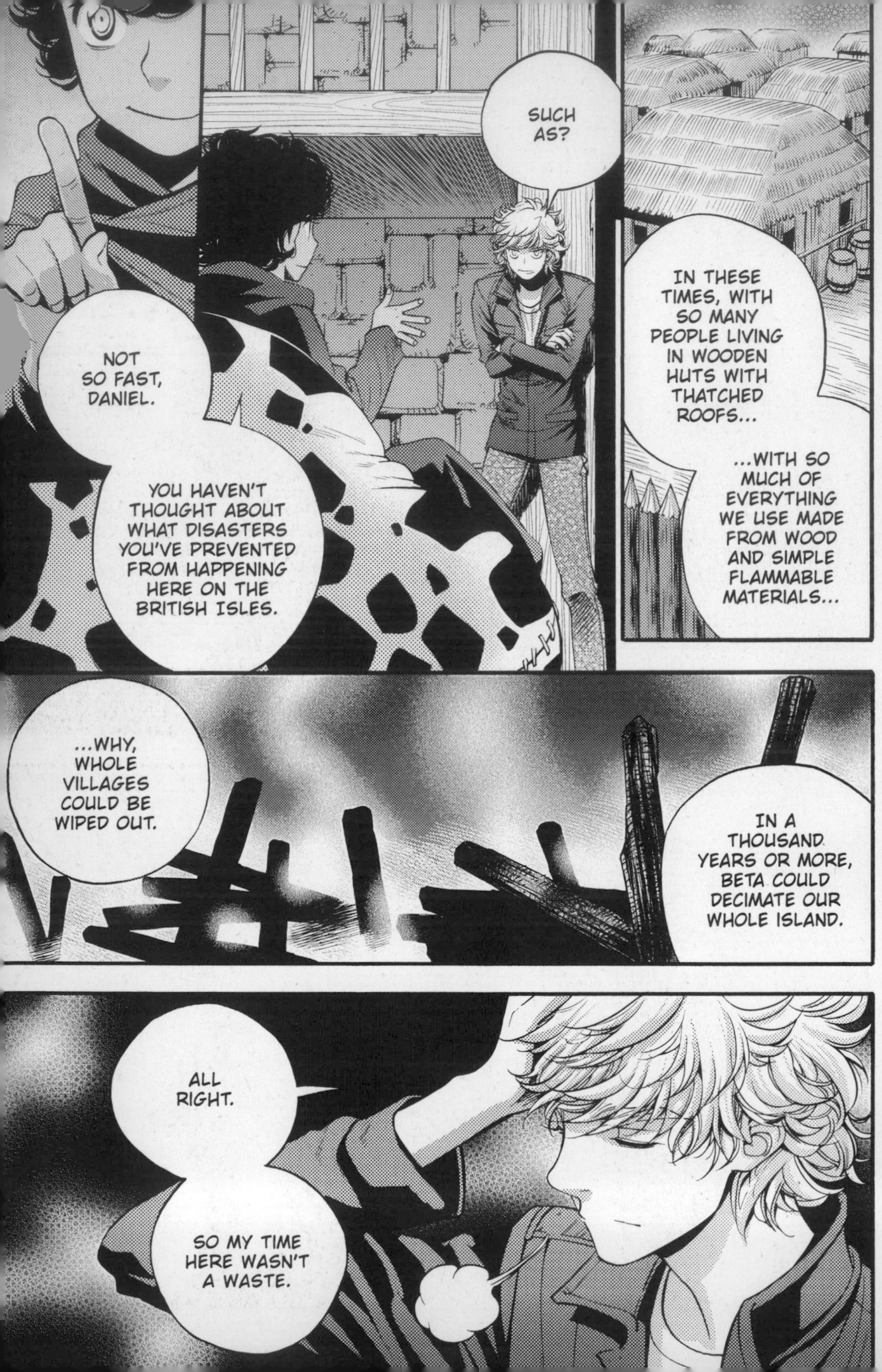
NOT SO FAST, DANIEL.
YOU HAVEN'T THOUGHT ABOUT WHAT DISASTERS YOU'VE PREVENTED FROM HAPPENING HERE ON THE BRITISH ISLES.
SUCH AS?
IN THESE TIMES, WITH SO MANY PEOPLE LIVING IN WOODEN HUTS WITH THATCHED ROOFS...
...WITH SO MUCH OF EVERYTHING WE USE MADE FROM WOOD AND SIMPLE FLAMMABLE MATERIALS...
...WHY, WHOLE VILLAGES COULD BE WIPED OUT.
IN A THOUSAND YEARS OR MORE, BETA COULD DECIMATE OUR WHOLE ISLAND.
ALL RIGHT.
SO MY TIME HERE WASN'T A WASTE.

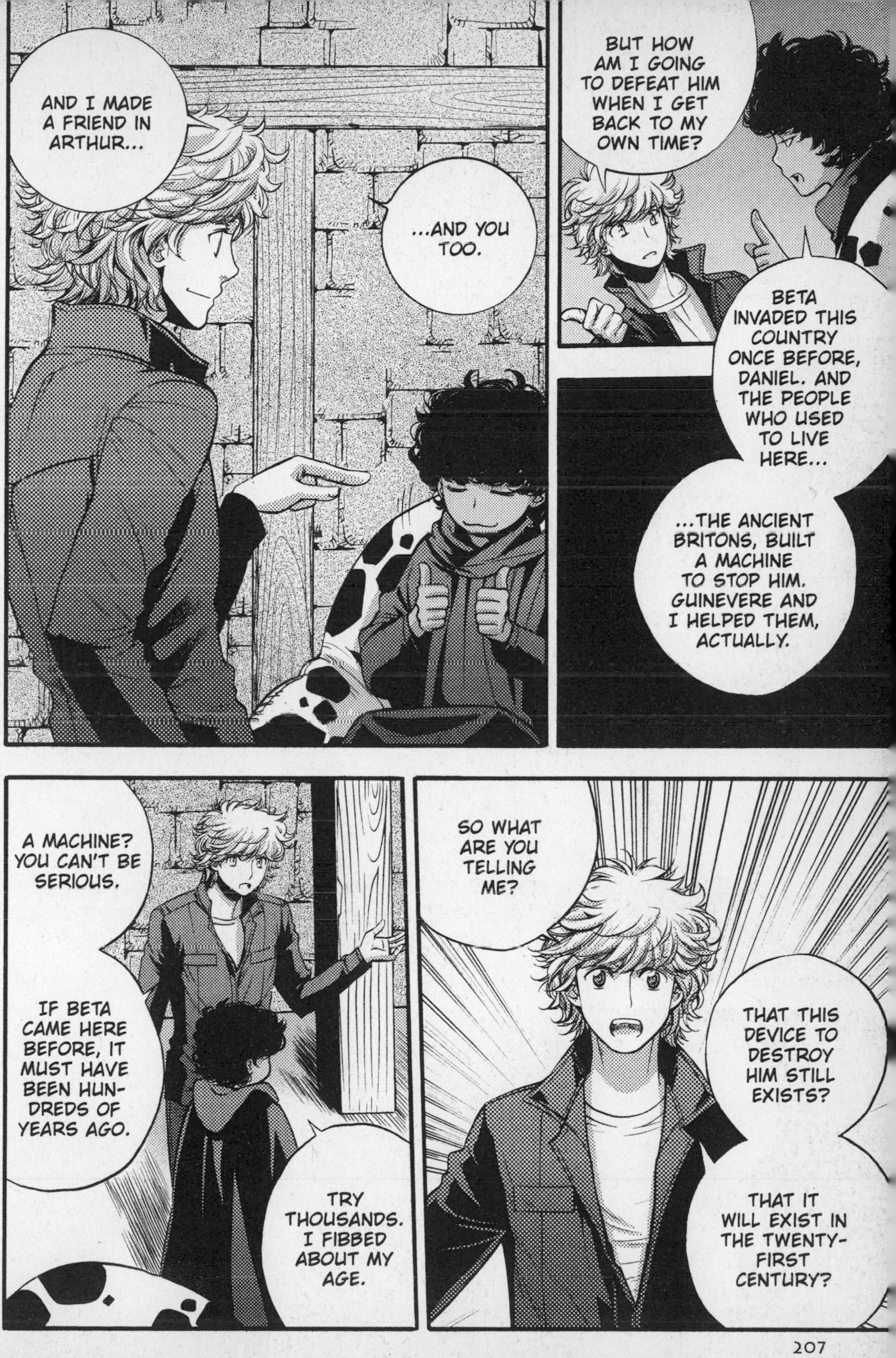
AND I MADE A FRIEND IN ARTHUR...
...AND YOU TOO.
BUT HOW AM I GOING TO DEFEAT HIM WHEN I GET BACK TO MY OWN TIME?
BETA INVADED THIS COUNTRY ONCE BEFORE, DANIEL. AND THE PEOPLE WHO USED TO LIVE HERE...
...THE ANCIENT BRITONS, BUILT A MACHINE TO STOP HIM. GUINEVERE AND I HELPED THEM, ACTUALLY.
A MACHINE? YOU CAN'T BE SERIOUS.
IF BETA CAME HERE BEFORE, IT MUST HAVE BEEN HUN-DREDS OF YEARS AGO.
TRY THOUSANDS. I FIBBED ABOUT MY AGE.
SO WHAT ARE YOU TELLING ME?
THAT THIS DEVICE TO DESTROY HIM STILL EXISTS?
THAT IT WILL EXIST IN THE TWENTY-FIRST CENTURY?

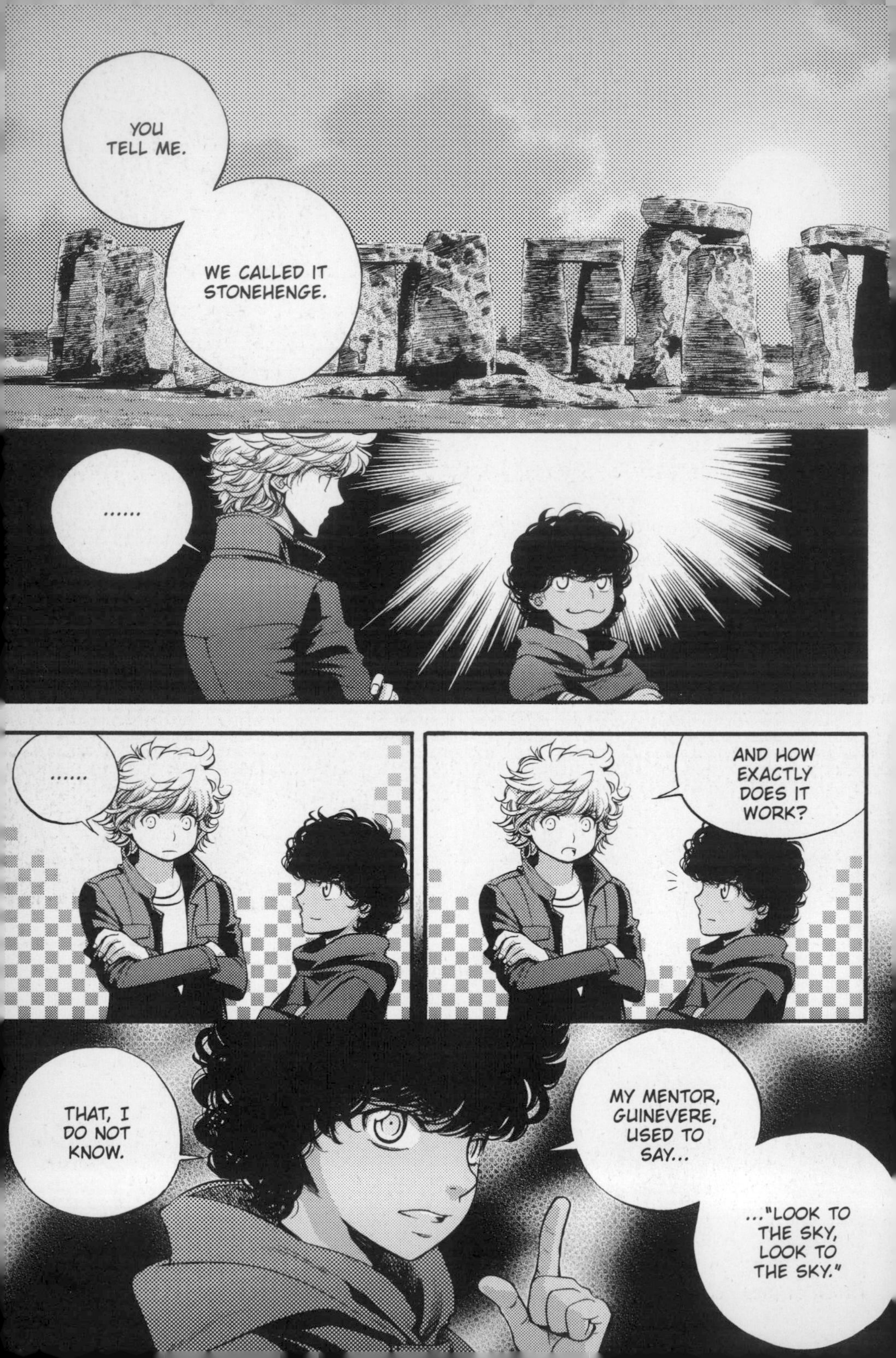
YOU TELL ME.
WE CALLED IT STONEHENGE.
......
......
AND HOW EXACTLY DOES IT WORK?
THAT, I DO NOT KNOW.
MY MENTOR, GUINEVERE, USED TO SAY...
..."LOOK TO THE SKY, LOOK TO THE SKY."

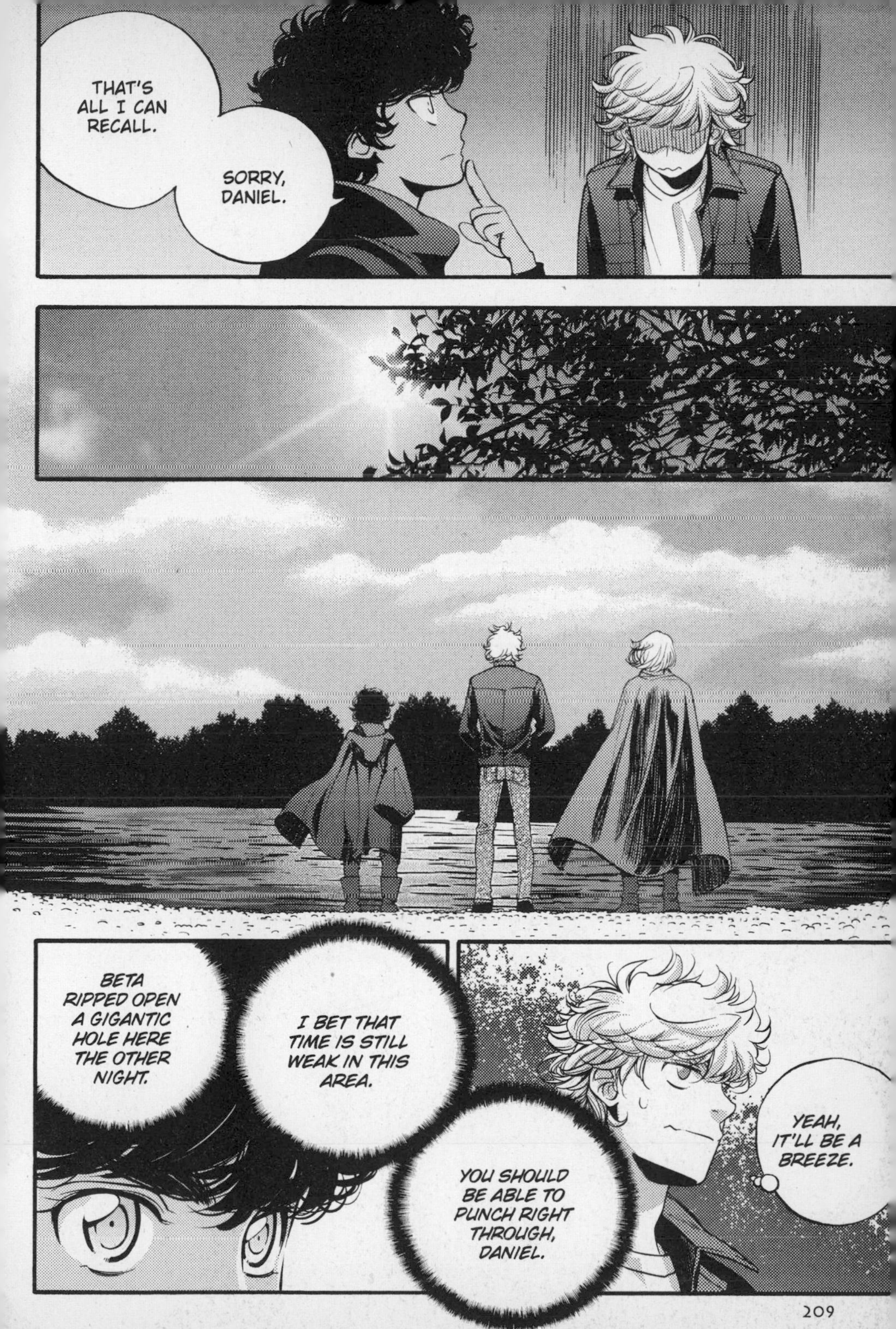
THAT'S ALL I CAN RECALL.
SORRY, DANIEL.
BETA RIPPED OPEN A GIGANTIC HOLE HERE THE OTHER NIGHT.
I BET THAT TIME IS STILL WEAK IN THIS AREA.
YOU SHOULD BE ABLE TO PUNCH RIGHT THROUGH, DANIEL.
YEAH, IT'LL BE A BREEZE.

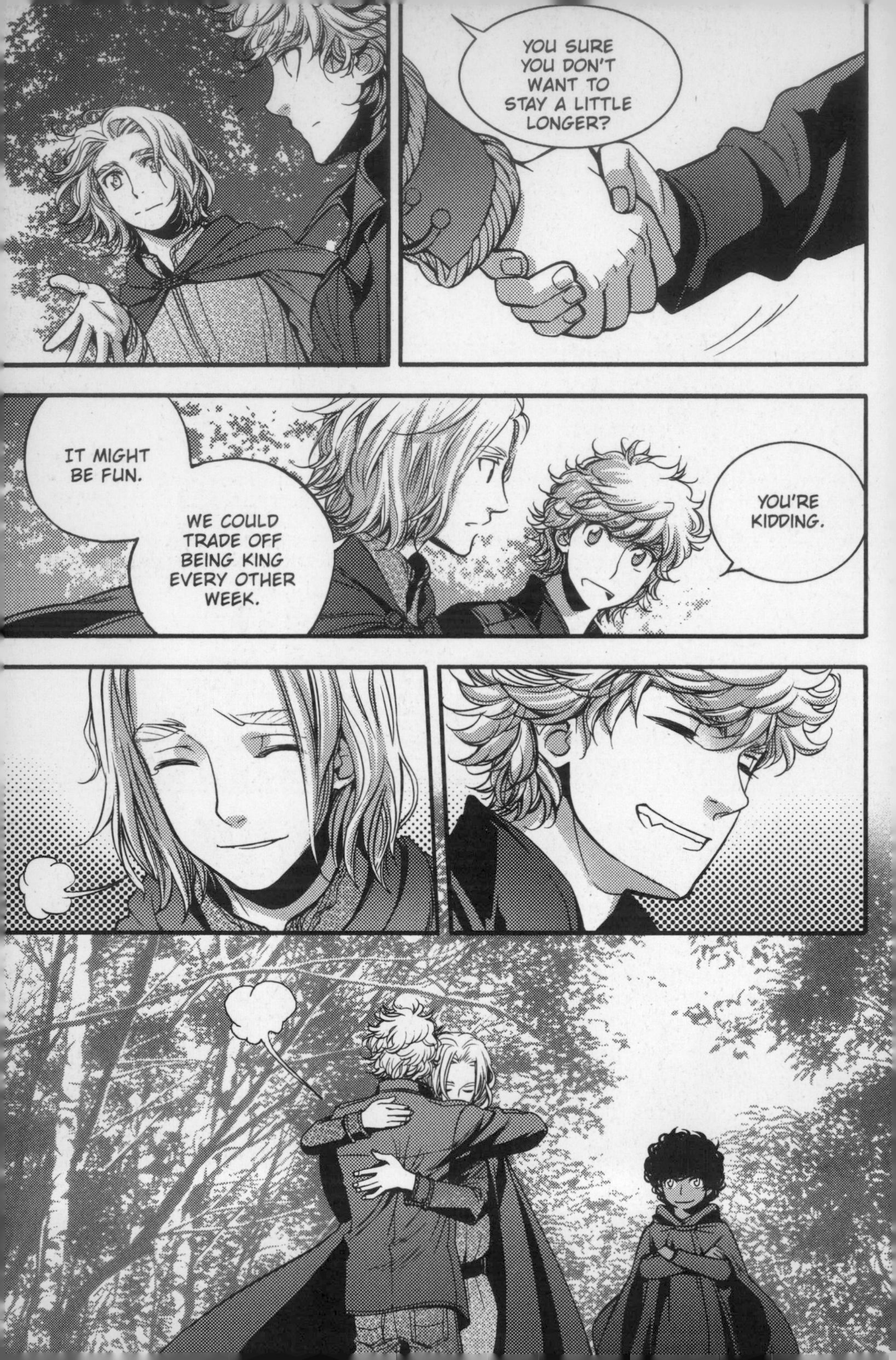
YOU SURE YOU DON'T WANT TO STAY A LITTLE LONGER?
IT MIGHT BE FUN.
WE COULD TRADE OFF BEING KING EVERY OTHER WEEK.
YOU'RE KIDDING.

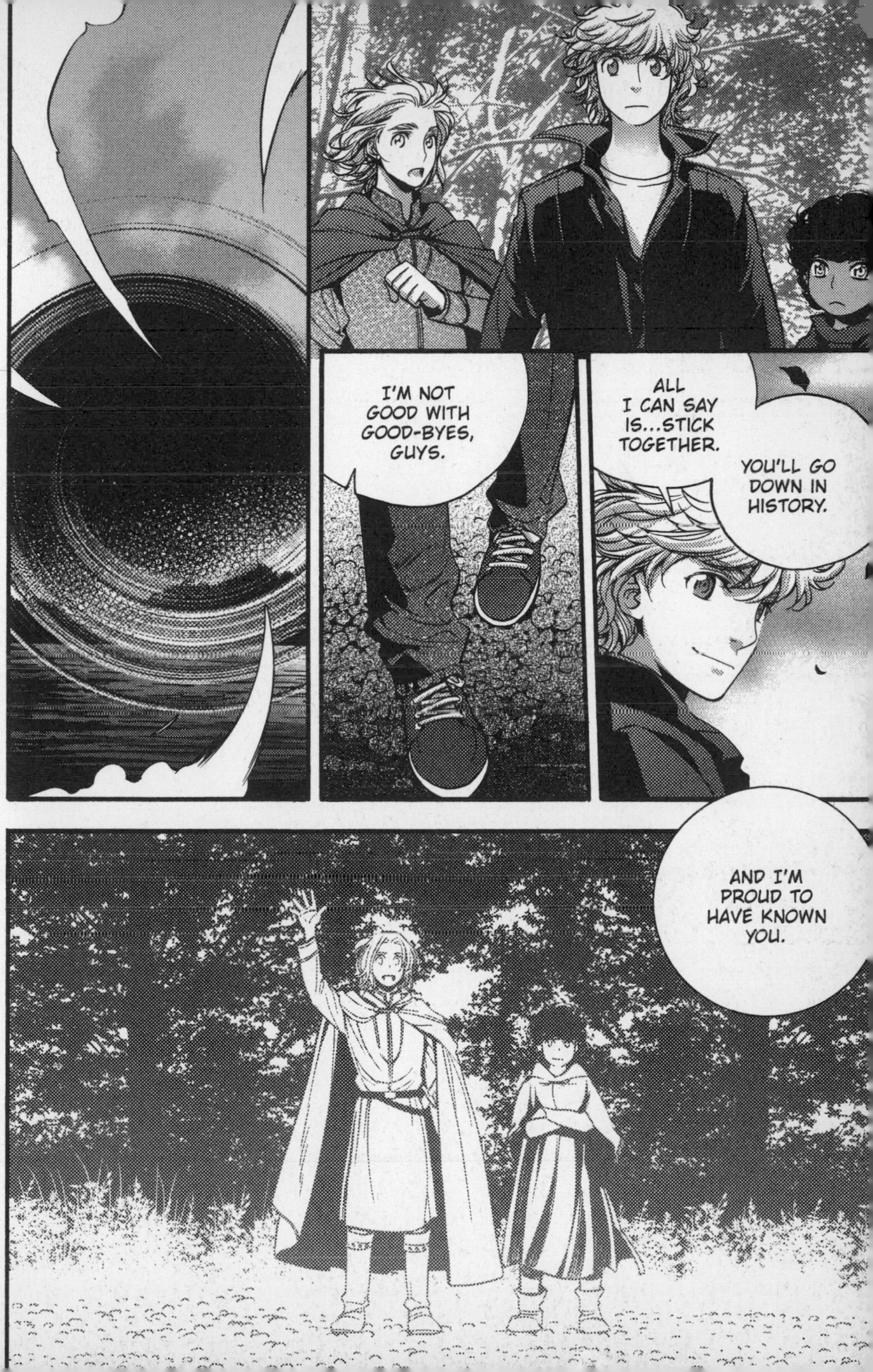
I'M NOT GOOD WITH GOOD-BYES, GUYS.
ALL I CAN SAY IS...STICK TOGETHER.
YOU'LL GO DOWN IN HISTORY.
AND I'M PROUD TO HAVE KNOWN YOU.

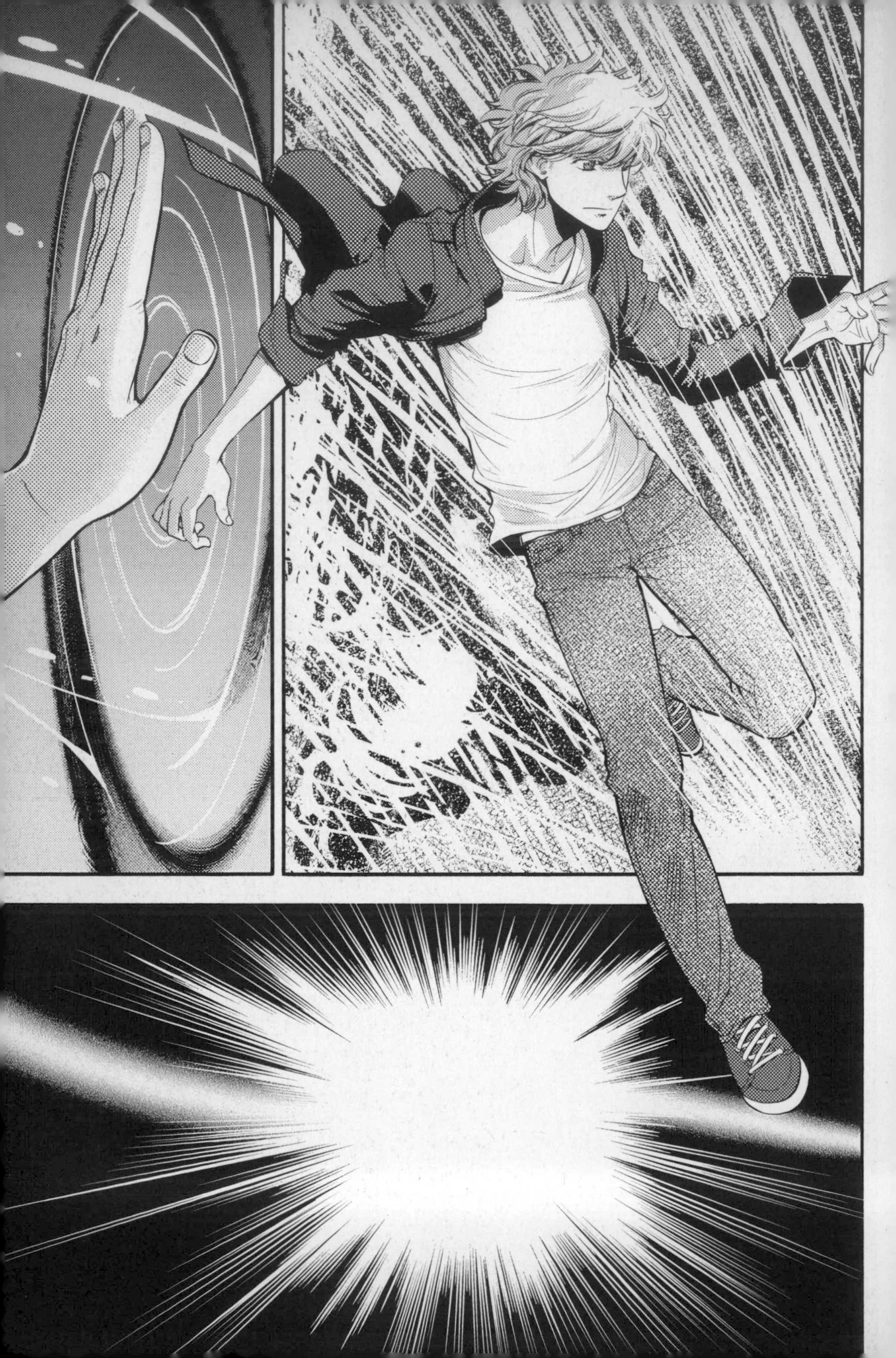

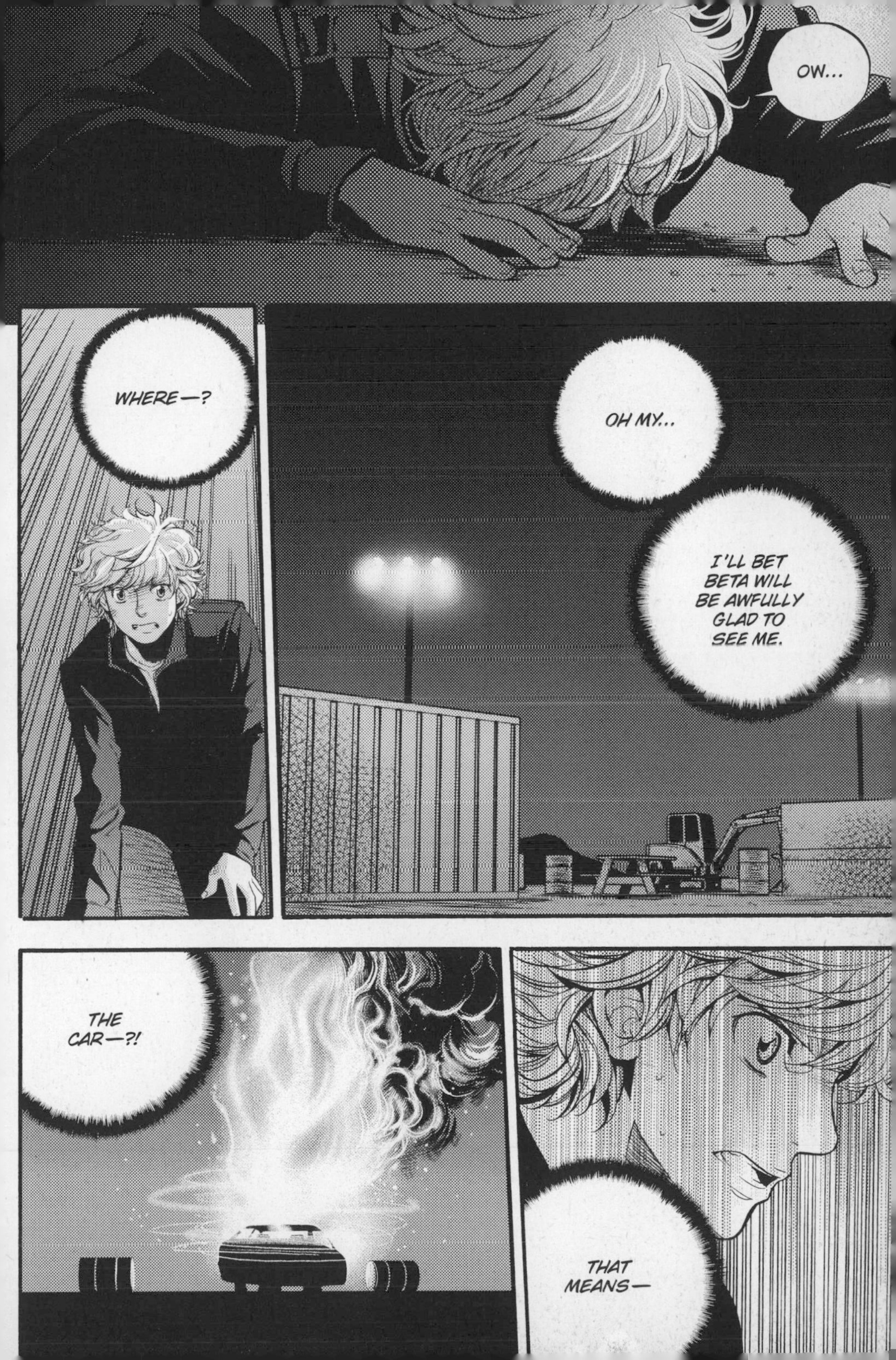
OW...
WHERE—?
OH MY...
I'LL BET BETA WILL BE AWFULLY GLAD TO SEE ME.
THE CAR—?!
THAT MEANS—

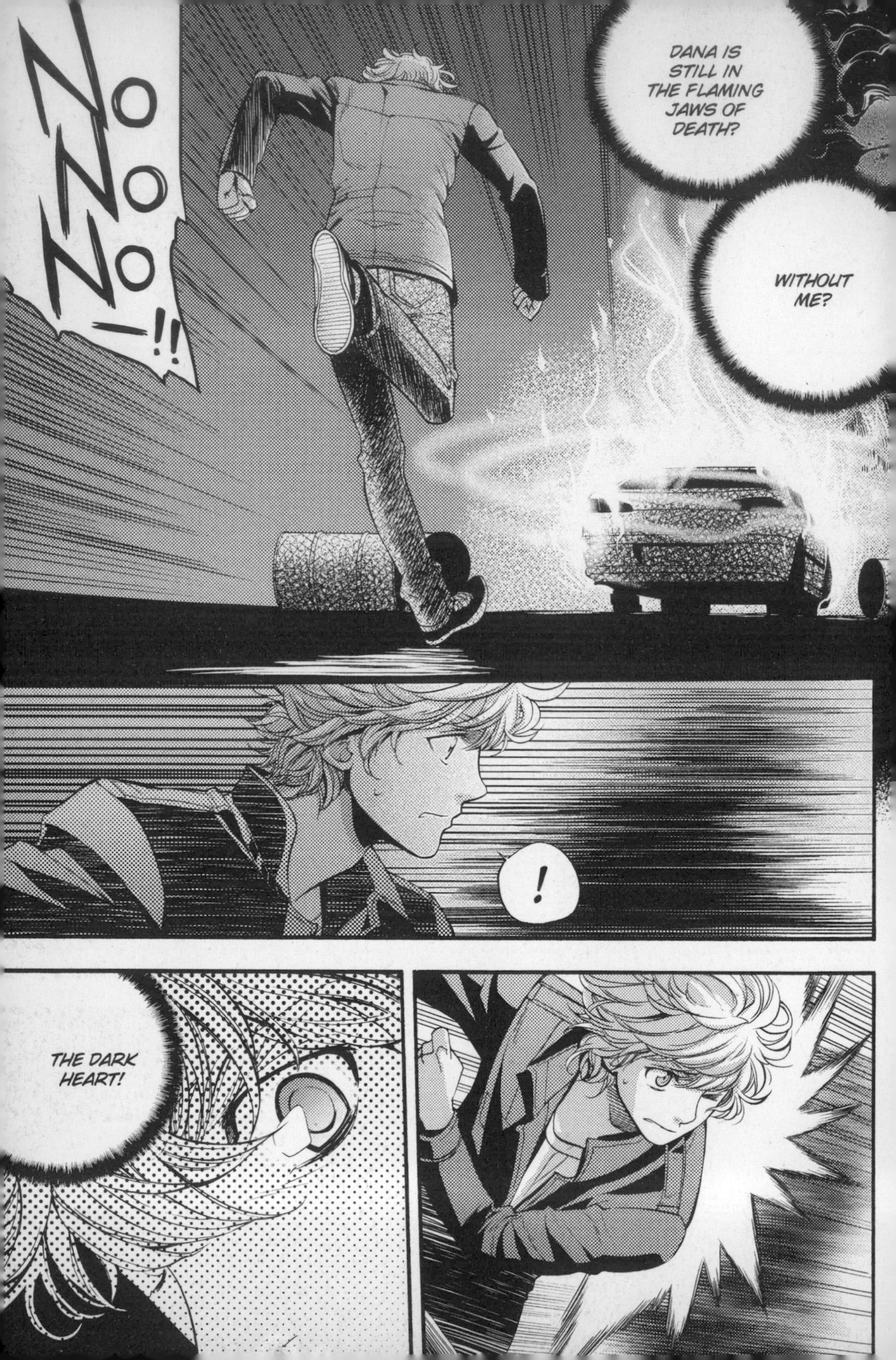
NONONO—!!
DANA IS STILL IN THE FLAMING JAWS OF DEATH?
WITHOUT ME?
!
THE DARK HEART!

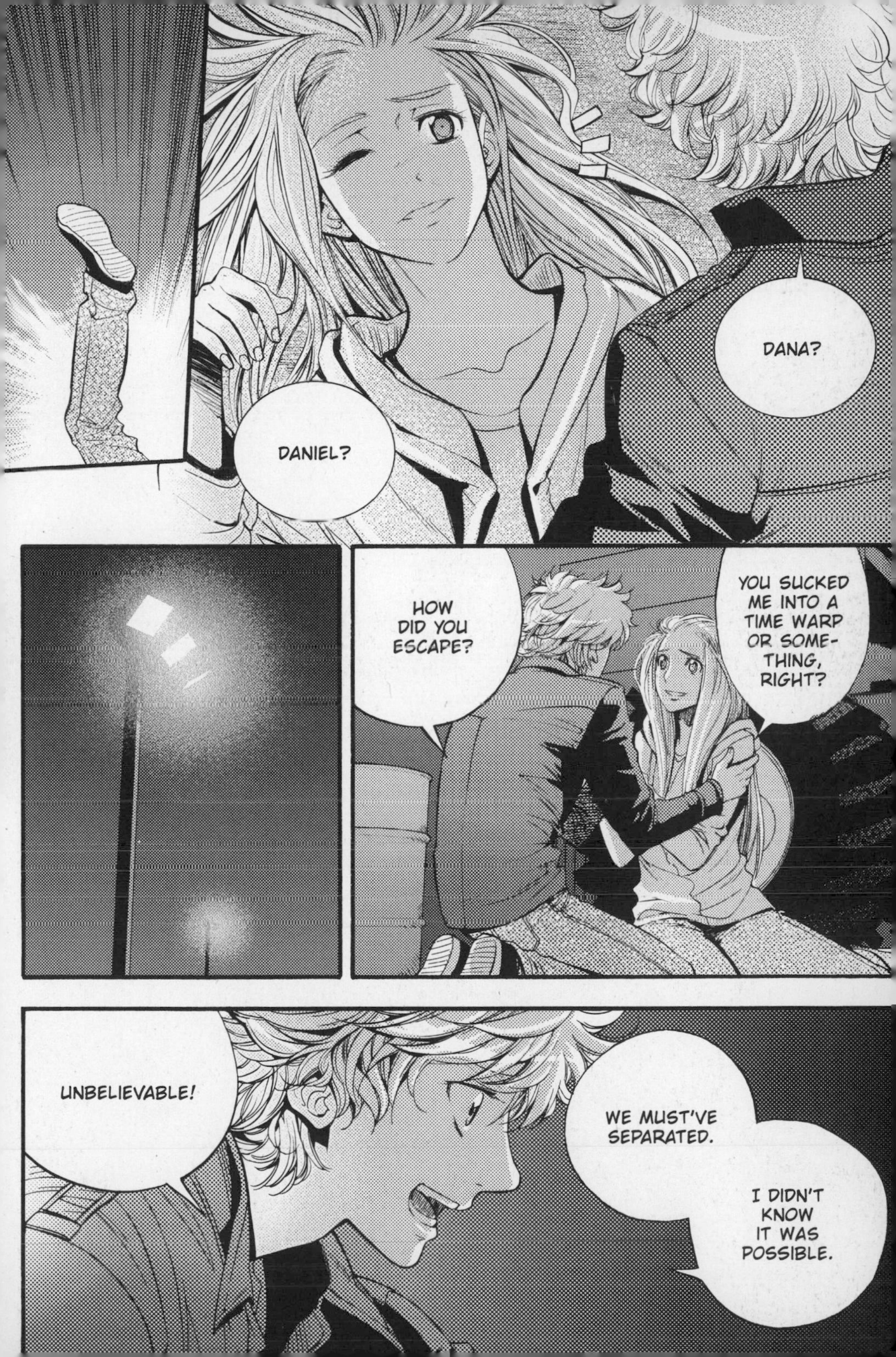
DANIEL?
DANA?
HOW DID YOU ESCAPE?
YOU SUCKED ME INTO A TIME WARP OR SOME-THING, RIGHT?
UNBELIEVABLE!
WE MUST'VE SEPARATED.
I DIDN'T KNOW IT WAS POSSIBLE.

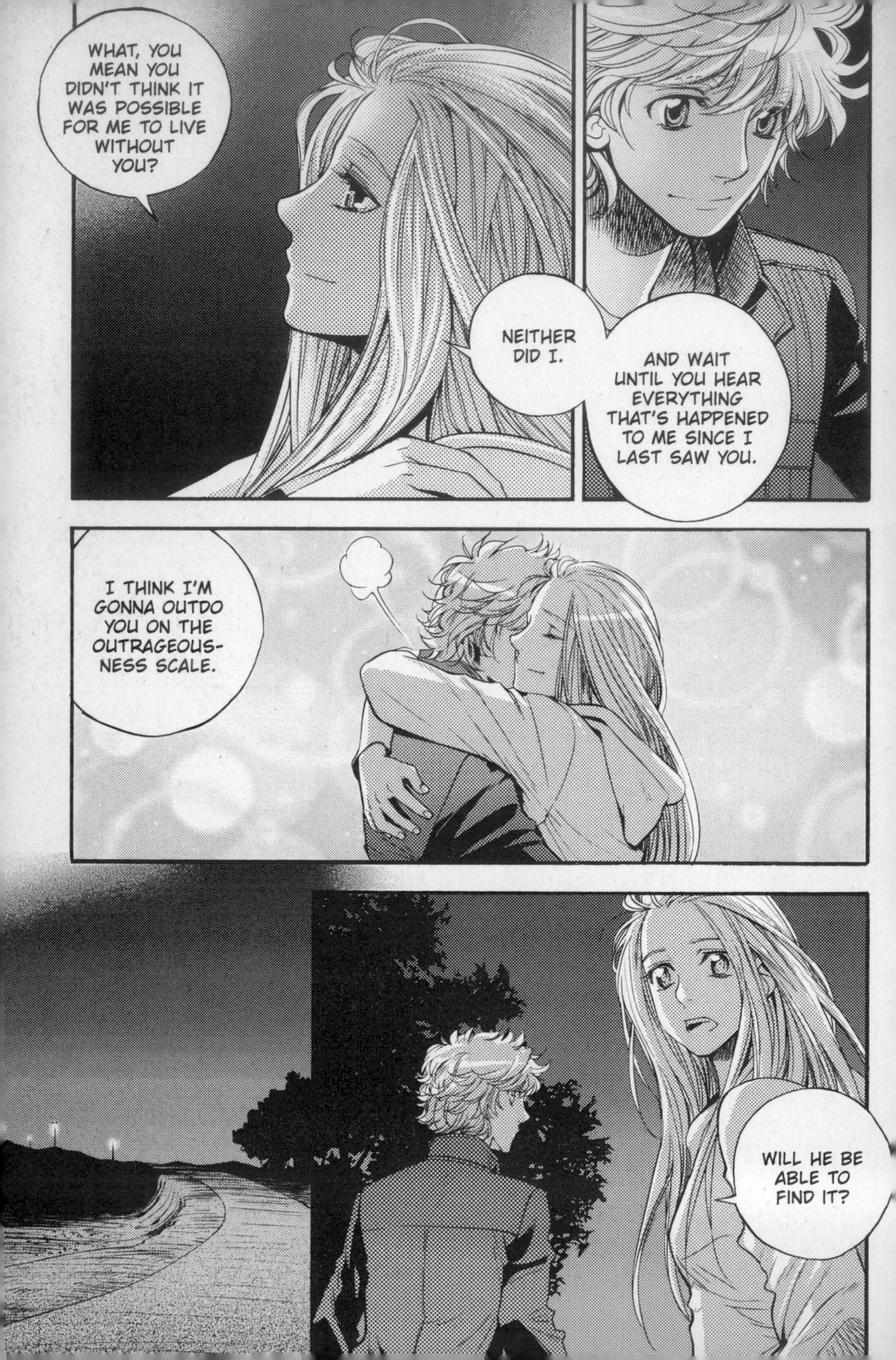
WHAT, YOU MEAN YOU DIDN'T THINK IT WAS POSSIBLE FOR ME TO LIVE WITHOUT YOU?
NEITHER DID I.
AND WAIT UNTIL YOU HEAR EVERYTHING THAT'S HAPPENED TO ME SINCE I LAST SAW YOU.
I THINK I'M GONNA OUTDO YOU ON THE OUTRAGEOUS-NESS SCALE.
WILL HE BE ABLE TO FIND IT?

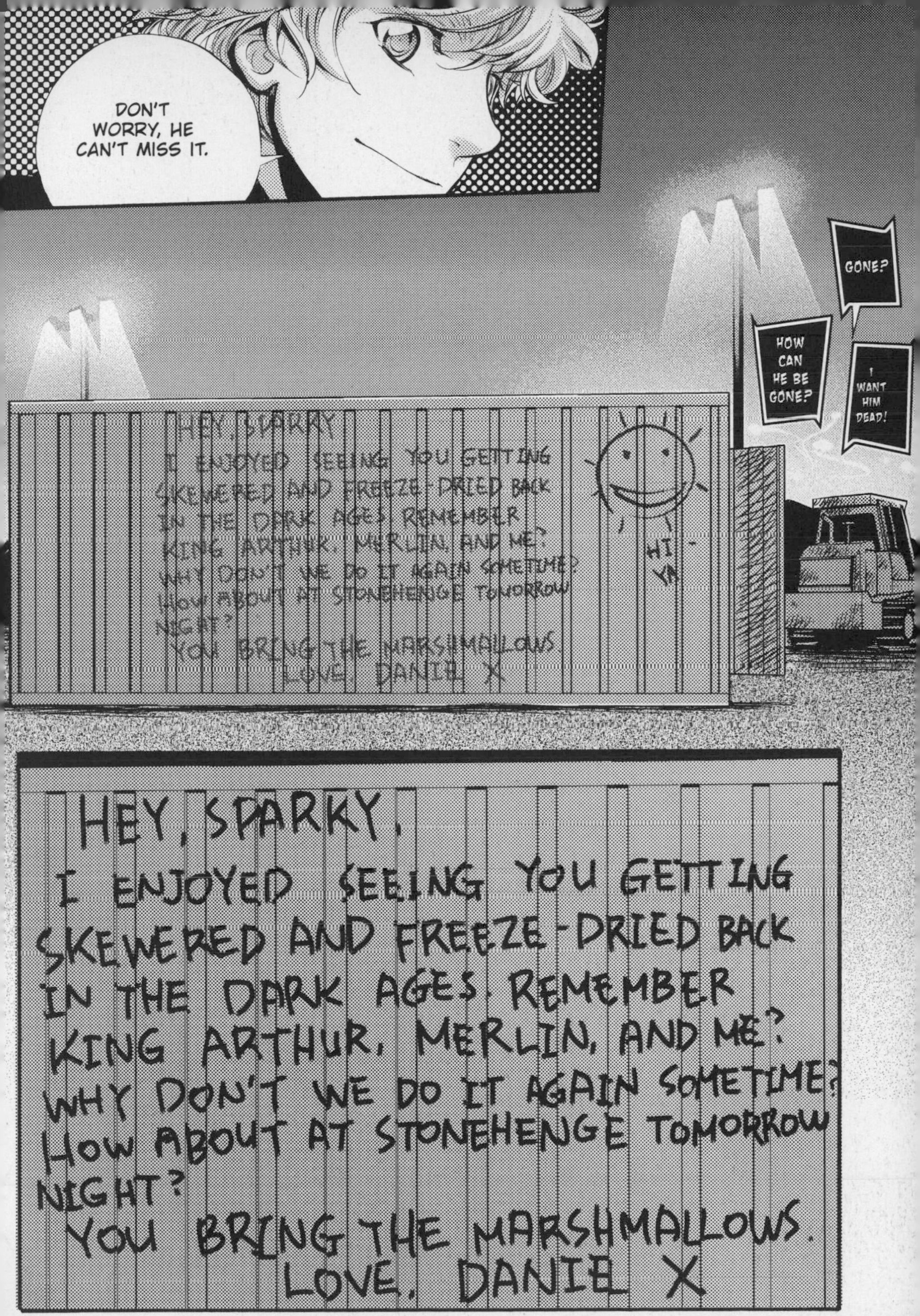
DON'T WORRY, HE CAN'T MISS IT.
HEY, SPARKY,
I ENJOYED SEEING YOU GETTING SKEWERED AND FREEZE-DRIED BACK IN THE DARK AGES. REMEMBER KING ARTHUR, MERLIN, AND ME? WHY DON'T WE DO IT AGAIN SOMETIME? HOW ABOUT AT STONEHENGE TOMORROW NIGHT?
YOU BRING THE MARSHMALLOWS.
LOVE, DANIEL X
HI - YA
GONE?
HOW CAN HE BE GONE?
I WANT HIM DEAD!

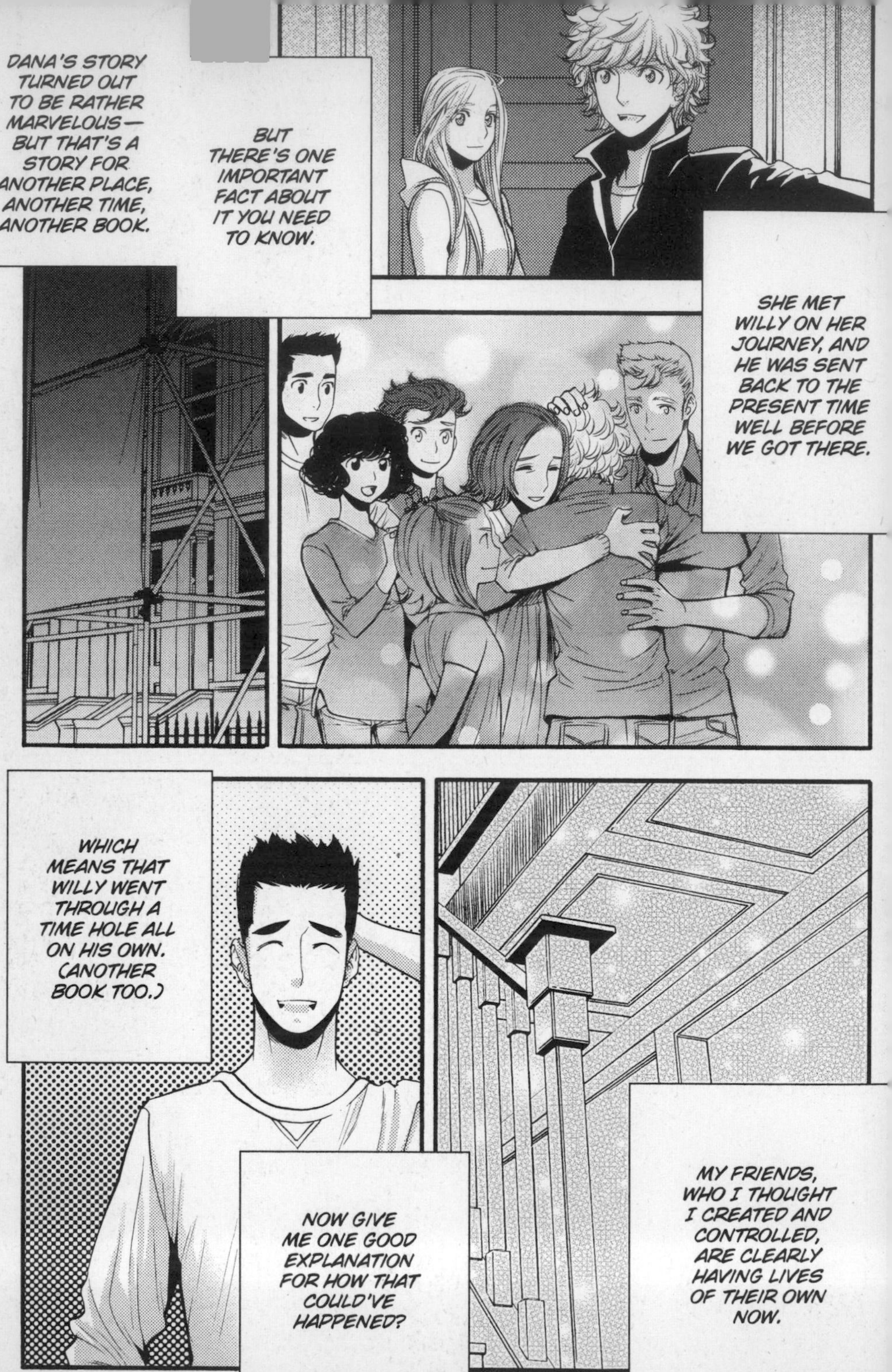
DANA'S STORY TURNED OUT TO BE RATHER MARVELOUS—BUT THAT'S A STORY FOR ANOTHER PLACE, ANOTHER TIME, ANOTHER BOOK.
BUT THERE'S ONE IMPORTANT FACT ABOUT IT YOU NEED TO KNOW.
SHE MET WILLY ON HER JOURNEY, AND HE WAS SENT BACK TO THE PRESENT TIME WELL BEFORE WE GOT THERE.
WHICH MEANS THAT WILLY WENT THROUGH A TIME HOLE ALL ON HIS OWN. (ANOTHER BOOK TOO.)
NOW GIVE ME ONE GOOD EXPLANATION FOR HOW THAT COULD'VE HAPPENED?
MY FRIENDS, WHO I THOUGHT I CREATED AND CONTROLLED, ARE CLEARLY HAVING LIVES OF THEIR OWN NOW.

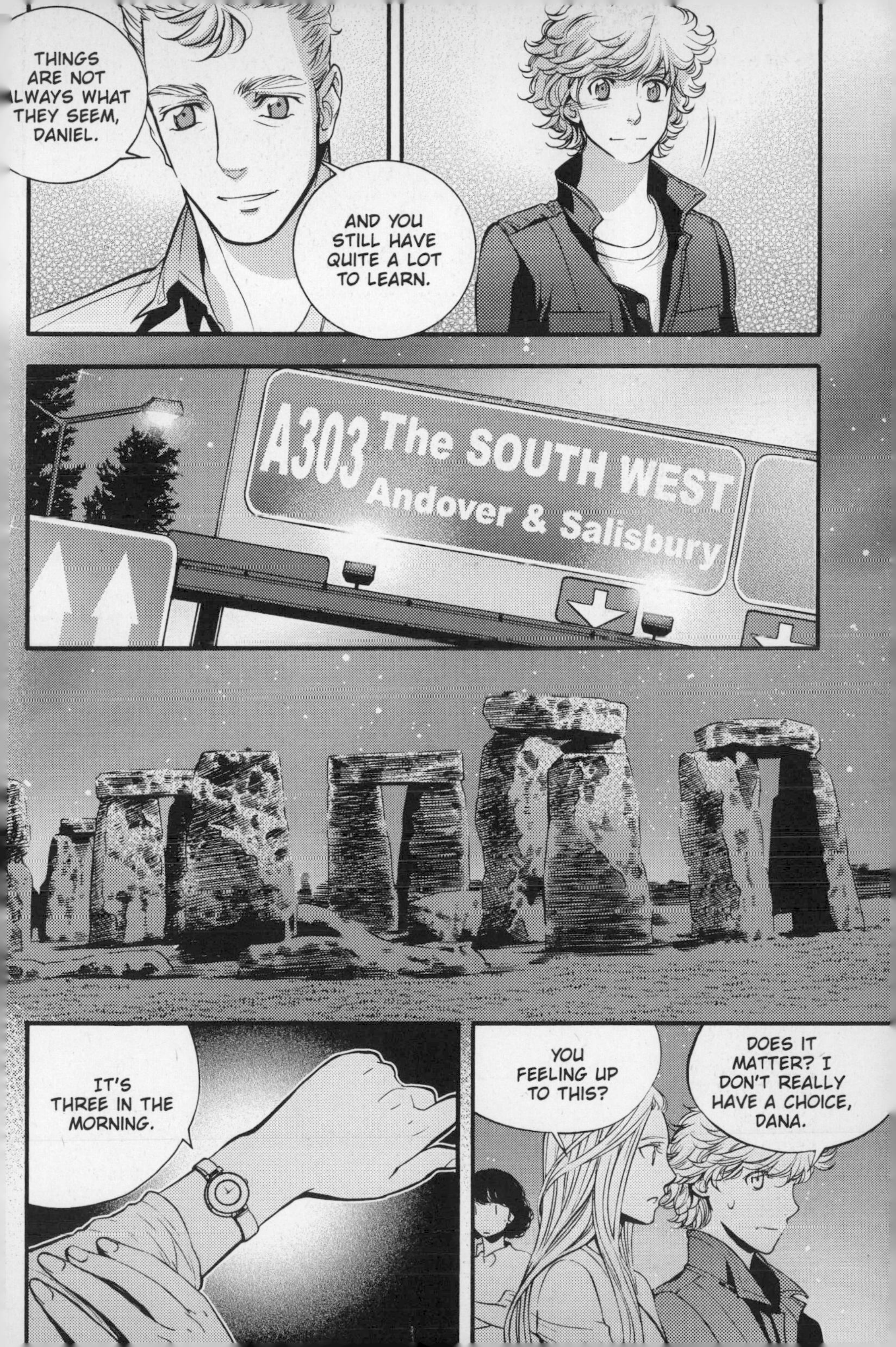
THINGS ARE NOT ALWAYS WHAT THEY SEEM, DANIEL.
AND YOU STILL HAVE QUITE A LOT TO LEARN.
A303 The SOUTH WEST
Andover & Salisbury
IT'S THREE IN THE MORNING.
YOU FEELING UP TO THIS?
DOES IT MATTER? I DON'T REALLY HAVE A CHOICE, DANA.

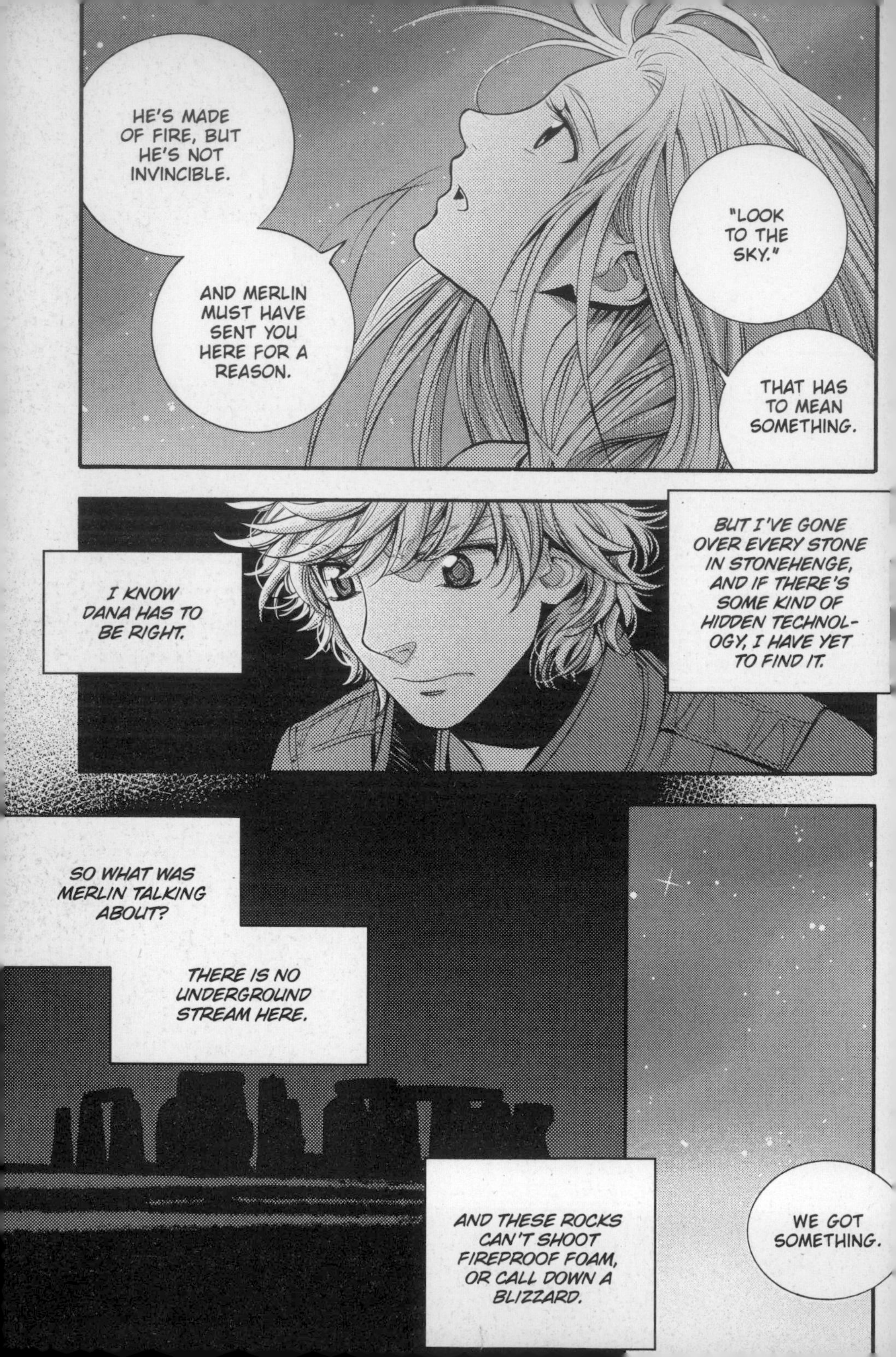
HE'S MADE OF FIRE, BUT HE'S NOT INVINCIBLE.
AND MERLIN MUST HAVE SENT YOU HERE FOR A REASON.
"LOOK TO THE SKY."
THAT HAS TO MEAN SOMETHING.
I KNOW DANA HAS TO BE RIGHT.
BUT I'VE GONE OVER EVERY STONE IN STONEHENGE, AND IF THERE'S SOME KIND OF HIDDEN TECHNOLOGY, I HAVE YET TO FIND IT.
SO WHAT WAS MERLIN TALKING ABOUT?
THERE IS NO UNDERGROUND STREAM HERE.
AND THESE ROCKS CAN'T SHOOT FIREPROOF FOAM, OR CALL DOWN A BLIZZARD.
WE GOT SOMETHING.

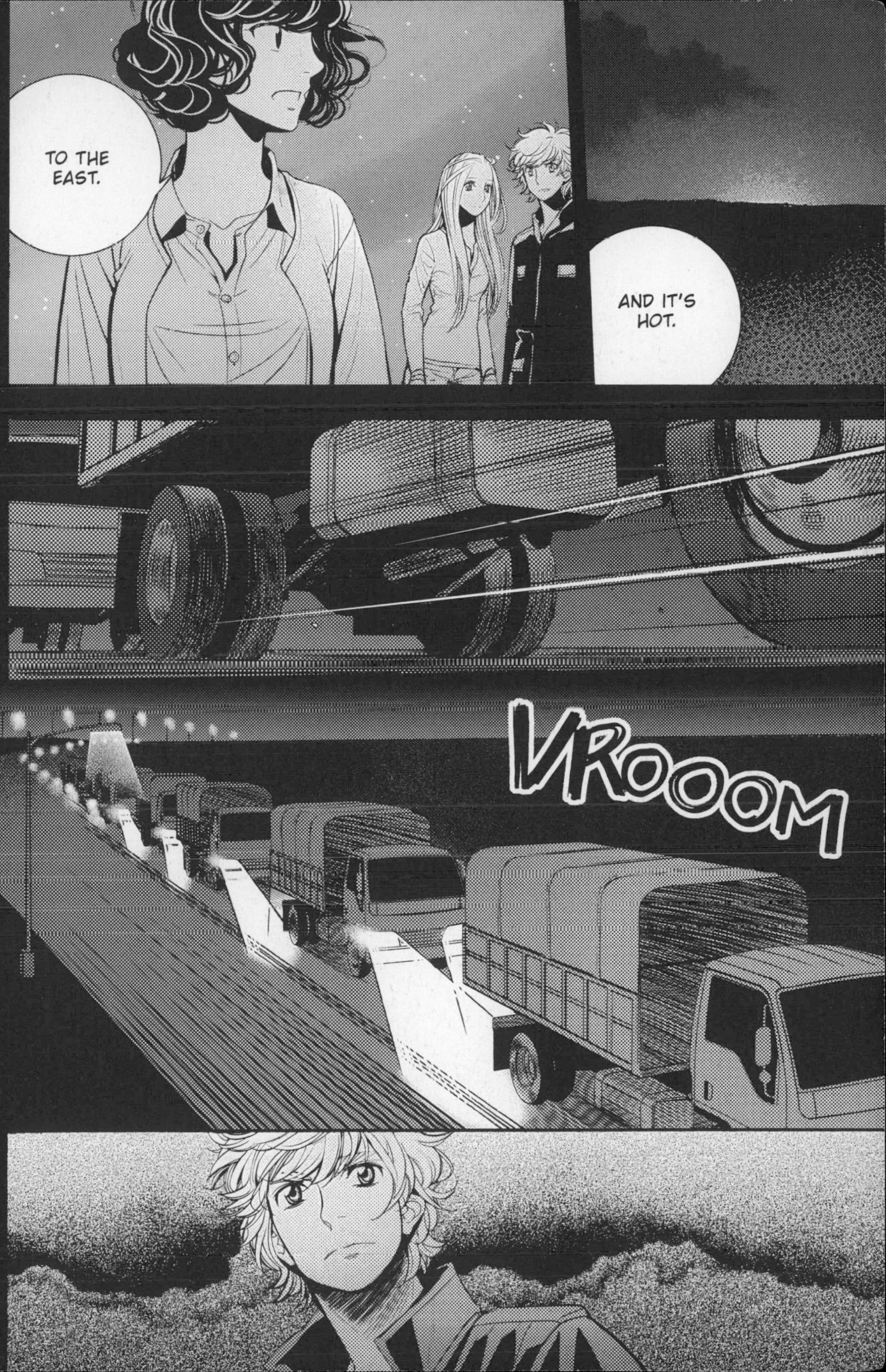
TO THE EAST.
AND IT'S HOT.
VROOOM

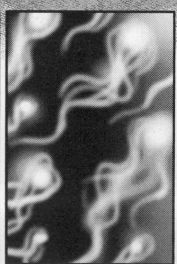

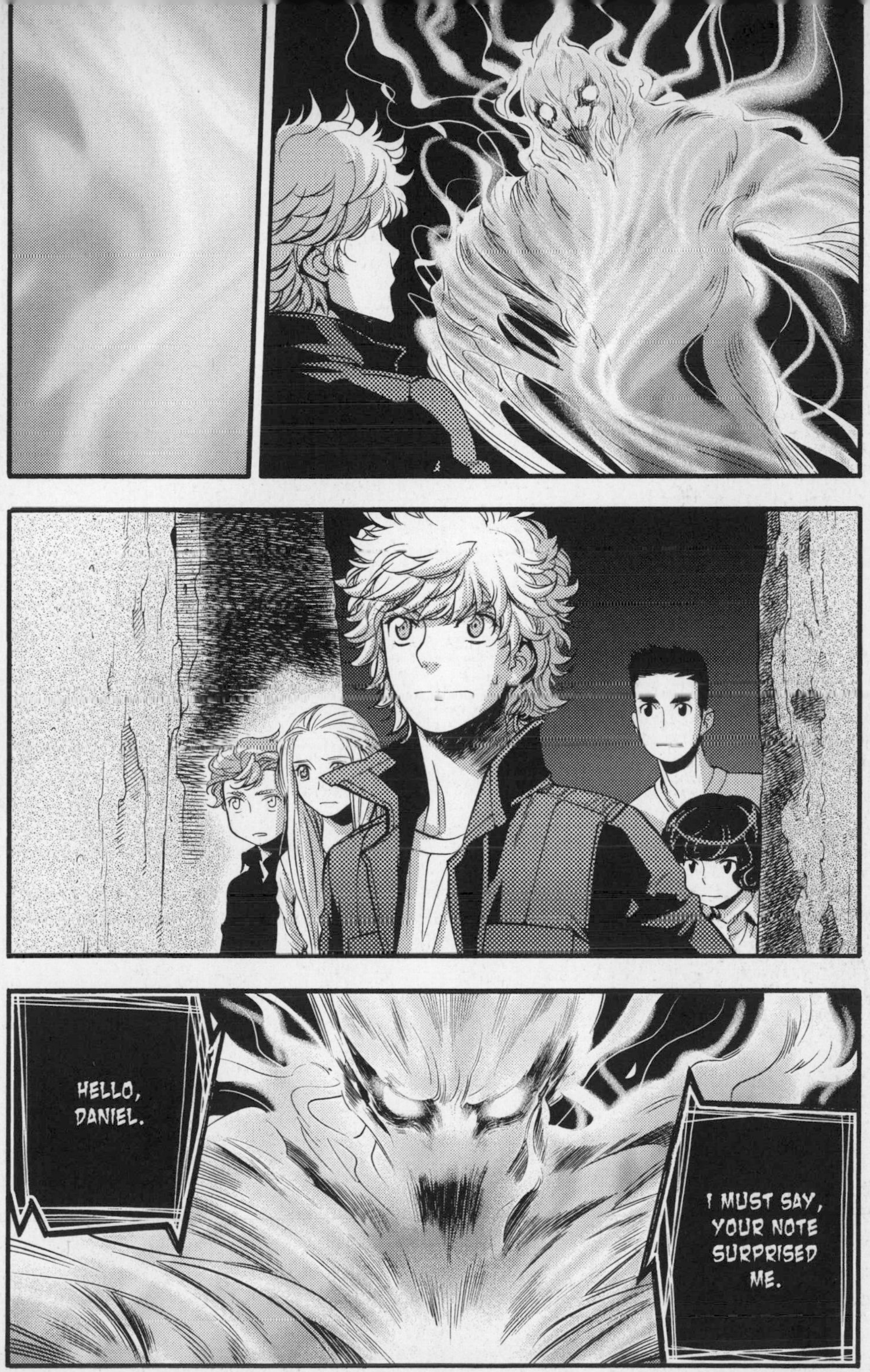
HELLO, DANIEL.
I MUST SAY, YOUR NOTE SURPRISED ME.

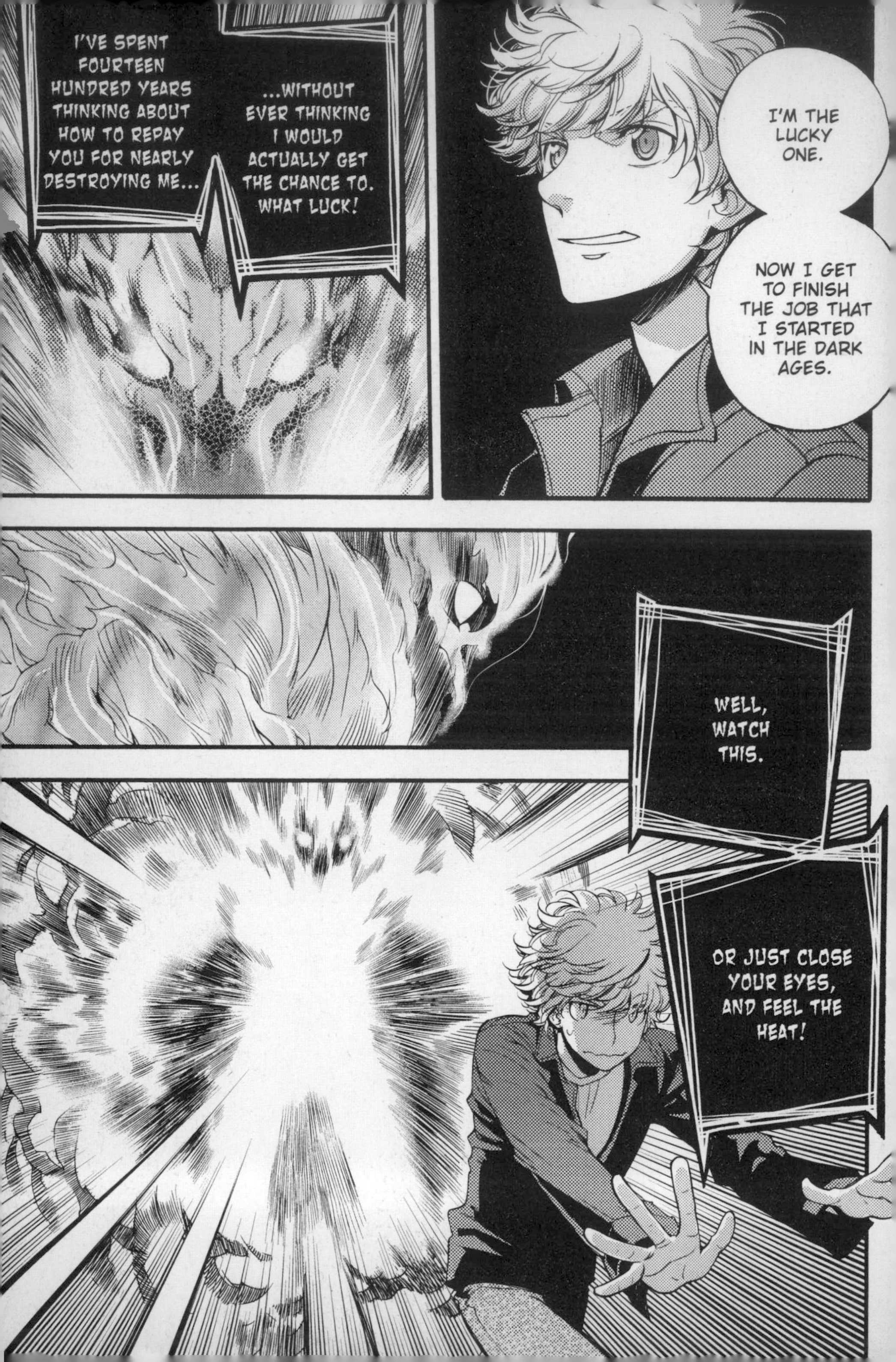
I'VE SPENT FOURTEEN HUNDRED YEARS THINKING ABOUT HOW TO REPAY YOU FOR NEARLY DESTROYING ME...
...WITHOUT EVER THINKING I WOULD ACTUALLY GET THE CHANCE TO. WHAT LUCK!
I'M THE LUCKY ONE.
NOW I GET TO FINISH THE JOB THAT I STARTED IN THE DARK AGES.
WELL, WATCH THIS.
OR JUST CLOSE YOUR EYES, AND FEEL THE HEAT!

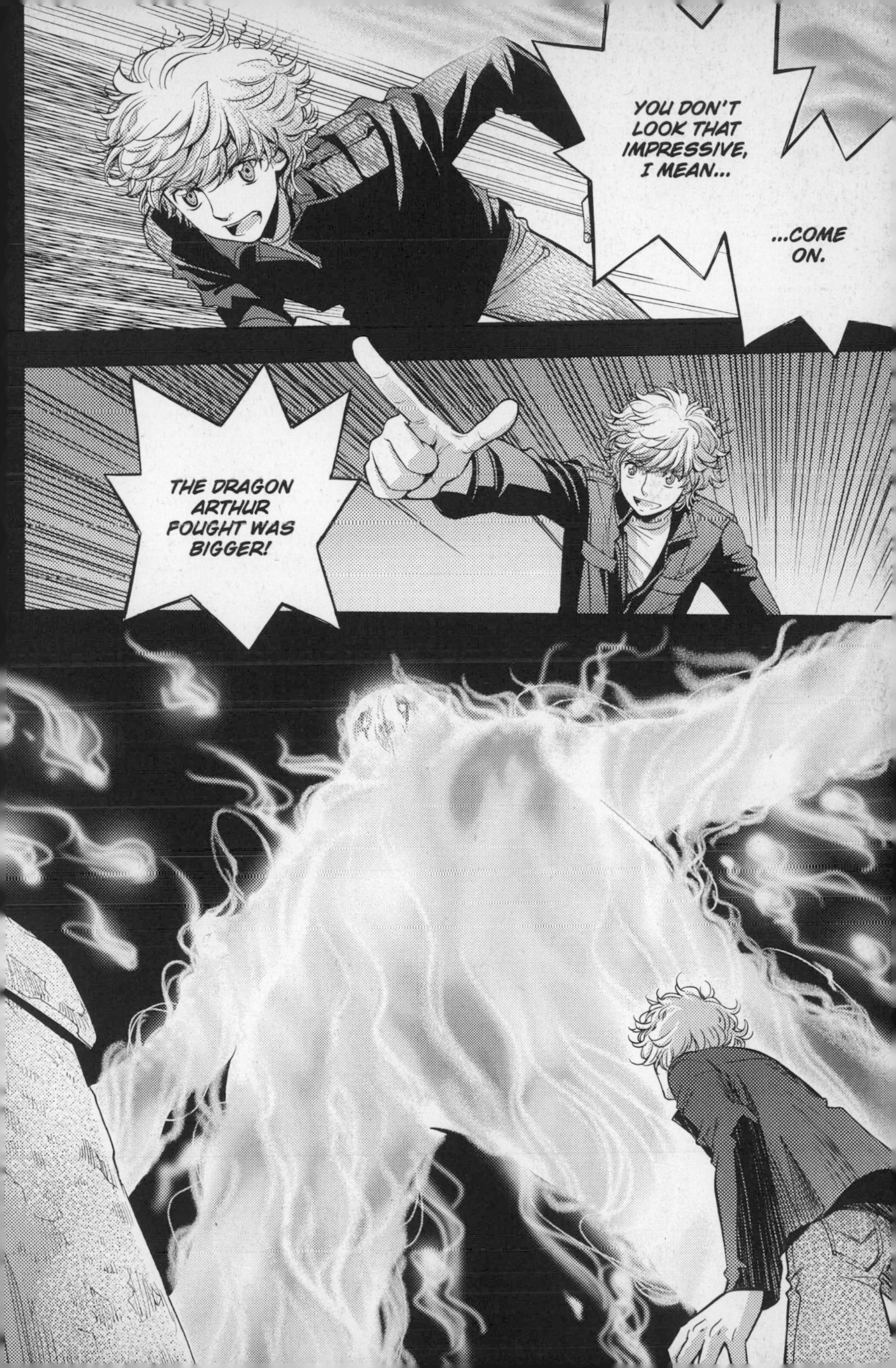
YOU DON'T LOOK THAT IMPRESSIVE, I MEAN...
...COME ON.
THE DRAGON ARTHUR FOUGHT WAS BIGGER!

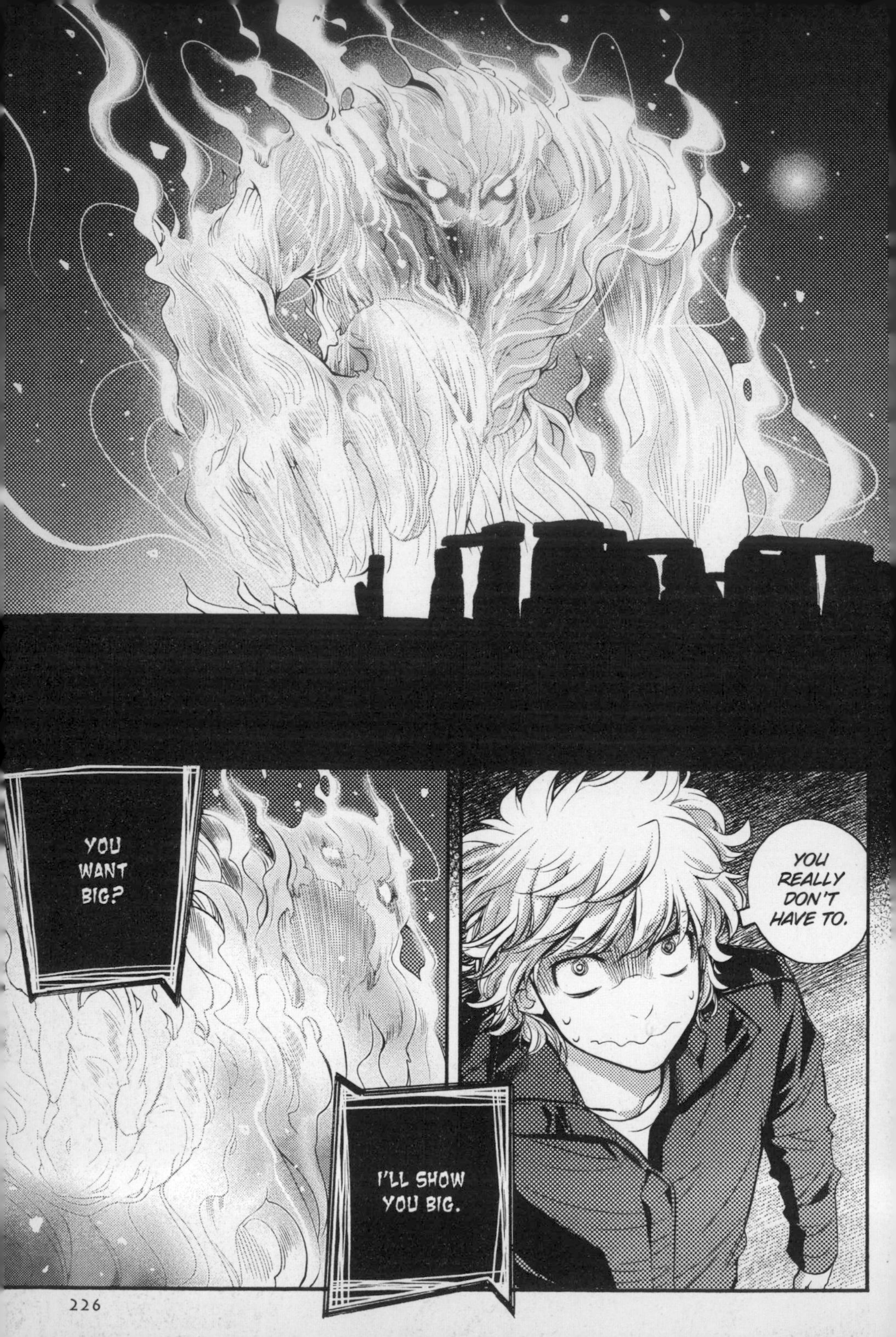
YOU WANT BIG?
YOU REALLY DON'T HAVE TO.
I'LL SHOW YOU BIG.

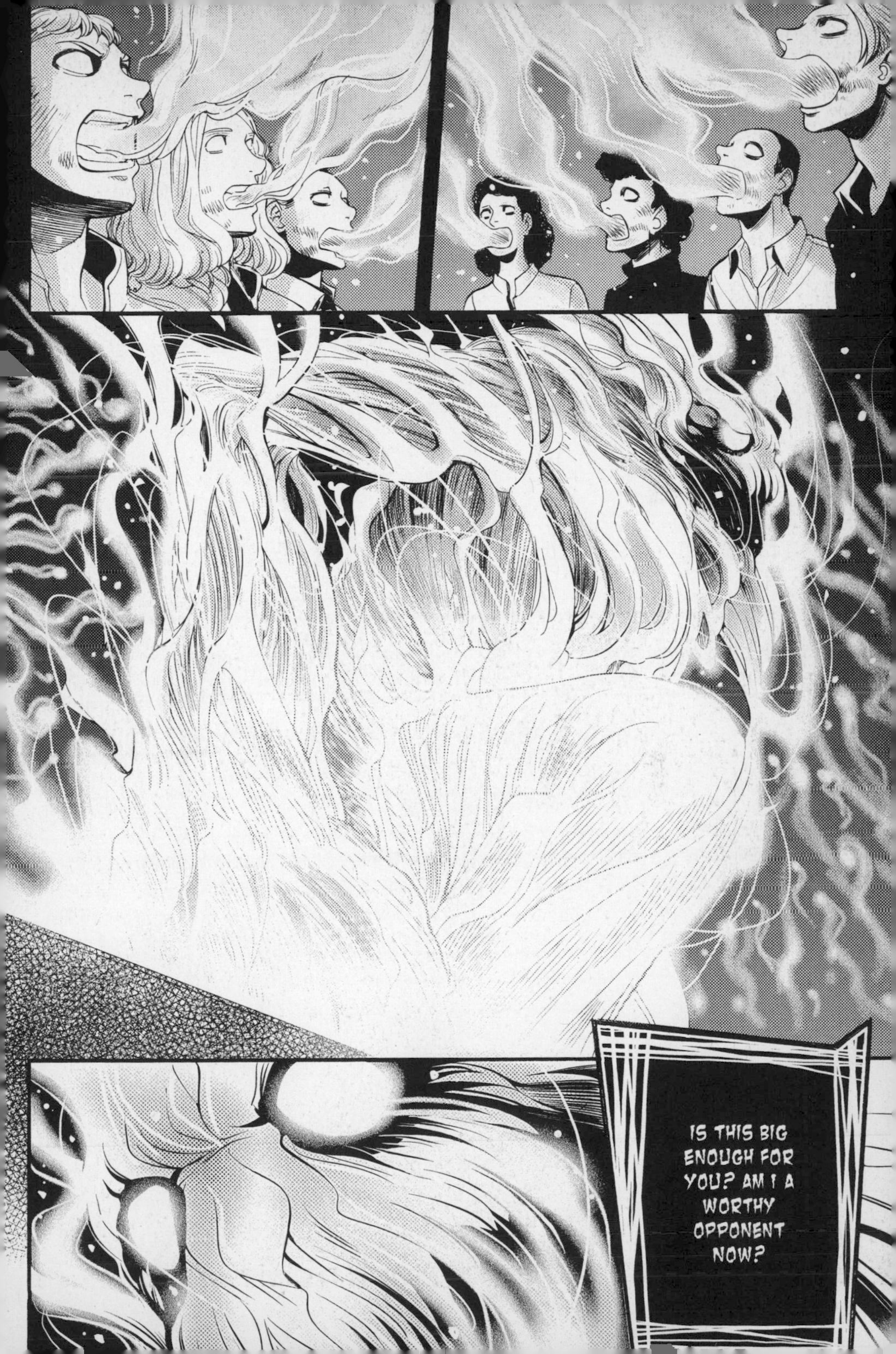
IS THIS BIG ENOUGH FOR YOU? AM I A WORTHY OPPONENT NOW?

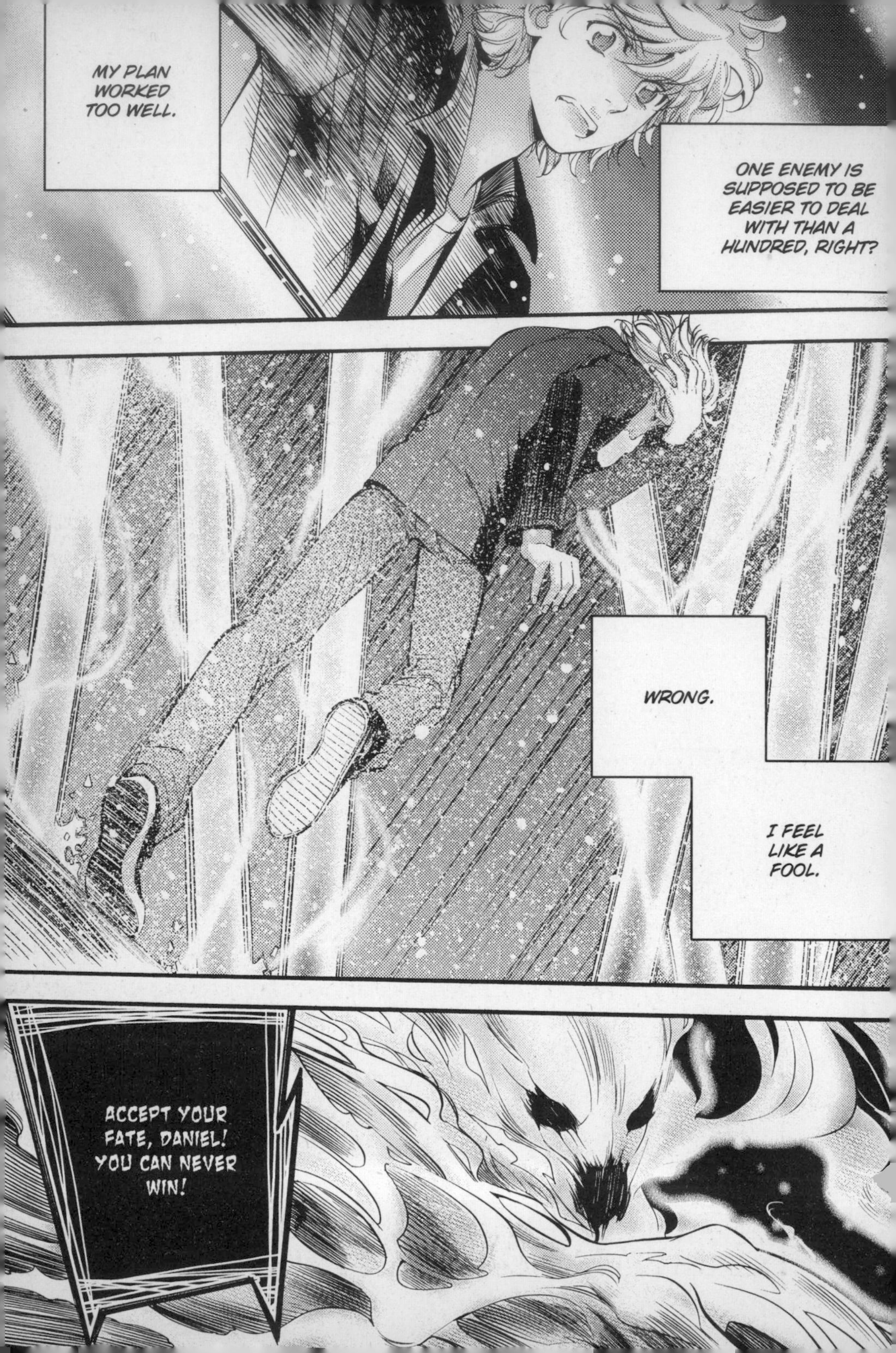
MY PLAN WORKED TOO WELL.
ONE ENEMY IS SUPPOSED TO BE EASIER TO DEAL WITH THAN A HUNDRED, RIGHT?
WRONG.
I FEEL LIKE A FOOL.
ACCEPT YOUR FATE, DANIEL! YOU CAN NEVER WIN!

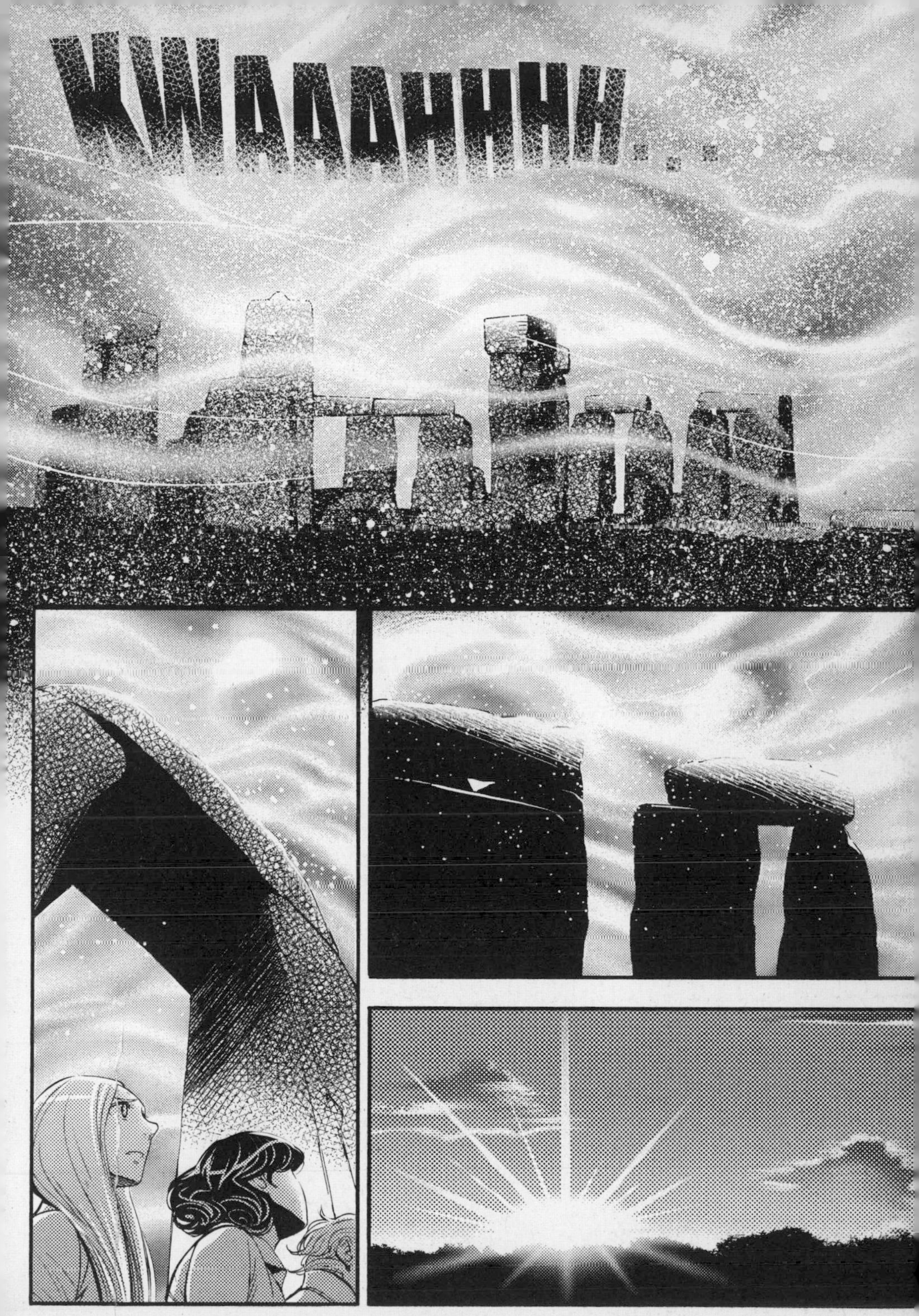
KWAAAHHHH...

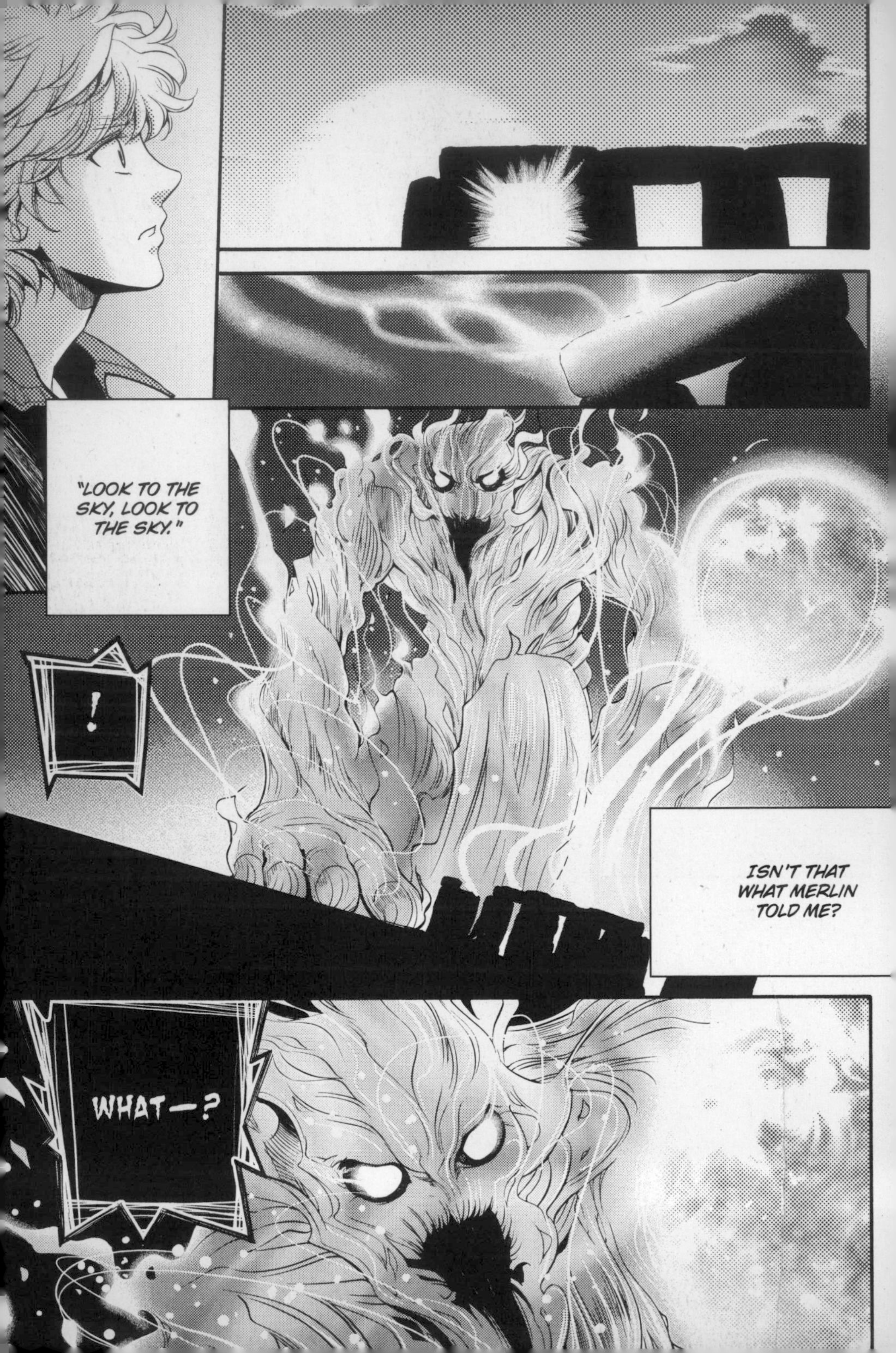
"LOOK TO THE SKY, LOOK TO THE SKY."
!
ISN'T THAT WHAT MERLIN TOLD ME?
WHAT—?

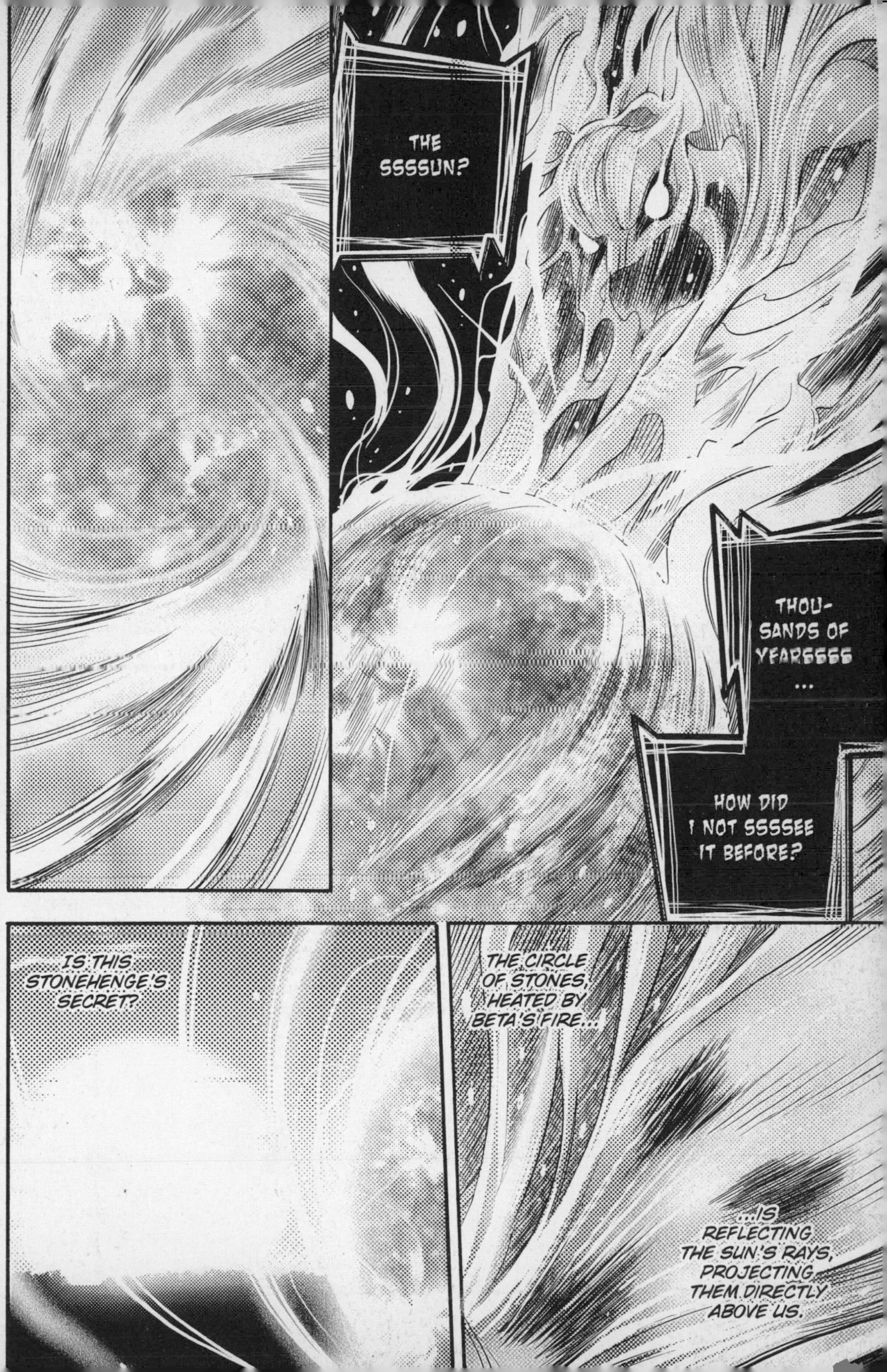
THE SSSSUN?
THOU-SANDS OF YEARSSSS...
HOW DID I NOT SSSSEE IT BEFORE?
IS THIS STONEHENGE'S SECRET?
THE CIRCLE OF STONES, HEATED BY BETA'S FIRE...
...IS REFLECTING THE SUN'S RAYS, PROJECTING THEM DIRECTLY ABOVE US.

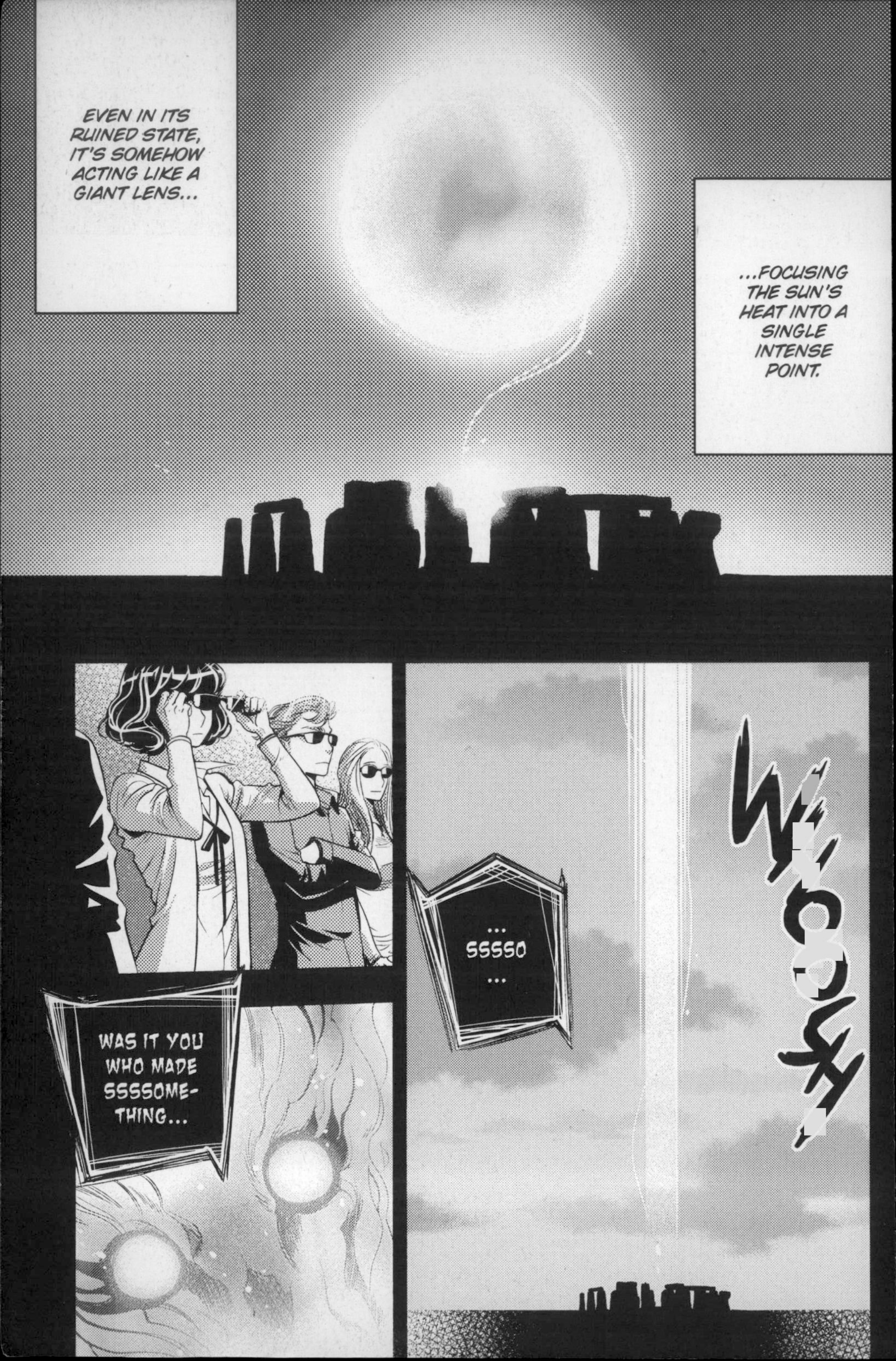
EVEN IN ITS RUINED STATE, IT'S SOMEHOW ACTING LIKE A GIANT LENS...
...FOCUSING THE SUN'S HEAT INTO A SINGLE INTENSE POINT.
WAS IT YOU WHO MADE SSSSOME-THING...
... SSSSO ...

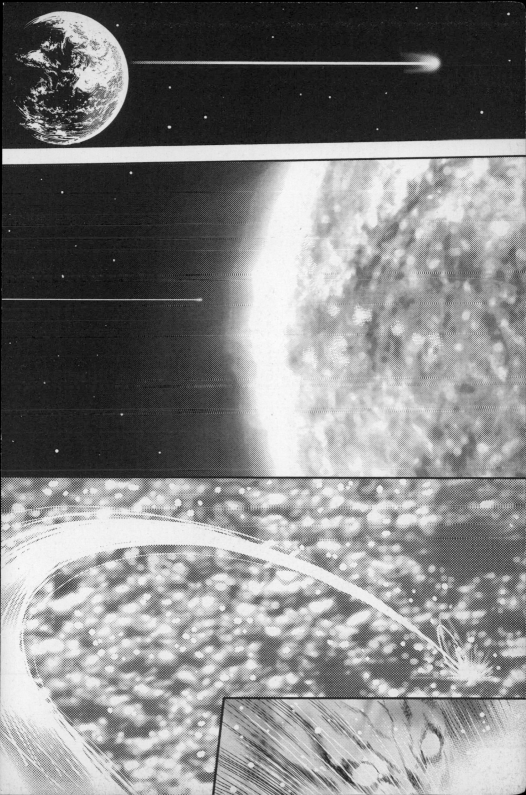

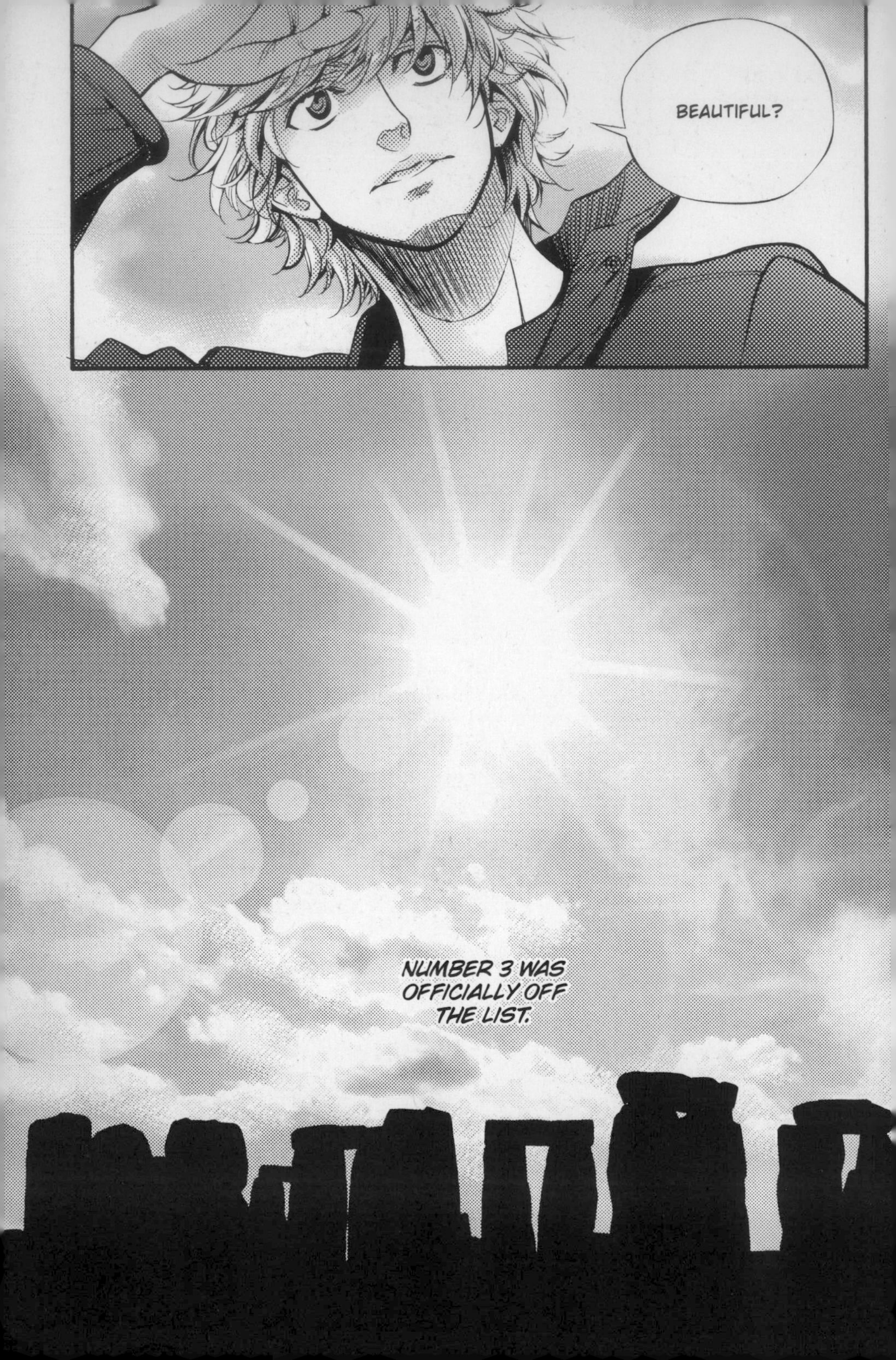
BEAUTIFUL?
NUMBER 3 WAS OFFICIALLY OFF THE LIST.

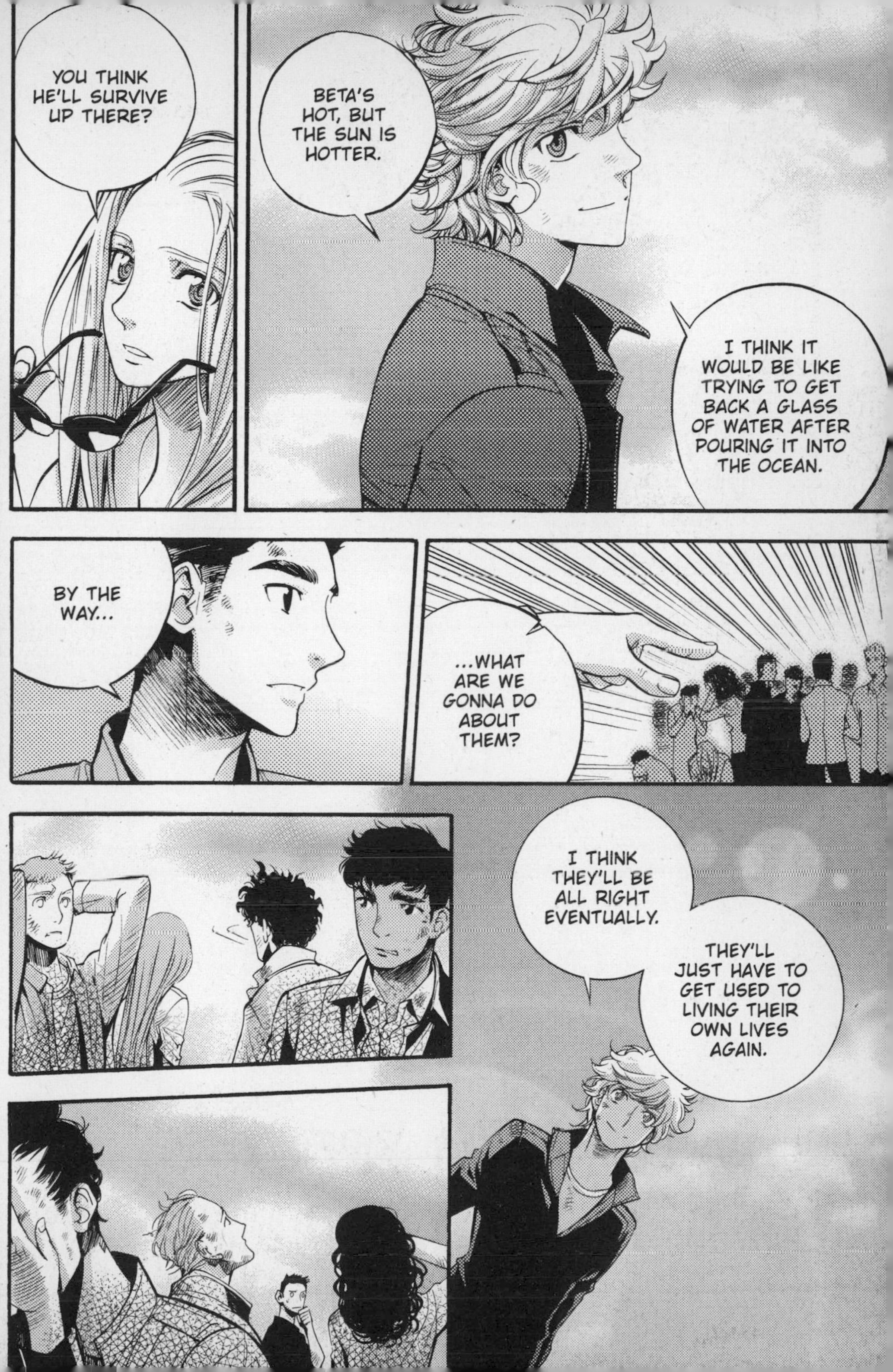
YOU THINK HE'LL SURVIVE UP THERE?
BETA'S HOT, BUT THE SUN IS HOTTER.
I THINK IT WOULD BE LIKE TRYING TO GET BACK A GLASS OF WATER AFTER POURING IT INTO THE OCEAN.
BY THE WAY...
...WHAT ARE WE GONNA DO ABOUT THEM?
I THINK THEY'LL BE ALL RIGHT EVENTUALLY.
THEY'LL JUST HAVE TO GET USED TO LIVING THEIR OWN LIVES AGAIN.

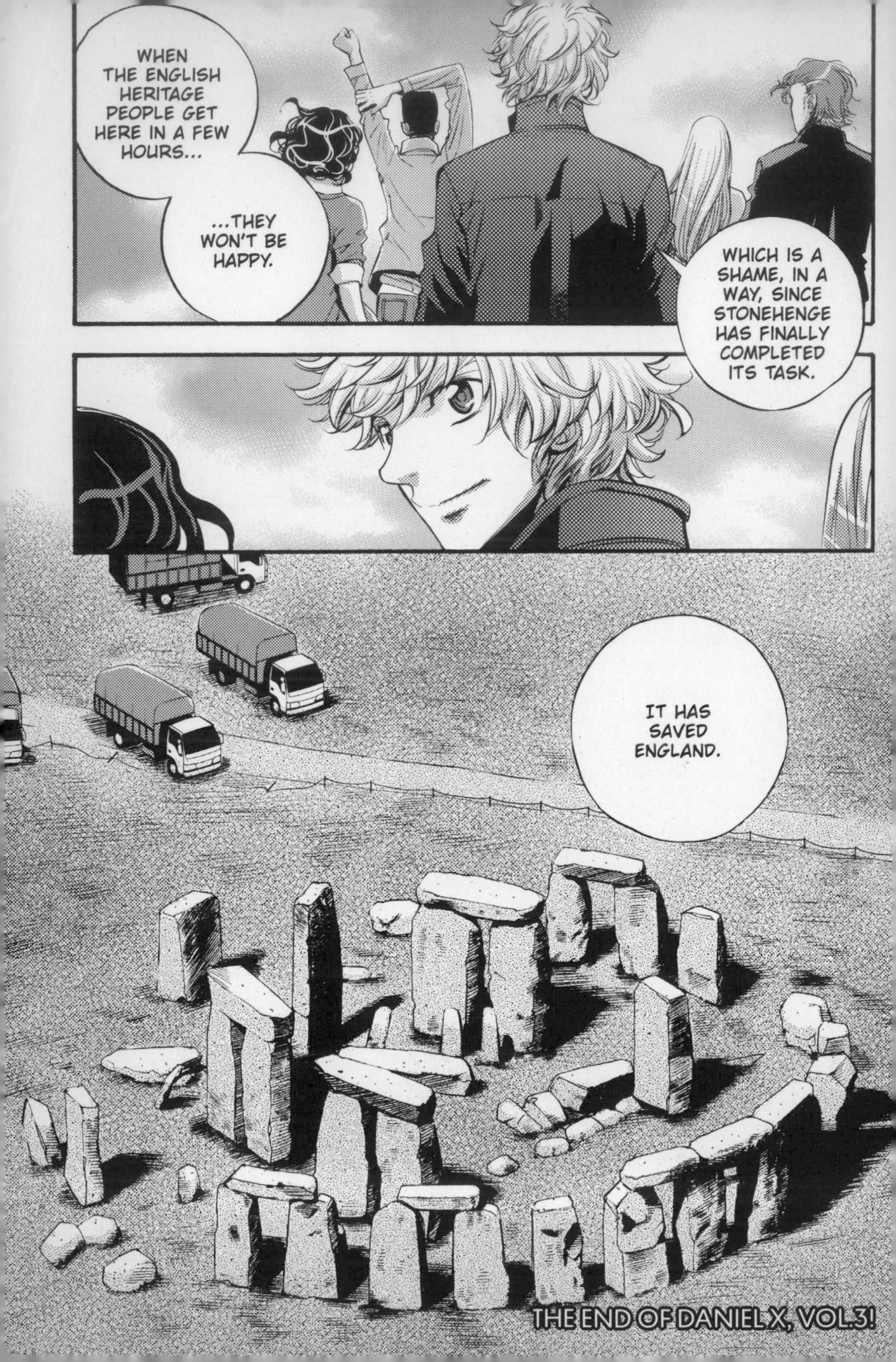
WHEN THE ENGLISH HERITAGE PEOPLE GET HERE IN A FEW HOURS...
...THEY WON'T BE HAPPY.
WHICH IS A SHAME, IN A WAY, SINCE STONEHENGE HAS FINALLY COMPLETED ITS TASK.
IT HAS SAVED ENGLAND.
THE END OF DANIEL X, VOL.3!

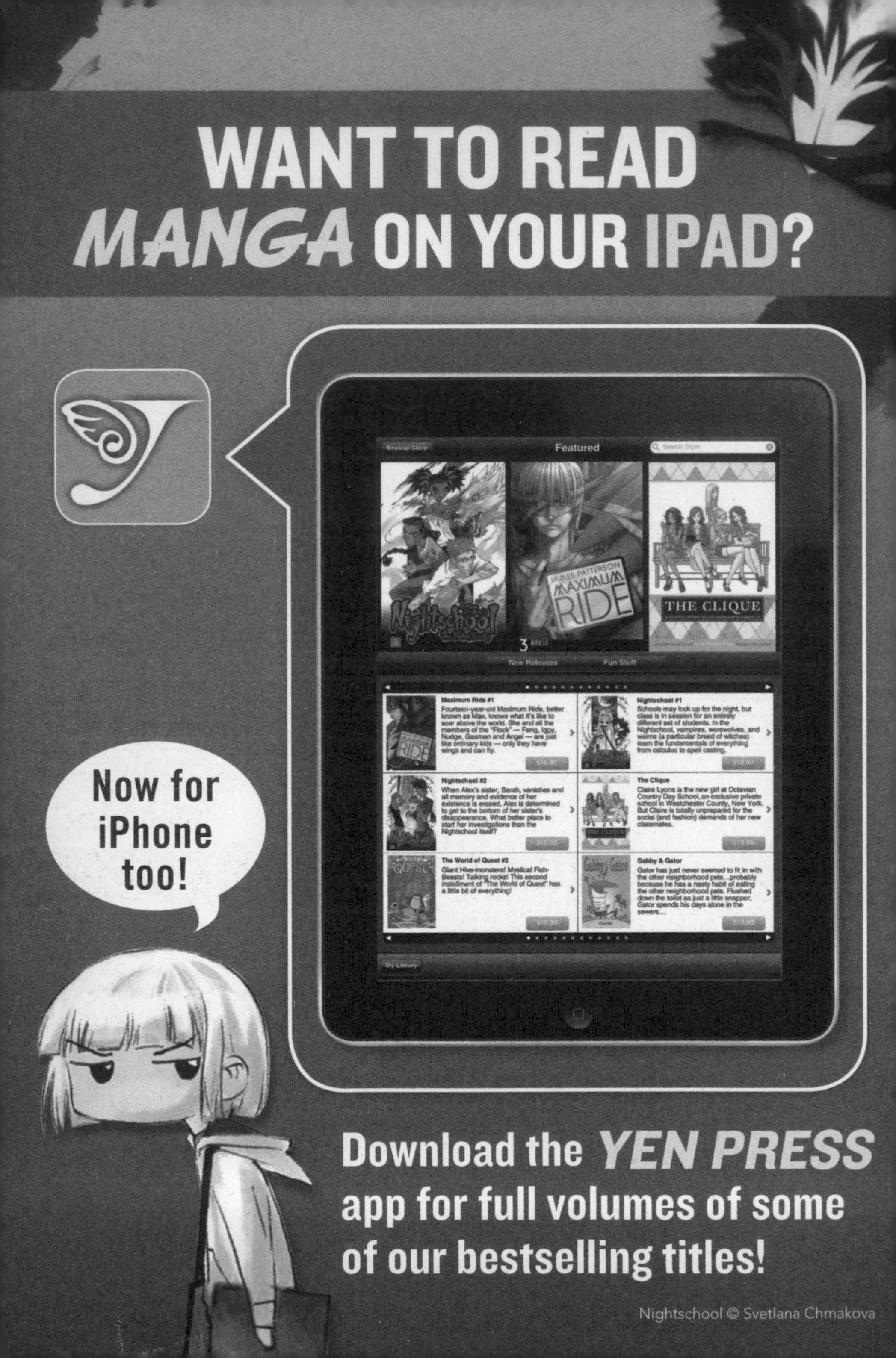
WANT TO READ
MANGA ON YOUR IPAD?
Featured
THE CLIQUE
JAMES PATTERSON
MAXIMUM RIDE
Nightschool
Now for iPhone too!
Download the YEN PRESS app for full volumes of some of our bestselling titles!
Nightschool © Svetlana Chmakova

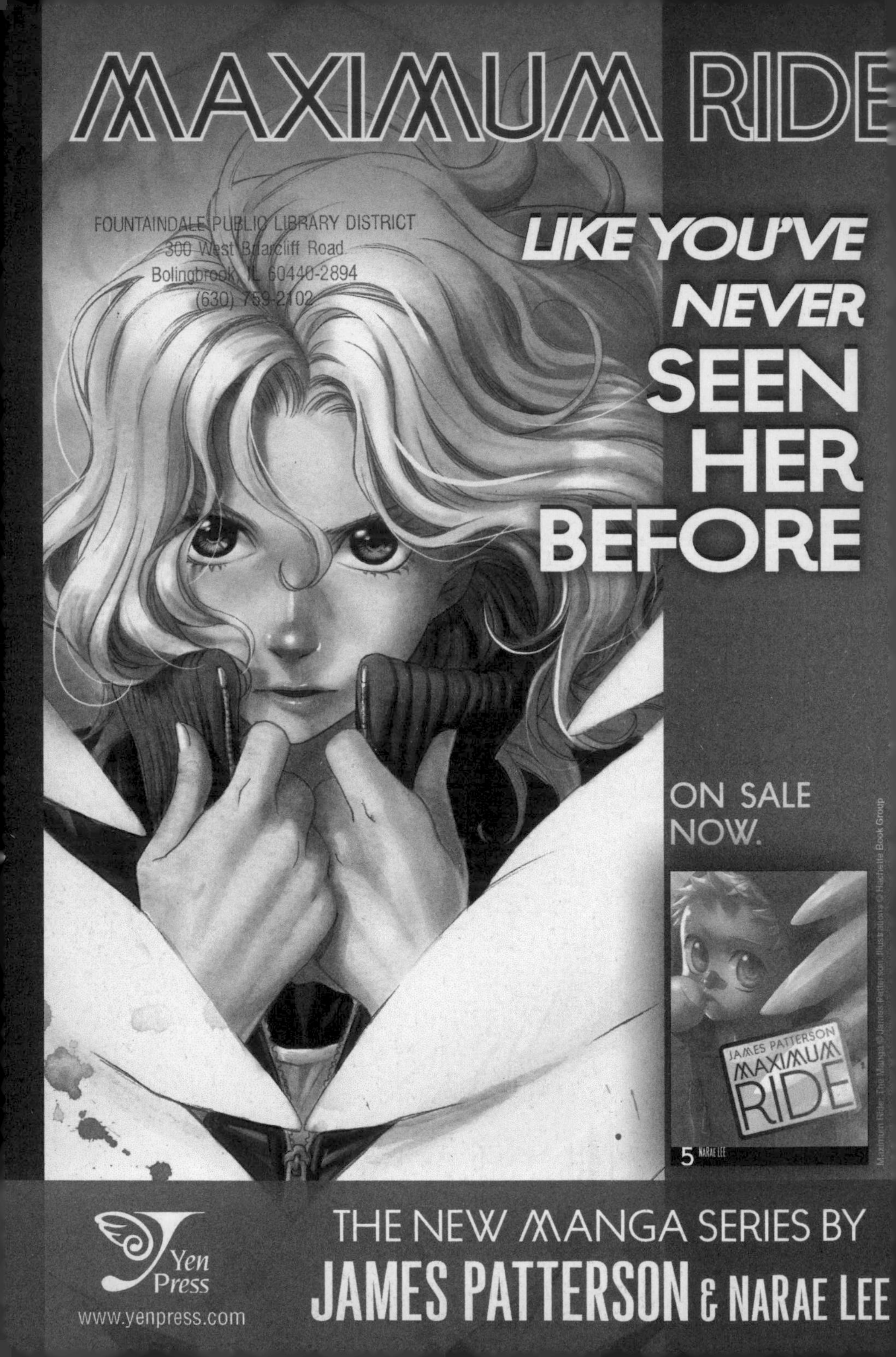
MAXIMUM RIDE
FOUNTAINDALE PUBLIC LIBRARY DISTRICT
300 West Briarcliff Road
Bolingbrook, IL 60440-2894
(630) 759-2102
LIKE YOU'VE NEVER SEEN HER BEFORE
ON SALE NOW.
JAMES PATTERSON
MAXIMUM RIDE
5 NARAE LEE
Maximum Ride: The Manga © James Patterson, Illustrations © Hachette Book Group
Yen Press
www.yenpress.com
THE NEW MANGA SERIES BY
JAMES PATTERSON & NARAE LEE

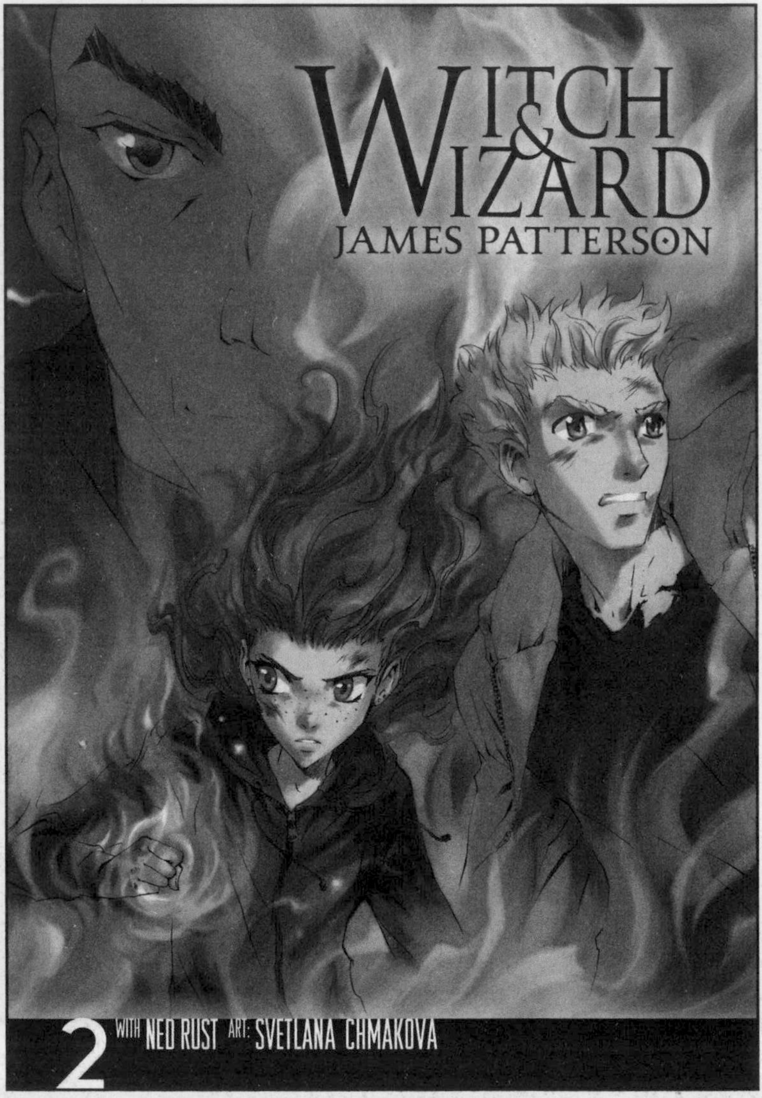
WITCH & WIZARD
JAMES PATTERSON
2
WITH NED RUST ART: SVETLANA CHMAKOVA

DANIEL X: THE MANGA ③

JAMES PATTERSON
WITH ADAM SADLER
& SEUNGHUI KYE

Adaptation and Illustration: SeungHui Kye

Lettering: JuYoun Lee & Abigail Blackman

DANIEL X, THE MANGA, Vol. 3 © 2012 by James Patterson

Illustrations © 2012 Hachette Book Group, Inc.

Yen Press
Hachette Book Group
237 Park Avenue, New York, NY 10017

www.HachetteBookGroup.com
www.YenPress.com

Yen Press is an imprint of Hachette Book Group, Inc. The Yen Press name and logo are trademarks of Hachette Book Group, Inc.

First Yen Press Edition: May 2012

ISBN: 978-0-316-07766-8

10 9 8 7 6 5 4 3 2 1

BVG

Printed in the United States of America